# Handbook of Financial Planning
and Control

# Handbook of Financial Planning and Control

*Edited by*

**M. A. Pocock** and **A. H. Taylor**

Gower

Published by
Gower Publishing Company Limited,
Gower House, Croft Road, Aldershot, Hants GU11 3HR, England


Reprinted 1983




British Library Cataloguing in Publication Data

Handbook of financial planning and control.
    1.   Corporations – Finance
    2.   Industrial management
    I.   Pocock, M A        II.   Taylor, A H
    658.1'5          HG4026

    ISBN 0–566–02127–7

Typeset by Inforum Limited, Portsmouth
Printed and bound in Great Britain at The Pitman Press, Bath

# Contents

## PART II CONTROLLING THE PERFORMANCE

## PART III THE MANAGEMENT OF CHANGE

# Contents

# Preface

This handbook is designed as an essentially practical exposition of the requirements of financial planning and control in the modern environment of business. It is intended to be as coherent as possible within the boundaries of so wide a specification. In places it is deliberately provocative and problems are examined for which specific answers are not readily available. The contributors are all experts in their respective fields, many of them of international renown, either as academics or businessmen. The book is primarily directed to business managers with corporate financial responsibility, but the breadth of approach adopted by many of the contributors should make the work of real value also to executives in non-financial functions and to advanced students of management. As Professor Robson points out in the opening chapter, managers are becoming increasingly numerate and those without a financial background are quite capable of appreciating the financial implications of their decisions.

A further objective of this handbook is to contribute to the interfunctional dialogue which takes place among the members of an alert management team. At the same time the book may help the industrial accountant to develop an awareness of the aims, parameters and problems of non-financial managers, and to improve the understanding by those managers of the inputs needed by the financial planners. For such reasons the book includes chapters on subjects not normally regarded as falling strictly within financial boundaries, e.g., forecasting and pricing. The integration of the material must to some extent be achieved within the framework of the reader's own experience.

The underlying theme of the book is that the fundamental business functions of producing and selling goods and services necessarily involve future planning and current control in financial terms. Since planning and controlling the affairs of a business are responsibilities of the management team, that team is entitled to the advice of the financial department expressed in the clearest and most unequivocal language. Above all that department must keep managers informed of the financial needs of the business for its survival, especially in relation to the availability of cash. The requirement of profit, or at least an acceptable rate of return on capital, also remains a condition for survival – at least for private industry – although in the modern age the concepts of profit and capital have lost precision.

The fight for survival in a world of fierce competition on an international scale alone justifies the development in a business of a strong financial planning function. Competition in the modern sense implies rivalry in price, distribution efficiency, technical competence and quality, innovation and service, combined with the financial strength to withstand the pressures of the game. These pressures derive not only from competitors and from the world economic situation, but also from the social movements which must be taken into account when formulating the business plan and when controlling its execution.

Many of the contributors to this handbook emphasise that the financial planning function must not try to exist in isolation, divorced either from the internal operations of the business or from its economic and social environment. For these reasons it may be thought that certain chapters, and sections of chapters, introduce a much wider meaning to financial planning and control than is customary. Nevertheless, the subject remains rooted in the fairly simple idea of cash flow and the rather more sophisticated ideas of profit, costs and capital. Through the examination of these ideas the handbook is concerned to inform general management and operating management of the means of combating competition and of improving efficiency.

Like many professions, accountancy has tended to become somewhat traditional in its outlook and stereotyped in its techniques. This is perhaps an inevitable result of the development and organisation of professional codes and standards. The tendency extends to some degree to that aspect of accounting – sometimes called 'management accounting' – which deals with the formulation of business plans, both short- and long-term, and the control of business performance. There is a danger, for example, that the product cost has, in some applications, become merely an arithmetical exercise in allocations and apportionments, nourished by the sacrosanct theory of the 'recovery of overheads'; and may have lost all basis in reality. In the first chapter Alan Robson urges the need for a much more widespread and positive use of marginal costing for control purposes. A later chapter by Richard Brown, reflecting his practical experience in cost control, isolates the circumstances where traditional methods simply confuse issues and misdirect management. These two examples alone reinforce the desirability of reappraising traditional methods.

In his chapter on inflation accounting Raymond Brockington shows how the protracted discussion on this vexed topic has inspired the business and academic worlds to raise searching questions as to the validity of the principles on which the practice of accounting has been based from time out of mind. In dealing with what has been unavoidably simplified by the term 'social accounting', Richard Dobbins and David Fanning refer to the social values and responsibilities which are implicit in any business organisation but which are subjected to the discipline of monetary measurement only with the greatest difficulty. The subject of change as discussed by Avison Wormald provides unmistakable warning of the need for the utmost flexibility of approach if the financial department is to measure up to the demands of modern times. Numerous references in other chapters insist that the accountant, and the manager he serves, meet the changes which are occurring by continuous reappraisal of hallowed ideas in accountancy as in other professions.

The contributions to this work reflect a rich mixture of academic thought and equally rigorous study and experience in the practical world of business. The arrangement of the contributions is intended to carry the reader through the main phases of a planning and control system in a logical and progressive manner; but the chapters frequently overlap as, indeed, functions in business overlap. In organising a series of contributions for a subject of such breadth and variety the editors have had to be selective to an extent that may offend some readers whose special interest may not have been fully discussed. To such readers we can only plead that, like business itself, the subjects embraced by a symposium of this nature must involve personal and debatable matters of judgement.

Part I of the handbook deals with the essential steps involved in the formulation of business plans. The opening chapters set up the background for the subsequent discussions by examining the importance of objectives; the need to analyse the resources of the undetaking – financial, material and others – and proceed to the forecasting of demand on which the budgets must be based. The problems involved in the formulation of budgets – income expenditure and capital – are reviewed by well known writers on these subjects. The first part concludes by a searching analysis of pricing policy which, although written by a marketing executive, makes it clear that the most impressive structure of financial planning can collapse as a result of an unsound pricing policy. As with other parts of the book, Part I is composed of contributions by an interesting mixture of eminent academic writers and business managers of wide experience, not exclusively gathered from financial fields.

Part II is concerned with the control of performance in relation to the forward plans, and the contributions again include those by businessmen and by academics. Professor Magee emphasises the importance of *post facto* assessments of business results, and this part includes a chapter on cost control as an occupation in which the controller must be prepared if necessary to forsake traditional methods. The vital importance of the control of funds is given stimulating and, in places, controversial treatment by an industrial accountant; and there follows a thoughtful exposition of the expanding function of internal audit.

Part III is a bold invitation to the reader to examine the management of change. This, of course, represents an aspect of management which has no boundaries or termination. The general requirements of financial planning in conditions of change, especially risk and uncertainty, are examined by Avison Wormald, whose experience of change would be difficult to surpass; change imposed by technological innovation is considered by the Director of the Manchester Business School Research Unit. Avison Wormald also writes on overseas development and although this will not constitute change for many businesses, it could necessitate a radical change for those who have not yet ventured abroad. The increasing impact of social factors on business performance is considered in the final chapter of this part.

Forward planning, control and change are all incorporated in varying degrees in Part IV and here the discussion ranges from the wider aspects of tax management from an international viewpoint to the immense revolution already accomplished by the computer and its predictable future. The significance of the smaller business unit is put in perspective and the part ends with the inescapable analysis of inflation accounting for which, we think, the conclusion has by no means been reached.

This handbook does not set out to instruct anyone in the mechanics of a system of accounting, costing or budgetary control. For such purposes many excellent books already exist; but not even the most thoroughgoing textbook can do more than offer some largely theoretical guidelines for adaptation to the infinite variety of circumstances present in the changing world of business. What we are asking the reader to do is to think afresh about the principles and practices of financial planning and control.

November 1980                                            M. A. Pocock
                                                          A. H. Taylor

# Notes on Contributors

**Richard Aitken-Davies,** BA, ACCA, ATII, (*Controlling the funds*), graduated in 1971 with an honours degree in Business Studies and has since held a number of administrative and accounting positions in industry. He is currently an assistant financial controller in the South Eastern Region of the Central Electricity Generating Board, where he is responsible for the full range of management accounting activities. He is the chairman and a founder member of the Ealing Business Graduates Association.

**Bryan Atkin,** BSc (Econ.), (*Pricing policy*), is a director of Industrial Market Research Limited and a frequent writer and speaker on marketing and market research matters. He has wide experience of the management and control of research surveys both in the UK and overseas, many of which have involved analysis of the purchasing process and the role of price in decision-taking. He was responsible for devising and implementing the important 'How British Industry Buys, 1974' investigation sponsored and published by the *Financial Times*, and co-authored a similar study of pricing practices 'How British Industry Prices' published by IMR Limited in 1975. In 1978 he spent six months on secondment to the Price Commission in charge of sectoral examinations into the bedding and road haulage industries.

**Professor Harold Bierman,** (*Capital budgeting*), is the Nicholas H. Noyes Professor of Business Administration at the Graduate School of Business and Public Administration, Cornell University. A Cornell faculty member since 1956, Professor Bierman formerly taught at Louisiana State University, the University of Michigan, and the University of Chicago. From 1964 to 1979 he helped the University of West Indies to establish a management programme.

His industrial experience includes work with Arthur Young and Company, Shell Oil Company, Ford Motor Company, National Can Corporation, and Boeing. He has been consultant to a wide variety of firms including Owens Corning Fibreglass and AT and T as well as the US government.

His teaching interests are in financial policy, investments and accounting. He is the author or co-author of ten books, including *The Capital Budgeting Decision, Financial Accounting, Managerial Accounting and Financial Policy Decisions*, and 100 journal articles.

**Raymond Brockington,** BCom, MSc (Econ.), FCA, (*Inflation accounting*), is currently lecturer in Finance and Accounting at the University of Bath. He has followed the debate on inflation accounting with great interest. He holds degrees from the Universities of Birmingham and London and is a Fellow of the Institute of Chartered Accountants in England and Wales. He has taught on a wide variety of courses in a number of educational establishments. An important research interest is in accounting education to which he has given practical expression over many years through his work for the Council for National Academic Awards. He believes firmly that problems such as those presented by inflation can only fully be resolved by a profession made receptive to ideas derived from research by an appropriate academic input to their education and training.

**Richard Brown,** BA, (*Cost control*), obtained an honours degree in Business Studies, awarded by the Council for National Academic Awards, the course being conducted at the School of Business, Ealing College of Higher Education. His business experience has been obtained exclusively in the financial departments of CAV/Lucas where he is now financial executive.

**Peter Chidgey,** BSc (Econ.), ACA, (*Internal audit and internal control*), lectures in auditing in the Department of Accountancy and Financial Control, University College, Cardiff. After graduating, he qualified as a chartered accountant with Touche Ross and Company. He is now Technical Manager with Stoy Hayward and Company.

**John Chown,** (*Tax planning*), is a director of J. F. Chown and Company Limited and of Reserve Asset Managers Limited, and a co-founder of the Institute for Fiscal Studies. He was educated at Gordonstoun and Selwyn College, Cambridge, winning the Adam Smith Prize and the Wrenbury Scholarship in Economics.

He was previously taxation correspondent of the *Financial Times*. Recent publications include: *Corporate Finance under Floating Exhange Rates* (Cityforum, 1979) and (with John Humble) *Tax Strategy for General Management* (Foundation for Business Responsibilities, 1978 – US edition *Tax Strategy for Multinationals* published by American Management Association, 1979).

**Richard Dobbins,** PhD, MSc, FCCA, AMBIM, FISB, (*Social accounting*), qualified as a certified accountant in 1968 after several years in professional offices, in industry and public service. He studied for his MSc in Management and Administration, and his PhD, at the University of Bradford where he was appointed Esmée Fairbairn research assistant in 1972, lecturer in Finance in 1973 and senior lecturer in Financial Management in 1979.

He is an active consultant and editor of the journal *Managerial Finance*. His special interests include the growth and impact of institutional shareholders, human resource accounting, disclosure of information to employees and modern approaches to the capital investment decision. He is the author of several articles and books including *The Growth and Impact of Institutional Investors* (with Richard J. Briston) published in 1978 by the Institute of Chartered Accountants in England and Wales.

**David Fanning,** BSc, (*Social accounting*), is lecturer in Accounting and Finance in the Department of Business Administration and Accountancy at the University of Wales Institute of Science and Technology in Cardiff. Prior to this appointment he was full-time research student at the Management Centre of the University of Bradford, researching in the area of financial management. His thesis topic was pension funding. He is a Business Studies graduate of the University of Bradford.

He has contributed a considerable number of articles and papers on topics in business, finance, accountancy and banking to newspapers, magazines and academic and professional journals. He has written *Marketing Company Shares* published by Gower in 1981. Jointly with Professor Roger Groves he is editing and writing a series of case studies in business finance, planned to be published in 1981. His earlier professional career included appointments in librarianship, market research and advertising.

**Desmond Goch,** FCCA, (*Income and expenditure budgets*), is the financial director of Coster Aerosols Limited and has held executive appointments in the aircraft, newspaper and packaging industries. He qualified as a certified accountant in 1955 and is a member of the Council of the Association of Certified Accountants. He is the author of the highly successful *Accounting for Managers* published by Pan Books Limited and has contributed many articles on finance and accounts to accountancy, financial and management journals.

**Philip Jones,** MSc, (*Computerisation of financial records*), worked in the motor industry for ten years before moving into higher education. His final position in industry was in Ford of Europe Systems Office where he was responsible for the design, development and implementation of management information systems in European plants. He qualified for the degree of MSc at the Cranfield Institute of Technology. He now teaches undergraduate and post-graduate students in the uses of computers in business and management studies.

**R. Y. Kennedy,** CA, FCMA, (*Analysing the financial resources of the business*), served in London with Peat, Marwick Mitchell and Co., the well known international firm of accountants after qualifying. He has acted as external examiner for the BA in Business Studies and was awarded a silver plaque by the Institute of Cost and Management Accountants for his services to that body. For ten years he was financial director of Winsor and Newton Limited before being elected chairman and managing director. Subsequently he joined the Reckitt and Colman Group as chairman of their Leisure Division and is now engaged in consultancy work.

**Professor Charles Magee,** FCA, BCom., (*Assessment of performance*), was Professor of Accounting and Financial Control at University College, Cardiff from 1970 to 1977, and Dean of the Faculty of Economic and Social Studies from 1973 to 1976. He is responsible for a continuous research project for the Department of Health and Social Security to develop procedures for a system of costing to be introduced into the hospital service in the UK. He is the author of standard textbooks on accounting and of articles on hospital costing and finance.

**Elwood Miller,** PhD, CPA, (*Accounting problems of multinational businesses*), is Associate Professor of the Department of Accounting in the School of Business and Administration at Saint Louis University, Missouri, USA. He has had extensive experience in international business operations and is the author of a number of publications including: *Accounting Problems of Multinational Enterprises*, Lexington Books, 1979; and *Inflation Accounting*, published by Van Nostrand Reinhold, 1980.

**Brian Murphy,** MSc, BA, IPFA, ACMA, DMA, AMBIM, (*Financial control of the smaller business*), is Head of the Department of Accountancy and Professional Studies at the Huddersfield Polytechnic. He is a frequent contributor to professional journals on financial matters and has written a book on management accounting. Before entering the teaching profession he obtained experience in the finance departments of local authorities.

**Alan Pearson,** BSc, (*Planning and control of research and development*), was in 1979 appointed director of the Management Course at the Manchester Business School, having previously held posts at that School concerned with Econometrics, Operational Research, Decision Analysis and, from 1967, as senior research fellow and director of the R and D Research Unit. Before joining the academic world he held appointments in industry with Pilkington Brothers and Simon Engineering. His career embraces an impressive list of appointments to various boards and committees, largely connected with R and D at home and abroad. His publications include numerous papers and articles as well as joint authorship of *Mathematics for Economists* (David and Charles 1975) and *Transfer Processes in Technical Change* (Sijthoff and Noordhoff, 1978). He has carried out consultancy and course design assignments with many leading UK companies.

**Alan Robson,** BSc (Econ.), FCA, FCMA (*Objectives and practice in financial planning and control*), is Professor of Management Accounting at the Cranfield School of Management, where he is chairman of Continuing Studies. He is also chairman of the Management Information Panel of the Institute of Chartered Accountants in England and Wales and author of a number of publications on management accounting and corporate planning. His early experience was in professional accountancy practice and in industry. Before joining the academic world he was finance office for the Engineering Division of the UK Atomic Energy Authority at Harwell.

**Maurice Sasieni,** BSc, MSc, PhD, (*Forecasting demand*), holds a first class degree in Mathematics from London University and a PhD in Operations Research from Case Western Reserve University in the USA. For the past several years he has worked in Unilever's Marketing Division and is currently employed by UIMC Limited, which is a Unilever management consultancy company.

**Heather Watts,** BSc (Econ.), ACA, (*Internal audit and internal control*), is a lecturer in auditing in the Department of Accountancy and Financial Control, University College, Cardiff. After graduating, she underwent training with Deloitte and Co.

**Avison Wormald,** BA(Hons), CBIM, (*Development overseas*), is executive vice-president of Lansberg, Wormald Humble y Asociados C.A., Management Consultants, Caracas, Venezuela; Professor of International Trade at the Universidad Metropolitana, Caracas; author of *International Business*, published by Pan Books. He was director and managing director of Fisons Limited, London from 1950 to 1962; chairman Grace Bros. Limited (W. R. Grace and Co.) and a director of many companies in six countries. He graduated from London University with first class honours and is a fellow of the British Institute of Management.

# PART I
# FORMULATING THE PLAN

## PART I FORMULATING THE PLAN

This part examines the essential stages involved in formulating the forward plans of a business and the expression of those plans in financial terms. The translation of the operating plans into monetary language will exercise a co-ordinating influence, as well as acting as a constraint, and will provide a measure of the extent to which the combined plans of the various functions are likely to achieve the business objectives. Furthermore the statement of the plans in terms of money will form a basis for responsibility accounting, and the establishment of standards and budgets for operating managers.

The opening chapter by Professor Alan Robson emphasises the prime importance of defining objectives, considering alternative courses of action, and setting up a system of appraising performance. He stresses in this connection that strategic and tactical planning must be differentiated, although they are of necessity inter-related. A further essential preliminary to sound planning is the analysis of the financial resources of the business, and this topic is developed by an experienced chief executive and accountant, Robert Kennedy. He also discusses the need to establish an effective organisation of the financial function, which must include a system for forecasting and controlling cash flow.

On such firm foundations the formulation of the business plans may be developed, and the first of such exercises is the forecasting of demand, as examined by Dr Sasieni, a marketing executive of Unilever. He points out that the demand forecast will be influenced by demographic and economic factors and eventually converted to an assessment of the attainable market share. The preparation of such a demand forecast will be aided by statistical devices as well as the application of judgement and experience.

On the basis of the demand forecast the detailed process of preparing budgets of income and expenditure will be inaugurated. The fourth chapter is thus concerned with the approaches to successful budgeting and here another financial executive, Desmond Goch, maintains that the budgets must be primarily directed towards the achievement of a satisfactory return on the *current* value of capital employed. Guidelines to budgeting for capital expenditure are given incisive treatment by an acknowledged expert on the subject, Professor Harold Bierman of Cornell University. The crucial problem of pricing policy is discussed by a director of Industrial Marketing Research Limited, Bryan Atkin.

# 1

# Objectives and Practice in Financial Planning and Control

A.P. Robson

*In this opening chapter the author seeks to clarify the objectives of financial planning and control as a means of assisting managers to choose between alternatives, plan action and check performance. He distinguishes between strategic and tactical decisions, emphasises the motivating influence of the exercise, and stresses the importance of discounted cash flow and marginal costing making proper use of techniques. The author gives due attention to human aspects and sees future developments resting largely on the growing body of financially numerate managers, growth in communications, development of more relevant management information and advances in computerisation. The ideas outlined by Professor Robson are taken up in greater depth, and with appropriate variations, by contributors to subsequent chapters.*

The financial planning and control function in an organisation has the main objective of assisting the management of that organisation. This assistance is directed primarily towards the planning and control activities of managers; but other activities will benefit as well, if the system is well conceived and used, for example, the co-ordinating and motivating aspects of management. A good financial planning and control system is one which is 'in context': what is done is relevant to the purposes of that particular organisation and the managers who work for it, whatever those purposes and however they may be measured and appraised. Inevitably, financial planning and control systems in practice fall short of this ideal, either in their design or in the way they are used. This chapter concentrates on those aspects of financial planning and control where improvements in practice might be made.

If a financial planning and control system is to assist managers, it will be useful to clarify, at an early stage, those activities which can receive particular benefit. They are: (a) choosing between alternative courses of action; (b) planning the action which is to be taken during a specified period of time; and (c) checking performance once action has been taken.

## ALTERNATIVE CHOICE DECISIONS

Choosing between alternatives is one of those activities which managers carry out several times every day. Every time someone comes into a manager's office and asks 'what do you think we should do about such-and-such?', the manager must either suggest doing nothing or recommend a course of action. In making his reply he is involved in choosing. But some of the issues he gets involved with are of sufficient importance to warrant some sort of formal financial analysis – and it is with these types of decisions that we are particularly concerned.

Two sets of these types of decisions may be identified. Each set has particular characteristics which give rise to the need for a specific kind of financial analysis.

The first set of decisions may be characterised as strategic. The use of the word 'strategic' indicates that these decisions are of sufficient importance to warrant the attention of relatively senior managers. 'Strategic' also implies that the decisions are likely to affect the organisation's survival and well-being in some fundamental way. Therefore, these decisions tend to have long-run effects, lasting over several years. Often they change the capacity of the organisation, e.g. by expanding or contracting the assets in use. Examples of decisions which have these characteristics are: the acquisition of an additional business; the closure of a factory; the closure of an activity accompanied by a switch to sub-contractors; the launching of a new product; and the re-equipment of a transport fleet.

A second set of decisions which managers are involved with may be thought of as being more tactical. This implies some sort of manoeuvring to achieve an improved result with given resources and a given organisation. 'Tactical' also implies the involvement of middle and senior managers, rather than senior and top managers. In many cases it is likely that a tactical manoeuvre will not commit the organisation for lengthy periods of time, since the essence of tactics is to be flexible in the face of a changing environment. Perhaps the most frequently found example of a decision in business which has these characteristics is the product-mix decision: a choice between alternatives, in which the managers have to decide which products they prefer to emphasise in their selling and marketing, so as to obtain whatever additional profit is latent in the market conditions which they face. Hotel companies which operate weekend holidays at lower than normal prices are examples of businesses involved in such a decision. They are trying to improve their profitability by filling the spare capacity which exists in the off-season. Their decision as to which hotel to include in the bargain rate scheme, and at what price, is aimed at securing whatever additional profit is available in a limited market. Should the decision appear to be wrong, the consequences are not too dramatic and can be reversed without undue delay and penalty. If the hotel is fully booked and inundated with enquiries, it is a simple enough matter to remove the hotel from the list in the next season's publication. Contrast this with the strategic situation where a company builds a new hotel of the wrong size, or in the wrong location or to the wrong design!

## ACTION PLANNING

Planning the action which is to be taken during a specified period of time is the second of the management activities listed earlier as likely to benefit particularly from the financial planning and control function. Planning of this type is much more detailed than the decision making first described. The extent to which the one type of planning is detailed and the other 'broad-brush' may be highlighted by the following simple example: suppose an organisation has an accommodation problem and has identified two possible sites for relocation of staff. Evaluating these alternatives is decision making of a relatively broad-brush nature, involving an overall appraisal of such issues as the capital and running costs of the two locations, their convenience from the point of view of access to Head Office, the amenities they provide, the spare capacity which they offer for future growth in staff numbers, etc. Once a particular location has been chosen, it will be necessary to prepare a much more detailed plan involving such issues as: surveyors' reports, legal negotiations, deciding on facilities to be provided, appointment of a project team to supervise contractors, appointment and terms of reference of a project manager. The project manager will, in turn, need a detailed plan covering such issues as the specification to be followed, the sequence of work to be performed, the time to be taken, and the cost to be incurred. He will need to plan the information he requires and the communication system he will set up. Of course, detailed action plans are required in organisations, not only to facilitate the implementation of strategic and tactical decisions, but also to ensure the smooth running of all those operations (probably the majority) which are to be carried on without any changes being introduced.

Preparing such a comprehensive action plan in an organisation of any size is obviously a considerable administrative task, involving many managers, and often spread over several months. If the organisation is to function effectively (in that it achieves its purposes) and efficiently (in that these purposes are achieved without undue loss of resources) the plan which the managers produce needs to be a co-ordinated one. Fitting the pieces together involves cutting and shaping the component parts, which usually means someone cutting and shaping someone else's plans. The object is that the organisation functions as nearly as possible as a harmonious whole, even though the task of managing the organisation is in the hands of individual managers who are organisationally subdivided.

Few activities are more liable to arouse heated debates than this, so that action planning is also tied up with motivating. If action planning is well handled, the managers in the organisation will acknowledge the interests of the organisation as a whole and will be committed to pursuing those interests even if this means some sacrifices on their part.

Another feature of detailed action planning is that it covers a specified period of time, in contrast to the decision making referred to earlier, where the planning period covers the expected life of the decision. Plans which repeatedly cover the same period of time become routine; and routine can become a chore and a nuisance. Unless the planning process is well managed, it can degenerate into a ritual of little effect, or an exercise which people undertake because they have to, rather than because they want to. While it is unusual for people to be indifferent towards the task of choosing between alternatives of a strategic or tactical nature, it is quite possible for these same people to be unenthusiastic about detailed planning. For this latter activity, creativity has to give way to bureaucracy; and initiative and imagination are seen to run into the dull, restrictive world of the administrator! Yet the issues covered by organisation-wide action planning are of considerable importance, dealing as they do with the acquisition, storage and consumption of resources in the supplying of services or products; the financing implications of this activity; and the cash flow consequences.

## PERFORMANCE APPRAISAL

Checking performance is the third major management activity which the financial planning and control function aims to assist in particular. This activity is clearly linked to the preceding ones, in that choosing between alternatives logically precedes action planning, which is logically followed by checking performance, which may, in turn, lead to re-choosing and/or re-planning, and so on. Checking performance implies the existence of a benchmark against which actual results can be compared. This is usually, but by no means exclusively, the current plan of action. Checking also implies highlighting people's failures as well as their successes: failure to set achievable plans based on accurate forecasts, or failure to act as they should have done. Checking also implies analysis of the causes of such failures and successes, and consideration of the action which will eliminate the failure and reinforce the success. All this relies on information being created which is relevant to the manager, in that it relates to his sphere of responsibility and deals with the key issues in his particular job; and, bearing in mind that there is no automatic control reaction on the part of a manager, the information should also invite a reaction from him as to what he proposes to do about the results he faces.

## FINANCIAL PLANNING AND CONTROL TOOLS

In attempting to assist managers in these areas the financial planning and control function has developed an impressive kit of tools. To use these tools effectively, both the manager and the management accountant need certain knowledge, skills and attitudes, which will enable them to recognise the potential and limitations of the tools; and also to avoid misusing them.

Two tools are of particular relevance to the manager who faces the strategic and tactical issues outlined earlier: discounted cash flow and marginal costing. Both are examples of applied logic in which the financial consequences of alternative courses of action are highlighted without reference to a number of the conventions of more traditional accounting.

## DISCOUNTED CASH FLOW

Discounted cash flow, as the name implies, focuses on the cash consequences of major change. These consequences are grouped under four main headings: more cash flowing out, less cash flowing in, less cash flowing out and more cash flowing in, all as a result of the change being contemplated. Cash is the focus because the change is being assessed, as far as is practicable, over the life of the venture. By focusing on the life of the venture and not on the individual accounting periods within that life, discounted cash flow greatly simplifies the collection of relevant information.

The contrast between the cash flow accounting which is needed for such an evaluation and the accrual accounting which is relevant to interim appraisal was perhaps more familiar to businessmen of a bygone age than to some businessmen today! For example, a group of merchants living in Venice who decided to trade in the Far East, could start their evaluation with the pile of gold which they possessed, and which they used to buy a ship and something to sell. They then would set sail; reach the Far East; sell what they had brought; buy something else; set sail for home; reach Venice; sell what they brought back; and sell the ship, ending up (they hoped) with a larger pile of gold than they started with. Profit equalled the difference between the pile of gold at the end of the voyage and the pile of gold at the start. There was no need for accountants (other than tax advisers); and above all, there was no need for accrual accounting. But if someone asked, in the middle of the Indian Ocean on the return trip, 'how much profit have we made so far?', then the whole complicated apparatus of accrual accounting would be needed, involving the preparation of a profit and loss account and a balance sheet, which could in turn involve problems of valuing the stock, matching expenses to revenues, depreciating the boat, etc.

It is possible that in the modern world this distinction between cash accounting and accrual accounting has become blurred. People are in danger of confusing decision-making appraisals with accounting for decisions. The danger points are the inclusion of 'sunk costs' and 'ongoing items' in decision-making appraisals. Vital though 'sunk costs' and ongoing items may be for other forms of accounting, financial numbers which are unaffected by a particular decision obviously should not enter into the economic evaluation of that particular decision – if I am stuck with something whichever way I turn, it does not help me decide which way to turn. An important consequence of this is that no matter how much money I have already spent on an asset in an organisation (a 'sunk' cost) and no matter how recently I spent the money, this asset's book value has no relevance to the economic evaluation of its disposal, looked at as an individual project in an ongoing organisation. Not all users (and, alas, not all producers) of financial information are convinced of the truth of these statements. In effect, some people appear to prefer to keep an asset simply because they have spent money on it, not because it is more economic to do so! If this is the case, they are confusing decision making with review of decisions, and this is more likely to happen when review leads to regret, i.e. when mistakes have been made in the past, and losses on disposal are coming home to roost.

## MARGINAL COSTING

Marginal costing in practice has always been fraught with difficulties. The commonest are probably the difficulty of determining the fixed or variable costs associated with a particular decision; an unwillingness to abandon one of the longest-serving members of the management accountant's list of ideas – the allocated and apportioned fixed overhead – and a failure to readjust to new percentage margins when setting selling prices. These are points which have been difficulties facing management accountants for many years. For example, some managers will equate fixed cost with committed cost, so that a fixed cost becomes 'one that cannot be altered at the discretion of management', as opposed to 'one that is not directly affected by a change in the level of activity being contemplated'. Similarly, some managers will confuse correlation with cause and effect, when considering variable costs. For them, advertising and order-getting costs generally are variables in that they usually move in relation to sales –

more advertising usually means more sales. On the contrary, of course, advertising is a fixed cost in the terms of the definition given above, leaving the word 'variable' to be reserved for those costs which are 'caused by volume changes', such as the postage cost in a mail-order business.

The allocated and apportioned fixed overhead is a concept of value in a number of settings, for example, as a component in making a pricing decision, and as part of a calculation designed to assess the economic viability of a venture. But, as a component in a marginal cost calculation, an allocated and apportioned fixed overhead, such as rent, has little, if any, place. Perhaps the reluctance which some managers feel about leaving out fixed overhead is born of the feeling that there is such a thing as *the* cost of something, so that a cost figure produced for one purpose is automatically seen as being useful for another. But, of course, a cost figure which is a valuable tool in one setting need not be a valuable tool in another – in the same way that, say, a hammer is a very useful tool for putting in nails but not much use for putting in screws! Perhaps management accountants should always ask their managers a question before supplying a cost figure: 'what are you going to do with it?'

Readjusting to new margins when the base number is on a marginal cost basis is, of course, another old problem. And yet, the finer points of accountancy can tend to get overlooked in practice, particularly when price competition is keen, so that contribution costing can be introduced, even though contribution pricing may be inappropriate, in that it yields too low a return on investment, or in terms of locking up spare capacity at low margins and perhaps preventing the organisation from accepting more profitable orders in the future.


## ADMINISTRATION AND MOTIVATION

It has already been seen that two important problems associated with action planning are administrative and motivational problems; and since budgeting and action planning go hand in hand, the former is as much subject to those problems as the latter. For example, preparing a set of budgets which includes figures relating to labour costs, purchases, stocks, material usage, overhead support in the factory, overhead support in administration, marketing, personnel, research and development and distribution – with all the detailed sub-schedules itemising the nature of these overheads, such as salaries, stationery, travel, etc., together with budgets for equipment, vehicles, debtors, creditors, cash flow, and fund-raising – all takes a great deal of organising, and often a great deal of time. Add to this the fact that most budgets go through an evaluation phase, whereby first drafts are criticised and amended, resubmitted and perhaps further amended before final approval, and the administrative task becomes even more evident. Most accountants are adept at this: arranging for the preparation and processing of paperwork is a task for which they are trained and for which they usually have the right temperament. But herein lies a degree of danger: that the preparation and evaluation of budgets will be seen to be primarily exercises in processing paperwork as far as the accountant is concerned. Even if the task is seen to include assisting in the development of alternatives so that budgets which are both achievable and desirable emerge, a main feature of the process will have been underplayed. This is, of course, the motivational aspect. Budgeting is part of the process of getting ready for action and as such should be considered as being clearly associated with leadership. What matters is not simply what figures are put together and whether all likely alternatives have been assessed, but also how the people involved feel about the outcome.

As already noted, co-ordination invariably means some sort of compromise whereby original proposals are modified in the light of other people's requirements, or in the light of externally imposed constraints. So, for example, the advertising manager may have to sacrifice some of his draft budget to the research manager, simply because top management feel that they cannot afford to spend all that was asked on developing business for the future, either because of cash constraints or because of likely reaction of the shareholders to the lower profit margins and lower return on capital which such expenditures will invariably bring, at first. But the alteration of one man's budget and not another's, or the alteration of a budget to accord with the interests of the organisation as a whole, is something which needs to be handled very carefully. Otherwise a nonsense, which takes place in some organisations, will be encouraged: the insertion of 'fat' into the figures at first draft stage, in anticipation of subsequent cuts, so that these cuts can be tolerated in the event. A system which then reinforces this, allowing people a budget in line with their previous year's actual (plus an appropriate allowance for staff and other changes such as inflation), is positively encouraging waste, as the 'fatted' budgets are spent so as to ensure a sufficiently large budget-base for next time. Techniques such as using a zero-base for budgeting are obviously useful in this connection, but they only provide an antidote to a problem which centres on the motivational aspects of financial planning and control.

## INFORMATION FOR CONTROL

Checking performance and the use of variance analysis is likewise an activity involving both accounting technique and psychology: accounting technique to distinguish such results as labour efficiency, rate and mix variances, materials usage, mix, yield and price variances, overhead expenditure and under/over recovery variances, etc.; and psychology to be able to use these results productively when they highlight, for an individual and his boss, what has gone wrong (as well as what has gone right).

In considering information which is being produced as a basis for control, it is essential to question if the information currently being produced is the most effective for this purpose. Control information needs to concentrate on key result areas. In so far as results in those areas can be measured, the numbers used need not always be financial; but if good results are being achieved on these numbers, then the organisation is a long way along the road to creating good financial results. For example, in the monitoring of the performance of branch managers in a commercial bank (where most of the local costs are commitments and many are determined by people other than the local branch manager), indices such as the value of month-end and monthly average credit balances, the monthly average value of approved loans, the number of new instalment loans granted, and the number of new accounts opened (excluding transfers from one branch to another) was felt by one bank to be more relevant for control purposes than preparing branch profit and loss accounts. Producing useful information for control purposes implies that the management accountant needs to adopt an imaginative approach which goes behind the balance sheet and profit and loss account to factors which determine financial results.

'Information for control must always be tailored to suit the circumstances' is a sentence which most accountants agree with, but not all practise. Deciding just what is a relevant information package for a particular manager in a particular job is not an easy task. This is a subject with which the academic accountant should concern himself as well, since there is an inadequate basis of ideas and information for the practitioner to draw on. Each location will have its own particular elements which need to be categorised and taken into account. For example, the different functional managers have different problems to cope with, ranging from the relative uncertainty and discretionary nature of the world of research and development, to the relative certainty and degree of commitment which forms much of the world of administration. Choosing a package of control information also involves choosing the criteria by which managers are to be judged by their superiors in the management hierarchy. These criteria must not only relate to the things that matter locally, but they must also encourage action (or inaction) in the interests of the organisation as a whole. Much has been written on this subject, of achieving what is often called 'goal congruence', especially in the context of divisionalised businesses where the division heads have a great deal of autonomy, and are treated as profit or investment centres. And the special case of the division head invariably raises the issue of transfer pricing. This, too, is an area which can repay attention in practice. In any event, the management accountant may well find that he is thrust into a discussion on what constitutes an appropriate transfer price for a particular set of circumstances, since the subject can arouse a great deal of emotion among the managers involved, and the management accountant can find himself acting as arbitrator between embattled transferor and transferee divisions.

Transfer pricing problems can also arise in practice in the area of decision making, where the system used to measure performance can give rise to unwise decisions, especially of the kind which involves weighing up whether or not to trade within the organisation. For example, in deciding whether or not to buy from inside the organisation, transfer prices will be a major element influencing the decision. The possibility of using a transfer price which encourages the wrong decision is obvious: for example, a decision to buy from outside, because it is 'cheaper' on a full cost basis, when what in fact ensues is a double cost (the additional cost incurred by buying outside *and* the ongoing cost of maintaining the (partly used) facility inside).

## FUTURE DEVELOPMENT

As all subjects are evolving in the field of management, it will be useful to consider some of the factors which are making for change in the area of financial planning and control.

One such element is a growing body of financially numerate managers, who are aware of the techniques in outline, know the jargon and are anxious to make proper use of their knowledge in their decision making, planning and control. Potential exists for a more fruitful relationship between managers and accountants, provided the latter are willing to respond and do not see the financially numerate managers as some sort of threat. Even greater potential would exist if management accountants were to make special arrangements for on-the-job training of these managers who are working in the other functional areas. An ideal would be for the managers who have attended a basic course in management accounting techniques also to attend an in-company course on the way these techniques are applied in the specifics of their own department, including the organisation and procedures that are adopted and the priorities which currently exist.

This is one aspect of employee communications as they affect the management accountant. Employee communications, generally, is a theme which is likely to increase in importance in the future. Already, companies have adopted varying forms of employee reports, and it is likely that developments will continue in this direction, so that there will be an increasing requirement placed upon the management accountant to make clear to the layman what financial figures mean. It is unlikely that the general mass of employees in an organisation will have received the same financial training as their managers; most will have received none. So this development in communication may pose a particular challenge for some management accountants whose orientation hitherto has been towards the preparation of figures, as opposed to their presentation and interpretation.

But even in the preparation of figures there are challenges to the management accountant, which are already with us and are likely to intensify. These stem from the growing influence of computers, not so much to perform complex calculations as to explore the consequences of alternatives. An obvious computer application of this type is when alternative assumptions are being made concerning a major project, and the computer is used to calculate the effect of variations in the financial outcome of the project. For example, the effect and likelihood of a delay in the start-up of the project, or the effect and likelihood of more or less buoyant sales can be rapidly seen by those involved in the project appraisal. This 'sensitivity testing' and 'risk analysis' is, of course, fairly common among larger organisations. With the advent of cheap computers, the practice of this type of calculation is likely to spread.

Similar approaches using computers may also be applied to the evaluation of budgets, other than project budgets. In the working capital area, for example, the effects of alternative stock, debtor and creditor policies and different cost and selling prices, either separately or in combination, can be quickly seen via the computer. Such calculations are not merely a speeding up, so that what took a week to do on a batch basis, now takes only a matter of minutes via a terminal or a table-top machine: the new dimension which has been added is the repeated interaction of calculation and judgement. As managers 'mull' over the issues, in the process of reaching a decision, they can explore alternatives, quickly see their likely effect if adopted, perhaps be surprised at the outcome and re-think their emphasis. There is potential here for considerably improved understanding of the economics of situations, leading to improved predictive ability and more soundly based decisions. Added to the administrative and motivational problems of budgeting already referred to, the management accountant will have to understand how to enable interaction between people and computers so that the judgement of the 'smoke-filled boardroom' and the rapid calculation of the computer reinforce each other.

# 2

# Analysing the Financial Resources of the Business

**R.Y. Kennedy**

*An important preliminary to the establishment of an effective system of planning and control is to define and analyse the resources available for implementing whatever plan may be adopted. The author of this chapter discusses the subject from the essentially practical viewpoint of his long experience in industry both as chief financial officer and managing director. He distinguishes between material and intangible resources and emphasises the need for careful analysis of the availability of finance as it affects long-term cash flow. The importance of cash flow, which has already been given prominence in the first chapter, will be referred to on many occasions later in this handbook.*

*Mr Kennedy highlights another resource of great importance to financial planning, that of the organisation of the financial department in a business and its division into various co-ordinated activities. He discusses the effect on planning of degrees of delegated authority and the special importance of dispersed operating units. An analysis of the significance of the smaller business unit is examined in depth by another contributor.*

A business in a free society exists to perform a service for the community in which it operates (including the gaining of foreign currency from exports) and in so doing to allow people working in it to earn a living. An employee cannot be forced to perform a specific task if he does not wish to. Nor can a customer be forced to buy if the goods do not appeal to him. The environment is always changing and what may have been a successful market for many years may disappear quite suddenly. Businesses do not exist in a vacuum – they must successfully interact with their environment. Some develop products which become household words for generations; others become famous for a time and then disappear; others again remain relatively unknown to the public but provide a service for many years.

It is the task of a company's financial organisation to ensure the availability of financial resources and to produce the financial information which will enable the business to succeed. Unless the revenue generated by a business exceeds its expenditure through time, the community will not allow it to continue indefinitely. Regardless of whether the business is operating within a free or a mixed economy, the community will either tire of filling its begging bowl and allow it to disappear or a new management will be appointed to reorganise it in such a manner that it will become profitable.

The environment tends to be hostile and the continued success of a business is always in jeopardy from one source or another. This gives rise to the element of excitement experienced by those engaged in the business. The information flowing from a company's financial organisation will not eliminate risk but it should provide data adequate to indicate trends on which action may be taken in time to avoid future dangers. The tasks of the financial organisation include ensuring the availability and control of finance; the evaluation of future plans in money terms; monitoring progress for the use of those responsible for controlling and co-ordinating the activities of the various parts of the business and the preparation of the annual balance sheet and profit and loss account for the information of the providers of finance and interested members of the public.

## BUSINESS OBJECTIVES

Any group of active people tends to fragment unless strong control is exercised from the centre. A business will, however, lose much of the enthusiasm of its executives if too many decisions are taken at the centre. Yet without general directives each executive will tend to develop his section according to his own interpretation of the future of the business, possibly in a manner different from that desired by senior management. This problem will be minimised by the preparation and adoption of parameters for the business in the form of business objectives. They should be described in a statement comprehensively and with adequate definition to cover inter alia such matters as:

1 The nature of the business, indicating products, services etc.
2 The sources of supply covering own manufacture, policy as to bought-in parts and sub-assemblies, quality levels etc.
3 Market levels to be exploited, e.g. top quality, specialist, mass market etc.
4 Promotion attitudes
5 Distribution methods, e.g. direct to the consumer, direct to the small retailer or through multiples, distributors, wholesalers, agents etc.
6 Staff welfare, discipline and remuneration policies.

Initially, though many difficulties will arise in drawing up the statement of business objectives, it is more important to have some statement, however inadequate, than none at all. The statement should err on the side of brevity. Experience alone will identify where improvements may be made but a lengthy document will tend to be ignored. At regular intervals all statements should be reviewed and amended to take account of changes in the environment and the development of the business. However, too frequent reviews may merely irritate and confuse members of the organisation, and it is therefore preferable that the statement should be limited to the permanent and more important aspects of the business. Although some authorities have advocated evaluation of business objectives in money terms, greater flexibility is achieved by using planning techniques for producing the necessary drive towards common goals.

## FINANCIAL POLICY

The financial organisation should analyse its role within the framework of the business objectives and should secure the approval of senior management. Such an analysis will be the basis of a statement of financial policy without which it would be impossible to make a meaningful assessment of the state of the resources of the business. The reports and recommendations emanating from the financial organisation will affect the activities of almost every executive and their justification must be related to agreed objectives, so that, though critical, they do not disturb good relations in the team.

The financial policy statement would cover such subjects as:

1 The owning and leasing of fixed assets
2 Borrowing
3 The desired level of profit in relation to sales volume and capital employed
4 The proportions in which profit should ideally be allocated to development, the suppliers of capital and the employees

and, if applicable:

5 Rules regarding inter-company pricing
6 The conversion rates of foreign currencies.

## THE STATE OF MATERIAL RESOURCES

In a small business, management is so intimately involved that members are subconsciously aware of the state of the material resources. This familiarity is impossible in larger businesses and to remedy the deficiency the financial organisation, with the assistance of experts in particular areas, should provide a statement of the material resources at regular and frequent intervals. Material resources give rise to upkeep costs and incur money costs as they represent finance tied up in the business. The advantages to be gained by a close control of the size of the investment in material resources may be illustrated in the following simplified example. If the general interest rate on borrowed money is 12 per cent p.a. and the business turns over its investment in material resources twice a year, then 6 per cent has to be added to the cost of the products to pay for the capital employed. This falls to 3 per cent if the investment is turned over four times a year.

The statement should give an assessment of the resources both quantitatively and qualitatively and should indicate the use made of the resources by the business as a whole. Where applicable, reference should be made to risk elements, measuring the risk in bands. When dealing with resources located overseas notes should be made of significant legislative and foreign exchange trends. A report should accompany the statement commenting on the assessment and making recommendations with a view to improving the effectiveness of the material resources investment.

The following notes on classes of material resources indicate aspects which should be considered in making the assessment.

## Land

Businesses engaged in such activities as building, mining, agriculture etc., depend on their tenure of suitable undeveloped land. Other businesses will benefit from their location near supplies of raw materials, availability of skilled labour and ready access to markets etc., in varying degrees according to circumstances. In such cases undeveloped land in close proximity to the established site is a hedge against the disruption and costs of moving to accommodate future expansion. Only a fixed fund of land overall is available, although its supply may be to some extent variable for particular uses, and competition for it will always be severe. The continued holding of suitable land is of great importance to a business. Reserves of undeveloped land to provide for expansion are always desirable and a necessity in the building and extractive industries.

## Buildings

Modern industrial buildings, and especially those designed to a plan which provides for the roof to rest on the external walls with a minimum of internal supports, remain valuable assets for many years provided they are regularly maintained. The relative advantage of purchasing, leasing or renting is a policy matter. Where the industrial process requires a specialised building, the risk element in providing the resource is considerable because the opportunities of realising the initial cost in the event of a subsequent sale are minimal, and it may be wise to treat the building as part of the plant.

## Plant and machinery

This group of resources is highly specialised and the operations executives should be invited to take a leading part in the assessment. Up-to-date plant registers, planned maintenance, and planned plant replacement will form the basic control. The actual time spent on installation should be controlled against the original estimates.

## Stocks

Stocks of goods will be found in all parts of the organisation. Each executive aims never to go short through lack of the materials necessary for carrying out his tasks and the total value of stocks held is usually a substantial proportion of the total investment in material resources. The ratio of stock held to usage is one of the best indicators for use in controls. Stocks no longer of value to the business are written off and should be disposed of to release space. Because stocks on consignment are held outside the business they call for special care.

## Trade debtors

Customers can be trained to pay promptly by the use of strict credit control. This enforces good accounting on them and the less efficient outlets are weeded out. Granting cash discounts is relatively expensive and would only be worthwhile if used as a marketing incentive, e.g. in lieu of additional trade discount. The twin controls of ageing individual debts, and the overall ratio of debtors to sales by markets are usually adequate if allied to a special check on the history of new customers. The assessment should include a review of the number and purpose of the issue of credit notes to ensure the adequacy of the system for billing customers.

## Trade investments

Circumstances may arise when it is advisable to invest in the businesses of suppliers and customers to secure preferential treatment, or as a preliminary to acquisition. Such investments tend to become permanent and the assessment of their value to the business should be rigorous to ascertain whether the original reasons for investing remain valid.

## Liquid resources

These are subject to a slightly different approach. They fall into three categories:

*Small funds* held by various individuals to meet out-of-pocket expenditure. They are controlled by imprest. The assessment should include reviews of the size and necessity for holding any funds at all. In total, they can add up to a sizeable figure and in practice they become fixed.

*Bank balances* held for the payment of purchases and expenses and the receipt of payments by customers. The timing of receipts and payments can vary widely during the year and as a result the total finance tied up may be considerable, particularly in a group. Appreciable savings can be effected by developing a central banking system in which all the group receipts and payments are balanced each day and surpluses invested on an 'overnight' basis. Movements of foreign currency can be handled in a similar manner, but this operation should be carried out by experts if losses are to be avoided.

*Reserve funds.* However excellent the planning system, the outcome of a year's operation does not equate with the planned profit and cash flow. The unexpected always intervenes. Some years everything goes well and in others a run of bad luck is experienced and the liquid resources have to bear the strain. Recourse is made to temporary borrowing and if this occurs in a period of recession, which is likely, interest rates will be high and their cost will increase the trading profit shortfall. The resources of the business should include funds to meet such contingencies. In good years the excess cash flow is invested outside the business to 'earn its keep' and to provide a resource to finance the years of cash shortages. The assessment should evaluate the size and effectiveness of the use of these funds.

## INTANGIBLE RESOURCES

Intangible resources emerge as a result of effort expended and are of permanent use to a business. In economic terms they have a value. However, the accounting convention treats such resources as of nil value on several practical grounds, e.g.:

1   Intangible resources have an exchange value only on a change in ownership, an event which is incompatible with the continuing business basis on which the annual accounts are drawn up.
2   The economic value of intangible resources tends to rise and fall in step with trading profits. Consequently changes in a value for such resources merely emphasise the ups and downs in trading profits.
3   There are no objective bases against which these resources can be measured; their valuation in money terms would be highly subjective and introduce undesirable obscurities.

Nonetheless, accountants have traditionally given values to the intangible resources listed below based on past expenses and/or profits modified by estimates of future profits. The Rolls-Royce debacle provided a dramatic illustration of the dangers of the application of the tradition.

Assessments of the state of intangible resources can be of assistance to management by determining the trend of their effectiveness through time.

### Research and development

There is no difficulty in recognising a successful completed project. But it is difficult in advance to assess whether or not the resources required for a new project will be wasted. It is hardly a matter to be left to the judgement of the Head of Finance, and his research and development colleagues are usually too involved to be able to take objective views. Once a project is running, a monitoring procedure should be instituted to assess the resources likely to be required, evaluating them in money terms, setting successive 'go'/'no go' decision points, and comparing actual expenditure with the forecast.

The assessment should investigate each completed project to obtain an indication of reasons for its success or failure. The data will assist in deciding the areas to be exploited and the methods to be followed in the future.

### Patents

One of the more difficult business decisions is to decide whether to make public the details of new products and obtain the right to attack plagiarists, or to allow competitors to deduce the new technology and copy it without fear of reprisals. Much will depend on an assessment of competitors' activities and strengths, and on the customs of the industry. Possibilities may exist for using patents aggressively to enter protected markets by offering licences for local manufacture and/or marketing in return for royalties. They can yield sizeable contributions toward the costs of research and development for a negligible outlay. The wider distribution should enhance an international reputation and reduce the opportunities available to competitors.

### Trade marks

Marketing policy may call for the registration of trade marks to deny their use to a competitor who might hope to persuade the public to buy his product if it carried a near imitation. This has happened frequently in overseas markets when the majority of customers were illiterate and bought on the basis of the designs. Registration fees are not high but the process of defending a trade mark in the courts can be costly. As the renewal periods of registration are infrequent and not uniform in all countries there is a tendency for the files to be neglected. The assessment of the value of trade marks will rely heavily on the strength of marketing opinion.

## Reputation (traditionally termed 'goodwill')

Profitable selling is much easier if the business has developed a good reputation for fair prices, reliable deliveries, consistent quality of product and generous settlement of grievances. A good reputation is not earned quickly but it can be lost overnight by changes which do not find acceptance with customers, e.g. new products which do not fulfill expectations, better or more acceptable products introduced by a competitor etc. An outstanding reputation may inhibit change and innovation from fear of adverse market reaction.

## Personal relations

A framework of good personal relations in a business will be provided by the introduction of adequate techniques to ensure good pay and conditions at each level, the welfare of employees, fair retirement benefits, comprehensive induction and training techniques, and sensible regulations for the settlement of disputes. However, it should be recognised that employees are quick to detect in their superiors bluff, sloth, unfairness, meanness etc., but they appreciate firm control, fair judgement, acknowledgement of extra effort and an intelligent interest in their affairs. A business is a closely integrated social group of human beings and attention to these factors is essential for the effective functioning of the techniques.

## Access to reliable sources of supply

Businesses depend on the effectiveness of their suppliers. Many large and successful businesses have spent much time, energy and money in assisting their suppliers to improve their manufacturing methods and techniques, recouping themselves by paying less for purchases and reducing stock levels as a result of more reliable delivery forecasts. They regard their suppliers of essential materials as an extension of their own business and have been known to assist in the provision of manufacturing facilities close to their own operations. This option is frequently preferable to incurring the capital cost and risks of entering new fields of activity in which expert knowledge is lacking. It is impracticable to adopt these procedures with all suppliers but purchasing departments can do much for the business by building up goodwill with suppliers' representatives. Good access to reliable suppliers of goods and services is a valuable business resource which is often overlooked.

## THE AVAILABILITY OF FINANCE

Finance has been called the life-blood of a business. Without an adequate supply of finance all the activities of a business are restrained and progress is impaired. It is not sufficient for a business immediately to have an adequate fund of finance; sources of further finance must be available to meet future commitments and survive inevitable setbacks. Lack of finance is a major cause of business failure.

A successful business will have less difficulty in obtaining additional finance when credit is freely available. But, like commodities, its supply and price may fluctuate. Its supply is particularly subject to changes in government policy. If proper steps are taken in the better times, finance will be more readily available for survival in the lean times. Consequently a business should keep its suppliers of finance informed of its financial progress, how it is dealing with problems arising from the state of the economy and what modifications it is making in its future intentions.

### Study of long-term cash flows

The experience of the rapid change in outlook which followed the investment boom of the early 1970s and the subsequent sharp rise in oil prices are a reminder to businessmen that they operate in an uncertain environment. Reserves of minerals, fossil fuels, etc. are dwindling. Developments in computer technology threaten to alter radically our way of life. On the other hand, man has consistently demonstrated his ability to adapt successfully to changing environments. Against this background a basic study has to be made of the probable levels of cash flow through the foreseeable future, for without such a study rational estimates of the timing and quantity of future requirements are impossible.

The length of the 'foreseeable future' is determined by the nature of the products being considered and the stability of the market. Ten years might be reasonable for an established general-purpose machine manufacturer, but three years could be too long for articles made for a newly developed fashion market. It is a subjective management estimate of the time which it will take to complete their current long-term programme.

## Borrowing finance

Although small businesses, particularly those starting up and proposing rapid expansion, often complain of difficulties in attracting the finance they require, surveys indicate that the amount of available finance is more than adequate. Applicants for finance tend to assume that the more optimistic they are, the more successful they will be; whereas the suppliers (the party to be convinced) look for realistic assessments of demand trends, costs and profitability, basing their assessments on their experience of similar businesses. Borrowers should always frame their applications for finance in a manner which will win the goodwill of the lender, without underestimating the difficulties of developing a successful business.

In a period of rapid inflation, the borrowing of finance for medium terms at fixed interest rates is often attractive compared with the issue of ordinary share capital. The cost of the dividends on the latter increases with the rising profits of the business, whereas the amount of interest paid on loans remains constant in money terms and becomes a lower and lower percentage of trading profit in a period of inflation. On the other hand if the rate of inflation drops, the borrower may find that he is paying relatively high interest charges out of declining profits.

Policies should be established for long- and/or short-term borrowing based on the study of cash flow and after review of the sources of finance.

## Long-term finance

Stock exchanges at home and overseas are the main sources of long-term finance for the larger businesses. Strict rules about conduct and disclosure of information have to be accepted by the borrower, but stock exchanges do give access to a continuing and broadly based financial source.

The form of long-term finance for an established business will be determined by a variety of factors including the existing capital structure, the stock market preference at the time of the issue reflecting an assessment of future currency inflation, the trend of interest rates, the incidence of taxation and the current degree of optimism. Rights issues are popular when the market is buoyant.

## Medium- and short-term finance

There are many sources including joint stock banks, merchant banks, finance houses, financial institutions, pension funds etc. Sources tend to specialise in particular outlets and businesses have the opportunity of choosing the source likely to be most satisfactory to them. There are advantages in cultivating more than one source of finance. The chosen sources should enjoy a substantial reputation, have some knowledge of the field in which the business operates, and be of a size relevant to the size of the borrowing business. A check should be made to ensure that the lender has access to reliable sources of new funds.

Lenders will expect to receive guarantees of good faith such as (a) preferential rights over some fixed assets, (b) guarantees of performance executed by a third party, (c) a share of the profits of the business by the issue of preference or ordinary shares or a mixture of such options.

## Other sources of finance

As an alternative to seeking additional funds, approaches can be made to any of a wide range of bodies prepared to share in the cost of specific material resources, such as:

*Central and local government and other agencies* whose function is to make available grants and subsidies or give preferential treatment at specified locations. Assistance is widely advertised and available to help achieve socially desirable objectives, e.g. reduction of unemployment where it is high, aid to an important sector of industry experiencing a cyclical slump, care of the disabled and elderly, housing to encourage people to move from overcrowded areas etc. The terms and conditions alter, often at short notice, as a result of changes in government policy. However, nothing is given free – the business will be required to forgo some of its freedom of choice. The only reason for offering special treatment is to tempt business to accept a course of action which it might not have followed otherwise. In many instances, a slight adjustment to planned decisions will enable a business to make successful deals in partnership with these agencies.

*Leasing.* A wide range of plant, machinery and equipment can be purchased by means of a leasing contract with one of the many finance companies specialising in this type of transaction. Contract details vary but the leasing company generally pays the supplier for the equipment on delivery and charges a fixed sum for an agreed term of years. The company offering the leasing contract compares the total cost of payments over the period of the lease with the estimated cost of other methods of financing the purchase. Savings may arise from the incidence of tax and interest rate charges. Benefits in the form of favourable repurchase terms and specialist advice on maintenance etc. are frequently offered. The implications of the contract terms should be carefully weighed as future changes in tax regulations, interest rates etc. may impose unfortunate liabilities on the party accepting the lease. The lease will run for several years and the outcome may well be different from that envisaged at the outset.

*Commodity 'futures'.* Commodity prices are subject to frequent and wide fluctuations due to changes in supply and demand. As a result the profits of companies which consume a large quantity of a particular commodity, e.g. wheat, copper, lead etc., will be seriously affected by changes in the buying price of their principal raw material. There are specialised markets dealing in the more important commodities on an international basis. Dealers in these markets, using their expert knowledge and experience, offer quantities of the commodity for delivery at a future date at a fixed price known as the 'futures' price. Companies using the commodity have the option of minimising the effects of commodity price fluctuations and variable storage costs by either a substantial investment in high stocks or placing forward orders through the commodity 'futures' market. The latter course saves storage and interest charges but the prices include the dealer's profit.

*Factoring trade debtors.* Companies offering this service purchase for cash about 80 per cent of the value of trade debtors at a discount and/or fee. They collect the money from customers when due, and remit the balance of 20 per cent to the business. Factoring can often be an advantage to a business but many managements who have organised an efficient control of credit are averse to losing personal contact with customers.

Borrowing for export

*Bills of exchange* are short-term instruments of credit and are inadequate for financing long-term, large-scale capital projects. The speeding up of international communications has lessened their use but the bill discount market is still very active and operates on narrow margins. Bills of exchange arising from a trade in which short terms of credit are granted can be discounted at very fine rates. They form a useful, continuing and flexible source of semi-permanent finance.

*Export credit guarantee department.* This government department was formed originally to provide a type of mutual insurance against the possibility of an overseas customer defaulting. Loans against export sales at advantageous interest rates are now available to those who use the department's services.

*Joint stock banks, merchant banks and others* have government support for the provision of special financial facilities to assist British exporters to compete in overseas trade. Consequently, they are able in suitable cases to provide finance to cover export trade at preferential interest rates and guaranteed terms.

## Internal generation of funds

In a discussion of the availability of finance, perhaps the most important rule is to reduce the need for it. The internal generation of a surplus cash flow is the cheapest source of finance. The level of investment in material resources should be strictly controlled. As much credit should be obtained from suppliers as is consistent with their own liquidity and the standard of service they are prepared to offer.

## ORGANISING THE FINANCIAL CONTROL

Businesses grow from a more or less well defined idea in someone's mind but finance must be available before the idea can become a reality. Financial backing is required to acquire those things necessary to give a physical structure to the business – the building, the equipment, the stocks of material and the people who will run the business. As the company develops, the original idea, if viable, will take on a unique form; control of the various activities becomes more defined and information about the efficiency of the organisation becomes increasingly essential. Experience has shown that the best general basis for the measurement of efficiency is in money terms and is achieved through an adequate system of financial control.

## The development of the financial organisation

In the early development of the business financial control will be rudimentary and little more than that required by every household in the conduct of its affairs. As the business grows in size it becomes a more complex entity, and a more structured form of financial control is needed to handle the increasing flow of information required in managing the business. Although the financial control becomes more important its role will always be to assist the business in achieving its objectives. In due course, the financial organisation will itself have to expand and the work pattern of the sections be reviewed in the light of developments and improved work techniques.

The staff should be asked for their ideas and several alternative solutions may be put forward. Some will involve substantial changes. The founders of the business probably held definite views on organisation and their influence may permeate the fabric of the company long after they have retired. The results of radical changes are often disappointing, partly due to a failure to appreciate the psychological and practical value of retaining continuity. Frequently the best solution involves only the essential changes. There are always difficulties which inhibit the will to institute changes and usually the best time to make alterations in settled routines is 'now'.

### Annual accounts

The developed financial organisation will provide the annual and interim reports which have to be made to shareholders and the wider public. In addition to the financial figures and supporting notes, the reports will include a varied selection of information regarding the company's corporate activities, such as internal reorganisation; provisions for health and safety at work; staff consultation; the policies being followed toward Third World countries; charitable, educational and sporting contributions made to the community at large.

### Internal reporting

In practice, however, the larger and more important work effort is directed toward the marshalling and recording of the flows of data and their presentation to management in a manner suitable for the control, administration and development of the business. In the larger financial organisations recording is carried out with the assistance of computers managed by a team of systems specialists, programmers and operators.

Data are marshalled at source in convenient groupings differentiating between capital and revenue for both income and expenditure. They are accumulated over four weekly or monthly periods. Special care is taken to ensure the accuracy of the originating data at this stage, as any errors will cause confusion in the subsequent output information. Unlike manual systems, computers are unable to recognise when output is nonsense unless they are programmed to reject information which lies outside the laid-down parameters.

*Services provided*. The computer configurations produce output designed to supply the various sections of the financial organisation with the information required in the desired format, e.g. operators' wages, staff salaries, payment for supplies, customers' invoices and statements etc. Collated reports are issued for the use of line managers covering such aspects of the business as the levels of income and expenditure actually achieved compared to budget, measures of output and efficiency etc. The economic service at headquarters will receive copies of the current results for incorporation in comparative studies of the progress of the business in relation to competitors' activities and general trade experience.

*Costing*. When profitability is measured only in terms of the units of the business, some products will tend to be overpriced and some underpriced in relation to a fair assessment of the proportion of expenditure attributable to them. A knowledge of the margin between the cost of a product and its selling price is an essential element of financial control. The amount of cost attributable to a product depends on the utilisation of the productive capacity of the factory, the prices at which the buying department obtains the raw materials, the efficiency of the work force, the qualities required of the finished product etc. The net price at which the product is offered for sale depends on a variety of considerations including the quantity to be purchased, costs incurred in effecting the sale and competitive prices. In quoting prices the marketing department relies to an important extent on the adequacy of the information provided by the costing department. A number of costing techniques have been developed to assist the preparation of product costs, e.g. marginal, standard, replacement and batch costing. The chosen technique should be the one most applicable to the needs of the business. Product costing involves a considerable amount of repetitive and detailed calculation which can be performed by a computer utilising data held in the memory store for other purposes. It may be preferable to limit the computer operation to routine calculations and print-out leaving to skilled accountants the interpretation of the output, which is a more complex and variable activity not usually suitable for relatively inflexible computer operation.

*Cash control.* The financial organisation can make a direct contribution to the profitability of the business by its handling of liquid resources. The units holding cash and bank balances should send by teleprinter to central control their opening balances, receipts and payments for the day and their estimates for the succeeding five days. Transactions involving foreign currency are reported separately. The information is collated at headquarters where the group's liquid resources are treated as one fund. Staff are in a position to maximise very short-term investment, hold back payments to even out cash flow and organise the timing of foreign exchange transactions. The system will have a beneficial effect on the manner in which the local accountants carry out their duties.

*Specialist activities.* A number of specialist activities are often treated as part of the financial organisation, e.g. registrar's duties relating to share transfers and dividend payments, taxation, insurance, pensions, patents etc. although in some companies these tasks are carried out by the legal department or outside specialists.

## Computers and centralised organisation

The increased standard of living in the industrialised countries led businesses to expand rapidly to satisfy the growing demand from consumers and to look for greater efficiency through economies of scale. To benefit from the advantages of large-scale operations they tended to centralise their activities in a small number of large locations. These large units required increasingly complex organisations which become unwieldy unless serviced by efficient financial departments. The volume of data was more and more difficult to handle by manual systems, and from the 1930s it became the practice to use the new electro-mechanical accounting machines which were then being developed.

In the early 1950s digital computers became available and commercial models were introduced into financial organisations. It was soon realised that they could speed up the collection and processing of data across the functional boundaries of the business and improve the effectiveness of centralised control. This vision led many businesses to embark on ambitious schemes based on computers. Many of these schemes foundered as a result of shortcomings of the hardware and lack of appreciation of the complexities of the systems which had to be developed. During subsequent years the new possibilities of obtaining economies of scale became a reality by the use of controls developed by the financial organisation.

However, largely as a result of the growth of centralisation in large businesses, shop-floor operators, first-line supervisors, office managers and their staffs began to feel so remote from those responsible for decision making that they saw themselves as mere cyphers in a vast impersonal organisation. In consequence efficiency and morale declined. 'Wild-cat' strikes were more frequent per employee in large organisations than in the small- and medium-sized businesses. Top management often felt out of touch with what the ordinary people in the business were thinking and doing. The development of greater consultation at all levels should ease the sociological problems, but consultation may, by its very nature, nullify a main advantage of centralisation, namely the ability of top management to put decisions into effect quickly and decisively.

Although a large computer system is a necessity in the financial organisation of a centralised business operating internationally, the system carries within itself factors which tend to inhibit its full potential. Systems planning is complex and calls for a rare degree of understanding of the interlocking nature of the various activities in the business. At no time are the systems in a settled state, for the business itself is continually changing in various small ways and the available computer hardware is constantly being improved. Computer staff tend to move readily from one installation to another and it is unusual for a systems analyst to complete a project. In practice it is seldom that a financial organisation reaps the advantages envisaged at the outset for any large systems proposal.

## Principles of the delegations of authority

The problems arising from a centralisation of activities as enumerated above indicate that a departure from full centralisation would improve industrial efficiency. This would involve a greater degree of delegation of authority for the taking of decisions than is practised in a centralised organisation.

As an administrative convenience the many activities within the financial organisation are accomplished through an adequate delegation of authority over the various specialist sections of the organisation. A manager is responsible to his superior for the proper carrying out of the duties assigned to him, and he in turn delegates to his subordinates. He will not delegate the responsibilities inherent in his job and those activities in which he is an acknowledged expert. He should agree with his assistant a clearly defined range of activities and pass to him the authority to take the related decisions. Some of these decisions may be ill-advised and it is the supervisor's task to minimise the effects of such decisions and encourage his assistant to learn by his mistakes.

The supervisor will find it relatively easy to arrange for his immediate subordinates to follow his directions but in situations where he is responsible for several command levels, particularly at separate locations, it is more difficult to ensure that his methods are adopted in first-line operations. Visits should be made to the various offices at regular intervals to talk to the staff at this level and observe weaknesses. Subsequently he should discuss his impressions with his immediate responsible subordinate with the object of encouraging him to improve working conditions in the office concerned.

The structure of the business described in the objectives of the business will determine the degree of delegation practised in the financial organisation. Preferences range from a predominately centralised system of control to a decentralised system but whatever the degree of centralisation, the foregoing principles of delegation will apply.

## Computers and a fully delegated organisation

Small computers capable of carrying out most routine financial transactions have been developed for small businesses, and the growth of silicon chip technology should increase their usefulness. They operate on standard systems with a wide range of applications and consequently can be sold quite cheaply. Since large organisations are in effect a large number of integrated small entities operating within a larger complex, small computers may be used to decentralise financial computer operations. The managers of the smaller entities remain in control of their own data collection at source, reducing errors which arise in transmission or from lack of understanding of specialised local conditions. Transmission of data to command levels and the centre is usually limited to significant totals in a standard computer format, thus substantially reducing the complexity of the central computer configuration. Provided the principles of delegation are observed, the controls provided by the financial organisation minimise the risks attendant in delegating almost complete authority to local management. The advantages of small business management combined with centralised direction of a large company may be brought nearer.

The search for the optimum balance between centralised and decentralised organisation control will continue but the possibilities presented by the wider use of small computers open up new vistas for improving industrial efficiency.

## Dangers inherent in an organised financial control

Two aspects of organised financial control may, if overlooked, involve the business in serious difficulties.

A well ordered and adequate financial organisation contains information on most of the vital aspects of a business: the state of its assets and liabilities; profitable and unprofitable activities; the progress being made toward the planned future of the business etc. When well organised, financial control can be the most far-reaching and effective management tool at the disposal of the chief executive. But it is a tool to be used with restraint and discretion lest it become the dominant function of the organisation, producing endless information with too little regard for the objectives of the business.

It is not yet fully appreciated to what extent the future will be affected by (a) the growing realisation of the limits of oil and other resources and (b) the developments in the use of micro-transistors in control mechanisms. Both will lead to basic changes in management practice. Financial organisations will be called upon to evaluate in money terms the effects of fundamental changes. They must be adequately staffed with assistants well qualified to assess ways of meeting the new challenges and able to present their findings to each management level in a clear unbiased manner.

## Financial control of dispersed operating units

The terms branches, subsidiaries, divisions, and groups are used to describe the departments of a business which operate at a distance from the centre. Joint ventures with other companies may be designated subsidiaries with minority shareholders, associated companies, consortia etc. according to the form of the relationship. Their operations may be carried out at home or overseas and will embrace a wide range of activities. A complete review of financial controls covering the range of dispersed operating units is beyond the scope of this chapter which has concentrated on a brief statement of a general approach to the problems involved in their control.

Complex structures are to be avoided as they give rise to differences in the interpretation of laws and regulations unconnected with the task of achieving business objectives. Subsidiaries are an example. They are legal entities structured according to statutes which define, among other things, the duties and responsibilities of the directors regarding separate financial accounts whereas a divisional structure enables managers to limit their attention to the general financial requirements of the total group. Matters are further complicated in situations where there are minority shareholders whose interests have to be safeguarded.

The basic, albeit oversimplified objective of the financial control of dispersed operating units is to enable management to deduce an answer to the question: 'Is the trend of returns satisfactory?'

To provide the information on which such an assessment can be based the financial organisation will be required to assist in establishing the tasks in terms of the local currency for the dispersed units to achieve in the immediate and more distant future. An accounting system will be developed to report, as a minimum, the values of monthly sales and profits compared with the forecasted tasks. The ratios of sales to profit, stocks and trade debtors will be calculated and compared with the ratios reported in previous periods and those used in the forecasts. A balance sheet of assets and liabilities with, in the case of jointly owned units, a local audit certificate would also be required.

Accounting conventions should be agreed. Although they will generally conform to accepted accounting principles it is important that they are agreeable to local practices and the needs of the business. This is particularly relevant in overseas units where national laws govern the methods of conducting business and preparing profit statements – some international companies which have raised capital overseas publish separate financial accounts for some of the countries in which they operate. The agreed conventions would cover such subjects as the bases on which profit is computed (depreciation; valuation of stocks; quantifying future liabilities; intangible and reserve assets; etc.) and the rules for inter-company pricing which would provide incentives to the manufacturing units and take account of the fiscal regulations of both the exporting and importing countries.

The financial organisation at headquarters would be responsible for converting the reports from the dispersed units stated in local currencies into consolidated statements by adjusting for changes in rates of exchange and inflation.

The method of financing the dispersed units, sharing profits and making distributions should be described in the agreement which establishes the unit. Local residents can assist in ensuring that alternative courses of achieving local objectives are not overlooked and there may be advantages in involving local residents in the financial management of larger units even where such a course is not obligatory.

# 3

# Forecasting Demand

**M.W. Sasieni**

*It is inconceivable that any business, or new venture in a long-standing business, could be successfully established without some forecast of the demand for the products or services which it is intended to supply, even if such forecast is purely intuitive and based upon the experience of one man. In more sophisticated situations, particularly where large-scale operations and heavy investments are involved, the forecast of demand on which the business plans are to be based will represent the result of a rigorous and scientific assessment of the future market. Such assessment will itself be founded upon a study of the economic and demographic factors which have affected and will continue to affect the demand.*

*Depending on the scope of the operations envisaged – or maybe the ambitions of the entrepreneurs involved – the forecast of demand will normally be followed by an estimate of the market share which the business aims to obtain. The extent to which that market share can be exploited and expanded will depend upon the several constraints on the organisation imposed by such factors as production capacity and the availability and cost of essential resources such as manpower, equipment and materials. One over-riding constraint will be the finance which can be made available. For the latter reason alone, the long chain of exercises leading from the forecast of demand to the eventual sales budget, although falling naturally within the ambit of the marketing function, must also be regarded as a vital element in financial planning, and justifies discussion in a work on that subject. Of equal importance, the subsequent financial control procedures should be directly related to the business plan which, it has been argued above, will logically be based initially on the forecast of demand.*

*In this chapter the author points out that for substantial businesses methods of forecasting have become somewhat specialised and, for that reason alone, require at least the general understanding of all members of the management team. The author refers,* inter alia, *to demographic factors, the level of economic activity, input/output analysis and demand/price elasticity. The discussion covers both consumer products and industrial products and particular attention is given to forecasting demand for new products. The technique of concept testing is examined and so are consumer trials and the application of various statistical devices. As a practising consultant Dr Sasieni acknowledges that judgement and experience may be vital factors in the accuracy of the forecasting exercise.*

All planning is a matter of assessing the task to be accomplished, deciding what resources this will require and making sure that the resources become available as and when they are needed. Financial planning is, of course, primarily concerned with a single resource – money – but it should be stressed that money alone will frequently fail to ensure that resources appear and tasks are accomplished on schedule. We only have to consider problems arising from crop failures to wartime shortages, from labour unrest to lack of technological and managerial skills, to see that while money is important it is by no means the only factor entering into planning and control. There are large organisations (including some state-controlled enterprises) that regularly and consistently fail to spend their capital budgets. The reasons are often complex, but they seldom include shortage of liquid assets.

Russell Ackoff (1965) has defined planning as 'anticipatory decision making' so that, by its very nature, planning is concerned with the future. It is therefore necessary that the planner has some understanding of the techniques available for forecasting, particularly for forecasting demand. Every business, whether privately or state-owned, and many government and local government departments are in existence to supply goods or services. To plan their future they need to understand how much of their goods or services will be required by customers. Of course the demand is partially within their control. We could say that the purpose of the large marketing departments, which exist in many organisations, is to ensure that demand reaches levels which the organisation considers acceptable.

Demand forecasting ranges over a continuum. At one end we have commodities at a worldwide level. Over the next few years what will the world's requirements be for wheat? for edible oils? for mineral oils? for coal, steel, etc? At the other end we may be selling chocolate candy bars under a particular brand name and we wish to know how many we will sell next year. In principle any technique can be used across the range, but in practice methods of forecasting have become specialised and some of these will be considered here.

## COMMODITIES AND INDUSTRIAL TOTALS

Even a small manufacturer is likely to find that the demand for his products varies directly with the total demand for products of a similar nature. On top of the variation associated with the commodity or industry there will also be changes brought about by the marketing activities of the manufacturer himself. These will be considered later, but first some of the factors which enter into predicting the demand for commodities will be reviewed. It should be realised that their relative importance depends on the timescale involved. Thus population growth may be of little consequence in next year's demand for say motor vehicles. It may be the single crucial factor in assessing demand for wheat or rice five to ten years from now. Changing demographics (by which is meant all aspects of population, including birth rate, age distribution, family size, level of education, geographic distribution etc.) are always candidates for consideration in forecasting demand over any horizon beyond the next year or two.

The second major factor is the general level of economic activity. This concept need not be defined here with any degree of precision. Suffice it to say that demand for most goods and services is likely to increase in periods of economic boom. There are exceptions; demand for cheaper substitutes is likely to be stimulated when times are hard. Such businesses are called counter-cyclical and may be much prized by companies with 'normal' products who wish to preserve a more uniform level of activity despite the ups and downs of the business cycle. The machine tool business is notorious for the way in which peaks and troughs exceed those of other industries. One firm discovered that during depression the government had a tendency to stimulate the economy with road-building programmes. By producing a range of medium-weight earth-moving equipment some of the worst fluctuations could be ironed out.

The use of economic activity to forecast, other than in a general fashion, is a highly skilled matter, and a discussion is beyond the scope of this chapter. However two techniques are worth mentioning. In principle a lead-indicator can be used. If some activity is found which moves ahead of the one it is desired to forecast, observation of the indicator can be used to predict. Thus changes in today's wholesale price index are likely to be reflected in retail prices three to six months hence. Current prices of raw materials will appear in wholesale prices later and so on. Unfortunately such indicators are not always easy to find and the relationship between them and the forecast variable may be weak. However they can be useful when our planning horizon is the next few months. Beyond this the only indicator may be population. After all, the adult population a few years hence already exists (partly as children) and a knowledge of death rates will enable a fairly good prediction of future age distribution, subject only to emigration and immigration.

A method which has received much attention over recent years is called 'input–output analysis'. Consider a particular industry, say steel, and ask what input from other industries is required to produce a ton of steel. Among other items there will be iron ore, coal and lime. There will also be less obvious requirements. Thus bricks and cement, motor vehicles, electric energy, even perhaps time on a computer will be needed. A table can then be drawn up, showing for each major sector of the economy the number of units of input required from others to produce a unit of output.

It can then be seen how changes in the output of any one industry affect all the others. Thus one ton of steel will require say one ton of coal. This in turn will require steel, bricks, cement, vehicles etc. Models of economic systems used to be built with perhaps twenty or so 'industries'. Nowadays, the availability of large computers has permitted models with hundreds of industries. The current limitations are probably the availability of data for deriving the input–output matrix, rather than computing resources.

One of the appealing features of this approach is its ability to model technological change. The data matrix represents current technology. Thus if steel is made in electric arc furnaces, the direct input of coal will be reduced and the input of electricity will rise. The coefficients can be changed to reflect beliefs about changing technology and thus forecast the impact of these changes on various industries.

It would not be appropriate to conclude this section without a reference to prices. In classical economics the major factor which influences demand at the commodity level is price. In practice there are many other factors, but price remains important. Unfortunately it is no easier to forecast price than demand, but sometimes both can be successfully predicted simultaneously.

Suppose that from past observations (world) production of a commodity against its price can be plotted, and in addition a relationship between demand and price can be developed. On the assumption that supply and demand balance in the long run the level of price and quantity at which equilibrium will occur can be determined. The effects of other factors can be allowed for, by envisioning them to cause a shift in either the demand or supply curve. Thus increasing popularity of coffee would cause the demand for tea at any given price to be reduced. The graph of demand versus price will be shifted downwards and to the left. Similarly a new production process may shift the supply curve so that the quantity produced at any specified price will change. Thus forecasting quantities and prices is reduced to understanding how these curves react to changes (see Figure 3.1).

## ESTABLISHED CONSUMER BRANDS

The volume for brands within established product fields is usually estimated in two stages. First a forecast is made for the product field (e.g. next year the German laundry detergent market will be about half a million tons) and then brand share within the total can be estimated. (This brand will obtain a share of 11 per cent). The simplest approach to forecasting is to say that the future will be similar to the past and the latest available share figure is a good guide to next year. If it is wished to predict for next year it would be as well to use share over a twelve-month period, because the latest monthly figure may reflect all sorts of temporary or seasonal fluctuation. The estimate is then adjusted in the light of any other relevant information. For example it might be known that a competitor was about to open a new plant which would give him increased capacity at a lower cost. Alternatively it might be known that distribution had finally been achieved through a retail chain which hitherto had not stocked the particular brand.

If a price change which could affect the volume is considered, more sophisticated analysis can help. To start, a graph of market share

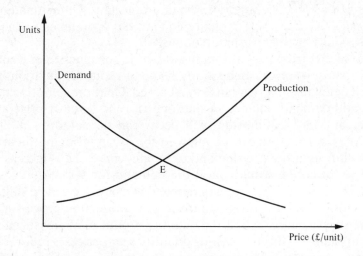

**Fig. 3.1  Supply and demand curves for a commodity**
Note: At the point E the quantity demanded just matches the production
and there is equilibrium.

against relative price[1] (i.e. price compared with competing brands)
would be plotted (see Figure 3.2). Then a 'price–volume' curve
which appears best to reflect their relationship would be sketched in.
All this can now be done automatically on a computer. Data on actual
volumes for the main brands and 'others' together with revenues or
prices are input. The machine not only computes shares and prices,
but in addition plots the necessary graphs and computes the
price–volume curve. It will also assess the statistical significance[2] of
the curve, and the price *elasticity*. The latter is a convenient and
widely used method of expressing the way volume varies with price.
Elasticity is the percentage gain (fall) in volume for a 1 per cent fall

---

[1] The use of relative prices and volumes usually eliminates problems of
seasonality and inflation.
[2] It is possible that even if price and volume were unrelated, sheer chance
would produce a plot in which a limited number of points lie on a line. It is
usually desirable to know the probability that this has occurred. If it is low it
reinforces the belief that price and volume are related.

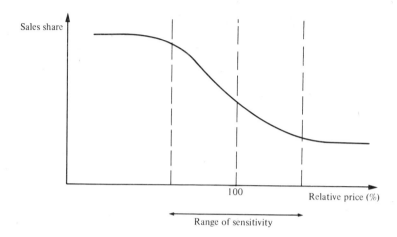

**Fig. 3.2 Price–volume relationship for a brand**
Note: Typically share is not price-sensitive at very high or very low prices.
Share may change markedly at prices near the market average (100 per
cent). Most brands usually operate within a fairly narrow price range and
within this range the curve can be treated as a straight line – plot the graph
and use a ruler!

(rise) in price. It has an immediate and important profit interpretation. If the variable margin per cent is divided into 100 and the
result exceeds the elasticity it will pay to decrease the price,[1] thus
increasing both gross profit and volume. On the other hand if the
result is less than the elasticity gross profit can be increased by
increasing the price.[1] There will be a decrease in volume and this is a
side effect that the profit gain may not be large enough to justify.

In some markets the only variable which has a measurable effect in
the short- and medium-term is price, but often several others should
be considered. Among potential candidates are:

---

[1] Recall that calculations were made in terms of relative price so that to
achieve the volume changes discussed a relative price change is needed.
Competitors may not permit this as they can easily change prices to match.

1 advertising levels
2 distribution
3 product quality (including packaging).

In practice distribution and particularly quality may not have varied in the past enough for their effects to be measurable (if there have been no changes, it cannot be said what the effects of changes would be). Of course the graphical plot will hardly serve if there are additional variables, but they present no special computational problems.

Product quality only enters the forecast if it is expected to change, either due to a change in brand, or to a change in a competing brand. When either is expected some allowance must be made. Often a change in brand is part of a relaunch by which it is hoped to give the brand a fresh impetus. Volume changes are often forecast by the well-known 'hockey stick' approach. This derives its name from its graph which resembles a hockey stick (see Figure 3.3). Such a graph may be wildly optimistic and examination of relaunches of other brands may yield a more realistic estimate of the likely gains.

Advertising differs in one important way from price. Experience shows that, much of the time, the effects of a price change on volume

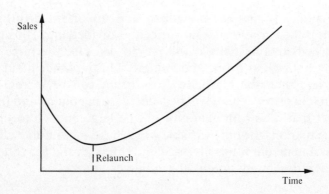

**Fig. 3.3  The hockey stick forecast**

are over within the month in which it occurs. This is in marked contrast to advertising effects which may persist for several months or even longer. In analysing how advertising affects volume these carry-over effects must be considered. Furthermore, while a straight line may be an acceptable representation of the way volume (share) responds to (relative) price, it may be expected that the effects of each successive pound spent on advertising will diminish.[1] This means that advertising response cannot be represented with a single straight line and more complicated curves are required. All these problems can be surmounted by a competent statistician, provided sufficient data exist. A complete understanding may require more than 60 observations. At one a month this means five years' data. Even if this much were available, market and economic conditions are likely to have changed so much as to make the early observations irrelevant. In these circumstances it is often best to settle for a simple model, which captures those aspects of the market which experience shows are important.

In many businesses established products account for the bulk of the turnover and profits. Any forecast of company performance will require their accurate assessment.

Although sophisticated analytical methods are available for forecasting, the results must always be 'hand polished' for those non-quantitative aspects which modify past history. The economic climate, competitive and retail trade activity, technological and political change are all likely to influence volumes, but often experienced judgement is the only way to incorporate them into forecasts.

## NEW CONSUMER PRODUCTS

Most businesses find that the demand for long-established products tends to diminish over time. This view has been enshrined in the so-called 'product life cycle theory' in which three stages in the life of

---

[1] People will already have heard the message. Since the number of good (TV) spots is limited, ever increasing funds will force buying of poorer spots.

There may be an opposite effect at very low budgets. Many writers claim that there is a threshold below which advertising has little or no effect. The evidence for this is not strong.

a product (or brand) are envisaged. First there is a growth period in which more and more people learn to use it. This is followed by a mature stage in which sales are steady; finally the item goes into decline and ultimately disappears altogether. The pattern fits many brands, but the reader can probably think of some notorious exceptions. Some brands, by constant modifications and improvement have been household names for 40 years and more. Be that as it may, there is no doubt that a firm that wishes to stay in business is likely to find it necessary to launch a stream of new and/or improved products. In planning it is clearly necessary to forecast demand for any proposed product.

At this point it is as well to distinguish three types of forecast which are frequently confused. Ideally the three should be estimated independently, and preferably by different people. Very often a single figure is used for all of them without any clear view as to which was the one actually estimated. The first forecast is the estimate of what the demand will prove to be. This will reflect the sum total of relevant experience and will take into account, as explicitly as possible, all the 'hard' evidence available. Such a forecast has nothing to do with how profitable the product will be, or whether the launch is desirable. It merely reflects the best thoughts about future demand.

This must be distinguished from an action standard. Very often there are a number of stages between the initial concept and final market success. At each of them a go/no go decision is necessary and frequently action standards are set as an aid to the decision process. Thus considerations of profitability might dictate that if the product fails to get 10 per cent in a test market it will not be launched nationally (or not in the test market form). Such a standard might be quite different from the estimate of what the actual share will be.

Finally there is the target figure. So much of the eventual outcome depends on the incentives, motivation and confidence of the staff involved that it is necessary to give them something to strive for, usually referred to as a sales target. It must be realistic, in the sense that while not so low as to be easily reached, it is not so high as to be considered impossible by those whose task it is to meet it.

In forecasting demand for a new product the purpose of the forecast needs to be understood, otherwise totally unsuitable numbers may be produced. For planning purposes the best estimate of actual sales will often be required, but sometimes action standards together with the chances of meeting them will be more appropriate.

This section concludes with brief notes on some of the techniques which provide relevant data for new product forecasting. Unfortunately none of them separately or in combination is infallible; there are many new products which fail and prudent financial planning will consider this possibility even if the sales manager's address to the sales convention does not!

## PRODUCT FORECASTING TECHNIQUES

### Concept testing

Once a product concept is considered a possible new entry by management, the next stage may be a group discussion. A small sample drawn from the demographic groups considered to be potential customers is invited to a meeting and a trained leader focuses the discussion on the product area. For example the groups might be asked to consider the problems of dirty dishes. From such a meeting the consumers' views as to the strengths and weaknesses of existing products will emerge for comparison with the new entrant. Quantitative estimates of sales volumes are not the normal outcome, but some feel for the potential can be obtained.

### Consumer trials

Once the product is available, even in very limited quantities, potential purchasers may be invited to try it and to comment. A group discussion could be used, but often a simulated purchasing situation will be more revealing. Respondents may be told they have so much money to spend (say enough for two packs of any brand in the product area) and they are asked to choose between the new brand and other existing brands. Usually any money remaining will be theirs to keep and they may keep all the money if they wish. Such a test involves pricing the new entrant, which is highly important to its ultimate success. The actual choice may be made from a catalogue list or from a mock-up of a real store.

Such a test is aimed at measuring repeat purchasing. The eventual sales depend on two factors: (a) what proportion of the population will try, i.e. buy, at least once; and (b) what fraction of their subsequent purchases will consist of the new brand. The first factor is called penetration and the second, repeat rate. The eventual share is the product of the two.

There are many ways of stimulating trial, including heavy advertising, free samples, special price offers and so on. However the repeat rate depends largely on the product itself, so that it can be estimated from test data of the sort described above. An attempt would be made to estimate penetration from previous experience of the proposed levels of advertising, promotion and sales effort. An important intermediate variable to be considered is the level of distribution (i.e. proportion of shops handling) which will be obtained.

If somewhat larger amounts of product are available, and if there are samples of the pack, a form of test, much closer to the real marketplace, is the mini-van. This is a van which calls on a selected panel of housewives at regular intervals and offers a fairly complete range of groceries at competitive prices. By accepting orders only on the special form provided a complete record of purchases is obtained. It is easy enough to insert new items into the range for test purposes. As far as the housewife is concerned, the van is merely a door-to-door selling operation, but it has been found to provide good estimates of repeat buying rates. It is less effective at estimating penetration, as it is difficult to simulate normal advertising activity, particularly television. Also missing are the effects associated with distribution levels. In some countries special mini-stores are used rather than vans.

The closest that can be come to the full national market is an area test market. Here the intention is to reproduce every aspect in a small area where the costs and risks are less than in a national launch. It is usually necessary to commission special market research in the test area to provide the required information. This is because routine sources seldom cover small areas in sufficient detail.

How well do test markets predict national sales? Apart from sampling errors associated with their size, there are some other problems. By their nature, small test areas may receive an undue level of sales-force attention. This should not happen but it does, because all concerned are aware of head-office interest. Competitive reaction is sometimes on a scale which could not be maintained on a national level. Finally the effects of regional differences must be considered. Different products do sell differently across the country and this too must be considered in grossing up to national sales.

Before leaving test marketing it should be noted that it cannot be kept secret (unlike a mini-van). Often competitors can learn just as much from a test market. If the product can easily be copied it may be preferable to avoid a test market altogether.

## INDUSTRIAL GOODS

Forecasting the demand for industrial goods differs in many ways from that of consumer products. The difference lies in the nature of the buyers, and often in the frequency of purchase. Typically the buyers are relatively few in number and technically competent to evaluate the objective properties of their purchases. This means that it is often possible to place prototypes with potential customers for evaluation.

Before this stage is reached it is usual to analyse the industrial uses of the product and to form estimates of the future development of the users. Thus the market for a new roof tile must depend on future housing starts, together with the rate at which existing roofs will require replacement. Once these estimates are available, they can be used together with the customer trials to estimate the volume we are likely to obtain.

It is likely that in estimating consumer sales potential, the bulk of the effort will go into field work to obtain data. In industrial markets a much higher proportion will be desk work in which data already published will be studied for the light they throw on the product.

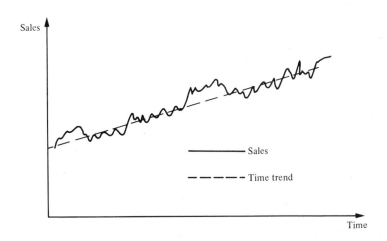

**Fig. 3.4   Actual sales and underlying pattern**

## ANALYTICAL METHODS OF SHORT-TERM FORECASTS

In all practical forecasting problems, the relevant information consists of a series of, say, monthly observations. These might be sales or
production data. At any point of time the past history of the series is
available and it is wished to predict the next few numbers. If the data
are plotted on graph paper two things will be noticed. There is a broad
pattern which relates the data to the passage of time – a pencilled in
freehand curve reflects this relationship. In addition there is a random pattern of deviations from this curve. To forecast, the freehand
curve needs to be extended in advance of firm information. To see
how accurate the forecast is likely to be, the pattern of the deviations
must be understood (see Figure 3.4).

### Moving averages

Intuition suggests that random fluctuations 'ought to average out'
and this leads to the simplest possible method of computing the
underlying time pattern. An appropriate number of observations is
averaged. Quarters might be taken, which means adding the first
three observations and dividing by three. Then observations 2, 3, and
4 and so on are taken. The result is a quarterly moving average. This
could be computed just as well by multiplying each observation by
one-third and adding the results in sets of three. The quantities
'one-third' are called weights.

Moving averages not only iron out random fluctuations; they also
iron out seasonal patterns, provided the length of the cycle is the same
as the number of observations being averaged. For this reason they
usually exhibit a much simpler pattern than the original data and it is
easier to 'guess' the next few moving averages for prediction purposes.

There is no reason why the weights used should all be equal and for
many purposes it is better to use unequal weights. Thus 60 per cent of
last month's sales might be taken, plus 30 per cent of the month
before and 10 per cent of the month before that. Such a weighting
system reflects the belief that recent events are more relevant to the
future than the remote past. Most of the currently available forecasting formulas are equivalent to some form of weighted moving
average, but frequently this is not readily apparent as it is convenient
to compute with other formulas.

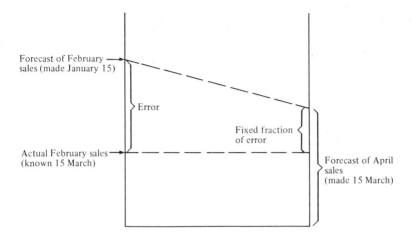

Forecast of February sales (made January 15)

Error

Fixed fraction of error

Actual February sales (known 15 March)

Forecast of April sales (made 15 March)

**Fig. 3.5 How smoothed forecasts are made**

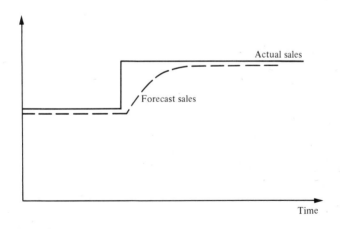

Actual sales

Forecast sales

Time

**Fig. 3.6 Tracking a step rise**

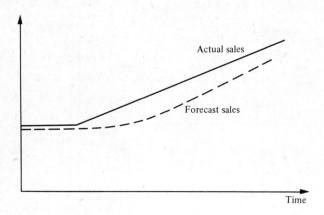

**Fig. 3.7  Tracking a trend**

Note: Unless the trend is also smoothed, the forecast will lag behind the actual sales.

## Smoothing models

As time passes more observations are obtained and the size of forecasting errors is ascertained. It seems reasonable to take past errors into account in making further forecasts. One way to do this is add a fixed percentage of last month's error to last month's actual sales and use the result as a forecast for next month. This is equivalent to using a weighted average of actual and forecast sales.

If there is a time trend the same can be done for the trend measure, which is defined as the difference between this month's and last month's actual sales.

Figures 3.5, 3.6 and 3.7 illustrate some possibilities with simple smoothing methods. Such methods seem to give quite good short-term forecasts, but perhaps too short-term for financial planning. They are very useful for production planning and stock control. As with any 'automatic' methods results can be improved by the judicious use of extraneous information. For example it might be known that this month's sales were affected by a strike or raw material problems; abnormally high sales might be anticipated next month because of a price offer.

## Large time series

The smoothing method just described can start with very few observations and will often settle down quite quickly to yield reasonable forecasts. When there are several years' listing more sophisticated methods can be used to determine appropriate weights. The best known of these is named 'Box–Jenkins' after its originators. It uses a weighted average of sales over several months, together with a weighted average of past errors. The system starts by using the data to determine how many months of each to take and then computes the weights. The basic criterion used is to make the (average) forecast error as small as possible, but Box and Jenkins recognised another principle which is helpful.

> As long as successive errors are not independent of each other, a knowledge of past errors could be used to predict future errors and hence to improve forecasts. Thus if calculation shows that errors are related to each other the forecast formula can be improved.

This approach not only permits the use of past history of a time series to forecast its future, but it can also be adapted to take into account other relevant information. For example in predicting sales it might be much better to use data on prices and advertising levels instead of sales alone.

## Causality and control

In order to forecast sales a lead indicator might be discovered and Box–Jenkins methods used to ascertain the nature of the relationship. This does not mean a cause of sales has necessarily been found or that altering the indicator would control or influence sales in any way. There may merely be a pair of variables which move together under the influence of a third, possibly unknown factor. Thus there is a major difference between forecast and control. The latter will require a much deeper understanding of the underlying mechanisms than the former. It is probable that control will require designed experiments to ascertain the nature of these mechanisms. A discussion of these points is beyond the scope of this chapter.

**57**

## REFERENCES AND ADDITIONAL READING

Ackoff, R.L. and Sasieni, M.W., *Fundamentals of Operations Research,* Wiley, 1965.

Gabor, A., *Pricing: Principles and Practice,* Heinemann, 1977.

Kotler, P., *Marketing Management: Analysis, Planning and Control,* Prentice-Hall, 1976.

Lewis, C.D., *Industrial Forecasting Techniques,* Machinery Publishing, 1970.

Wilson, A., *The Assessment of Industrial Markets,* Cassell/ABP, 1973.

Worcester, R.M. and Downham, J. (eds), *Consumer Market Research Handbook,* Van Nostrand Reinhold, 1972.

# 4

# Income and Expenditure Budgets

## Desmond Goch

*We now assume that the business has defined its objectives, considered its resources, and assessed the demand for the goods and services which it was set up to supply. The next major stage in the planning process is to formulate the budgets of income and expenditure, for both revenue and capital items. The author of this chapter deals with income and expenditure on revenue account and the succeeding chapter will examine capital budgeting. He divides the process of revenue budgeting into (a) long-term strategic planning, incorporating the forecast demand changes referred to in the preceding chapter, and (b) short-term, tactical planning. The author refers to the budgeting process as representing 'a distillation of experience and judgement . . . of the management team', thus echoing a similar thought expressed by Dr Sasieni when examining the forecasting of demand. Another significant comment by the present author on the budgetary system is that it should combine 'an element of motivation with a dash of scepticism'.*

*Emphasis is given to the importance of the objective of a profit target based on the current value of capital employed (for further discussion of the assessment of current values the reader is referred to the chapter on inflation accounting); and of reconciling the sales and production viewpoints. One of the key planning considerations in preparing the sales budget is to give priority to those product ranges from which the greatest contribution will be derived. The importance of sound pricing policy and the need for control of research and development are referred to by Mr Goch and taken up in greater depth in later chapters.*

Business planning can usually be divided into two broad categories.

One of these is the long-term strategic planning which is primarily concerned with forecasting and shaping the future development of the business to ensure that it is equipped to deal with perceived changes in the market for its existing products or services and to be ready to exploit new commercial opportunities and technical innovations whenever they arise. This kind of planning may have a time-horizon that extends forward for a decade or more, particularly where the industry concerned is one that requires a lengthy gestation period for its major capital expenditure schemes before they begin to make a contribution to profits. For example, an oil refinery or a complex chemical plant is usually subject to lengthy environmental planning permission procedures and even then the ensuing design and construction phases will be spread over several years. In these kinds of circumstances forward planning entails looking a long way into the future.

The second kind of business planning – with which we are concerned in this chapter – is the shorter-term tactical planning which reflects the current trading environment and makes its impact through the annual trading budget. With its much shorter time-horizon – usually no more than a year ahead at a time – it aims to assess the business outlook over this period and to plan accordingly so as to make the most economic and profitable use of resources in exploiting the potential market opportunities. This budgeting exercise imposes a discipline on management by requiring this kind of regular appraisal of the way in which the long-term planning objectives are being met and by determining the standards by which subsequent performance will be measured.

It needs to be emphasised at the outset that the preparation of a trading budget of this nature is an exercise that should, where possible, involve all those line managers who will subsequently share responsibility for seeing that it is implemented. Although the budget is ultimately expressed in financial terms, it is essentially concerned with planning the effective and profitable use of the human, physical and financial resources of the business during the period under review. It should accordingly represent a distillation of the experience and judgement of a range of opinion within the management team and in this way it is more likely to be accepted as representing an achievable target.

In the sense that the targets set by the budget should be ones that demand a concentrated effort to achieve, the planning process should

aim to combine an element of motivation with a dash of scepticism –
the latter being required to act as a counterweight to the over-
optimism that sometimes pervades the discussion when sales and
production targets and potential market opportunities are being considered. Although such optimism should not be too hastily dis-
couraged, there is a need for an entirely objective assessment of the
trading possibilities and the underlying strategy within the parameters of the economic environment if the budget plan that eventually emerges is to provide a sound base for the consequential
decisions that may have to be made in relation to providing additional
production facilities and possible working capital requirements.

## THE PLANNING OBJECTIVES

One of the starting points for the budget planning operation will be
the determination of the trading objectives and to a large extent these
will obviously reflect the strategy defined in the long-term plan. For
many businesses this budgetary objective can be summarised as a
requirement to earn a minimum target rate of profit and all the
ensuing detailed planning will be directed towards meeting this
requirement.

However, the concept of a profit target needs to be related to an
acceptable base figure and it is frequently expressed as a rate of
return on the capital resources employed in the business expressed in
monetary terms. This 'return on capital employed' yardstick (ROC)
for measuring performance is most appropriate where the undertaking is of a kind that requires investment in the form of buildings,
plant and machinery and of working capital to finance trading stock,
materials, work in progress and customer credit, in order to carry on
the business. Since the capital funds which have to be provided to
finance this investment require to be remunerated in the form of
dividends, loan interest and, perhaps, bank interest, then the test of
commercial viability and managerial efficiency is the ability to earn
enough profit to meet these commitments after tax has been paid and
to provide sufficient surplus thereafter to meet the additional capital
requirements for progressive expansion in the future.

In setting this financial objective a decision must be made as to
what is the appropriate rate of return to be expected from the employment of the capital funds in this way. One approach is to express

the target rate in relation to rates being achieved by comparable businesses in the same or in similar industries and this information can usually be obtained from an examination of published annual reports or by studying comparative financial statistics compiled by one of the agencies that nowadays specialises in providing this service. An alternative possibility is to relate the required rate to an established datum point such as bank minimum lending rate, although this is a less realistic yardstick as it is subject to short-term fluctuations and takes no account of industry sector experience. The first approach is probably the more equitable one to use and is more likely to be accepted by managements as offering a fair comparison with performance elsewhere.

In determining the value to be placed on the physical assets component of the figure of capital employed to be used for setting the profit target it is becoming increasingly common practice to adopt current costs rather than the historic costs at which they are normally shown in the balance sheet. Where the calculation of current values is not a practical possibility, then consideration could be given to adjusting the historic cost figures by reference to an appropriate index of prices.

So as to ensure comparability between their various manufacturing establishments or operating divisions, some companies calculate the capital employed base for this purpose on the assumption that premises are occupied on a tenancy basis (irrespective of the actual circumstances) and thus a notional rent is charged against the budgeted profit and the capital value of the buildings (if any) is excluded from the calculation. The advantage of this method is that the managements of individual operating units are not unfairly penalised when their profit targets are being assessed by being burdened with the capital value of premises which they are required to occupy as a matter of overall company policy but which may not be the most economical choice from a purely operational viewpoint.[1]

A profit target expressed as a rate of return on capital employed is not appropriate to every type of trading activity, particularly where the nature of the business does not require the investment of significant amounts of capital in buildings, plant, machinery and similar kinds of physical assets. In a business such as an advertising agency or

---

[1] A specimen 'capital employed' computation is shown in the appendix to this chapter.

an architectural practice another yardstick will need to be adopted and this may be one which is expressed simply as a target percentage rate of net profit on sales turnover or gross fees, as appropriate.

The overall financial target may, of course, be a composite of varying rates of return required of individual divisions or profit centres within the main trading unit, and from the viewpoint of encouraging greater involvement of individual departmental managers and instilling a proper element of motivation there is every advantage to be gained from this approach. If managers are made responsible for preparing or contributing to the preparation of their own trading budgets, they are thereby encouraged to accept a deeper sense of commitment to achieving their targets.

A corollary to this sectionalised approach to budgeting is the existence of a logical and clearly defined management structure. Responsibility for spending and profit must follow the line of the management chain of command and must take into account the limits within which individual initiatives can be exercised. The individual manager is thereby encouraged to 'run his own show' and to be prepared to answer for his actions based on the results he turns in at the end of the year.

## THE KEY PLANNING CONSIDERATIONS

Notwithstanding the principle of delegation of financial and budgetary responsibilities, there is an overriding requirement for centralised guidance and control and in the typical business this oversight can best be exercised through a budget planning committee comprising senior management personnel representing the principal line and staff functions – marketing, production, finance, personnel, etc., with the chief executive acting as chairman of the group.

The starting point for the planning exercise should be an appraisal of the proposed budget strategy in the context of the economic and trading environment at that time and the marketing conditions that are foreseen for the budget period. There is no rigid set of rules to be observed in making this appraisal as the strategy will be conditioned by the business climate and factors such as the degree of competition to be expected from overseas suppliers and the strength of consumer demand. The nature of the industry will, of course, be a material factor in determining the precise approach. Different considerations will apply when forecasting the potential demand for a range of fast-selling consumer products compared with, say, the prospective order book for specialised machinery being sold in overseas markets against worldwide competition.

Most forms of business activity are affected to some degree by the external environment and the level of economic activity in the territories where business is planned. A key factor in assessing market possibilities and shaping the trading budget will therefore be the accuracy of the assessment of the probable course of the national economy during the budget period under review. Whether the business be one of organising and selling foreign holiday package tours or of involvement in marketing high-technology electronic equipment to overseas customers throughout the world, the chances of finding sufficient customers to take up the potential output or production capacity on offer will be influenced to a marked degree by the state of the internal economies of the countries in which they are situated. In some instances, of course, the underlying political stability of national governments will be a material consideration in deciding where to concentrate marketing effort. There may also be a need to take account of difficulties likely to be encountered in remitting back to the home country the proceeds of sales made in territories where the government imposes rigid foreign exchange restrictions.

Where the business is one with a markedly seasonal pattern of demand, the success of the trading forecast on which the budget is to be based may be conditioned by the potential buoyancy of trade in the immediate months ahead. An example of this kind of business is the toy manufacturing industry which has a large part of its annual sales turnover concentrated into the pre-Christmas shopping period. The level of demand in the shops at that time is to some extent influenced by the amount of disposable income in the hands of parents and other relatives when the Christmas-present buying season is at its height. If at that time the economy is running at a strong level and there are no major adverse influences such as transport strikes to mar the spending spree, then there will be every likelihood of a good selling season for the toy industry.

However, the decisions about which toys to produce, and at what level of output, have to be made many months beforehand and at the time when these production programmes and sales campaigns are being planned the economic outlook may seem to be very much less favourable. In such circumstances the budget planners will need to consider the views of the more reputable and influential economic forecasting institutions and of available surveys of business opinions such as those conducted by the Confederation of British Industry. Equally important, of course, will be such feedback as can be obtained from customers who are visited on a regular basis by sales representatives as this will give an indication of opinion within the industry in which the business operates. A further view on the prevailing industrial climate can usually be supplied by the senior marketing executives and their contribution to the budget planning sessions is often the most sensitive guide to the probable course of trade.

It is against this backdrop of external economic factors and intelligence gathered about the known intentions of competitors, actual or potential, that the budget planners will have to make their assessment of the prospective order book and the market opportunities that are likely to present themselves. If the company is a divisionalised or multi-product business, then this task should be delegated as much as possible to those managers who are responsible for the marketing operations at these sub-levels and their individual assessments can be presented for scrutiny and discussion by the main planning group so as to encourage the formulation of a broadly based view on the likely trend of trade.

## THE SALES/PRODUCTION EQUATION

Where the assessment of potential demand and market opportunities indicates that there is an element of choice in deciding which sectors and product ranges should be given priority, then this requires close consultation with the production management executives (or the executives responsible for procurement and supply where the organisation does not manufacture) and also with the financial members of the planning group.

In such circumstances the selling effort should be concentrated on those product ranges that will yield the highest contribution to profit and a close analysis should be made of the kind of sales mix that will best achieve this objective. The profit contribution per unit of output represents the difference between the revenue yield and the directly related incremental costs arising from production and it is commonly referred to as the 'contribution margin'. By way of example, if the unit of sales is a canned food product, the incremental costs would consist of the cost of the bought-out can and the cost of the ingredients that go to make up the contents. When assessing the relative profitability of this product compared with an alternative, it is essential to determine their respective contribution margins after taking into consideration the hourly production rates and assuming that they are both capable of being produced on the same preparation and canning line.

The following example based on this imaginary food product will serve to illustrate this important concept of the contribution margin as a factor when making a sales/production decision in such circumstances. It is assumed that the management of the production unit has only limited capacity on its can-filling lines and it has to choose between three alternative products when planning the production programme. The three products are sold to wholesalers and large retailers and the respective contribution margins have been calculated in Table 4.1.

**Table 4.1**
**Contribution margins of three products**

|  | Product A | Product B | Product C |
|---|---|---|---|
|  | p | p | p |
| Net sales revenue | 11 | 12 | 14 |
| Incremental costs: |  |  |  |
| Can | 2 | 2 | 2 |
| Ingredients | 3 | 4 | 5 |
| Other direct costs | 1 | 1 | 1 |
|  | 6 | 7 | 8 |
| Contribution margin | 5 | 5 | 6 |
| Hourly production rate | 3,600 | 3,400 | 2,800 |
| Contribution per hour | £180 | £170 | £168 |

It will be seen from this example that although Product C has the highest unit selling price and the highest unit contribution margin, it is Product A with the lowest unit selling price which yields the highest contribution on an hourly basis and it is the differential in the hourly production rate which is the deciding factor. Since it is the contribution margin that represents the gross profit from which the production overheads, the selling, distribution and administration costs and the net profit margin have to be found, there is obviously considerable importance to be attached to maximising it by choosing that product mix that will best achieve this objective.

Although this example has been based on a manufactured product, the same principle applies in distribution and service industry organisations. A retailer will obviously look very carefully at the gross profit margin (a synonym for the contribution margin in this context) when deciding which ranges of goods to give prime selling space to when planning counter and window displays.

## MATCHING DEMAND TO RESOURCES

In planning the sales budgets for individual products an essential part of the exercise is to ensure that the forecasted offtake can be matched by the productive capacity of the organisation. It may be that when the sales requirement is related to potential capacity in this way it will be found that the targets could not be achieved without bringing into use additional capacity and in this event it will be necessary for the budget planners to examine the implications so far as it might entail incurring capital expenditure on plant and also additional operating costs.

If, on the other hand, it is found that there is likely to be a surplus of production capacity, then it may be possible to plan for the introduction of new product lines or services so as to gain a higher utilisation of plant and other facilities. An example of this approach to the exploitation of under-used capacity is to be found in the magazine and periodical publishing industry where new titles are launched, or existing ones are re-launched, so as to take up printing capacity that would otherwise be standing idle. Thus, when the Trafalgar House Group took over the Beaverbrook Newspapers organisation, the new management decided that rather than risk an inevitably bitter confrontation with the trade unions if it attempted to cut the labour force so as to deal with the overmanning that had been a contributory factor to trading losses, it would instead strive to achieve a higher plant utilisation. The outcome of this approach was the launch of a completely new daily newspaper (*The Star*) that could be printed on the existing presses and using substantially the same publishing-room staff and distribution facilities.

A comparable situation in a service industry might be in the holiday travel business where the more popular resorts have reached their capacity in terms of available hotel accommodation and so the marketing effort is turned to promoting the virtues of newer centres which have not hitherto attracted a large tourist following. In this way the travel companies and the air charter firms are able to maintain full utilisation of aircraft and other facilities that have been committed on time charters or other contractual arrangements.

When the broad outline of the sales/production plan has been agreed, it will then be necessary for the production members of the planning team to break it down into manageable sectors so that the manpower and materials requirements can be allocated to the departments involved and costed out in financial terms. This part of the budgeting exercise is probably the most complex aspect as it entails translating physical output into terms of manpower requirements and machine-loading programmes. In addition, an appraisal has to be made of the back-up facilities that will be needed in the form of setting and maintenance personnel and toolroom services. Most of the major problems in this area are likely to arise when a new production facility is being created or a major product change is necessary.

It is possible, of course, that where the pattern of sales has seasonal or other cyclical characteristics, then the production programme may be planned on the basis that goods are made for stock at times when demand is at a seasonally low ebb. On the other hand, where output is produced on the basis of forecasted demand from retailers, rather than manufacturing against specific orders, provision may have to be made in the labour budget for possible overtime working at peak periods when demand is high. Peaks and troughs in demand can make for difficulties in production planning and the ideal solution – though often unattainable – is to develop products or sales outlets that fit into the slacker periods in the present programme.

Having translated the production requirements into physical and manpower resource terms, it is necessary to determine appropriate control factors for monitoring subsequent performance against the budget. If standard costing methods are already in use they will provide the basic data for building up a system of flexible budgeting. Such a system is valuable where budgeting assumptions have to be made within a range of possible output levels as some items of overhead will fluctuate in proportion while others will vary hardly at all. Indeed, it is often the case that in the short term very few overhead expenses will vary with output – with the possible exception of some consumable materials and the variable element of the power charge for electricity or gas. With longer-term variations in the level of activity there will, of course, be pressures to reduce items of overhead that are left untouched in the short term. Thus it may be advisable to classify the various items of overhead expenditure as either 'fixed' or 'variable' so that the budgeted expenditure limits can be flexed according to the level of activity.

## BUDGETING FOR OVERHEADS

Concurrently with the planning of the sales and production pro-grammes, an analysis will have to be made of the expenses that go to make up the remainder of the operating expenditures under the general classification of factory overheads. In the case of a manu-facturing organisation these expenses will embrace a multitude of individual items, from period costs such as capital expenditure amor-tisation charges to the day-to-day spending on maintenance spares, loose tools, consumable materials and similar items.

The periodic budgeting exercise provides an opportunity for a detailed scrutiny of many items that throughout the rest of the year are usually lost among the nooks and crannies of overhead expen-diture and accordingly a careful appraisal should be made of the justification for perpetuating recurring commitments before they are included again. An examination of the telephone accounts sometimes discloses charges for rental of equipment that is no longer in use and the same may be said of some equipment-leasing agreements.

For many companies the payroll comprises by far the largest category of expenditure and in addition to the direct wage and salary costs there are all the related costs such as national insurance con-tributions, superannuation scheme contributions, sickness benefit and medical insurance schemes, employer's liability insurance and

similar commitments. It therefore follows that with labour costs
becoming such a large element of total costs for many companies,
particular attention needs to be given to the planned use of labour
resources and to any aspect of the budget that might entail recruiting
additional employees. Indeed, there is much to commend the practice
of many companies of drawing up a total manpower budget which,
when approved, represents the limit of the organisation's payroll
commitment and which cannot be exceeded without the specific
authorisation of a senior management executive.

Planning the labour element of the budget is one of the most crucial
phases of the whole exercise as there is a perfectly human tendency
on the part of many departmental managers to seek to justify as large
a manpower establishment as can be negotiated. Underspending
being so much easier to justify than overspending, and with the
possibility of absenteeism and sickness in mind, they will sometimes
seek to hedge their bets when asked to state their manpower
requirements for inclusion in the budget. When evaluating manning
requirements for production line work it is not too difficult to assess
the strength of a case for additional people but rather closer scrutiny
and a degree of scepticism is needed when the request is for indirect
employees. Jobs such as storekeeping, quality control, packing,
labouring, cleaning, etc., have a tendency to multiply and swallow up
the profit margins unless they are closely controlled and a similar
approach is usually needed in the case of administrative personnel. In
all these areas there is a need for applying the control of the strict
manpower budget, but leaving the individual departmental managers
to decide which jobs to fill within their allocation of posts.

## ACTIVITY BUDGETING

For some types of businesses the planned level of business activity
may need to be capable of significant variation as the year progresses
if new opportunities are presented. For example, a multiple retailing
organisation operating a chain of outlets in major towns and cities will
often find that the opportunity arises at short notice to acquire new
premises or to take over suitable existing premises and this may
represent an expansion of trading levels and profit expectations
beyond those envisaged in the original budget plan.

For this type of business the approach to budgeting would probably
be based on the assumption of a target rate of turnover and gross

profit from each shop calculated according to its floor space and any new acquisitions during the year would be added to the budget totals on the same basis. Similarly, of course, any closures of outlets during the year would be withdrawn from the time when they ceased to trade.

The sales staff payroll budget and the shop-related overheads budget could also be built up in the same way, according to the number of shop units, and the emphasis of the budget plan would thus be directed at the operating level of the retail selling units rather than at the consolidated results of the company, such as would be the case with a large manufacturing organisation. Indeed, with this kind of multiple retailing organisation the essence of sound budgeting and control would be the formulation of appropriate budget standards based on experience gained in operating the more efficient outlets.

The principle of applying predetermined budget standards has, of course, other applications including the virtue of combining the forecasting of operating costs with the setting of standards which can be applied as yardsticks for judging subsequent performance. It may be possible to devise similar cost control factors to those applied in many manufacturing businesses and thus to relate target cost levels to the degree of activity. Companies employing a force of outside sales representatives might well adopt a similar approach in forecasting and controlling selling costs in terms of salaries and expenses and the same technique can be applied to operating costs for a vehicle fleet measured on a volume/mileage basis.

## RESEARCH AND DEVELOPMENT BUDGETING

For many companies – typically those in the aerospace and pharmaceuticals industries – long-term survival depends on the ability to maintain a technical or scientific edge over competitors and this entails supporting a continuous programme of research and development. The nature and extent of this commitment will vary considerably, but in many instances it will entail financing the cost of a permanent research establishment with all the attendant running expenses that it involves.

At the end of the day, of course, the expectation is that such an investment will fully justify its existence in the form of new products and improvements to existing ones. During their commercial lifetime they will thus contribute to earnings on a scale that will more than recoup the expenditure incurred in running the research facility and at the same time enhance the company's reputation as a leader in its industry. Setting up such a facility often represents an act of faith in the future as there can never be absolute certainty that such an investment will pay off in simple financial terms. Inevitably some projects will prove to be abortive and only a proportion may offer the hope of commercial exploitation.

However, having made the decision to set up such a facility it can be assumed that the parent organisation has accepted a commitment to finance a research programme and the next question to ask is how much expenditure can the business afford to commit on an annual basis for this purpose. It is entirely understandable that the staff employed in these kinds of establishment should feel that their work is best carried on away from the day-to-day pressures of the production units and thus they do not alway so readily understand the need to accept the kind of financial disciplines and cost constraints which are normally imposed elsewhere in the organisation. It will therefore make for a better working relationship between the senior management of the company and the senior research staff if there is a clear appreciation on both sides of the broad objectives of the research and development programme and of the financial limitations within which it has to be conducted.

To achieve this end it is essential that the research establishment should be fully integrated within the annual budgeting exercise. To the extent that the main research establishment budget will comprise premises and payroll costs, these elements of the total financial allocation can be readily evaluated in financial terms. In addition, it is probable that there will be some non-recurring expenditure to be incurred on specialised test equipment and possibly on projects placed with outside research organisations and universities. In quantifying the likely expenditure in these sectors it is desirable that the head of the research department should be asked to outline the year's programme so that this can be costed in terms of the staff employed and such other expenditure as can be foreseen. The costed programme can then be submitted through the central budget committee for approval by the board of directors and when so accepted it will form the year's research budget.

Although this budgetary discipline will almost certainly seem bureaucratic and irksome to the staff of a research and development department – as, indeed, it will to staff elsewhere in the organisation –

it nevertheless provides them in the long run with a greater measure of personal security and assists them to define priorities that are consistent with the commercial objectives of the company. For many industries a sound research and development programme is essential to the future wellbeing of the organisation but it must be carried on at a level that the company can afford – and hence the need for soundly-based budgeting.

## THE OVERALL BUDGET REVIEW

When all the individual departmental projections have been completed they will have to be assembled by the finance department representative on the budget planning team in a format that corresponds with the presentation adopted for the organisation's internal management accounts so that the overall result can be studied and evaluated according to the broad strategy and the financial and commercial criteria which were determined at the outset of the budgeting exercise.

It would be surprising, indeed, if this first draft were to be found to present an acceptable statement of projected trading results and the budget planning team will have to pass their judgement on the planned performance for each department. It is not practicable in a general review of budgeting procedures of this nature to define precisely the kind of yardstick that would be applied for this purpose, but obviously the assessment would take in key factors such as the forecasted rate of profit on sales turnover and, where appropriate, the return on capital employed. Most important, however, is to examine very closely the underlying assumptions as to the level of projected sales, which must always be the keystone of the whole financial and budgetary edifice. How does it compare on a physical volume basis with earlier years and is any assumption as to growth – both absolute and relative to the market share – founded on reasonable arguments? Does any assumed increase in the share of the market take account of the known plans of competitors and their probable reaction to this attempt to capture some of their business? Are the assumptions as to growth in the total market consistent with national economic trends and other market indicators? These are the kinds of question that need to be asked by the central budget planning team so as to test the validity of the projections on which the sales forecasts are based.

So much for the demand side of the equation – but what about the supply side? Here again there is a need for fairly rigorous scrutiny of the assumptions about the level of output that will be needed to meet the selling requirements. Any significant increase in the sales volume requirement must be looked at in the context of the existing plant capacity. If the demand on resources is going to be such that additional capacity will need to be installed, then this will have to be available in time to make good the extra volume needed. Failing that, does the budget make realistic provision for any extra overtime that may be needed to meet the target from the existing plant? Do the production plans ensure an adequate supply of bought-out materials and components?

In the light of replies given by the departmental and divisional managers to these kinds of question, it may be necessary to re-examine certain sectors of the budget plan so as to get the balance right. At the end of the day, of course, the total plan must indicate a level of profit that is acceptable in relation to the capital and other resources employed in the business. It may be, of course, that as a result of the budget appraisal consideration will have to be given to the case for withdrawing from those trading activities that show little prospect of earning an adequate return when measured in this way.

One of the major hazards of budget planning in the contemporary business environment is deciding the extent of the provision that has to be made for cost inflation during the review period. Where the business operates in an industry whose wage rates are negotiated on a national basis, it will be necessary for the planning team to formulate a view on the likely level of the annual settlement. On the basis of this view, an appropriate allowance must be built into the budget.

In the case of a manufacturing business the likely trend of prices of its major raw materials can be difficult to forecast with any confidence, particularly where they are traded commodities such as cocoa or wheat or where metals such as steel or aluminium are involved. The problem is compounded, of course, where such materials are imported and buying prices are governed by fluctuations in foreign exchange rates. However, despite these complications, a best estimate has to be made to give some indication of the likely outcome of trading.

When these various cost inflation contingency factors have been incorporated into the budget forecasts a view can then be taken on the probable effect on profit margins and thus on the prospective pricing strategy. Trading budgets which are subject to these kinds of variable can, of course, be criticised for being little more than an informed guess at the future course of business and those managers who have had extensive experience of participating in budget planning will concede the element of truth in this view.

However, despite these reservations, the fact remains that a soundly constructed budget that has been based on rational assumptions provides an invaluable means of monitoring trading activity. As the business moves forward into the trading period covered by the budget and the actual out-turn can be compared with the forecast, it acts as an early warning system and indicates those areas where action may need to be taken to deal with any adverse trends.

Finally, the planning exercise itself imposes a mental discipline on individual managers in that it requires them to make a rigorous appraisal of their department's performance and its prospective contribution to profitability over the coming year. By being involved in the planning processes across a wide spectrum they are encouraged to take a broader view of their responsibilities, thereby aiding the development of latent talent within a controlled environment.

## APPENDIX – RETURN ON CAPITAL EMPLOYED

Where the nature of the business is such that it requires a substantial investment of capital in land, buildings, plant, machinery and in working capital to finance stock, work in progress and trade debt, then a profit target expressed as a predetermined rate of return on the funds so employed is an appropriate basis of calculation for budgeting purposes.

In determining this capital employed base it is reasonable to make an adjustment to the historic cost figures at which the fixed assets are normally shown in the balance sheet so as to reflect current cost values. For the sake of simplicity this adjustment can be calculated by reference to an appropriate index of prices such as those published by the Government Statistical Service.

The following specimen balance sheet of an imaginary company is used to illustrate the calculation of a capital employed base figure for this purpose. It is assumed that the relative price index for 'Land and buildings' stood at 115 at the date of purchase and at 140 at the date of the balance sheet – thus showing an increase of 22 per cent. The 'Plant and machinery' index stood at 125 at the date of purchase and at 169 at the date of the balance sheet – an increase of 35 per cent.

### XYZ Ltd – Balance Sheet at 31/12/19XX

|  |  | £ |  |  | £ |
|---|---|---|---|---|---|
| Capital and reserves |  |  | Fixed assets |  |  |
| Share capital |  | 800,000 | Land and buildings |  | 750,000 |
| Reserves |  | 400,000 | Plant and machinery |  | 280,000 |
|  |  | 1,200,000 |  |  | 1,030,000 |
| Deferred taxation |  | 200,000 | Investments |  | 100,000 |
| Current liabilities |  |  | Current assets |  |  |
| Creditors | 150,000 |  | Trading stock | 200,000 |  |
| Taxation | 70,000 |  | Debtors | 400,000 |  |
| Bank overdraft | 120,000 | 340,000 | Cash | 10,000 | 610,000 |
|  |  | £1,740,000 |  |  | £1,740,000 |

The adjustments made to the balance sheet figures to determine the capital employed base figure are as follows:

| | Balance sheet | Excluded assets | Indexing factor | Adjusted values |
|---|---|---|---|---|
| | £ | £ | | £ |
| Land and buildings | 750,000 | 100,000 | 1.22 | 793,000 |
| Plant and machinery | 280,000 | — | 1.35 | 378,000 |
| Investments | 100,000 | 100,000 | — | — |
| Trading stock | 200,000 | — | — | 200,000 |
| Debtors | 400,000 | — | — | 400,000 |
| Creditors | (150,000) | — | — | (150,000) |
| | Adjusted capital employed | | | £1,621,000 |

For the purpose of this illustration it has been assumed that not all the land and buildings represented in the balance sheet are employed in the activity covered by the profit target and hence an adjustment has been made to exclude the appropriate book values. The current cost indexation has been applied to the adjusted book value. Similarly, the book value of the investments has been excluded as not being a part of the capital employed for this purpose.

It will be noted that the bank overdraft figure has been excluded from the calculation as it should be regarded as a source of capital rather than a current liability for the purpose of determining the capital employed base figure.

The appropriate target rate of return required by the budget (see text of this chapter) would be applied to the above adjusted capital employed figure of £1,621,000.

## REFERENCES AND ADDITIONAL READING

Cave, Stanley B., *Budgetary Control and Standard Costing*, 3rd edition, Gee & Co, London, 1973.

Heckert, Josiah B. and Willson, James D., *Business Budgeting and Control*, 3rd edition, Ronald Press, New York, 1967.

Rautenstrauch, Walter and Villers, Raymond, *Budgetary Control*, 2nd edition, Funk & Wagnalls, New York, 1968.

Scott, J.A., *Budgetary Control and Standard Costs,* 6th edition, Pitman, London, 1970.

Welsch, Glenn A., *Budgeting: Profit Planning and Control,* 4th edition, Prentice-Hall, 1976.

Willsmore, A.W., *Business Budgets in Practice,* 5th edition, Pitman, London, 1973.

# 5

# Capital Budgeting

**Harold Bierman, Jr**

*This is a subject for which there is already a voluminous literature, by no means all of which reflects recent developments. In this chapter Professor Bierman reviews the progress of thought on the subject.*

*The author sees the capital budget as the specific plan of action which allocates resources for the long-range plan. The objective of the process is firmly stated to be to maximise the net present value of the stockholders' position. The errors which result from using for capital appraisal purposes the accounting concept of profit are clearly exposed, and accrual accounting is compared with the simpler idea of cash flow. Capital projects are considered under the two essential headings of independent investment alternatives and mutually exclusive investments and we are informed – perhaps to our surprise – that 'there is no reliable objective way to rank investments'.*

*The author explains the defects of using return on investment and payback techniques of assessing capital projects, and compares the present value method with the internal rate of return. A particularly interesting section is the discussion of risk; 'there is no reason for assuming that risk is compounded through time' and the author maintains that it is incorrect to take risk into account via the discounting technique, but indicates how a risk premium may be quantified and refers to the capital pricing model of William Sharpe.*

*In a later chapter on the assessment of performance, Professor Magee, of the University of Wales, takes up a development of capital budgeting by emphasising that a post audit of each project is an important function of financial control.*

After the top management of a firm has completed its planning exercises, the resulting long-range plan has to be translated into a specific plan of action which actually allocates resources. This specific plan may be called the capital budget and the process of arriving at the plan may be called capital budgeting.

It is convenient to divide investments into two general classifications. The first category is all investment opportunities that are economically independent of each other. Thus a firm might consider replacing its automobile production line with a more labour-efficient set of machines, or it might consider entering the airline industry. These are two independent investment alternatives.

Once the independent investments have been determined, the second type of classification must be considered, that is to gather information on all investments which perform the same economic function. These are 'mutually exclusive' investments.

Once it is decided that the airline industry should be investigated as a possible investment all the different investment possibilities in aeroplanes that are mutually exclusive have to be considered. That is, there can only be one type of aeroplane fleet. The fleet might actually consist of a mixture of types of plane, but there can only be one type of mixture at a given time.

The objective of the capital budgeting process is to make accept-or-reject decisions involving independent investments (they can all be undertaken if they are desirable) and 'best of the set' decisions involving mutually exclusive investments (only one of these investments can be undertaken). In making these decisions there is implied some known and agreed objective for the firm.

As a first step it should be clearly indicated what objectives are not affecting the capital budgeting process. The aim is not to maximise total sales or percentage share of market. Growth is not the goal (though it might occur if the correct decisions are made) nor are earnings per share and total earnings being maximised. It will be seen that the goal is to maximise the net present value of the stockholders' position and it is assumed that in doing so wellbeing of the stockholders is being maximised. The decisions are being made from the point of view of the stockholders and it is assumed that their interests are best served by a procedure that systematically assigns a cost to the capital that is utilised in the production process.

The capital budgeting process that is recommended must take into consideration a cost on the capital that is being utilised or more generally the process must take into consideration the time value of money. As a second step, after enough sophistication to include complexities is gained, it can be recognised that the process must also take into account the existence of uncertainty and adjust for the risk of the project being considered.

Capital budgeting decisions generally involve immediate (or nearly immediate) outlays and benefits that stretch out through time. In some cases the benefits may be deferred for many years. The primary problem facing management responsible for making capital budgeting decisions is to incorporate time value and risk considerations in such a manner that the wellbeing of the stockholders is maximised.

This chapter will first review briefly the development of capital budgeting decision making over the last 25 years and then describe the present state of theory and practice. Most importantly, the basic principles of capital budgeting about which theoreticians are in general agreement will be described.

## THE PAST BRIEFLY REVIEWED

In 1951, two important books were published, one written by Joel Dean and one by Friedrich and Vera Lutz. These books immediately started people thinking about investment decisions and first a trickle and then a flood of papers and articles was written. At the time of publication of the two books the largest number of business firms were using a mixture of payback, a naïve return on investment (average income divided by average investment) and in the machine tool industry some variation of the MAPI[1] formula was just being introduced. An article in the *Harvard Business Review* by Dean (1954) was particularly important in bringing capital budgeting to the notice of business managers. In this paper Dean recommended the use of the rate of return method. This method consisted in finding a percentage (rate of discount) that caused the sum of the present values of the cash flows to be equal to zero and was a particularly important measure since it described the profitability of an investment in terms that were analogous to the yield of a bond or other

---

[1] Machinery Allied Products Institute

monetary investment. This was intuitively appealing to practical business managers. The internal rate of return technique rapidly became accepted by a wide range of industrial firms (the chemical and oil firms led the way), but there was some confusion about the relative merits of the internal rate of return (a percentage) method and the present value (a dollar amount) method. A famous issue of the University of Chicago *Journal of Business* described the confusion that existed, and the classic paper by Lorie and Savage (1955) summarised difficulties associated with the internal rate of return method in evaluating mutually exclusive investments, and in other situations where investments had to be compared.

The confusion between present value and internal rate of return persisted in theoretical literature until Jack Hirshliefer published a paper in the *Journal of Political Economy* (1958) which drew heavily on the classic book by Irving Fisher (1930), *The Theory of Interest*. In this paper Hirshliefer laid the foundation for understanding the similarities and differences between the present value and rate of return methods of making capital budgeting decisions. Later Bierman and Smidt (1975) published *The Capital Budgeting Decision*.

William Sharpe (1964) published a classic paper that introduced the capital asset pricing model. Since that time scholars have attempted to link that model to the capital budgeting decision problem. Particularly important links have been forged by Hamada (1969), Fama (1968), Lintner (1965), Mossin (1966), and Stapleton (1971). Future progress will build on these foundations.

The remainder of this chapter will describe the basic elements of capital budgeting and in the process will indicate how the conflict between present value and rate of return may be easily resolved.

## RANKING OF INVESTMENTS

Some managers think it useful to classify investment decisions as being of three types:

1  Making accept-or-reject decisions involving investments whose cash flows are independent of each other.
2  Choosing the best of a set of mutually exclusive investments; that is because of their characteristics only one of the investments can be undertaken (for example, you only place one roof on a factory).
3  Ranking of investments in order of their desirability.

This third classification requires explanation. While investments can be ranked subjectively in the same manner that one can rank the ten best movies of the year, there is no reliable objective way to rank investments. This disclosure is generally disappointing to managers who like to rank investments in order of relative desirability and then cut off when all investable funds are committed. In fact, some 'solutions' have been offered which claim to accomplish such rankings. Unfortunately, no simple exact solution exists.

However, all is not lost. Most importantly the investments can be separated into two classifications, acceptable and not acceptable. If a manager then wants to rank the acceptable investments using subjective or quasi-quantitative techniques, given the degree of uncertainty that exists in the world, this practice is relatively harmless. Second, the need for a ranking can be avoided by a 'programming' technique that chooses the best set of investments, given the resource limitations and a well-defined objective (such as maximisation of present value).

In some very well-defined situations investments can be ranked, but these cases are not likely to be frequently encountered in the real world.

## USE OF CASH FLOWS

The investment analysis should be performed using the after-tax cash flows of each period as the inputs into the calculations. The results are consistent with the use of a theoretically correct income measure and easier to compute since they do not require a measure of depreciation expense and other accounting accruals and assumptions.

The debt flows are generally excluded from the measure of cash flows. Thus profitability measures are obtained that are independent of the method of financing. For some purposes the decision maker may want to include all debt flows (not just interest) to obtain stockholder equity profitability measures. These measures must be used with care since they are not comparable to measures that exclude the debt flows. A major error is to include some of the effects of debt, but not all.

The accountant measures yearly earnings based on complex 'accrual' concepts. The cash flow calculations of capital budgeting decisions are much simpler. The net amount of cash receipts and expenditures for each time period need to be found (an implicit cash outlay will be included, as when an office space is used rather than rented out). Conventionally the cash flows are those of the investment excluding the financing cash flows.

Why can cash flows be used for the capital budgeting decision? The objective is to evaluate the investment over its entire life and there is no need to determine the year-by-year profitability (as with accounting) in order to decide whether or not the investment is acceptable.

## Discounted cash flow

The discounted cash flow (DCF) methods of evaluating investments have now gained acceptability and are used by almost all the largest industrial firms and their use is spreading among the smaller firms. Twenty years ago less than 10 per cent of the Fortune 500 firms used these procedures (the estimate is from the Stanford Research Institute study published in January 1966). Today it is difficult to find a Fortune 500 firm that does not use one or more of the discounted cash flow procedures.

All firms face capital budgeting decisions where the timing of the cash flows and the uncertainty of the cash flows of an investment are relevant factors. For many years managers did not know how to take time-value into consideration in a theoretically correct manner. Now two basic methods are widely used and they are both DCF methods. One method is to find the average return on investment earned through the life, where the average is of a very special type. The second method is to apply a rate of discount (interest rate) to future cash flows to bring them back to the present (finding present value equivalents). The first calculation described will be called the 'internal rate of return' method and the second calculation 'net present value'. A wide range of different titles is used and there are also different variations of calculations, but these two methods are the most common and the most useful.

## THE TIME-VALUE FACTOR AND INVESTMENT EVALUATION

All investments have three basic elements that an investor is likely to take into account in some fashion:

1   The time-value of money; funds at different times have different values.
2   The outcomes are uncertain; attitudes towards risk are relevant.
3   The value of the information; the uncertain flows are spread out through time and at present there is no information as to the outcome.

It is not surprising that there are markets that enable different individuals to attain their own preferences relative to the three elements listed. There may be some people whose near-term plans are completely independent of the actual outcomes of an investment, so they would pay nothing for information relative to the outcomes of an investment. Others (say someone planning the education of children) may be very concerned with the fact that they will not know the outcome of their investment for a number of years. The same types of differences among the individuals with respect to time-value of money and risk lead to a conclusion that exchanges will take place if there is a market for such exchanges.

The conventional net present value method of making capital budgeting decisions takes the time-value of money into account using the firm's cost of capital as the discount rate. The essence of this approach is that the average cost of a particular source of capital is defined as the discount rate that makes the present value of the expected proceeds that will be received by the capital supplier equal to the market value of the securities representing that capital. With a business corporation, proceeds expected to be received by the capital supplier have some degree of uncertainty. This is clear in the case of equity capital; and so long as there is a probability of default, it is also true of debt. The excess of the cost of corporate capital sources over the discount rate that applies to default-free cash flows presumably reflects an adjustment for risk. Raising the discount rate to compute present values may not be an effective or useful way of allowing for risk of an investment in a real asset.

It will be assumed that it is wished to take the time-value of money into consideration and that initially the uncertainty question does not exist.

**Pitfalls of bypassing time-value**

Consider the following two investments:

|  | Cash Flows ($) at time: | | |
|---|---|---|---|
|  | 0 | 1 | 2 |
| Investment $A$ | -10,000 | 1,000 | 11,000 |
| Investment $B$ | -10,000 | 11,000 | 1,000 |

A casual inspection reveals that the second investment is to be preferred to the first (the total amount received is the same for both investments, but the second investment receives some cash earlier than the first). Several methods of evaluating investments will fail to reveal the superiority of $B$ to $A$. For example, the total income over the life of either investment is $2,000 and the average income is $1,000 for an average investment of $5,000. This is a 20 per cent return on investment (ROI) and both investments have this return. The ROI measure cannot detect the superiority of $B$. Either of the DCF methods will reveal that $B$ is better than $A$.

## Time-value calculations

It is well-known that money has value and that a dollar in hand today is worth more than a dollar to be received one year from today. For example if money can be borrowed and lent at 0.10 per year then $100 held today and invested to earn 0.10 will be worth $110 one year from today. In like manner $100 to be received one year from today has a present value now of $90.91 ($90.91 invested to earn 0.10 will earn $9.09 interest and will be worth $100 after one year).

Assuming that we can lend and borrow at an interest rate of $r$, the following formula enables us to move back and forth through time:

$$A = (1+r)^{-n}S$$

where $r$ is the interest rate

$n$ is the number of time periods

$S$ is the future sum to be received in the $n$th period from now

$A$ is the present value or present equivalent of $S$.

If $r, n$ and $S$ are properly specified then one is indifferent between $S$ dollars at time $n$ and $A$ dollars now.

For example assume a firm is to receive $1,000,000 two years from now and $r$ is 0.10. Then

$$A = (1.10)^{-2} 1,000,000 = \$826,446$$

The firm is indifferent between a security offering $826,446 now or a security offering $1,000,000 in two years. The following calculations show the indifference:

| | |
|---|---|
| Initial sum | $826,446 |
| Year 1 interest | + 82,645 |
| | 909,091 |
| Year 2 interest | + 90,909 |
| | $1,000,000 |

If $r = 0.10$, the present value of $1,000,000 due in two years is $826,446. Tables give the present value factors for different values of $r$ and $n$. To find the present equivalent of a future $S$, multiply the appropriate present value factor by $S$. Values of $(1 + r)^{-n}$ are contained in tables or alternatively most hand calculators can be readily used to determine the values.

## METHODS OF CAPITAL BUDGETING

There are many methods of capital budgeting used by business firms, but just about all of them are based on one of four methods to be described here.

Care is needed with the terminology in this area. The same words are used differently by different people (including authors). In this chapter terms will be used consistently but this does not mean that the next time the terms are encountered they will be used in the same manner.

The most widely used method of making investment decisions is the 'payback' method. The length of time required to recover the initial investment is computed and this measure is compared to the maximum payback period. For example, an investment costing $1,000,000 and recovering $250,000 per year would have a payback period of four years. Well-informed managers will state that they understand the limitations of payback (not considering the time-value of money and the life of the investment after the payback period) but they use the payback measure as an indication of the amount of the investment's risk (a payback of one year would indicate less risk than a payback of four years). Unfortunately, payback is not a reliable risk measure. For example, gambling at Las Vegas has a shorter payback period than the purchase of a US savings bond but it has much more risk.

The second most popular method of measuring profitability of an investment (though it is rapidly losing ground to better measures) is return on investment (ROI). The ROI of an investment is the average income divided by average investment. Since the income and investment measures used are conventional accounting measures, the ROI measure fails to take effectively into consideration the time value of money. The conventional ROI measure is a very unreliable way of evaluating investments; however, there is an even worse way of applying the technique. A common practice in industry is to compute the ROI of the first complete year of use. Since this ROI, as conventionally computed, will tend to understate the actual return on investment, this creates a bias against accepting investments that should be accepted.

The other methods that require explanation are the several discounted cash flow measures. These measures are more reliable measures of value than the payback and ROI measures described above. The discussion in this chapter will be limited to the rate of return and the present-value methods. These two measures are chosen since they are widely used and also because they will do everything that alternative methods will do and in some cases will avoid errors introduced by these other measures.

## The present-value method

The present-value method of evaluating investments has been increasing in use for the past 20 years. It is now difficult to find a large industrial firm that does not employ the present-value method (it is generally used in conjunction with other measures), somewhere in its organisation.

The first step in the computation of the net present value of an investment is to choose a rate of discount (this may be a required return or 'hurdle rate'). The second step is to compute the present-value equivalents of all cash flows associated with the investment (on an after-tax basis) and sum these present-value equivalents to obtain the net present value of the investment.

The net present value of an investment is the amount the firm could afford to pay in excess of the cost of the investment and still break even on the investment. It is also the present value of all future profits, where the profits are calculated after the capital costs of the investment.

## Example

Consider an investment costing $902,740, that promises cash flows of $1,000,000 one period from now and $100,000 two periods from now. Using the present-value factors for $r = 0.10$ we have:

| Time period | Cash flows ($) | Present-value factors (0.10) | Present-value equivalents |
|---|---|---|---|
| 0 | −902,740 | 1.0000 | −902,740 |
| 1 | 1,000,000 | 0.9091 | 909,100 |
| 2 | 100,000 | 0.8264 | 82,640 |
| | | Net present value | $89,000 |

The firm could pay $89,000 more than the $902,740 cost and break even (that is, would just earn the 0.10 capital cost). Thus the $89,000 is in a sense the 'excess' incentive to invest and is a measure of the safety margin that exists.

Assume the following arbitrary depreciation schedule (any other schedule would give the same present value of income):

| Year | Depreciation ($) |
|---|---|
| 1 | 842,740 |
| 2 | 60,000 |

The following incomes then result:

| Year | Revenues ($) | Depreciation ($) | Income before interest ($) | Interest on book value ($) | Income ($) | Present-value factors | Present value ($) |
|---|---|---|---|---|---|---|---|
| 1 | 1,000,000 | 842,740 | 157,260 | 90,274 | 66,986 | 0.9091 | 60,900 |
| 2 | 100,000 | 60,000 | 40,000 | 6,000 | 34,000 | 0.8264 | 28,100 |
| | | | | | Present value of incomes | | $89,000 |

The present value of the after-interest income is $89,000 which is the amount of net present value of cash flows obtained above. This value is independent of the method of depreciation.

The argument is sometimes offered that the present-value method is difficult to understand. Actually it is the simplest of the procedures to use. If the net present value is positive the investment is acceptable. Also, the interpretation of the measure is easy and useful. The net present value is the amount the firm could pay in excess of the cost and still break even, and it is the present value of the income after capital costs.

## The internal rate of return method

The present-value method gives a dollar measure. Some managers prefer a percentage measure that is most frequently called an investment's internal rate of return. Other terms applied to the same measure are yield, DCF or discounted cash flow, return on investment, time adjusted rate of return, profitability index, and to complete the circle, present value.

The internal rate of return can now be defined as the rate of discount that causes the sum of the present value of the cash flows to be equal to zero. This definition can then be used to compute an investment's internal rate of return. The internal rate of return is found by a trial and error procedure (when the net present value is equal to zero, the rate of discount being used is the rate of return).

Continuing the above example, the net present value is found equal to zero using a 0.20 rate of discount. For discount rates larger than 0.20 the net present value would be negative (see Table 5.1).

### Table 5.1
### Present values with different discount rates

| Time | Present value: 0.00 | Present value: 0.10 | | Present value: 0.20 | |
|------|---------------------|---------------------|---|---------------------|---|
| 0 | −902,740 | 1.0000 | −902,740 | 1.0000 | −902,740 |
| 1 | 1,000,000 | 0.9091 | 909,100 | 0.8333 | 833,300 |
| 2 | 100,000 | 0.8264 | 82,640 | 0.6944 | 69,440 |
| Net present value | +197,260 | | +89,000 | | 0 |

The internal rate of return of an investment has several interesting and relevant economic interpretations. For example, it is the highest rate that the firm can borrow, use the funds generated by the investment and repay the loan. Assume funds are borrowed at a cost of 0.20. The following repayment schedule would then apply:

| | |
|---|---|
| Initial amount owed | $902,800 |
| Year 1 interest (0.20) | +180,500 |
| | ———— |
| | 1,083,300 |
| Repayment using cash flows | −1,000,000 |
| | ———— |
| | 83,300 |
| Year 2 interest (0.20) | +16,700 |
| | ———— |
| | $100,000 |
| Repayment using cash flows | −100,000 |
| | ———— |
| Amount owed | 0 |

The cash flows generated by the investment are just sufficient to pay the loan costing 0.20.

If incomes and investments are properly measured taking time-value into consideration then the ROI (that is, income divided by investment) of each year will be equal to the internal rate of return of the investment. This will not occur using conventional accounting.

The decision rule to be used with the internal rate of return method is that all investments with an internal rate of return greater than the required return be accepted (this assumes the cash flows are those of a normal investment, that is, one or more periods of cash outlays followed by cash inflows).

## THE NET PRESENT-VALUE PROFILE

For any investment we can compute its net present-value profile. Figure 5.1 shows the net present-value profile for the example of this chapter. On the X axis are measured the different rates of discount and on the Y axis the net present value that results from the use of the different rates of discount. The intersection of the net present-value profile and the X axis defines the internal rate of return of the investment (the net present value is equal to zero).

Inspection of Figure 5.1 shows that for a normal investment

**Capital budgeting**

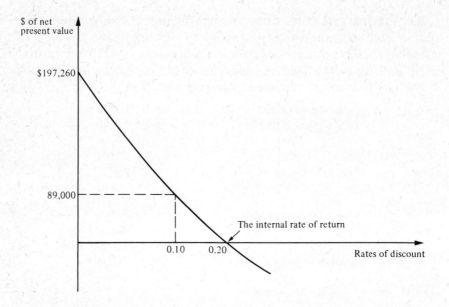

**Fig. 5.1 Profile of net present value for an investment**

(negative cash flows followed by positive) the present-value profile slopes downward to the right. Thus for an investment with an internal rate of return greater than the required return the net present value will also be positive. Thus with normal independent investments the present-value method (a dollar measure) and the internal rate of return method (a percentage) will give identical accept and reject decisions.

## COMPARING PRESENT VALUE AND INTERNAL RATE OF RETURN

Figure 5.2 shows why internal rate of return and present value may seem to recommend different alternatives.

The curve $AA$ represents the net present-value profile of investment $A$ with a rate of return of $r_a$. The intersection of the curve with the $X$ axis is defined to be the internal rate of return. Investment $B$ has an internal rate of return of $r_b$. The present value of the investments is measured on the $Y$ axis for a given rate of discount. It can be seen that $B$ has a larger internal rate of return than $A$. However, for

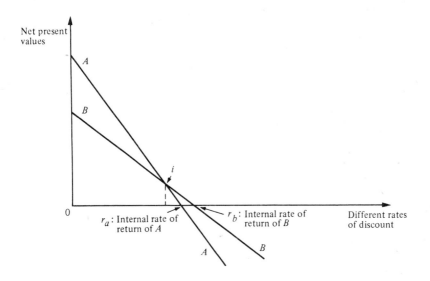

**Fig. 5.2   Two mutually exclusive investments**

all rates of discount less than $i$, investment $A$ has a higher net present value than investment $B$. Thus, if $A$ and $B$ are two mutually exclusive investments (only one can be undertaken), the internal rate of return criterion incorrectly indicates $B$ is to be preferred. The present-value method indicates that $A$ is preferred if the appropriate rate of discount is less than $i$.

If the investments are independent and if the required return is less than $r_a$ then both investments are acceptable. With independent investments the internal rate of return and the present value procedures both give consistent results. If the internal rate of return is larger than the required return, then the present value will also be positive. If the required return is greater than the internal rate of return the investment is not acceptable and the present value is negative.

Table 5.2 is a concrete example of the type of situation shown in Figure 5.2. Assume $A$ and $B$ are mutually exclusive.

Investment $B$ has a larger internal rate of return than $A$ but if the appropriate rate of discount is 0.10 investment $A$ has a higher present value. At a 0.233 rate of interest the investor would be indifferent.

## Table 5.2
## Two mutually exclusive investments

| | Cash flows | | Time | |
| Investment | 0 | 1 | Rate of return | Present value (0.10) |
|---|---|---|---|---|
| A | -80,000 | 100,000 | 0.25 | $10,910 |
| B | -20,000 | 26,000 | 0.30 | $ 2,364 |

## RISK AND INVESTMENT

It is not correct to assume that it is appropriate to take the risk of an investment into account via the discounting (and compounding) procedure. There is no reason for assuming that risk is always compounded through time, and that $(1+r)^{-n}$ can be used to take risk and time value factors into consideration in one computation.

Assume an investment is available that costs $100,000,000 and promises to return either $200,100,000 or $0, the events both having 0.5 probability. The pay-off occurs in a time period shortly after the outlay. The expected rate of return is thus very large. While this investment is 'obviously' acceptable using the criterion 'accept when the expected rate of return is greater than 0.10', it is not all clear that investors who are currently expecting a return of 0.10 for a moderately risky firm would want this investment accepted because of the 0.5 probability of losing $100,000,000.

William Sharpe published a paper (1964) that introduced the capital asset pricing model (CAPM). The CAPM is relevant to capital budgeting since if investors are well diversified, certain types of risk are less important than other types. With perfectly diversified investors, risks that are specific to the firm can be diversified away by the investor and thus are not relevant to the decision maker. The risk that is relevant to the investor is how the investment's profitability is correlated with the return of the other investments available to the investor.

This can be translated mathematically into an expression that allows us to quantify risk premiums. The inputs into the calculation are the measures of the market return risk trade-off (analogous to the use of the market interest rates to measure the time-value factor), and a measure of the degree to which the profitability of the investment is correlated with the market return. Other problems arise in application because many investors are not perfectly diversified, and more will have to be learnt about the importance of this consideration and how to handle it. Another complication is that there are other parties (such as managers) who have interest in the firm's continuity of existence, and care must be taken to consider their welfare as well as the welfare of the common stockholders. Finally, the specific mathematical models only apply to certain limited probability distributions or utility functions. Thus it does not appear that the CAPM will supply easy exact solutions to the problem of making capital budgeting decisions under uncertain conditions.

## CONCLUSIONS

In the career span of one manager a move has been made from the use of measures (payback and return on investment) that failed to consider effectively time-value to an acceptance of a discounted cash flow measure, rate of return. This measure was then found to give faulty directions in situations involving mutually exclusive investments and the present-value procedure was found somewhat easier to apply and gave results that were somewhat more reliable indicators of value.

While the cost of capital has been recommended as the discount rate or the hurdle rate to be used by firms, and was used by a large number of firms, the measure implicitly incorporated both time-value and risk considerations, and the compound interest calculation using the weighted average cost of capital did not result in a reliable value measure.

A default-free time-value factor followed logically from the conclusion that risk did not necessarily compound through time. However, this left risk considerations out of the analysis. Sensitivity analysis and simulation, while giving useful insights, did not lead to explicit accept or reject recommendations. Finally the capital asset pricing model was offered as a possible solution to the problem of how to include time-value and risk. Unfortunately, the calculations require unrealistic assumptions and the model is not apt to apply to the specific investment of the firm being analysed.

Despite the limitations of the capital asset pricing model, business managers should be aware of its existence, because they will be hearing more and more about this theoretical construct for the remainders of their careers. It offers a way of quantifying and incorporating risk considerations if the facts of the situation fit. Investments rejected under conventional analysis using the cost of capital would become acceptable, and investments previously considered to be acceptable would be rejected because of their 'systematic' risk, that is, the risk that they will go down in value if the general market conditions deteriorate.

Capital budgeting is too big a subject to be covered in one chapter. The objective of this chapter has been to make clear the nature and uses of the basic discounted cash flow methods. Some complexities in their use have been omitted as have descriptions of alternative, but inferior, calculations. Too frequently managers have been unnecessarily confused about the basic nature of the present-value and the internal rate of return methods, and are thus reluctant to use them. The net present-value profile graph makes clear the relationship of present value to internal rate of return and why they may lead to different recommendations in cases involving mutually exclusive investments.

The DCF calculations are powerful tools for evaluating investments. This chapter has not attempted to deal with all the complexities of using these tools, nor has it fully explained their wide range of uses. It is hoped that the reader will feel he should become more familiar with these tools. They are extremely useful. While the uncertainty questions occupy the largest part of the academic literature, the operating business person should realise that the basic DCF calculations are still the most reliable way of evaluating investments, and are an important tool in deciding whether or not an investment is acceptable.

## REFERENCES AND ADDITIONAL READING

Bierman, H. and Smidt, S., *The Capital Budgeting Decision,* 4th edition, Macmillan, New York, 1975.

Dean, Joel, *Capital Budgeting*, Columbia University Press, New York 1951; 'Measuring the Productivity of Capital', *Harvard Business Review,* January–February, 1954, pp. 120–130.

Fama, Eugene F., 'Risk, Return and Equilibrium: Some Clarifying Comments', *Journal of Finance,* vol. 23, (March 1968), pp. 29–40.

Fisher, Irving, *The Theory of Interest,* Macmillan, New York, 1930.

Hamada, R. S., 'Portfolio Analysis, Market Equilibrium, and Corporation Finance', *Journal of Finance,* vol. 24, (March 1969), pp. 13–31.

Hirshleifer, Jack, 'On the Theory of Optimal Investment Decision', *Journal of Political Economy,* August 1958, pp. 329–352.

Lintner, J., 'The Valuation of Risk Assets and the Selection of Risky Investments in Stock Portfolios and Capital Budgets', *Review of Economics and Statistics,* vol. 47, (February 1965).

Lorie, J. H. and Savage, L. J., 'Three Problems in Capital Rationing', *Journal of Business,* October 1955, pp. 229–239.

Lutz, Friedrich and Vera, *The Theory of Investment of the Firm,* Princeton University Press, 1951.

Mossin, J., 'Equilibrium in a Capital Asset Market', *Econometrics,* October 1966, pp. 768–775.

Sharpe, W. F., 'Capital Asset Prices: A Theory of Market Equilibrium Under Conditions of Risk', *Journal of Finance,* September 1964, pp. 425–442.

Stapleton, Richard C., 'Portfolio Analysis, Stock Valuation and Capital Budgeting Rules for Risky Projects', *Journal of Finance,* vol. 26 (March 1971), pp. 95–118.

# 6

# Pricing policy

**Bryan Atkin**

*Financial executives will surely agree with the author of this chapter when he says that the pricing decision represents perhaps 'the most delicate and important of the problems facing a company'. Those who are responsible for financial planning and control will also be acutely aware that 'relatively small differences in price can have a dramatic effect on the profitability of a product or service'. For the latter reason alone an error in establishing the price can nullify at one stroke the reality of the forward plans and the most efficient control of the subsequent performance.*

*Pricing policy is therefore an essential element in the financial planning of a company's affairs. The many and diverse implications of establishing that policy are proper subjects for study by financial executives for it may well be incumbent on them to give advice, from their particular viewpoint, of the financial effects of that policy or, indeed, to assist in the framing of the policy.*

*Nevertheless, the determination of price is generally the direct responsibility of the marketing, commercial or contracts department, if only because that exercise involves so many interacting and complex aspects of marketing policy. Thus it was appropriate that this chapter should be written by one who essentially takes the marketing viewpoint although throughout he acknowledges the critical influence of financial considerations.*

*The chapter discusses economic theory related to price, especially the concepts of elasticity and break-even levels. The author accepts the importance of economic theory in analysing the general way in which markets behave, but finds it of little help in the practical business of determining a price.*

*The chapter is concerned with pricing strategy as a long-term aspect of the subject, and with pricing tactics as representing shorter-term manoeuvres. Whereas in principle the strategy should exercise a broad influence on the tactics, there are circumstances in which the constraints and the opportunities arising from the tactical situation demand a review of the long-term strategy.*

*Although the writer is largely concerned with marketing tactics and strategy, he takes the attitude that those aspects of the general subject must be applied to achieving corporate objectives and long-term profitability. He carefully examines the role of costs but implicitly recognises the old adage that 'cost is a convention and price a policy'. He pays due attention to the alternative policies of 'skimming' and 'penetration' pricing in relation to new products, and analyses both the benefits and the short-comings of market research. His discussion of the possibilities inherent in mathematical models and computer simulation of pricing mechanisms will be of particular relevance to those interested in the potentialities of those approaches.*

A pricing decision is part of an intricate network of relationships, those between, for example, one product and another, between one enterprise and another or between one enterprise and the body controlling it, between different buyers and consumers, between different decisions to invest in plant or jobs. (Price Commission, 1980).

Setting and maintaining the right prices for its products is perhaps the most delicate and important of all the problems facing a company. Price is, after all, the specific mechanism by which the cost-generating activities of firms (in the form of production, capital investment, marketing and promotion, administration, etc.) are translated into revenue and, therefore, into the profits which form the basis of the company's continued existence and growth. Whatever other things impinge on sales volume and on profitability, the pricing executive can be sure that the consequence of *his* decisions will be reflected in his firm's financial performance. However successful a firm may appear to be, poor pricing will inevitably result in sacrificed profit either through loss of sales or loss of margin or both. The importance of the pricing decision is, moreover, not diminished by limitations faced by the individual firm in its degree of flexibility in setting prices – even relatively small differences or changes in price can have a dramatic effect on the profitability of a product or service.

It is, however, a reflection of the paradoxes inherent in the realities of business life that there is probably no area of business activity in which practice differs so widely from theory as the area of pricing. The simple – and well attested – truth is that in a great many firms, large as well as small, prices are set in a way which is disorganised, inconsistent and often just illogical. The reasons for this are not hard to find. Pricing decisions, even under the best of conditions are difficult to make and frequently have to be taken against what can often seem overwhelming odds – inadequate information; time pressures; corporate demands; changing and sometimes unpredictable competitive situations; higher than budgeted R and D and other overhead costs; inflationary pressures on labour, material and other production costs. Added to this, those responsible for pricing in the firm are often managing directors, sales or marketing managers or financial managers who face a great many other demands on their time.

The purpose of this chapter is not to describe at length theories of pricing, which are well covered in other texts, but to provide a framework within which the reader can evaluate the opportunities for greater profitability available to his own firm through the development of a more rational pricing policy and implement the practical procedures leading to the shaping, introduction and control of this policy.

## ECONOMIC THEORY AND THE PRACTICAL BUSINESSMAN

There is a substantial body of economic theory dealing with price and pricing. The practical businessman can, however, expect little direct help from the academic in applying economic theory to the solution of everyday pricing problems. Certainly, theories of price are effective in describing *in general* the way markets behave: demand and to some extent supply volumes do respond to price approximately as predicted by theory and markets do vary in the degree of responsiveness to price changes (as provided for by the concept of price elasticity[1]). The problem is that the theory breaks down when applied

---

[1] Technically, price elasticity is measured by dividing the percentage change in the volume of demand (or sales) brought about by a change in price by the percentage change in price. 'Elastic' markets are ones where demand increases (or decreases) by more than a proportionate price change and 'inelastic' markets where a change in price is greater, proportionately, than the effective increase (or decrease) in demand.

in particular cases largely because the assumptions on which theoretical calculations are based turn out to be inappropriate in real life. For one thing firms rarely possess, or are able to generate, the empirical data required to construct actual demand or revenue curves for their products and are often unable to distinguish costs sufficiently clearly to construct cost curves. Second, the goals which businessmen set themselves and the constraints which surround their achievement are usually far different – and less rational – than the idealised principles and responses of the theoretical firm. Third, markets do not in practice display the assumed characteristics of perfect competition and rational purchasing behaviour on which theory is based.

Nevertheless, since it has long enjoyed a certain popularity, an adaptation of economic theory worth mentioning at this point is the concept of 'breakeven'. The concept, in its simplest form, purports to show the minimum quantity of its product(s) a firm has to sell simply to cover its costs. Figure 6.1 shows the classic breakeven chart in its most widely reproduced form.

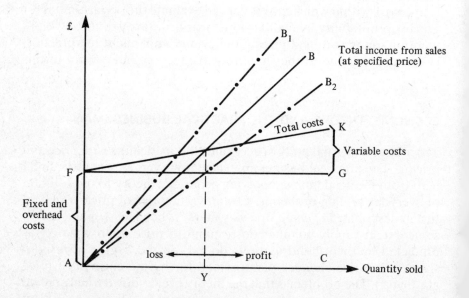

**Fig. 6.1:   Simple 'breakeven' chart**

In the chart the line AB represents gross revenue from unit sales at a specified price and line FK the total cost of making those units made up of fixed costs (incurred whether or not the product is produced and sold at all) and variable costs (which vary according to the number of units produced). The intersection of lines AB and FK represents breakeven – the point at which gross sales income is exactly equal to the costs involved in producing those units (Y) for sales. At the price set, the firm makes increasing losses with every unit as sales fall short of Y and an increasing profit with every unit in excess of Y. The chart can be developed to show alternative breakeven points at assumed different selling prices (represented by lines $AB_1$ and $AB_2$ in Figure 6.1).

The attractiveness of the 'breakeven' idea – which in principle can be applied both to individual products and to the firm as a whole – is obvious in the context of a chart on the managing director's wall dramatising what the firm has to do to stay in business *once selling price has been determined*, by indicating the volume of sales which have to be achieved to reach breakeven. However, the concept is of little help to the pricing executive in actually setting prices because of the crude and unrealistic assumptions which the basic theory assumes about the level of, and relationship between, price, demand and costs. Thus:

1    The sales income line (AB) takes no account of the price elasticity of demand. The breakeven quantity (Y) is a 'formula' calculation not a forecast of actual sales which would still need to be made to determine the profits likely to be generated at a particular price (or indeed whether breakeven were achievable at all at that price).

2    The assumptions that variable costs increase proportionately with unit output (as represented in line FK) and that fixed costs remain the same irrespective of the level of output are poor representations of business reality.

Gabor (1977, p. 49 et seq.) describes a more sophisticated variant of the concept which takes account of the relationship between price and quantity in drawing the curve of gross sales returns but goes on to observe that its practical value is similarly diminished by the lack of information on costs and demand elasticity[1] available to the average firm.

---

[1] One of the problems in applying the concept of elasticity in practice is that the theory assumes a constant relationship between demand volume and price when in fact research has repeatedly shown that consumers (and

At best the 'breakeven' concept – which is closely associated with cost-based pricing formulae described later – is mostly of value as a simple 'rule of thumb' method for evaluating pricing options in the context of other market-orientated information on (potential) demand and competition.

## PRICING POLICY, STRATEGY AND TACTICS

Before looking in more detail at pricing decisions and the way they are arrived at, it is useful to draw a distinction between three terms often used rather interchangeably by businessmen – in so far as they are used at all! These terms are *pricing policy, pricing strategy* and *pricing tactics.*

*Pricing policy* refers to the framework of rules and constraints within which, and perhaps by which, pricing decisions are taken. The nature and scope of this framework and the degree of formalisation or precision can vary widely from one firm to another, on no better basis than management preference or style, even within the same industry or between firms with apparently similar pricing problems. At one extreme pricing policy can be little more than a rationalisation of rule of thumb judgements or historical practice. At the other end of the scale can be policies devised and spelled out in considerable detail. An example is the policy operated by the Metal Box Company (1978) described by the Price Commission as comprising the following elements:

1  an immediate objective of raising return on capital to 17 per cent;
2  through the discount structure to pass on to large customers the cost savings commensurate with the scale, continuity and stability of their demand;
3  for non-standard containers to price these at a level related to the operating costs of the lines while producing these containers;

---

*(footnote continued)*
industrial buyers) respond differently to the *size* of price changes particularly when these are measured in a competitive (one brand versus another) rather than a global (total market change) context. Depending on the circumstances therefore a market can be both elastic and inelastic in terms of response to the pricing activities of the individual firm – a paradoxical situation requiring sound judgement and market knowledge.

4    to ensure that customers share with the company the benefits arising from productivity improvements and reductions in specification;

5    in the case of new business, selling prices are to be set on the basis of (achieving) 70 per cent capacity usage of (production) equipment (If demand fails to reach target volume, a decision has to be taken whether to increase selling price or to eliminate the product.);

6    to obtain high export prices wherever possible but retain flexibility to use marginal cost techniques for opportunistic business;

7    regular review of standard margins to ensure equity across the range

Simply having a pricing policy, however formal, does not imply that it is either logical or sensible in the broader arena of the market place. Nor does the existence of a policy guarantee that it will be observed in practice – policies are often more honoured in the breach than the observance. Indeed it is entirely feasible for a firm to trade without a pricing policy at all or for decisions to be justified by reference to a policy which is to all intents and purposes a *post hoc* rationalisation. This is often the case with small companies where pricing, like many other decisions, is in the hands of one forceful personality – a situation in which whim, prejudice and ignorance can easily play a powerful role.

Whereas *pricing policy* is the outcome of largely internalised objectives of a financial or other corporate nature, or statements of pricing principles, *pricing strategy* reflects the (longer-term) market-orientated (or externalised) objectives of the firm. In effect *pricing strategy* involves the systematic manipulation or planning of pricing decisions and policies over a period of time in the context of achieving the broader objectives contained in corporate and marketing plans. It implies recognition of the role of price as an active, and important, component of the overall marketing 'mix' rather than a largely intractable obstacle which marketing has to overcome in order to compete successfully. In so far as pricing policies and strategies are the expression of needs and objectives over different time periods and on different planes it is not unusual for firms to have a pricing *policy* but no pricing *strategy*.

While pricing strategy is 'the art of projecting and directing the larger pricing issues within a marketing campaign in the longer term (i.e. ignoring short-term fluctuations in market or trading conditions)' (Wilson, 1972, p. 132) pricing tactics are concerned with the manipulation of prices themselves and the way they are presented in order to achieve the optimum response in a competitive situation from a targeted customer group, and take as much from an interpretation of the psychology of the buyer as from more rational 'economic' judgements. Tactics are, by their nature, often short-term and may be changed several times during the life of the strategy of which they form a part – the practical means of responding on a more day-to-day basis to changing conditions in the market place. In practice pricing tactics, of which there are a great many variations (some are described later in the chapter) are often mistakenly elevated to the level of pricing strategy.

Oxenfeldt (1960) sees the pricing process as one involving a series of sequential decisions which can be taken over a period of time rather than as a single all-embracing solution. The six steps he proposes are:

1  Identification of target markets
2  Choosing an appropriate image
3  Constructing the marketing mix
4  Selecting a pricing policy
5  Determining price strategy (and tactics)
6  Definition of a specific price.

This multi-stage approach has a particular relevance to new product development but can be recycled wholly or in part as a means of reappraising existing products. The approach is particularly interesting in the emphasis it gives to broader issues of market segmentation and planning the marketing mix as the essential framework for pricing decisions.

## PRICING POLICIES AND TECHNIQUES

Wilson (1972) has observed that pricing 'is an exercise which must be undertaken on two dimensions. First it is necessary to think in terms of establishing the right price and second of using the correct methodology for arriving at it.' In a way this observation neatly encapsulates the practical dilemma facing most firms with respect to pricing. At one level the pricing process take place within a framework which is the product of a variety of factors and influences, both internal to and external to the firm itself. These factors, which provide the basis for defining pricing policy, strategy and tactics, include:

*Internal*

*External*

Corporate objectives and business goals – both generalised and specific

Cost structures – direct and indirect

Existing prices (e.g. of other products in the same or other product lines)

Historical practice and precedent in price setting within the firm

Degree of market knowledge (or ignorance) of key executives

Pressures from feedback of other individuals within the firm, e.g. salesmen

Levels of R and D and pace of new product development.

The nature, strength and pricing behaviour of competition (direct and indirect; existing and potential)

The role and importance of distributors and their attitudes and needs relating to price (including need to create/maintain acceptable margins)

(Pressure from) suppliers of raw materials, components etc. used in the product

The size, structure and perceived price sensitivity of demand

The purchasing procedures and motivations of (potential) customers

Existing and anticipated government policies

General conditions prevailing in different markets (especially where export markets are concerned).

At the second level the pricing process involves (or more correctly, perhaps, should involve) the application of a sensible and coherent procedure for actually determining the final price at which the product will sell. That this procedure or methodology needs to be conceived and operated within a broader framework of attitudes and subjective judgements which may not always be logical and may even be in conflict, is simply a reflection of the facts of commercial life.

However, pricing policies and strategies do not necessarily define, or even imply, a particular methodology or technique for arriving at the selling price itself. In many cases this is set as much by guesswork, trial and error, historical analogy and simple entrepreneurial judgement as it is by some more formal procedure or formula.

There is no single 'correct' methodology or golden rule for arriving at the right price. For example, the pricing decision process and the degree of flexibility available to the pricing executive in setting prices are heavily conditioned by whether prices are *declared* or *negotiated* (the pricing system). At one extreme the executive responsible for setting catalogue or list prices is in theory at least creating a structure of 'ruling' prices for his products which will remain in force for all or a substantial proportion of sales until a change is notified; at the other the executive involved in contract or tender pricing is faced with a new pricing decision with each new order or customer. The apparent coherence and stability of published prices have to be seen, however, in the context of the discounts, concessions, rebates, differentials and other devices employed by firms to manipulate the prices actually paid by customers. In a substantial number of firms list prices can be said to exist mainly as a basis for discounting with the bulk of turnover being generated from sales at discounted and negotiated prices (Atkin and Skinner, 1975). An apparently logical framework of declared prices can, therefore, be rendered meaningless and misleading by the reality of a haphazard system of discounts and/or individual negotiations with strong customers. (See Discounts and discounting pp. 133).

The 'right' price is not necessarily what theorists would call the 'best selling price' in the sense that it maximises profits for a given product considered by itself. In any meaningful sense what is 'right' can only be assessed in the context of what the firm identifies as its general strategic or operational goals. Because these differ according to the size, product range, historical development, future ambitions, geographical trading pattern, financial resources and management philosophy of individuals so the concept of the 'right' price will also vary.

The precise combination and weighting of factors determining pricing policy and price setting will depend on the product, the market and other circumstances. The following paragraphs look in more detail at five categories of factor which both shape pricing policy and contribute to a greater or lesser extent to the process of actual price setting. To the extent that one of these categories may carry the greatest weight in the pricing process it is possible to talk about pricing which is profit, cost, competition, demand (or customer) or distribution system orientated.

## Profit targets and other corporate objectives

Perhaps the most widely quoted of all business aphorisms is that it is the objective of every firm to maximise its profits. The most cursory examination of this proposition in the light of actual business practice, however, shows it to be one which should not be taken too literally. Firms rarely set out even with the *theoretical* objective of maximising profits (or return on capital employed) and often introduce criteria into pricing strategies and policies the deliberate effect of which is to contain profits at a level which is below that which otherwise might be achievable.

Few would deny that, in a free market economy, a firm exists to make a profit and, indeed, needs to make a profit to exist. More fundamentally, perhaps, the profits generated by the firm have to be sufficient to satisfy the providers of the capital – shareholders, bankers, etc. – on whom the firm's existence and future ultimately depend. Simply making a profit does not itself guarantee the continued flow of funds required to renew current plant and invest in facilities for producing new products. Equally, given the scarcity and cost of capital, it is nonsense to suggest that a firm would be able, even if it wished, to continue to pour capital into the production of a product until the last drop of profit has been extracted from the market.

Profit (which can be defined as total gross sales returns or revenue minus the total of fixed and variable costs, before tax) is therefore a less meaningful criterion for judging business performance in the longer term than return on capital employed or 'return on investment' (which is usually taken as the relationship between a firm's profit before tax and the whole of its assets).[1] Thus the Price Commis-

---

[1] The actual value of the calculation is affected by the way in which the assets are valued – at historical cost or at current cost. The issues and controversy emanating from these different accounting procedures are dealt with elsewhere in this book. They do not, however, alter the basic point of principle concerning the need to make sufficient profits to produce an acceptable return on capital employed.

sion commented with respect to UG Glass Containers Ltd that 'for [the company's] profit to be adequate it must be sufficient after paying for the cost of capital to fund all expenditure on fixed and working capital necessary to maintain the fabric of the business and to make a contribution towards capital required for expansion' and went on to state that the company's corporate strategy provided specific targets relating to pre-tax profit and return on capital employed to be 'achieved and maintained' (UG Glass Containers Ltd, 1978).

The question of time dimension also needs to be considered. A quick glance at the city pages of any national newspaper shows that profits achieved by even the largest firms fluctuate from year to year for reasons, often connected with the general economic environment and trading conditions, over which the firm has no control. Financial objectives can therefore be expressed both as long-term and immediate.

Longer-term financial objectives tend to be set in the context of achieving a targeted average level of return on investment or profit for the whole of the company which is considered by the firm to be 'reasonable' taken over a period of years (and across all products). This is usually expressed as a percentage but could also be a money sum. Judgement of what is reasonable is in this context largely a pragmatic affair, owing more to general perceptions within society of what might be considered as 'fair trading profit' or to historical experience or analogy, than to the projection of a mechanistic formula. In the short term, different targets may be set either for return on capital for profit or for margins or contributions (difference between selling price and *direct* costs usually expressed as a percentage) which reflect prevailing economic and market conditions in individual years or even short planning periods.

As we have indicated earlier, however, financial objectives are not the only determinants of corporate policy and are therefore by no means the only factor underlying pricing decision. Other considerations affecting either individual price decisions or the internal climate within which decisions are made include:

1 *(Market) growth aspirations*. Targets relating to achievement of an annual percentage rate of growth in revenue and/or volume terms or of an overall target for a period of time, e.g. five-year plan.
2 *Market share*. Targets relating to achievement either of some

specific share of total industry sales (or consumer uptake) of some or all of the company's products or of some more vaguely defined objective such as 'market leadership'.

3 *Corporate stability/expansion*. Development of products and businesses to achieve more broadly conceived goals concerning the longer-term stability and growth of the firm as a whole with implications for balancing investment decisions, R and D expenditure and other aspects. Decisions which appear unattractive from a purely financial standpoint in the short term may have important longer-term implications for the firm's financial health either individually or as part of a framework of such decisions.

4 *Corporate image*. Pursuit or rejection of a course of action in the light of judgements – objective and subjective – about the way the company wishes to be seen in the market place. This may be related to protection of an existing image e.g. where a manufacturer of a range of products with a reputation for quality, rejects the chance of selling a range of popularly priced goods (however profitable potentially) because of the risk of tarnishing a carefully fostered image. Or it may be related to development of a targeted image (e.g. for product reliability, speed of after-sales response, innovative design) which has attendant implications for costs and prices.

5 *R and D*. This can be both the lifeblood to and a leech on corporate profitability depending on the extent to which it is controlled and goal-orientated. Where R and D, especially in fast-moving high-technology industries becomes tied up with the image and reputation of a company it is possible to generate sunk costs which for reasons of competition or strength of demand are difficult to recover through the prices the company is able to command in the market place.

6 *Costs and efficiency*. Corporate plans often contain cost reduction and efficiency objectives linked to opportunities that provide for keen competitive pricing and/or greater margins.

7 *Customer/public opinion*. Winning and retaining the regard of customers and perhaps of a broader public through performance or specific design, e.g. safety aspects of equipment for which profit may be a secondary consideration, or by being seen to be trading 'responsibly'.

8 *Competitive arena*. Implementation of strategies for pre-empting, containing or meeting competition.

9 *Capacity*. Gearing of pricing and marketing strategies to achieve acceptable level of use of production capacity.

An example of the way various strands of corporate policy link together to affect prices can be found at BOC Limited.

> The company's central thinking is based on the need to manage a portfolio of businesses. Essentially, this is to invest for market growth and to increase market share on the assumption that scale benefits on costs will be obtained. This gives the investor market dominance based on competitively low cost which in turn provides the power further to secure market position by keen pricing. When the growth slackens off the rate of investment can be reduced to yield a positive cash flow which may be reinvested in another growth market . . . (BOC Ltd, 1979).

## The role of costs in pricing

It has often been claimed that the pricing of industrial products is derived from or based on costs and very little else – a process which Wilson has derided as 'faith, hope and fifty per cent'. The argument runs that the cost accountant and the engineer have dominated the pricing process and that neat formulae based on cost are most easily comprehended by these types of executive whose knowledge of, and exposure to, the market place itself is limited. Research into pricing behaviour has tended to support this view of the pricing process: when asked directly about the pricing of their products firms will indeed claim that they arrive at their prices largely by the application of some formula related to costs.

How rigidly companies stand by such formulae or, indeed, whether they actually have a formula at all, is very much open to doubt. Gabor claims that 'pricing is not in fact carried out by the alleged mechanistic application of cost-based formulae' and goes on to quote Edwards: 'the manufacturer has a "hunch" as to the price at which his article can be sold and makes use of "costing" or "estimating" to justify that price'. In other words a price 'derived from cost' can often be in effect the reverse procedure with margins and contributions justified *post hoc* by reference to costs when in fact they are subsumed from price. Nevertheless if prices are rarely based exclusively on cost, it is equally rare for costs not in some way to form the starting point or platform either for calculating prices or for evaluating the profit consequences of various prices indicated or set by reference to other factors.

Indeed, in so far as goods ultimately have to be sold at a profit for the firm to survive, it is inevitable that costs will enter into the pricing equation in some form.

In order to use costs at all in the pricing process it is obviously necessary for the firm to have a clear idea of what its costs are and how these should be allocated to individual products. This is all very well for the firm producing only one product since all costs are, by definition, attributable to that product. Where more than one product is concerned, as it is for most firms, the issues of cost allocation can be exceedingly complex and the solutions at best arbitrary. The costs of producing and selling a range of products can be classified broadly into three main components:

1   *Variable (including direct) costs* – costs which vary in relation to output, e.g. materials and components, labour, advertising.
2   *Fixed costs* – costs which do not vary in relation to output except in the longer term, e.g. buildings, machines, vehicles.
3   *Overhead costs* – costs attributable to management.

The problem of allocating management overheads will be obvious but what of variable and fixed costs? *Shared costs* are a common feature with respect, say, to vehicles and buildings but can also occur with respect to materials and labour. Consider, for example, the furniture factory which uses the same labour force, the same machinery and to some extent the same materials to make beds, wardrobes and dining room tables. Add to this a constantly changing balance of production volume between these different product lines – and within each product line between different model ranges – and the problems of allocation assume daunting proportions. The cost accountant might be able to devise an acceptable formula for allocation if each product was always produced in the same proportions but the formula becomes increasingly unworkable and arbitrary where these are constantly changing. Basing a formula on historical experience is equally undesirable as it makes pricing for the future dependent on past and possibly greatly outdated sales levels. The scale of difficulty increases still further where several products are produced by the same process (as in oil refining or dairy processes) and therefore incur, not so much shared costs as *joint costs*, or where a marketable product is a by-product of the production process for another good.

The problems outlined above become highly relevant when costs are used as a means of calculating price. There are two main concepts or procedures for cost-based pricing – *absorption or full cost pricing* and *variable cost or incremental cost pricing.*

*Absorption cost pricing*, to put it simply, involves the principle of adding a predetermined mark-up to total unit costs derived from the formula

$$\frac{\text{total of fixed and variable costs}}{\text{attributable to the product}}$$
$$\frac{}{\text{total units produced}}$$

By this procedure, sometimes known as 'cost-plus', each product produced by the firm is made, in theory, to cover all of its costs and make a known profit on each unit of sale or order.

*Variable cost pricing* is based on the principle of relating prices not to total costs but to variable costs only with the mark-up on costs (or the price less variable costs if the price is set by a procedure independent of costs) making a *contribution* to fixed costs and to profit, the scale of which depends on sales objectives being achieved. Gabor distinguishes two variants of variable cost pricing: one is based on average variable costs (for a predicted level of output) and the other, which he calls incremental cost pricing, is based on the incremental or additional cost of producing a particular batch of the product which may be different from the variable costs of total production when considered in unit terms. Incremental cost pricing is a concept particularly appropriate to pricing individual orders, in cases where demand is made up of discrete orders or batches, or in evaluating the relative contribution of alternative possible orders where the price available is fixed by some other means perhaps beyond the firm's direct control.

Absorption cost pricing is a method which has had particular appeal to the firm with a substantial proportion of its total costs in the form of fixed costs and overheads, since it places all products, in theory, on a sound profit footing and eliminates cross-subsidisation and below-cost trading. It is particularly useful in tender or contract pricing as a reference basis for pricing where there are no other useful indicators and in setting some practical limits to prices of new products with no relevant competitors. However, absorption costing has a number of major drawbacks as the basis for pricing. The arguments can be summarised as follows:

1   It is, as has already been shown, not always easy to isolate the total

costs attributable to a particular product where there are several, possibly disparate, product lines and ranges. Depending on the conventions and assumptions used to apportion costs, the outcome of the application of absorption cost pricing techniques could be substantially varying price levels for individual products.

2   There is, anyway, no compelling reason why any particular segment of the business, individual product, or specific order *should* be made to bear its proportionate or 'fair' share of overheads even where these can be calculated. Looked at in an overall corporate sense, the ability to offer a full product range, stability of production, attraction or retention of a major customer, response to a change in the competitive environment and many other factors may in individual cases and pricing decisions be considered to carry greater weight.

3   Absorption costing takes no account of demand. The fact that a price can be computed by this method does not guarantee that consumers will buy the item at that price or at the predicted volumes. Nor are firms willing in reality to implement one of the apparent implications of the method which is to *raise* prices when demand falls short of expectations or declines from a previous level (since total costs will be spread over a smaller volume of output). The inclination of most firms in this situation would be to *reduce* prices.

4   Absorption costing takes no account of competition. No firm can guarantee that its competitors will play by the same rules either by adopting the same method of costing or by allocating its overhead and fixed costs to particular products on the same basis. The firm rigidly applying absorption cost pricing would find its products highly vulnerable to a competitor using direct or incremental cost methods or simply pricing irrationally.

The proponents of incremental cost pricing tend to use arguments which are the obverse of their criticisms of absorption cost pricing emphasising the flexibility of the method as a means of responding to (changing) demand and competitive conditions. Thus it is pointed out, for example, that since market conditions vary between different industry segments of a given national market and even more, perhaps, between different national markets it is logical to seek (or accept) prices which reflect those conditions. Using a direct or an incremental cost approach enables the firm to operate at different prices in different markets while maintaining overall control over the aggregated contribution derived from sales to these various markets and a means of assigning supply priorities between them in the event of demand outstripping capacity. Similarly the method enables the firm to consider and respond to individual orders in a way appropriate to specific circumstances. Thus, for example, at times of high demand a means is provided of selecting orders or pieces of business which yield the greatest contribution and at times of low demand of indicating how far the firm might reduce its prices before an order ceases to make any contribution at all.

Despite its apparent pragmatism, variable or incremental costing is not without its attendant dangers. In the first place, it has been said with some truth that all costs become variable if the firm is to survive – that is, in the end, the firm depends on making sufficient revenue from its sales to cover all costs incurred whether variable, fixed or overhead. Incremental cost pricing cannot therefore be pursued unchecked. As we have seen earlier it must be conducted within some framework or yardstick of required contribution based on profit targets or targets for return on capital invested.

Second, firms using incremental cost pricing to justify accepting an order at reduced contribution may find they have made a rod for their own backs in subsequent dealings with the same customer. However logical the concept of variable pricing might be to the seller, the buyer is given a weapon which he will be all too willing to use in subsequent negotiations, if he can, when general demand conditions have improved and the firm has been able to command higher prices. If the seller gets to the point of refusing an order offered at too low a price there is a danger that the buyer may simply eliminate him from future consideration or allow a competitor to gain entry.

Third, there is always a risk of provoking price retaliation from competitors resulting in reduced margins all round and a steep hill to climb back to acceptable profitability in a market environment which can become accustomed with remarkable rapidity to low prices.

Finally, it must be appreciated that it is not always easy to determine clearly either the variable costs attributable to a particular product or the incremental costs associated with a particular batch or order. Some so-called variable costs are not, in fact, more than marginally variable, at least in the shorter term. Few firms are able or willing, for example, to manipulate the size of their labour forces constantly to reflect changes in the level of orders. Unionisation and a natural desire on the part of firms to keep a trained and effective work force together play an important role here. It is easy for firms to delude themselves therefore as to what the incremental or marginal unit cost of a product actually is. Similarly, taking on an additional order in certain circumstances may have its own 'hidden' incremental costs in the form of overtime working, loss of efficiency in output in machines pushed closer to maximum capacity, extra 'blocks' of production space requiring heating, lighting and maintenance and many other items.

Pricing is not only difficult in practice to base entirely on costs but even should it be feasible it renders the firm vulnerable in other respects. In a strictly competitive sense it hardly matters a jot how reasonable a profit mark-up or contribution target a firm sets in relation to its own costs if these costs are higher than those of competitors. Indeed it has been observed that the costs which ultimately matter are those of the lowest-cost producer. Of course, most markets support producers who vary in efficiency, but the greater the disparity in efficiency, the greater is the pressure exerted on the least efficient producers.

More broadly, cost-based pricing formulae often provide little encouragement to company management to consider the prospect for improving margins by reducing costs as distinct from raising prices. The degree to which costs are in themselves controllable will depend on individual production circumstances and quality of management. Firms rarely explore as rigorously as they might the various ways in which costs might be cut, from better materials purchasing to tighter control of office costs. This is not, however, the only way costs can be cut and here we return again to the need to be alive to *market* needs and conditions. Research has consistently shown over the years that products and services can quite simply be 'over-engineered' – that is contain features to which the user attaches little economic significance in the purchase decision or which are designed to a quality standard which exceeds customer needs. By eliminating these features from the product or changing the product specification the firm may well be able to make considerable savings in costs without reducing prices, at least to anything like the same extent.

### Competition and pricing

There are few products or services indeed for which there is no effective competition. Even when a firm has no direct competitors –

as in the case of an innovative product – it usually has to take into account products capable of acting as alternatives or substitutes in some way, or the prospect of competition developing.

Long-term monopolies are therefore rare outside the realms of state enterprises but it is possible for short-term monopolies to develop on the basis of new products, particularly where high technology is involved. Firms may be able to protect themselves for a time from direct competition by the taking out of patents – as Xerox Corporation did with plain paper copiers and Polaroid Corporation with instant photography – but in the end competition will come either through expiry of patents or through a competitor finding a means of entry which does not infringe the patents (as Kodak did with instant photography). The short-term monopolist needs to consider pricing in the context of the breathing space he has to establish himself in the market place before competition develops, rather than in terms of the apparent freedom of action of the true monopolist.

At the most fundamental level, the product competes on the basis of its usefulness or value to the buyer compared with the many other items on which income or resources can be expended.

Price acts as an element in competition therefore at up to three levels: it can help determine whether or not a product is bought at all (or whether the decision to purchase is taken now or at a later date); it can help determine in which of a number of alternative ways a particular need is satisfied; and it can help determine which supplier's product is selected.

It is not surprising then that in most cases prices are set and maintained with some reference to the general level and range of competitive prices. In a more specific sense, however, pricing against competition can become in itself a technique of pricing. This can work in one of two main ways:

1   By establishing the prices being charged by all (or a selected cross-section) of the competitive suppliers active in the market and positioning one's own price to occupy a certain position in the range. This may reflect either 'safety' pricing (pricing in the middle of the range) or 'aggressive' pricing (pricing at either extreme). In the latter case particularly, given that price variations reflect product differentiation, the adoption of competition pricing also tends to imply judgements about demand response and price segmentation in the market (see below).

2   By gearing prices to those charged by a specific competitor on the basis of achieving parity with them or of achieving a designated discount or premium. This approach is often used where one company has achieved a position of such pre-eminence in the market place that both sellers and customers accept its prices as a reference level. An example is the market for open-top containers in relation to which the Price Commission commented that 'where prices are negotiated by individual contract they are set by reference to Metal Box levels'.

In so far as competitors' prices are declared or easily established, competition-orientated pricing is relatively straightforward and has the advantage of placing prices within the known parameters of the market place. The price structure of markets is not, however, always easy to establish. Published price lists often give a highly misleading guide to actual price levels which may be arrived at largely by discounting or special negotiation. Further, buyers are frequently reluctant to indicate even to independent researchers, let alone company salesmen, the terms of a bargain struck with a competitor. There is always a danger therefore that prices may be set on the basis of a competitive price structure which is different in reality from that assumed.

The extent to which firms are willing and able to take a competitively independent line in setting and maintaining prices is partly a reflection of factors such as market share, established reputation, financial strength, distinctiveness of product and relative costs of production, and partly a reflection of competitive psychology. Many writers on pricing have drawn attention to the fact that price competition often tends to be of a muted and controlled nature in which a few (perhaps only one or two) dominant suppliers (price leaders) both set the price levels and pricing systems around which competition is fought, and determine the timing and scale of price changes. Other firms (price followers) are essentially content to respond – raising and lowering prices in line with the price leaders. Markets operating on this basis can become highly conservative and regulated structures in which price competition is to all intents and purposes eliminated. In certain industries, typified by large commodity-type businesses such as cement, animal feeds and tyres, the institutionalisation of competition among a small number of large companies has resulted in prices fixed and maintained at very similar levels with price rises taking place in rounds under the 'leadership' of one company – a situation to all intents analogous to the outlawed 'price ring'.

In theory, price leaders 'undertake' to behave in a responsible manner with respect to price setting and act as 'policemen' for any firm threatening to take a more aggressive and independent pricing line. However, in practice the *status quo* is protected more by mutual compliance than any genuinely effective sanction which the price leaders can bring to bear. As Japanese companies have demonstrated repeatedly in European markets, complacent and conservative competitive environments – which in turn lead to reduced interest in increasing efficiency and cost savings – are highly vulnerable to a bold and determined aggressor.

## The attitudes and motivations of the buyer

Price is rarely, if ever, the only factor entering into the purchasing decision and is sometimes only secondary. The success of pricing decisions is therefore highly dependent on the ability of the firm to comprehend and respond to the purchasing environment into which its products are sold. Many ineffective, even disastrous, pricing policies can be traced back to misconceptions about the attitude of buyers to price and the role of price in the purchase decision. These misconceptions are often rooted in a popular industry folklore the credibility of which has been reinforced by constant repetition to a point at which the desire or willingness of firms to go against this conventional wisdom has been almost totally sapped. The philosophy of price cutting as the only effective means of competition which pervades some industries is often due more to uncritical acceptance of this folklore than to a sober analysis of marketing options.

Distinguishing fact from fiction in the market place is therefore the first task of the would-be rational pricing executive. Some of the elements bearing on the role of price in the purchase decision will now be considered. The most important of these is the concept of 'product differentiation'. This relates to the differences in functions, performance, design and other product-related or physical attributes which a manufacturer can introduce to distinguish his products from those of his competitors. The greater the differentiation, it is argued, the more invidious direct price comparisons by the buyer become, thus giving the firm greater flexibility in turn to gear its prices to the value it believes, or can persuade buyers to believe, attaches to the features or benefits it is offering. In many industrial markets this is characterised by the weighting attached by buyers to factors such as 'technical specification' and 'quality'. The range of price competition in such markets reflects the fact that buyers vary in the importance they attach to different product features in relation to price. The principle of segmentation – designing and pricing products to cater to a particular target group of customers within the market as a whole – derives from the concept of differentiation.

Economists usually assume, in theorising on purchasing behaviour, that the buyer, being rational and efficient, will tend to purchase at the lowest price prevailing in the market place, for the product which best fits his needs and requirements. Where there is little or no product differentiation, such as in the case of electrical cable or industrial fasteners, he might be expected to look for the lowest price *per se*; where there is substantial differentiation such as in an industrial engine or a conveying system, then the buyer will weigh up all the economic aspects of the alternatives available to him to arrive at the product which offers him the highest cost–benefit. As consumer goods companies and advertising agencies have long appreciated, the domestic consumer is neither rational nor efficient but there is a widely held belief that the industrial buyer, being a 'professional', cannot be deceived as easily and will go unerringly to the 'bottom line'. Research into the buying decision has consistently shown this simply not to be true when considered in any detail.

In the first place, economic factors are not the only criteria employed in the purchase decision. Even in the case of non-differentiated products, many other factors can intrude to justify purchases at other than the lowest price which may be available. These include:

1  Delivery (firms are often prepared to pay more for fast delivery or guaranteed delivery or for a delivery particularly convenient to the purchaser).
2  After-sales service/availability of spare parts.
3  Previous good experience of the product or other things produced by the same manufacturer.
4  Proximity of supplier to the purchaser.
5  Security of supply/risk spreading (e.g. by dividing requirements between two or more suppliers).
6  General reputation of supplier/advice and recommendation of own staff and other firms in buyer's industry.

7  The volume of other goods purchased from the same supplier.
8  Good personal relationship with salesman, technical staff and other aspects of the supplier's organisation.

Second, economic considerations can go far beyond the 'price' of the product. In the case of a capital product such as a commercial vehicle, a forklift truck or a machine tool, the purchase price of the product is only one of several cost-related considerations such as running costs (in terms of fuel and power, cost of spare parts); 'whole life' cost (the estimated total cost of the machine or vehicle over the whole of its operational life taking into account length of expected operational life, reliability in service, running costs and disposal value); cost as method of financing the purchase (are credit or deferred payment terms available? Is a leasing or rental facility available as an alternative to purchase?).

Third, industrial buyers are perfectly capable of being irrationally influenced by factors such as a persuasive salesman; clever advertising; cosmetic product features such as design; fashion trends within the industry and simple prejudice. A manufacturer of circular knitting machines for whom the author once carried out a research project found it hard to accept that many customers rejected his technically well-engineered but old-fashioned looking product in favour of a streamlined, push-button import with, by objective standards, an inferior price/performance relationship. Various writers have drawn attention to cases where new products have been unsuccessful initially because they were priced too cheaply, thus creating buyer suspicion, and became successful when the price was brought more into line with what the buyers expected to pay! Differentiation is therefore feasible at a level well short of genuine product differences.

Finally buyers rarely have perfect knowledge of the markets for all the products they have to buy. Thus the buyer for a fabrications firm may have an extensive and systematically compiled knowledge of the suppliers and prices for the steel products which make up a substantial proportion of his firm's costs but has neither time nor the inclination to develop the same knowledge for less significant items he may also be responsible for such as paper clips and toilet rolls.

It has rightly been said that the price the final buyer is prepared to pay for a product is, in the end, the best guide to optimum pricing. Because it is the best guide, however, it is inevitably the most difficult concept to employ as a practical technique in pricing. The attraction of cost-based pricing formulae and using competitors' prices as a yardstick for price setting can be attributed at least in part to the fact that they are simple to understand and employ information which, in theory at least, is readily to hand or easily generated. By contrast it is often exceedingly difficult to establish in a direct way how much customers for a product are prepared to pay for it, or put another way, how many customers would be won at different alternative prices, given the variety of factors which affect the purchase decision of individual buyers. Nevertheless it is within the capacity and resources of most firms to develop sufficient information from their own knowledge and experience of trading in particular market places or by talking to some potential customers, or by some experimentation or by extrapolating the results of market research surveys. Then they can make broad assumptions about the size and structure of demand for a product and responsiveness to price in a competitive context which can be used to narrow the limits within which price should be set and define the strategy and tactics which best fit market conditions.

## Distribution structure

Where a product is sold direct from manufacturer to end user, as many industrial products are, the pricing executive has only to consider pricing at a single level. The situation becomes more complex when distributive intermediaries – agents, wholesalers and retailers – are involved, as he then has to consider not just the price at which the product is sold to his immediate customer, say a wholesaler, but also the price at which it ultimately sells to the final consumer after it has passed through one, two or even three sets of hands each of which have added their own mark-up. Wholesalers and retailers tend to price by adding a designated percentage mark-up to the price they buy-in the product in order to cover overhead and sales costs and yield a profit. It is, however, relatively unusual for a single fixed percentage to be applied to all products. Rather the percentage mark-up is manipulated between products according to circumstances or design around some overall average (which may itself reflect long-standing practice or folklore in a particular industry rather than any independent judgement on the part of the distributor).

Since the ending of resale price maintenance the manufacturer is unable to dictate the ultimate selling price of his products (and therefore in effect distributors' margins). Distributors may therefore manipulate margins in a way which favours or disfavours the products of the individual manufacturer and therefore impacts on ultimate sales. Pricing to the *distributor* but with an eye to reselling prices is therefore a special component of the art of pricing.

It should also be recognised that the effect of passing on, say, a reduction (or an increase) in the cost of materials or components is heavily affected by the length of the distribution chain. Not only might the change be much smaller proportionately in respect of the final selling price than it is to the ex-factory price but distributors can choose to pass on the change across a spectrum of options ranging from no price adjustment at all to one in excess of that made by the manufacturer.

## AIDS TO PRICING

### Models and computer simulations

In the main, however practical or logical the basic technique adopted, pricing decisions tend to involve a great deal of individual judgement by the pricing executive. Because the individual has to apply precise weightings to the many influences bearing in practice or in theory on this decision, the final outcome is at best an approximation of the best selling price and is as good, or as bad, as the quality of judgement applied to it. Various attempts have been made to construct 'models' of a more formal nature designed to help the firm fix the optimum price of its products under actual competitive conditions. These models differ widely in their nature, purpose and origin, but most frequently relate to the pricing of goods for retail sale (particularly fast-moving goods such as baked beans and washing powder) and pricing in a competitive bid or tender situation.

Basically, all models work by simulating, in terms of mathematical relationships, the interaction of the variables – company-, competition- and demand-related – which govern the pricing decision. They share therefore inevitable problems in defining and assigning a value to each variable. Their success depends on the quality of research or of the market knowledge or insight the firm is able to feed into the model, and on the manipulation of the variables which normally requires access to a computer. The cost and complexity of model building has tended to make it the preserve of the largest firms only at present, although it is possible with the development of modestly priced small computing systems and more effective pricing research techniques that some elements of modelling may come within the compass of a great many more firms in the future.

## Market research

Whether or not a pricing model is being developed, firms still require information on customers and competitors to help them reach sensible pricing decisions. This information is rarely readily available 'off the shelf' and some level of active information gathering is therefore predicated. The most widely employed source of intelligence is the salesman (Atkin and Skinner, 1975). The reasons for collecting information via the salesman are, naturally, seductive: the salesman is already employed by the firm 'on the road' and he is in constant contact with customers. In theory he ought to be particularly alive both to competitors' prices and to the price sensitivity and purchasing considerations of the buyer. In practice, however, salesmen are a highly unreliable source of pricing intelligence and tactical judgement. Research into the pricing of industrial products has suggested that it is not unusual for salesmen to convince themselves that they have lost orders on the basis of price when in fact other factors were of greater or equal importance in the purchase decision and it seems likely that many buyers use price as an excuse for not placing an order with a particular firm rather than give the real, possibly more contentious, reason.

While it is not suggested that firms should give up monitoring price through feedback from salesmen, it would seem prudent that where key pricing decisions are concerned, such as pricing a new product or a change in pricing strategy, information should be generated where required by means of more systematic market research conducted by a reputable and competent consultancy with experience in asking and interpreting questions about price and setting these in the context of other data on market structure and the purchasing process. Market research can make a valuable contribution to the analysis of pricing situations and the selection of appropriate strategies and tactics, although in view of the difficulties in collecting detailed information on prices actually paid and in measuring likely response to hypothetical price levels, it is not usually a tool for setting actual selling prices.

## DEVISING PRICING STRATEGY AND TACTICS

### Entry strategies

The concept of pricing strategy as a means of using price as an element in the achievement of specific marketing goals was mentioned earlier. This involves the co-ordination of pricing decisions in the context of their longer-term impact and implications rather than their short-term or tactical benefits and requires the firm to take an extended view of such factors as probable product life; volume and price sensitivity of potential demand; opportunities for segmentation of demand by price and the optimum phasing of segmentation; pace of likely consumer acceptance taking into account competitive, alternative and substitute products; build-up of production capacity and the opportunity for scale economies in unit costs; timescale for recovery of R and D costs.

The most sensitive, and probably the most important, time for strategy formulation is before the launch of a new product – whether or not the product concerned is an innovative or unique one with no direct competitors or is a new brand entrant to an established market place. It is frequently stated that at the stage of market entry the firm has a choice between two basic strategy options known as *skimming* and *penetration*.

*Skimming* strategies involve the deliberate setting of an initial price which is high in relation to anticipated long-term price levels towards which the price will be progressively lowered as competition and demand conditions change. The benefits of this strategy derive from the high gross margins achieved at the outset against which R and D and other 'sunk' costs and often heavy initial promotional costs can be set and from the flexibility afforded for using subsequent price changes as a means of controlling market expansion (since, setting aside inflation, the direction of price changes will be downward) and meeting emerging competition by aggressive pricing. Skimming enables the firm to cream off that component of demand prepared to buy the product at its highest price before attacking the broader potential market which may exist for the product at a lower price. In so far as the progressive effective price reductions can be implemented on a 'step-wise' basis, the market may be, in effect, creamed off at different (and progressively larger) levels. The firm employing a skimming entry strategy also gives itself the option of approaching the anticipated longer-term downward adjustment in price by introducing variations of its original product or even a different brand rather than by simple price reduction, thus enabling it to maintain a premium price on its original product. This strategy might be termed progressive segmentation. A further advantage of skimming which should not be overlooked is that it conforms to the well attested dictum that it is easier to correct a pricing mistake in a downward direction than in an upward one.

*Penetration* strategies are intended to generate the highest possible volume of sales from the outset by keen (low margin) pricing. In practice they can be divided into two categories – demand-orientated and competition-orientated strategies (see Table 6.1). Demand-orientated penetration strategies are based in the main on a combination of an expected high level of price sensitivity among potential buyers and a need for a high volume of demand to justify plant investment or achieve projected economies of scale in production (i.e. some products have to be produced in volume or not at all). Competitively they have the advantage of potentially creating a strong market position or an image as market leaders before competition emerges (although this will depend on the speed and strength of the competitive response).

One specific variant of demand-orientated penetration strategies is worth mentioning – this might be called the 'razor and razor blades' strategy. Basically it involves pricing a unit of hardware (e.g. razor, labelling gun, copier, abrading machine) at a level which achieves the maximum market penetration or placement so that profits can be achieved on repeated sales of related consumables. If the consumable can be made unique in some way to the hardware, at least initially, a curious combination strategy of penetration for the hardware and what amounts to skimming on the consumable presents itself.

Demand-orientated penetration strategies usually assume a slight underlying downward trend in prices under the impetus of further economies of scale and competitive pressure. This assumption is not necessarily true of competition-orientated penetration strategies. Penetration pricing in the broadest sense can be regarded as a means of deterring potential competitors by pressuring the margins which can be achieved to offset the costs of entry implicit in product development, investment in production facilities and marketing/ promotional efforts. To this extent bold penetration pricing might be employed to pre-empt the (immediate) risk of competition. Even so the strategy may still call for prices to be kept, in relative terms, around the launch level or even drifting lower to keep up the deterrent.

Two situations exist, however, where the strategy may be one of low entry price and an underlying plan for either a sharp or gradual increase in price. First, where a new product is being launched in a market where the competition comprises substitute or alternative products, price has been used as a means of persuading potential users to try the product (about which they may have, for example, technical doubts) on the assumption that when it has proved itself they would be prepared to pay a price equal to, or higher than, the existing alternatives. The second example concerns the use of a low entry price as a means of displacing or forcing out entrenched competition from an established market place or of gaining a substantial market share on the basis of which prices can subsequently be increased to a more profitable level. This highly aggressive strategy is one which has been successfully employed by Japanese companies in European markets for a wide variety of products. An example is marine engines. 'The prime target for the Japanese ... was the European market and the view in the trade was that their strategy would follow the familiar pattern of gaining a large initial market share at cut prices, forcing the opposition out and then raising prices' (*Marketing*, 1979, Oct., p. 32).

The temptation to use price as an entry wedge becomes increasingly great the more difficult it is for the firm entering a well established existing market to differentiate its product sufficiently clearly from those already available to ensure achievement of a satisfactory foothold on other competitive grounds. It can, however, be a high-risk strategy: if competitors have the resources to fight a rear-guard battle or even to step up the price war or if customers do not respond to the entry price as expected, the firm employing this strategy might find itself blocked, forced even to lower prices with consequent loss of profit margins all round or even faced with a situation in which serious resistance is encountered to the subsequent price rises implied by the strategy.

In general terms the more innovative the product the more the firm is likely to incline towards a skimming rather than a penetration strategy, particularly if R and D costs have been high and production capacity is limited, at least in the short term. However, the right strategy will depend on the firm, the product and the market.

**Table 6.1
Evaluation of entry price strategy**

| Skimming | Penetration – demand-orientated | Penetration – competition-orientated |
|---|---|---|
| Anticipated short product life (technological changes, fashion) | Anticipated long product life | Anticipated need to tempt users to try new product rather than continue with existing functional alternatives (gain foothold especially where differentiation not immediately clear to, or valued by, consumers) |
| Slow initial consumer acceptance (new applications, new technology) | Belief in rapid consumer acceptance/high price elasticity | |
| Uncertainty over ultimate scale and elasticity of demand | Economies of scale in output – threshold sales level before economies can be achieved | Pre-emption of competition – exclude prospective competitors by raising entry costs/establishing entrenched position |
| Market segmentation – 'cream' those prepared to pay high price before moving to mass market (perhaps with lower priced variants) | Expectation of rapid competitive response – establish sound market position/market leadership before competition can develop | Displacement of entrenched competition by aggressive pricing in directly competitive market (market launch of similar or identical product) |
| Inelastic production costs/capacity constraints | Exploitation of established reputation/sales, marketing, distribution strengths | |
| Recovery of high R and D costs | | |
| Generation of funds for mass marketing | Create platform for continued sale of related products e.g. labelling machines and labels | |
| Competition slow to develop due to patent protection, research lead time, high production entry costs | | |
| Exploitation of established reputation/differentiation aspects of product | | |

## Reviewing strategy after entry

Although pricing strategies are conceived as operating over a period of time, ignoring short-term fluctuations or pressures which may demand a tactical response, this does not mean that the strategy does not need to be kept under regular review. Nor that it is not necessary for strategies to be changed if conditions in the market place become sufficiently different from those that prompted the original plan.

The firm which has adopted a skimming strategy is faced with the need to decide when to implement the price cuts envisaged by the strategy and how large these should be on each occasion. There can be no hard and fast rules to guide these decisions. Depending on the pace at which competition develops – and this may be slowed down by patent protection, high entry costs and other factors – a high initial price might be retained for some considerable time before it needs to be reduced. On the other hand it can be advantageous to make the first cut well ahead of competition as a pre-emptive measure. Equally the timing and size of the cut may be best related to taking advantage of the demand interest opened up by initial entry to boost sales by a substantial cut in price justified by reference to cost savings from increased scale of production and greater efficiency. Similar considerations apply to subsequent cuts.

The firm which has implemented a penetration strategy has less room to manoeuvre in terms of price adjustments in the face of developing competition. The major problem facing pricing executives is maintaining a long-term view of price developments when competitive pressures appear to be forcing the firm into a growing number of reactive or short-term tactical decisions most probably associated with price cuts. In order to maintain its strategic grip the firm must be able to retain a broader view of the development of demand, its sensitivity to price changes and its susceptibility to non-price differentials.

It is probable that for many products, pricing decisions shade from the strategic to the tactical in the longer term whichever entry strategy is adopted as competition develops, as product differentiation becomes increasingly difficult to sustain and as sales approach saturation. Even so it would pay the firm to be alive to the opportunities which exist for using a deliberate change in strategy to revitalise its position in the market place or improve profits. The variations of strategy option are legion but include:

1   Switching from a skimming strategy to a penetration strategy to exploit mass market potential of a product initially pioneered at a high price – perhaps by introducing a simplified and cheaper version rather than by cutting the price of the original product.

2   Introduction of replacement or second generation products which can be differentiated sufficiently to command a premium price (return to skimming strategy).

3   'Re-packaging' of products in a way which takes them out of the competitive arena. A good example is the development of 'electronic office' concepts linking more conventional pieces of equipment in a unique total way (return to skimming strategy).

4   Concentration of attention on more profitable market segments even at the cost of volume – diversion of released production resources into other products.

5   Improve margins by concentration on cost savings through more efficient production rather than by increasing prices (although the ability of the firm to use this strategy is limited by the long-term tendency of all production methods to ape the most efficient).

## Tactical considerations

In theory, strategy precedes tactics in the pricing process, the latter providing the short-term dimension to the implementation of strategy which governs the actual prices charged and the way these are expressed to the customer. In practice it is not always easy to separate the two. Tactics can be considered at two levels. First there are tactical decisions which relate to gearing actual price levels, and the form they take, to what might be termed the 'psychology' of the customer and the nature of the purchasing process. Such tactical considerations, in so far as they hold true over a period of time, in effect form part of strategy.

The semantics of such pricing tactics tend to be those of the consumer market and retail pricing. However, many have a more universal relevance whatever the product or service being sold. Probably the most widespread tactical device is discounting and this is considered in more detail below. However, mention might also be made of such tactics[1] as:

---

[1] Based on Wilson, 1972.

1 Offset – low basic price, 'lost' margin recouped on extras, replacement parts or consumables.
2 Diversionary – low basic price on some products (in range or line) developing overall image of low cost.
3 Discrete – tailoring of price to bring product within the purchasing competence of a given seniority of buyer (relevant where the location of purchase decision is determined by corporate price ceilings).
4 Price lining – price kept constant but quality of product or extent of service adjusted to reflect changes in costs.
5 Financing – alternative options to purchase such as leasing and rental (can be used as a specific means of extracting greater profit by changing the bases on which 'price' is assessed by the customer); might be coupled with special credit terms, trade-in allowances and special offers.

The above tactics are basically concerned with price. However, these need to be considered alongside what might be termed non-price differentials – ways of competing which command customer loyalty outside the framework of direct price competition, such as delivery services, after-sales support, technical back-up and advice and advertising and promotion effort.

In addition to these 'tactics of strategy' there are tactical questions of a more practical day-to-day level: what is the best way to pass on a price increase forced by rises in costs? Should ways be sought of keeping prices stable by modifying the product? Is it better to make price changes at regular and infrequent intervals (as until recently was mainly the case) or often in line with cost changes (as inflation is increasingly forcing on firms)? Should prices be changed to take into account positions of short-term strengths or weaknesses in the market place? How should the firm react to changes in competitors' pricing – is it necessary to react at all? By how much?

The combination and application of tactics requires, if they are to have the desired effect, a detailed knowledge of the customer groups to which they are applied and the way these take purchasing decisions as well as a good appreciation of the likely response from competitors and the tactics which they are using themselves.

## DISCOUNTS AND DISCOUNTING

The principle of discounting, whether formal or discretionary, is entrenched in most sectors of manufacturing industry where list prices of some kind or other are employed. The variations in discounting practice in everyday use are numerous. Four main types of discount: quantity discounts, trade discounts, cash discounts and seasonal/load shedding discounts are summarised in Table 6.2. Other types of discount include those based on geographical factors (e.g. zonal pricing based on delivery distance); delivery method (e.g. discounts for customer collection); trade-in allowances on old equipment; 'free' supply of related consumables (e.g. labels used in price marking equipment). There are various ways also in which discounts are actually effected: they can be based on physical volume or money sales; be a percentage discount or a cash difference from a 'list' price; be shown as a flat sum rebate or a net price; be made 'on-invoice' or 'off invoice'. Finally discount structures can be formal (with details published for customer use) or discretionary (in the form of guidelines within which sales managers can negotiate) or a combination of the two.

Special contract or 'net price' arrangements with key customers are, in effect, an extension of the discounting principle but with the essential difference that the terms of the sales agreement are usually the result of direct negotiation between buyer and seller rather than a development of the existing discount formula. Prices are inevitably keen but how much so will depend in individual cases on the bargaining strength of buyer and seller at the time and can be obscured by the introduction of product modifications, non-standard delivery arrangements and other special conditions. Special terms can come to dominate sales, for example, approximately 80 per cent of the sales of the Metal Box Company (open-top group) in 1977 were covered by special arrangements.

Of course in theory and in practice there are excellent reasons for operating a discount policy, some of which are indicated in Table 6.2. Carefully operated and controlled, discounting provides firms with a flexible facility for fine-tuning response to (changing) demand and competitive conditions while retaining the overall integrity of catalogue and list price structures. The danger of discounting as general practice is that it can lead to inconsistency and lack of control. Special terms to important customers can individually be defended

## Table 6.2
## Types of discount

| | Method of operation | Reasons for use |
|---|---|---|
| Quantity or discount/ rebates | 1 Single order – discount based on physical volume purchased at one particular time | 1 Respond to individual purchasing power of customer in a competitive environment |
| | 2 Cumulative – discount based on physical volume purchased over a fixed period of time (usually one year) | 2 Pass on cost savings involved in servicing larger orders (economies in packaging, transportation, sales, administration) |
| | 3 Guaranteed offtake – version of cumulative discount involving commitment by the buyer to take up either a fixed minimum quantity over the period as a whole or in specified amounts at fixed intervals (e.g. monthly) or both. Sometimes penalties in the form of surcharges are made for exceeding a contract offtake as well as for falling short. In other cases bonuses can be paid for exceeding contract minimum | 3 Encourage customers to purchase in larger quantities than they might otherwise do<br><br>4 Discourage small orders which are expensive to process or unprofitable<br><br>5 Promote repeat purchasing<br><br>6 Create stability in demand and foster greater regularity and consistency in supply (benefits in stock-holding, organisation of transportation, operation of product lines, etc.) |
| Trade discounts | Usually percentage discount from a specified 'list' price, designed to represent the distributors' operating expenses and profit. Alternatively may be represented as net trade prices available only to recognised 'trade' customers.<br><br>Where more than one level exists in the distribution chain, discounts may discriminate between levels | 1 Aid in controlling or guiding final selling price (subject to legislation)<br><br>2 Means of discriminating between different types of distributor, e.g. wholesaler and retailer; general distributor and special distributor who may offer |

| | | |
|---|---|---|
| | (e.g. between wholesalers and retailers) | additional or enhanced service |
| | Trade discounts may be characterised as a flat rate trade concession (e.g. 25 per cent to trade, list to other buyers) or combined with a quantity discount | 3 Simplicity – easily understood by distributors<br><br>4 Economy – reduce need to keep changing catalogues (since discounts, not 'list' prices can be manipulated)<br><br>5 Protection of distributor against direct buyers |
| Cash discounts | Deductions offered by the seller if payment of an invoice is made within a specified time period | Encourage immediate or early payment thus saving costs involved in the extension of credit and management of overdue accounts |
| Seasonal discounts/ load shedding | Differential prices according to season, day of week or time of day, where demand has a cyclical pattern and supply is fixed or intractable – most appropriate in consumer markets | Encourage spreading of demand, diversion of peak loading, boosting of demand at low periods<br><br>Examples – electricity, coal, hotels, cross channel ferries, public transport, cinemas |

on the basis of pragmatism and expediency but add up in total to a jungle of prices which inevitably becomes perpetuated in successive deals with the same customers.

Discounts and special details in effect represent the reality of pricing while formal price lists and formulas represent the theory. The greater the flexibility or informality of the discounting procedure, and the more discretion which is granted to individual sales executives in negotiating actual prices, then the more the difficulty the company faces in maintaining a firm grip over the effects of its pricing activities. Anticipating revenues and profit is a basic component of financial budgeting and control. However, the ability to make realistic forecasts and impose meaningful controls is directly related to an appreciation of the way prices are actually arrived at, the extent and 'mix' of sales at discounted prices and the relationship these prices have with formal price structures.

The firm operating discounts should keep asking itself:

1 *Do we need to discount at all?* Tradition and convention often play a major role in the operation of formal discount policies and structures. Yet firms have successfully fought the weight of conventional practice. For example, one major US-owned manufacturer of office furnishing systems has successfully operated a list price only policy for sales of whatever size in a market where discounting is notoriously widespread.

2 *What types of discount should we offer?* The types and scales of discount appropriate in individual cases cannot be embodied within a general set of rules. These will depend on the markets concerned, on the cost structures faced by the firm, perceived customer sensitivity to price changes, on the competitive situation and many other factors. What is important is that discounting procedures are subjected to rational evaluation of all the factors involved and kept consistent with changes in cost, sales structure and the market environment. Discount structures have a habit of becoming entrenched so that they remain in force long after they have ceased to be relevant to the firm's business. A manufacturer who has switched from selling through distributors to mainly direct sales does not, for example, need to offer trade discounts pitched at a level which encourages heavy stocking.

3 *What proportion of sales will be made at discounted prices?* Company management should be aware of the sensitivity of revenue and profit to the extent and level of discounting. This should include a particular appreciation of the role of special terms negotiated with large customers and the impact of a wide flexibility or discretion in fixing discount prices.

## PRICING AND NEW PRODUCT PLANNING

It can be said that the only time a firm genuinely has complete discretion in pricing is before it has committed itself to developing and marketing a new product at all! Once resources start to be committed to R and D, and even more once production facilities have been invested in, the pricing options available to the firm become progressively narrowed by practical considerations: the costs 'sunk' in bringing the product to market; the fixed costs represented by the scale of plant laid down to produce it; the direct costs of production consequent on choice of production process and scale of production; the constraints imposed by demand and competitive conditions and by the pricing of existing product lines with which the new product might be expected to interact.

New product development has always been a high-risk activity – various studies in the USA have shown failure rates among those actually launched running as high as 60 per cent. Many others are abandoned before they reach the production stage after large sums have been spent on R and D. The risks are moreover tending to become greater on average as the pace of technological change and competitive pressures force up development costs. The more greedy on resources new product development is, the more careful the firm needs to be that the products selected for development are those standing the best chance of achieving a good rate of return on investment when the product finally goes into production. Many writers on new product planning have emphasised the need for establishing clear frameworks of controls, systems and guidelines for appraising the relative merits of new product ideas so that management time and resources are channelled to those products offering the most attractive investment opportunity.

The process of new product appraisal is one which involves a large number of corporate and marketing considerations. However, anticipation of the price ranges at which the product is likely to sell and the market conditions or assumptions underlying those ranges is something which should normally take place at the earliest stages of product planning and be held under review throughout the development process. In effect it is argued that firms should think far more concretely about gearing new product development to a broad target selling price derived in turn from a realistic evaluation of potential demand and the nature of competition than they do at present. This would have several major benefits:

1   It would contain the tendency in R and D to 'over-engineer' products (since the price target will also imply production cost targets which would have to be met if satisfactory profits are to be made).

2   It would prevent the development of products based on unrealistic assumptions about likely sales volumes (which often result from the use of cost plus formulas to project price, at the planning stage).

3   It would provide a framework for 'fine-tuning' the product

during the later stages of development to maximise competitive success within the selected price range.

Admittedly this approach is not easy to apply to the product which is itself a dramatic technological breakthrough or creative innovation for which existing price indications in the market place are inadequate and hypothetical testing of consumer responses at best unreliable. However, the great majority of new products do not fall into this category but relate in some reasonably direct way to established applications and existing products against which price targets can reasonably be set.

## PRICING AND PRODUCT LINES

A great many pricing decisions take place in the context of product lines or ranges rather than as entirely independent exercises. Product lines or ranges comprise individual products linked together in some identifiable way – by a common function, by a common design or structure, by a common production process, by a common user group or application area. An office equipment manufacturer may, for example, offer a range of copiers of different print speeds or output capacities; within each model type a choice of features, e.g. automatic or manual operation; ranges of other office products, e.g. typewriters, word processors and facsimile transceivers.

The basis for product-line policies and the justification for offering different models, lines and ranges is a subject in itself. It is sufficient to note here that the existence of product lines raises particularly complex issues of pricing because of the way demand for each individual product interacts. Product lines as a whole may be mutually supportive but individual products within the line can easily be competitive with each other, particularly if encouraged by lack of care in pricing. Simply applying a common mark-up to each individual product is clearly unsatisfactory since it is probable that each product will vary in its production and marketing cost profile and in the opportunities and constraints implied by demand and the competitor environment it is selling into. This argues for a pricing policy which provides for each product in a line to be individually priced according to costs and market conditions subject to certain broad principles of consistency to minimise the risk of anomalies leading to the firm competing with itself.

Even so the firm faces sensitive issues each time a product line is extended, supplemented or modified by introduction of revised models or when a new product line is introduced. An example of the dangers faced, in the author's own experience, is provided by a building board company which tried to launch a new and superior grade of board at a premium price in a market which turned out to place much less value on the higher quality offered by the new product than the company expected. The result was that as the price of the new product was forced down to a level close to that of the firm's existing range of building board, buyers of the original range simply switched allegiance to the new product forcing the price of the original range still lower in order to maintain sales. What started off as an exercise in market segmentation turned out to cause disastrous loss of profit all round.

## SUMMARY

This chapter has sought to demonstrate why pricing is perhaps the most complex and demanding – and least clearly understood – of all tasks facing company management. Some conclusions are now drawn which might help the financial executive, in particular, contribute more effectively to pricing policy formulation and price setting.

1 *Pricing is much more of an art than a science.* There is no universal formula or golden rule for arriving at the right price. Those responsible for price setting have to balance and allow for a variety of factors and influences both internal to and external to the firm itself which, far from the ordered and rational world of the theoretical economist, may not always be logical and may even be in conflict. Nevertheless, profitability can significantly be enhanced by injecting greater coherence into the rules and principles, whatever these may be, which govern the way prices are fixed and maintained. The financial executive has an important part to play in the preparation and implementation of pricing policy.

2 *Successful pricing decisions cannot be based on costs alone.* Prices are far less often arrived at by the mechanistic application of cost-based formulae than is widely believed. Even so, costs and cost-related profit targets remain a major obsession of many firms in pricing, particularly in the case of industrial products. Financial

executives have tended on the whole to encourage and reinforce this essentially inward-looking approach. The success of pricing decisions is, however, highly dependent on the ability of the firm to comprehend and respond to *market* needs and conditions. The contribution of the financial executive to pricing decisions would be substantially enhanced by greater recognition of the role of such factors as competition, buyer attitudes and motivations and the impact of distributive systems in optimum pricing.

3 *Price is a much neglected and potentially powerful element in the marketing mix.* Price is widely treated more as a handicap which has to be borne rather than as a positive tool for achieving designated marketing goals. This chapter has looked at the ways pricing can contribute to overall marketing plans both in the longer term (pricing strategy) and in the short term (pricing tactics). The financial executive should be prepared to be 'sufficiently flexible in his own advice and policies not to inhibit sales and marketing personnel from manipulation of price as a marketing weapon'.

4 *Pricing considerations are a key element in product planning.* Anticipation of price ranges and market conditions are an essential precondition to effective investment and product planning. The financial executive should seek to ensure that pricing factors are introduced at the beginning and not at the end of the planning cycle for new products.

**REFERENCES AND ADDITIONAL READING**

Atkin, B. and Skinner, R., *How British Industry Prices,* IMR, 1975.
Price Commission, *Compressed Permanent Gases and Dissolved Acetylene Sold in Cylinders, Cylinder Rentals and Fixed Charges* (BOC Ltd), HC 223, 1979.
Gabor, A., *Pricing, Principles and Practices,* Heinemann, 1977.
Price Commission, *Open Top Food and Beverage Cans and Aerosol Cans* (Metal Box Ltd), HC 135, 1978.
Oxenfeldt, A. R., 'Multi-Stage Approach to Pricing', *Harvard Business Review,* July/August 1960.
Price Commission, *Report for the period 1st February to 30th April 1980.*
Price Commission, *Prices of Glass Containers* (UG Glass Containers Ltd) HC 170, 1978.
Wilson, A., *The Marketing of Professional Services,* McGraw-Hill, 1972.

# PART II
# CONTROLLING THE
# PERFORMANCE

## PART II CONTROLLING THE PERFORMANCE

Part II assumes that the business plans have been formulated. The efforts of the management team must now be applied to measuring the performance in relation to the plans and taking whatever action is necessary to correct deviations from the plans. In this stage of the exercise, as many writers point out, it will also be incumbent on the management to consider whether the plans, rather than the operations, need redirection, because of unforeseen contingencies or errors in the original forecasts.

In the construction of a work of this nature it is convenient and orderly to set out the several phases of the exercise of planning and control as being each self-contained, one following the other in apparently neat chronological progression. In fact, as practising managers are well aware, there is inevitably a great deal of overlap between the functions of planning, measuring the results and controlling the operations; and to some extent this overlap is bound to be reflected in writings on the subject which profess to have an applied rather than a purely theoretical emphasis. Thus Part I contains reflections on measurement and control whilst Part II will from time to time refer back to the principles and assumptions on which the forward plans were based.

Bearing in mind the qualifications mentioned above, the four chapters of Part II deal with the assessment of performance in general but nonetheless realistic terms, cost control, funds control, internal audit and other methods of internal check.

# 7

# Assessment of Performance

**C.C. Magee**

*Professor Magee begins the discussion on the assessment of performance by pointing out that, in spite of popular impatience with past events, the* post facto *assessment of the financial results constitutes a salutary exercise for the managers who were involved in the formulation of the original plans. Thus, in comparing forecasted and actual results 'there should be no automatic congratulations for managers who exceed their target'. Nevertheless in making such comparisons it is important to separate controllable from uncontrollable factors. The assessment of performance must also embrace investment projects and should relate to the basis on which they were originally approved. It will be recalled that the principles and techniques for appraising projects of a capital nature were examined by Professor Bierman in an earlier chapter.*

*The chapter then pursues questions arising from the use of the return on capital as a standard and a measure of achievement; the rate of return to be used for such purposes to accord with the social responsibilities of the business. Likewise the capital base, preferably represented by total assets, needs precise interpretation. The author discusses the apparently conflicting roles of profit and cash flow in the process of measuring results and concludes that the two concepts must be regarded as 'complementary and not substitutional'. Profits are essential for the purpose of financing future activities. The chapter lays stress on the need for sound accounting principles to be applied, particularly in respect of the valuation of assets, if the dependability of comparisons over time is to be assured.*

An important area of management control is the *post facto* assessment of the financial results of the organisation as a whole, that is the examination in retrospect of the financial effects of earlier decisions to invest. Management must regularly commit resources for both long-term and short-term purposes and, because this commitment will always involve risk, a careful assessment of the anticipated results of any project on the financial position should be made before a decision is taken, and before resources are irrevocably committed.

A periodic evaluation is needed, after resources have been invested, to report what has been achieved, to examine the amount of the profit, or the extent of the loss, and to consider the effect of implementing the plan on the financial state of the business, in particular to note whether financial stability has been maintained or alternatively the extent to which it has been impaired. Information on all these aspects of the finances of the business is needed to permit management to assess the quality of earlier plans, the quality of past decisions at strategic level and the effectiveness with which they have been implemented. Finally it is important that an informed base of financial knowledge should be developed from which future activities can be planned.

Production managers in turn require detailed financial information at tactical level about the activities for which they are responsible. General management must be informed about the financial results of all these different areas of activity, with just enough detail to permit it to make a fair assessment of the financial contribution made by each to the overall health of the business. Perhaps emphasis should be placed on the need for information about the extent to which conflicting departmental interests have been responsible for reducing the total profit, and perhaps for introducing some element of financial instability.

Profit is an important test of success, but the test can only be satisfactorily applied if profit is one element in a comparison. Profit must be considered for example in relation to a forecast, to the amount of capital resources used to produce it, or to the profit record of a preceding year. Additional comparison may be made in a larger business between the results of different divisions in a particular year, and changes in these relationships over time may be very significant for the long-term health of an undertaking. Profit should be earned at a level that is regarded as adequate in relation to the relevant elements in a comparison, for example to capital employed, and this expected rate of profit is a factor to be taken into account at the forecast stage.

While profit is a good indication of success or failure, however, the accounts that report it give little information about the factors that contributed to its result. An analysis of expenditure will show what items have varied in relation to a forecast or in relation to a previous year, but it provides little evidence of the reason for the change that has taken place.

Explanations of poor results, of reasons for what has happened, must be made available, and the information can then be used to support and interpret what the figures show. This evaluation of the financial results may then be used as a basis for a decision which attempts to bring about an improvement in an unsatisfactory situation during a subsequent period, for example an increase in the profit to produce the expected return on capital. Explanations are just as important if the results are good, perhaps showing an improvement on expectations, and a guide is needed to indicate the steps that should be taken to keep production and profit at this satisfactory level.

An explanatory report on results that differ from expectations is also needed as a point from which to test the forecasting ability of the various groups who contributed to the build-up of the estimates. Results which are better than expected must be subject to the same level of scrutiny as those which fall below the forecast, and this inspection is particularly important when managers who are responsible for operations themselves prepared the data on which the estimates are based. It is not unknown for forecasts to be set deliberately at a low level in order to make achievement easy, and by this means to allow a comfortable margin for the production of an apparently satisfactory result. There should be no automatic congratulations for managers who exceed their target. A failure to forecast a high level of activity may well have made it difficult to produce the goods to meet demand; it may have caused unnecessary expense such as high-cost overtime working, or buying out components. The effect of a higher rate of expenditure, caused by the need to meet this unexpectedly high level of demand, because it is reflected in increased costs, must be to bring the profit down to a level below the potential of the business.

Managers who fail to reach their target must expect to be called on for an explanation. The real responsibility for failure may not be theirs;

higher costs may be caused by factors which affect the rate of expenditure but which they are unable to control, and an analysis of data with the object of separating controllable and uncontrollable changes in cost, in order to pin responsibility or to exonerate, is an important exercise in financial control. Systems of standard cost and of budgetary control have been developed as accounting tools which will help to provide information about revenue and about costs on a responsibility basis, and it should be possible, if these procedures are installed and effectively operated, to establish as the result of further enquiry what has gone wrong and, if the fault lies within the organisation, who is responsible for what has happened. The variances that emerge will normally be investigated if the amount is material, as a part of the ongoing process of detailed assessment, but their effect is likely to become clearer when the comprehensive accounts of the business, showing the reported profit and the general financial position, are under review.

The operation of appraising the results of past investment decisions is important where large sums of money are committed over long periods of time, and discounting is widely used today as a method of selecting the most attractive of a number of different investment possibilities. The mathematical techniques employed can only be put to work on the basis of the data prepared by the accountant or by the budget department and while the mathematical calculations may be perfectly correct, the use of wrong estimates as the basis for these calculations will result in the production of forecasts that can never be correct. The discounting procedures to some extent help to minimise the effect of wrong estimates, especially when they are made in respect of periods that lie well in the future, but they cannot eliminate the impact of such errors completely. Large sums of money are often at stake when long-range business plans are put into effect, and the continued financial health of the business may well depend on the accuracy of the calculations on which decisions to invest are based. Error of a significant amount, especially in connection with receipts and payments which fall in the early part of the period covered, may spell disaster.

There is no way of eliminating error from forecasts, but past experience should be used in the attempt to build up the necessary expertise within a particular business. The quality of the forecasts can only be tested satisfactorily if past results are closely scrutinised and compared with the original estimates to discover what discrepancies exist, what has gone wrong and where. This exercise is a first step that must be taken to establish the cause or causes, to suggest remedies for the future, and to provide an assessment of the expertise within the field of forecasting that is available to an organisation. The difference between forecast and achievement is not necessarily the result of an operating failure; it may be produced just as easily by a forecasting error, and one that could have been avoided had greater accuracy been achieved when the estimates were prepared in the first place. It should be possible to reduce the risk that a forecasting error will recur and although the exercise will not recover what has been lost, it should at least help to provide more reliable estimates for future planning.

Aids to investment decisions, mathematical or otherwise, are important tools of management, but they do not provide a complete answer because they must depend on forecasts of the future rate of cash receipts and cash payments. Estimates may be wrong *ab initio* or the expectations on which the forecasts were based may change as the result of events that could not have been predicted when the forecasts were prepared and the foundations on which the exercise is built may be completely destroyed. A comprehensive evaluation of the financial results of decisions after the event is needed not only as a check on the accuracy of the calculations on which action was based, but also on the reasons and the responsibilities for an error. Financial reports on the results of individual investment decisions should be produced, in so far as it is possible to identify and analyse the data, but the problem of joint costs often makes it difficult to ensure that adequate allowance has been made for all expenditure relevant to a particular area of activity. There is a very poor case for attempting to analyse joint costs on some arbitrary basis, but there is a very great danger of swinging too far in the opposite direction, and allowing so much attention to be focused on the amount of the contribution provided to meet joint costs that their full impact on profit may be neglected.

There is a wide range of general overhead and administrative expenditure, which may or may not be charged against the operating revenue produced when individual investment decisions are implemented, but which must be covered by the surplus earned from all productive activities. The results of all the investment decisions taken by the management of a particular business must be considered in the light of the profit derived from all operations after all costs have been charged against all revenue. Profit is normally calculated on a period basis and revenue must be charged with all expenditure which has been incurred and which is able to make no future contribution to profit. A decision to carry forward to a future accounting period any part of expenditure which has already been incurred may only be based upon a reasonable expectation that it will provide some future benefit or advantage. Subjective judgement is necessarily involved in any calculation of the amount to be carried forward, that is in quantifying it, but there must exist some objectively established expectation of benefit to justify any carry-forward.

The benefits received from a particular investment plan will not normally be limited to one accounting period, and any analysis of profit on the basis of origin should cover a period of years if it is to permit a full assessment of the results. The analysis must include sufficient detail to identify the revenue derived from each different project together with the expenditure to be matched or charged against it. An important point that must be emphasised is that comparisons of the financial results of individual investment decisions over time must be comprehensive, and they can only be satisfactory if the individual financial results are regarded as an integral part of those produced by the operations of the whole enterprise. Any fragmentation of figures, taking individual items of revenue and of expenditure out of the general context of total income and total expenditure and appraising them as if they represented the results of independent entities, must produce the risk that some items of expenditure will be overlooked and as a result the profit reported from individual projects overstated. The danger of overlooking revenue is usually much smaller.

The contribution of a particular investment decision to profit is the total benefit it provides during the effectiveness of the expenditure incurred. An evaluation of the results will only be complete however if recognition is given to the total costs, including those which have not been allocated directly to any individual project; these costs must be met before profit emerges, and some undefined part of such expenditure is a legitimate charge against revenue. It may be impossible to charge out some items of cost, but their impact must be recognised.

An important purpose of the appraisal of results is to confirm whether or not the project has produced the expected cash flow. The main function of the financial accounts of a business however is to measure the results in terms of profitability and it is on the basis of success or failure measured in these terms that management will be judged. The resources committed must produce a return calculated on an annual basis at least as good as that which would have been produced by an alternative investment, and this return is measured by reference to actual income available within each year to pay whatever dividend is appropriate and to provide a surplus for reinvestment which it is hoped will in turn be profitably committed.

The evaluation of the results of long-term investment decisions, and in particular the importance of establishing whether or not they have provided an adequate contribution to fixed costs and to joint costs, in short, whether they have been profitable, must be clearly distinguished from the approach to a short-term decision on whether to accept an order which will only provide a small contribution. Long-term expenditure is relevant to an evaluation, anticipatory or *post facto*, of the long-term decision; sunk costs are of no consequence to a short-term decision, and if the business will be worse off by refusing to accept a contract which will do little more than cover marginal costs, the contract should be accepted. The evaluation of long-term expenditure on a long-term basis calls for different considerations and for a different approach.

## PROFIT AND FINANCIAL STABILITY

The primary function of business management is to employ the resources committed to it in a profitable manner. The immediate objective is a profit sufficient to cover a dividend on the invested capital, together with a surplus which will be at least sufficient to ensure continued financial stability. A normal expectation today is that the surplus will also be enough to support expansion and development. The longer-term objective is to keep the business alive for the foreseeable future and the profit target must be set with this aim in view.

The level of profit sought must be reasonable in relation to a number of significant factors, financial, material and human, and the target must be one that in practice is possible to achieve. The aim must be clearly defined at the outset; it may be modified or changed subsequently in the light of experience or altered circumstances, but at all times the target must be kept in sight. It must be attainable, and its existence must be known, understood and accepted by all the senior members of the managerial team.

Some concession is made to social policy when the aim of continuity is accepted; the availability of jobs for people is an issue here and continuity of business activity provides them. It may therefore be argued that a moderate level of profit should be the aim of management, because such a level is consistent with continuity, and it follows that a moderate level for dividend and for profit retention is implicit in such a choice. The pursuit of maximum short-term profit, and of efficiency in its extreme form may be socially objectionable, but it is important to note in addition that financial stability may be an early victim of an aggressive profit policy.

The important virtue of retained profit to the business is that it provides an addition to the resources, and therefore to the assets, under the control of management. These additional assets may and should be used for expansion; they should themselves generate additional profit, and although there may be setbacks its average level over a period of years should steadily increase. Management which is able to provide resources for expansion out of profit must also demonstrate an ability to employ them fruitfully and the proof of this ability will be a steady rise in profit commensurate with the additional assets employed.

A profit which falls a little short of this desirable level suggests a lower degree of success, and any shortfall must result in a decline in profit retention if the dividend is maintained, or in dividend paid if an attempt is made to stick to preconceived views of profit retention. A more significant fall, which cuts the dividend and eliminates retention, or vice versa, poses more serious problems. Failure to remunerate capital will make a new issue of shares more difficult; failure to retain profit will make a new issue more necessary.

An important financial fact is that the increase in net assets that results from profit will first of all appear in liquid form; retained profit, subject to any investment decision taken by management, will produce a steady increase in the balance at the bank. The new liquid resources provided by profitable activity come under direct managerial control; they are available for, and normally they will be used for further development and, unless they are to remain idle, a series of investment decisions must be taken with this object in view. It is possible, however, for a successful company to anticipate the availability of new resources produced by profit, to borrow on short term to finance intended development, and to repay as profit emerges. It is normally regarded as unsound financial policy to provide for long-term investment on the basis of short-term finance and, because the profit from the new venture is unlikely to be enough by itself to repay such a loan within the two or three years' credit period, an advance of this type is quite certainly an undesirable method of financing developments in the case of a new business. The profit that can be expected from the general activity of a well-established and successful business, however, introduces an advantage and provides a series of expectations very different from those existing in a new business. The expected results over the next few years can be calculated by projecting the activity of the recent past into the future. The result of this projection and the anticipated profit from the new investment may together provide a very satisfactory expected source of repayment for a short-term loan.

How much can be borrowed if repayment out of profit is to be completed over two or three years, on the assumption that profit from current activities will continue to accrue at its past rate and that there will be a little extra from the new project, is simple to calculate. The retained profit for one year, that is profit after tax and dividend, is the basis of the calculation; three times this amount can be repaid in three years or in a shorter period if additional profit can be expected from the new venture, provided no new investment is made. It may be preferable to omit any profit from the new venture in the loan repayment calculation until the venture has proved itself.

In practice the amount available for repayment each year is increased by the annual depreciation charge, part of the positive cash flow, and the effect is to permit the repayment of more than three times the profit in three years on the assumption that no resources are needed during the period for replacing plant that wears out and no new investment decisions are taken. The extent to which such assumptions are valid in a mature and widely based business must be closely considered and all these factors would need to be very carefully assessed before a decision to borrow is taken.

A very different situation will exist in the case of a business that has suffered a loss, even a short-term one; it is significant of rather more than the fact that there is nothing available for dividend, since it results in an actual decline in the resources under managerial control. If the previous level of resources was satisfactory, their total after a loss will not be adequate to allow the enterprise to carry on without some restrictions on its rate of activity. An attempt to evade the logic of the situation will produce a decline in liquidity, and this is likely to be at the expense of external creditors, unless and until the loss is made good by profit in a later period. A short-term loss means only a temporary set-back, but unless the amount is small and the trend of results is quickly reversed, its implications are clear and must be recognised.

If losses persist over several years, a steady and continuous drain on resources must impair the ability of the enterprise to continue. The first impact of loss is on liquidity, but there is a limit to the extent to which it can be reduced and still allow the business to continue to operate, not only at the current but indeed at any level. Additional outside resources will be needed to fill the gap, but they will be harder or even impossible to obtain because of the very circumstances which make them necessary. It will be difficult, if losses have been heavy and sustained, to take advantage of the prospect of profit if it should emerge. Available resources may have been reduced to so low a level that they are no longer adequate for the job they are intended to do. Purchase of additional plant etc. that may be necessary to take advantage of any change in circumstances may be quite impossible, working capital may already be very small or even non-existent. The development of a situation such as this calls for closing down the business, or if the prospects of future profit are sufficiently real, for a reorganisation or transfer of the business to a new group with available resources, but one which may be unwilling to commit them to the enterprise as it exists, to the particular managerial group in control.

## RETURN ON CAPITAL EMPLOYED

An enterprise is established to make profit by employing in a productive manner the assets committed to its charge. Profit is therefore the test of success; profit is needed to enable management to continue functioning and to fulfil the duty imposed on it of servicing the capital with which it has been endowed. An additional surplus, retained profit, is useful as a basis for development; indeed it is very nearly in the category of an imperative, and many members of both management and ownership groups would regard as unsound an enterprise unable to provide a reasonable amount of retained profit, enough at a minimum to act as a financial stabiliser against adverse conditions.

Some measure of the extent to which the profit is adequate for these objectives must be developed. Profit must be at least large enough to give a satisfactory rate of return on the invested capital, a basic figure below which it must not be allowed to fall, on average over a period of years, if the business is to continue in satisfactory competition with its rivals. Its ability to raise capital in future will depend, first, upon the extent to which the business continues to produce the minimum profit which will enable it to pay a dividend that satisfies investors on the basis of comparisons they are able to make with alternative investment possibilities and, second, because retained profit must act both as a stabiliser and as a basis for expansion, upon whether a sufficient surplus emerges to meet these requirements.

The figure of capital on which the expected return should be made includes not only subscribed capital but also retained profit, i.e. the ownership interest, the effective capital of the business at a particular date. It may be expected that retained profit will be capitalised from time to time and that the separate balance carried forward on profit and loss account will be kept at a low level. Capital employed may also be defined to include long-term loans or sometimes as total assets.

The amount of the expected profit, covering intended dividend and retention, may then be expressed as a percentage on capital employed, e.g. the ownership interest. This approach is widely used today as a method of assessing the adequacy of the profit in relation to the resources committed to producing it. The standard is reasonably objective, in the sense that it can quite easily be used as a base for a comparison to judge whether investment proposals are satisfactory, and subsequently how achievement measures up to estimate. It can also be used to compare results over time and with results achieved by other businesses, which can themselves be translated into the same language and so provide material for an assessment of the relative levels of the profit return. Care must be taken to define capital employed in the same sense for all elements in a particular comparison, i.e. as the interest of the ownership group, the interest of this group plus long-term loans or as the total assets. The definition chosen for capital employed will depend at least to some extent on the purpose for which the percentage return is needed and the type of assessment that is being made, and it is probably wise to be flexible in this matter.

The possibility of variations in the definition and interpretation of the term 'capital employed' must receive careful attention when the concept is to be used to make some assessment of progress. Adjustment to the recorded value of assets to allow for such facts as changes in the general level of prices is common practice today, but no generally agreed procedure has been adopted, and the calculations made by different enterprises will not necessarily be on the same basis; the effect of alternative choices would need to be examined in practice, before any conclusions are reached from a comparison of the rate of return on an inter-firm basis.

The significance of the definition of capital employed becomes apparent when it is related to the financial structure of the business. Development is often financed on the basis of long-term loans and if profit expressed as an average rate of return exceeds the interest payable to the lenders, there will be a surplus available for the ordinary shareholders. A substantial surplus may emerge in good times from such an element of gearing, and this will provide a valuable addition to the profit available to ownership; the reverse will be true in bad times and it may even be difficult to meet the interest payment to lenders. A business which is financed to any significant extent by means of long-term loans may produce a better return on capital employed, interpreted as the ownership interest, than another company which depends entirely on share capital and retained profit. The return produced by the first business may however be lower than that of the second if capital employed is defined to include long-term loans. There is probably a case for avoiding the rather narrower definition of capital employed as the ownership interest and accepting the rather wider one which includes long-term loans. The use of this definition of capital employed will help to eliminate the distorting effects of differences which result from the various mixtures of capital resources from which an enterprise can choose.

The problem of comparison may be further aggravated if a company depends very heavily on short-term credit to finance its work. A company which expands unilaterally the credit terms it gets from its suppliers because it pays no interest on such resources should be able to produce a larger return than another business which maintains a more normal credit situation. The fact is that a business which plays on its creditors in this way may be able to increase its profit without expanding the base for the return on capital calculation, and as a result may produce a more favourable rate of return than might have been expected, but financial stability will suffer. The excessive use of short-term credit, the extension of the normal credit terms, must produce financial instability; it is indeed one sign that this stage has already been reached, that a potentially dangerous financial situation has developed and the company may be forced to cut back its rate of activity.

The method of calculating the return on capital can of itself have no effect on the financial stability of the business, but it is not impossible that a base could be chosen that masks a very pedestrian out-turn, and perhaps one that is deteriorating. It could be argued, for this reason, that the total of the assets in use provides the most satisfactory basis on which to calculate the return; indeed it would be reasonable to go further and to call for a revaluation on a current price basis.

An additional factor must be borne in mind if an attempt is made to compare the trading results of one enterprise with those of another similar business. There is a surprising lack of exact comparability between the work of two apparently very similar enterprises. Most businesses operate on a mixed basis in the sense that each relies on a variety of different products, and the range of products on which A depends may differ substantially from those on B's list despite considerable overlapping. The differences between the two businesses may be on the fringe, and account for no more than say 20 per cent of total production, but there may be wide variability and significant differences in the profit returns from these marginal activities; these differences may be sufficient in their effect on the final return, on the average rate of return on total capital employed, to render comparisons of doubtful value, if they are used as the sole method of assessing relative efficiency in the use of resources. Variations in profit mix may have a similar effect, and it may be difficult for outsiders to identify such a change. The analysis of turnover and profit produced by different lines of product can be very useful to other managements attempting to make comparisons.

The use of return on capital as a good basis for inter-firm comparison is affected by the fact that both profit measurement and asset valuation are always to some extent a subjective process; the problem is discussed in the last section of this chapter.

## CASH FLOW

The term cash flow is widely used today and refers to and includes all the cash that comes into the hands of management and is available for spending during a particular period of time. The concept of a rate of cash flow, the rate at which resources become available, is a relevant factor in any assessment of the current and expected financial stability of an enterprise. The significance of this concept is that management has control over the destination of liquid cash that comes into its hands, and if the flow is at a sufficiently high rate, management should be able to meet the commitments which it has accepted and which are judged to have a prior claim on the available resources. Any failure to meet claims as they fall due is likely to damage the credit image of an enterprise and consequently its ability to fund its activities.

Much of the cash flow that comes under the control of management is earmarked to pay for raw materials, wages, salaries and other running expenses. It is a fact of economic life that if the enterprise is to remain in business it must continue selling and meet the consequent costs. There is thus a continuous flow of goods etc. into and out of the business, and because this movement is in both directions the cash flow which follows it is largely repetitive and the outward movement is in many ways mandatory. A management wishing to stay in business enjoys no effective right of decision over the disposal of that part of the inward cash flow that must be used to meet this repetitive demand for payment to cover the cost of its sales. Failure to meet such a demand on any significant scale must mean that the continuity of the business itself is in danger, although changes in the nature of its activities are not precluded.

The significant element of cash flow inwards that is relevant to managerial decision is the part that is free for disposal, in general the surplus that is not required to meet the repetitive demand for expenditure necessarily incurred to earn revenue. The basic constituent of such systems is profit which produces the increase in net assets, initially a surplus of liquid resources. Profit is a residue, an excess of revenue over costs and by definition it is not required to meet payment for expenses incurred in the earning process. These expenses have been deducted before the profit is measured. The cash received from sales has first been used to meet the total periodic cost, and the residue, the surplus, remains available in liquid form for spending.

There is however a second element in net cash flow measured on a periodic basis. The earlier discussion about the repetitive element in outwards cash flow assumed that such expenditure was met by the early payment of cash. There are, however, important exceptions, sometimes referred to as 'non-cash' expenses, because the payment does not take place during the period covered by the profit calculation. This non-cash element of expenditure covers all the depreciation charges together with the amounts written off any other item that has been capitalised, e.g. research costs.

A cash outflow to meet the total cost of the asset, a part of which is periodically charged against revenue, did of course take place, but at an earlier date and within an earlier accounting period. Management did exercise its prerogative to use resources to buy a long-term asset, such as new plant, but the cash, perhaps produced by retained profit, was spent in an earlier year. The immediate charge against revenue did not include the full cost as in the case of the repetitive payments; some part, e.g. 10 per cent or 20 per cent, was treated as a period cost and the surplus was carried forward to be charged against the revenue of each of those later years in which it was expected to make an effective contribution to production. The total cash outflow in this first year must have substantially exceeded the depreciation charge in that year. The position is reversed in the later years of the asset's life: the cash outflow is less than the total costs charged against revenue, and the net cash inflow available for managerial decision is the total of the net profit plus the non-cash expense, as defined above, charged against revenue.

Effectively the amount available to management is the net profit plus the depreciation charge. That charge of itself however does nothing to create inwards cash flow. The existence of this flow depends entirely upon whether enough goods are sold at a sufficiently high price to cover the cost of materials consumed, wages etc. as well as the non-cash expenses, and to leave a surplus or residue of profit. If a loss has been suffered the cash flow measured by the depreciation charge will of course be reduced by the amount of the loss and it may even disappear.

The projection of the future or expected cash flow is an important part of the procedure for forecasting and budgeting. The expected receipts for a given period and the rate of receipt will be estimated and compared with the anticipated payments and the rate of payment; any gap, particularly important if it is a deficit, will be estimated in advance. The ability to use a cash surplus to advantage and to take steps to ensure that a deficit is covered are important elements of financial management. Permanent capital should be invested profitably, but held at the lowest level consistent with permitting the business to develop unhampered by a shortage of resources. Short-term deficits should be anticipated and covered by arrangements for an overdraft to be available as the gap emerges. It will be easier to make the arrangements if there is reasonable anticipation of any shortage.

An advance calculation of profit is a second important element in the forecasting procedures but it does not provide all the data needed for the calculation of a cash surplus or deficit, partly because it makes no allowance for payments of a capital nature, and there may also be non-revenue receipts. There is the additional problem implicit in the profit calculation that expenditures incurred are not necessarily chargeable costs in the periodic income calculation. The cost of raw materials purchased is not the same as the cost of raw materials used; the point becomes very significant when finished goods, in which the raw materials and other costs are embodied, are the subject of valuation and particularly when totals of stocks vary substantially from one period to another. A case can be made for sticking to cash receipts and cash payments when advance calculations or forecasts are prepared because this avoids the contentious problem of stock valuation and the depreciation charge which necessarily intrude into the area of profit measurement. The calculations of cash flow are of a much more factual character and while forecasting always presents problems of valuation, the forecast of expected profit is more difficult than that of cash receipts and cash payments because of difficulties such as choosing the correct methods of valuation; in short these are additional problems which appear when profit measurement is attempted, but which are absent when cash flow is being calculated.

It must be accepted, however, that while calculations of cash flow and the measurement of profit overlap, they are essentially two distinct exercises, and the information provided by each has its own specific purpose. The calculations are complementary, not substitutional, and there are normally good reasons why both should be undertaken; the effect of the additional element of valuation on the profit calculation must however be understood when an appraisal of the expected results is being made, but there is no case for suggesting that because the two statements produce similar or overlapping information it is better to choose the one which may be the more accurate. The flow of funds statement as a method of communicating information of financial significance is widely used today and it has become an important accounting report in the area of *post facto* assessment, but it supplements rather than replaces the profit and loss account. The total amount of information available is expanded by the production of these two reports and they should both be used if a wide and critical analysis of business activity is to be undertaken.

Two different purposes are fulfilled by the documents. The profit and loss account, despite the problem of valuation, provides the information on facts that must decide whether a business is viable in the sense that it has provided, and is therefore likely to continue providing, a satisfactory expansion from internal sources. No other accounting report provides the data for the assessment of the probability of long-term viability, the most important element in the life of any business. The historical account cannot predict results over the long-term future, a feat which no accounting report or mathematical calculation is capable of doing: these long-term possibilities depend as much as anything on the quality of present and future management. A good current profit-making enterprise, however, provides by its existence a clear indication that there is a public interest in and demand for its product, that good management is there to produce it at a low enough cost and that the business therefore possesses the recipe for long-term success.

The cash flow statement, and especially its projection into the future, provides information that is not available in the profit and loss account, information of a different type which supplements what appears there. The statement is concerned basically with the need for financial resources, with their origin and with their use by a business in the context of the ability of the business to meet its commitments, short- and long-term, as they fall due; the emphasis is on the maintenance of, and on the expected maintenance of financial stability. The statement is used as a guide to the desirability of accepting further commitments on the basis of the financial resources currently available or, if this appears to be unreasonable, to the need for procuring additional financial resources before any fresh commitments are accepted.

The most satisfactory way of using such accounting reports and forecasts as profit statements and flow of funds statements is a joint use. Profit or the likelihood of profit in sufficient quantity is a justification for the use of financial resources. Reports on past activity will indicate the extent to which it has been possible to produce a profit with a balanced use of resources; estimates of future results will indicate the extent to which profitable activity is possible on the basis of the resources likely to be available or whether, because the level of activity is expected to exceed certain limits, more resources will be needed. Potential profitable use of resources is a justification for getting them, but provision of resources does not of itself produce a profit. Consideration must be given to the prospect of existing resources proving adequate, to the prospect of resources expected from retained profit over a period meeting an existing or an emerging shortage, to the prospect of a temporary overdraft bridging a short-term gap and to the possible need for additional permanent capital. The absence of a hope of future additional profit provides no justification for seeking additional resources; decisions about the future can only be taken satisfactorily if, before they are made, both aspects of enterprise activity, profit and cash flow, are taken into account.

A reasonable profit in relation to the resources committed is one ingredient necessary to justify a decision to invest, and a cash flow that will permit the maintenance of financial stability is the second ingredient. The *post facto* assessment must pay attention to both factors and in both cases will review the extent to which expectation has been fulfilled.

## REFERENCES AND ADDITIONAL READING

Anthony, R., *Financial Accounting*, Irwin, 1980.

Goch, D., *Finance and Accounts for Management*, Pan Books, 1980.

Kohler, E. L., *Accounting for Management,* Prentice-Hall

Magee, C. C., *Financial Accounting and Control,* Allen and Unwin, 1968.

Magee, C. C., *Framework of Accountancy,* Macdonald and Evans, 1979

Magee, C. C., *Rowland and Magee's Accounting,* Gee, 1971.

Solomons, D., *Divisional Performance: Measurement and Control,* Irwin, 1968.

# 8

# Cost Control

**R.J. Brown**

*The preceding chapter considered the broader implications of the control system and attention is now directed to a specific aspect of the general subject, that of cost control. The author of the following chapter has had many years' experience organising the cost control systems of a large manufacturing plant. He looks upon the subject as being of the nature of profit control which should be examined under each of the following headings: the production situation, the project situation and the lossmaking situation.*

*In the production situation the investigation of standard cost variances can be of some assistance so far as direct costs are concerned but the author regards standard costing as of little practical benefit in the control of overheads. He emphasises the importance of constructing efficient procedures for the control of overheads because this classification of business expenditure is tending to increase as a proportion of total costs. He regards more direct methods of controlling overhead costs, such as by actual limitation of inputs, as being most effective.*

*Likewise there are limitations on the typical use of budgetary control in the project situation, and here the initial budget should be formulated on the basis of cost saving or profit enhancement elsewhere. The author thus sees severe limitations on the effectiveness of the traditional techniques of standard costing and budgetary control, but his criticism is constructive and he makes a number of other practical and specific suggestions for the control of costs and the improvement of profits.*

The process of setting the objectives for a business and formulating the plans to achieve them, which has been dealt with in previous chapters, can be likened to deciding on a ship's destination and plotting the intended course on the charts.

To continue the nautical analogy, the process of 'cost control' can be compared with the problems encountered at sea in navigating with the least possible deviation on the course which has been set and coping with the day-to-day problems of tide, currents and weather together with the practical performance of ship and crew.

In many ways, it is too sweeping to refer to this whole process as 'cost control', since the purpose of an enterprise is usually the earning of profit, in which the control of expenditure is but part of the process.

The types of situation which a business encounters in dealing with the day-to-day control of profits fall broadly into the following categories:

1   *The 'production situation'*
    In this case, the output is clearly the product or service which is being sold, and the concern is to minimise the inputs or expenditure involved in creating the product or service.

2   *The 'project situation'*
    In this case, money is being spent in the expectation that a profitable output will emerge, but with the detail and dimensions of the results being largely uncertain. Research, development and advertising expenditure are included in this category but in practice it embraces virtually all items of overhead expenditure involving people, plant or services.

3   *The 'lossmaker situation'*
    Every now and again, a voyage will commence where there has been an error or misjudgement in plotting the course, or the ship or crew prove insufficiently equipped or experienced to make the journey, or the conditions at sea were rougher than expected, and the ship and crew risk foundering. In such situations, decisions need to be made as to whether to carry on to the destination or return to port, and if so by what means, or in the extreme situation whether to abandon ship! In a business, the economic conditions may, at times, be as unpredictable as the weather, and the business plans are inevitably less precise than the course plotted for a ship. In this situation, the 'rules' have changed, and the approach to it needs to be quite different from that used in the 'production' or 'project' situation.

The types of action which can be applied to all these situations fall basically into two categories:

1  Physically limiting the inputs or expenditure incurred by the business.
2  Maximising the 'efficiency' of the operation of the business. Within this, a major requirement of the process is a careful and accurate diagnosis of the problem in order that attention and action can be centred on remedy.

In either case it is necessary to develop yardsticks on the basis of which the appropriate action can be taken.

Against the background of this general perspective on day-to-day cost control, it is now appropriate to consider the suitability and limitations of the various specific techniques which can be used to deal with the situations.

## THE PRODUCTION SITUATION

The conventional technique used in controlling the profitability of production situations is standard costing. This rests on the basis that the standard cost is a predetermined yardstick of what output 'ought' to cost, and actual costs are then related to this yardstick; the points of difference or 'variances' which emerge identify the areas of inefficiency enabling action to be centred on remedying them.

In practice, standard costs are established for each operation performed on each component produced, building up in total to a standard cost for the final product. The standard cost normally comprises three separate elements:

1  *The material element*
Self-evidently, the standard material cost of an item is a function of the amount of material which ought to be used in the production of the item, and the price which ought to be paid for that material in whatever quantity it is purchased. Inevitably, some discretion has to be exercised in determining whether it is expedient or meaningful, in a particular situation, to attribute all material consumed in the production of an item specifically to that item, or whether to treat some as general 'overheads', e.g. cutting oils, paint, solder, electricity.
2  *The direct labour element*
This element relates to the cost of those people whose work

should result in the direct and immediate creation of output. The time which such individuals ought to spend in the performance of a particular operation is determined, and this combined with the rates of pay they ought to receive, enables the direct labour element of the standard cost to be computed.

3   *The overhead element*

In essence, this is computed by taking all costs incurred by the business, other than material and direct labour costs, and attributing them to individual operations. The total amount to be recovered is normally that defined in the annual budget or forecast. This total amount is often then apportioned between various cost centres within the production process, e.g. a type of machine or production department. The level of activity anticipated in the forecast for each cost centre is then expressed in an appropriate unit such as machine or direct labour hours or some dimension of material used. From this, a standard cost of overheads per hour (or whatever) for that cost centre is established. The overhead element of the standard cost of an operation is then derived by multiplying this overhead rate by the hours etc. which ought to be taken in the execution of that operation.

Provided that what has been produced in a given period is identified, that output can then be expressed in terms of what it ought to have cost in total, and also separate the labour, material and overhead elements of that total.

By comparing the actual expenditures under the same headings, the areas in which costs have been higher or lower than they ought to be can be identified. In addition:

1   If the difference between the price actually paid for material and the amount allowed in the standard is recorded, the cause of any variation in material costs can be further analysed into whether it is a function of the amount used or the price paid.
2   Similarly, if the actual hours worked by direct labour in a period are recorded, any variance in direct labour cost can be analysed into whether it is a function of the efficiency of labour or the hourly rate paid to that labour.
3   Finally, if actual overhead expenditure is related to the forecast, then any variance in overhead cost can be analysed into whether it is a function of the amount spent, or a difference in the level of activity (recovery).

This approach to analysing the causes of variances can be carried on virtually indefinitely. Provided that effort and expense are available to measure one variable, the other can always be deduced. Typically, a business may thus identify the effect of using non-standard materials and the creation of scrap on material variances; the effect of waiting time, scrap and higher than standard skilled labour on labour variances.

If the business is fairly large, it is obviously essential to ask the question not only 'what?' but 'who?' is the cause of these variances, since it is individuals who must take action to remedy the problems. A global result for the business as a whole does not help to resolve the problem since it cloaks a large number of varying items. It is probable that the analysis will need to be carried down at least to departmental level, and in the case of labour analysis, conceivably down to that of the individual operator.

Bearing in mind that the objective is profit control, standard costs are also applied in the analysis of the profit and loss account. By relating actual and forecast sales turnover to the actual and forecast standard cost of those sales, the extent to which sales volume, sales prices and product mix have affected total actual profits relative to forecast profits can also be established.

Through the technique of standard costing a reasonably objective analysis of the historic performance of the business is obtained, although it should be recognised that the counting, evaluation and analysis required itself involves an on-cost to the business, and this on-cost will increase directly with the amount of analysis required.

Given that the information is available, it is perhaps worth considering its application in controlling rather than simply analysing profits. The following points can be made.

1   It needs to be recognised that the question relates to what has already happened, and assumes that if action is not taken, the problem will recur in the future. While this assumption may have some logical limitations, it is sound enough in practice to use as a working hypothesis.

The essential requirement is that the information is produced as soon as possible after the event has occurred, thus minimising the period over which the loss is occurring before action is taken.

This comment is particularly appropriate to the material usage and labour efficiency types of variance which both reflect areas where performance can go 'off the rails' very quickly. With variances such as overhead recovery, gross profitability, sales volume and labour and material prices, the need for rapid reporting of actual results is perhaps less pressing, since the problem ought to have been foreseen and action taken accordingly. On this point more will be said later.

2   In the area of overhead control, standard costing, of itself, is of little practical benefit. Overhead expenditure variances are, in fact, identified by the budgetary control process. So far as overhead recovery variances are concerned, it is feasible to evaluate factory output programmes, and in the event of an under-recovery to determine whether it is a function of low demand or inadequate achievement against that programme. As noted before, however, it is suggested that the effect of a fall in demand on a factory's performance can, and should, be anticipated rather than measured in hindsight.

3   It is a fact of business life that increasing proportions of total costs are inevitably being incurred in the area classified as overheads. This has been brought about by two trends.

First, there is a trend towards the replacement of direct labour by the use of machines in virtually all spheres of industry.

Second, there has been a corresponding growth in the number of employees supporting the production process rather than being directly involved in it. The substitution of machines for men has increased the requirement for production engineers and setters. The accelerating advance in technology has demanded the involvement of more people in research and development, since a company which produces an obsolete product very quickly becomes obsolete itself. The increased level of fixed overheads involved in both the mechanisation and staff only indirectly involved in production makes the maintenance of sales volumes particularly critical, and thus yet more people have become involved in the process of marketing the products of the business.

Because of this trend, and because of the inadequacy of standard costing techniques as a mechanism for controlling overhead costs, it is suggested that standard costing is becoming less relevant as a technique in profit control than has previously been the case.

A final feature of the practical problems which can be encountered in the application of standard costs to overhead control is that the more remote an overhead is from the actual production process, the more arbitrary does any allocation of that cost to the product become, and the less meaningful the variances which are computed against the standard. The trend is for those overheads which are directly related to the production process to form a decreasing proportion of the whole.

4    In the area of direct labour costs, the increasing mechanisation of the industrial process has resulted in the output of direct operators being determined not so much by their own efficiency and effort, but by the 'cycle time' of the machines or the speed of the conveyor. As a result, the effort of the individual is likely to be a less significant factor in the creation of variances than has been the case previously, and in many situations, factors such as attendance and industrial relations problems assume much greater significance. Since the identification of the remedial action in these cases does not rely on the application of standard costing, the technique itself is of less significance in profit control.

There is also, perhaps, an inherent danger in the principle of standard costing which considers labour as being a variable cost where in practice the description 'hourly paid' no longer means that such employees can be dismissed at will. This is of more relevance in considering the lossmaker situation.

5    The process of increasingly sophisticated mechanisation has made the usage of materials more predictable due to quality becoming more consistent, and usage being more carefully governed. This tends to minimise the size of the variances, and thus the significance of standard costs in profit control.

6    A final point of concern is that the standard costing technique can result in a rather fatalistic approach being taken to profit control. If the price of material becomes more expensive, the standard cost of the material element is in turn revised. If the wage paid to direct labour is increased, the standard rate of the direct labour element is revised in step.

The standard costing approach does not immediately direct attention to the fundamental questions such as whether these increases are out of line with the general trend of cost increase or whether some alternative approach to the production of the product would not prove more cost effective, e.g. could an alternative type of material be employed, or could the method of manufacture be changed?

With overhead rates, the process is even more insidious, since by definition the standard overhead rate is that which has to be applied to recover what are expected to be the actual costs. It does not attempt to deal with the question as to whether those actual costs are reasonable.

Even in the field of labour efficiency and material usage variances, there is a tendency for this 'drift' in standards to occur. In practice, a gap will nearly always occur between what an item 'ought' to cost, and what in practice it does cost. This gap soon becomes recognised as normal, and thus attention ceases to be centred on it, as a result of which a less stringent yardstick is effectively created.

These features do not, of themselves, negate the value of the standard costing technique, but it does need to be recognised that the standard itself is by no means immutable, and that almost as much attention needs to be paid to the way standard costs inflate, as is paid to the variances which the standard costs reveal in analysing actual performance.

It must be stressed that the foregoing points do not argue for the abandonment of standard costing as a technique for profit control; they simply attempt to put its limitations in the modern business situation into perspective. The area of profit control quite apart, standard costing continues to fill a virtually indispensable role as a basis for stock accounting and for the evaluation of output of multi-product concerns. It also is often the only practical starting point for price setting when a very wide range of products is handled, and where no clear market demand pattern can be established.

What can be said is that due to the increasing proportion of total costs being represented by overheads in modern industry, the need to find approaches to deal with 'project situations' is becoming more urgent, while the conventional 'production situation' is one which is diminishing in significance.

The control of project situations is dealt with in the next section, but the techniques for dealing with the profit control of production situations are by no means limited to standard costing. Some supplementary approaches which can be taken are as follows:

1   Perhaps the most obvious control which can be exercised is by limiting the inputs into the 'production situation'. For example, the recruitment of labour can be limited to the level which it was projected ought to be capable of handling the factory programme; controls can be exercised on orders on suppliers for materials before they are released, so as to identify and query situations where an above-

standard price is to be paid; controls can be applied to ensure that only sufficient material is issued from the stores as is required to produce the programmed output by the 'standard' methods of efficiency. It can be argued that these controls are exceedingly crude in that, of themselves, they provide no assurance that the required output will be achieved. They are, however, highly effective in ensuring that a limit is placed on the total costs that are incurred, and thereby direct attention to the efficient use of the inputs, having disposed of the problem of the inputs themselves being potentially too great.

2   As noted before, as far as possible an approach should be taken which prevents a variance occurring and initiates the right action to avoid or minimise the financial costs or maximise the opportunities. In this area, the data may not be 'financial' in the strictest sense of the word, but their consequences must be perceived in a financial way.

Given that in many industries there is a lead time, which is measurable in weeks rather than hours, between an order being received and a sale occurring, the most obvious area of attention should be the order intake. The volume of work which this represents should dictate the short-term policy of a business as to whether it engages additional labour, or replaces vacancies as they arise and whether overtime is worked or not. The unit selling price of each order should be 'vetted' before it is accepted, and its impact on future trading results projected. The acceptance of substantial volumes of orders at lower than forecast rates of profitability signals a red light for the pricing policy of a business or its original perception of the nature of the market. A buoyant state of incoming demand should direct the attention of a business to being selective in prices accepted, giving production priority to the higher-margin business, and considering which orders use the least of the scarcest resources, in so far as these options are open in a practical commercial sense.

The business must be alert to external influences affecting the order intake. In domestic markets, government fiscal policy and activities by competitors are areas which can affect demand in a relatively short period of time. In overseas markets the effects of movements in rates of exchange, and the political and economic stability of the countries concerned, are significant factors. The fact that these can rarely be quantified with any accuracy, and that the business can rarely influence the course they take, does not minimise the need to see them as significant inputs into the process of controlling profits and costs on a day-to-day basis.

Likewise, an industrial relations problem needs to be assessed in terms of its effect on future profits. Not only should a financial view have a bearing on the way the problem is resolved, but the action which needs to be taken to overcome the financial consequences of the dispute needs to be formulated as it occurs, not after its effect has been measured.

3   A final point which perhaps needs to be made is that all controls and systems within a business have a financial implication, even if they do not actually form part of the accounting records of the business. As part of the process of profit control, it is not only reasonable, but almost imperative, that a financial view is taken on the adequacy of such mundane activities as production control, stores recording systems, wages booking and buying office procedures. It is within these activities, after all, that many of the causes of the phenomena which are blandly described as cost variances actually occur.

## PROJECT SITUATIONS

Project situations were earlier defined as being those where for a finite input or expenditure, a direct and immediate effect on output or sales would not be expected to occur, i.e. most items classified as fixed or semi-variable overheads. The classic technique for dealing with such situations is that of budgetary control.

Within this definition falls a tremendous variety of costs, ranging from those which could be considered unavoidable in the short term, such as rent and rates, through those which are fundamental to the production process, such as the costs of power, tooling, transport and stores, to those which are more concerned with the evolution and development of the business, such as the costs of advertising, design and development, methods improvement and systems analysis.

Budgetary control is relatively straightforward and involves two stages. First, there is the establishment of the budget which determines the amount of money which a particular department or activity (with an individual identified as responsible) ought to incur in a period of time; and second there is the process of measuring and controlling actual expenditure in relation to the budgets.

The essence of the budgets is that they identify who is to be accountable for the item of expenditure. Where the item involves the cost of employees, the budget will be expressed both in terms of the numbers of individuals employed in a particular department, and in the sums of money which will be spent on the employment of those people, covering not only their salaries and associated costs, but also such incidentals as travelling, entertainment and stationery costs.

Cost such as plant and building maintenance, rents, rates, power, advertising, will be expressed in finite sums of money, but within each heading it is quite possible that major individual items of expenditure will be specifically identified.

Such budgets normally establish, in total, the limit of expenditure for a period of a year, and within that year an assessment of the proportion of that budget which is likely to be spent in each month, or quarter.

Sometimes these budgets are considered conditional on some other variable, such as sales, being as forecast, in which case the technique of flexible budgets is employed.

Businesses differ in their views on the way their managers should be accountable for the expenditure which they have to control. Some consider it sufficient for a manager to contain his overall expenditure within the total amount budgeted; others expect managers to contain expenditure on each individual item in the budget to within the amount allowed.

The practical control of actual expenditure within this budget occurs in two ways:

1 Actual expenditure is recorded on a regular (normally monthly) basis, and is related to the expenditure which was budgeted to occur over the same period. Significant variances are identified as a result, and on the principle that problems which have occurred in the past are likely to occur in the future, attention is centred on particular areas in order that appropriate action can be taken.

2 Of rather more direct impact is the process of only allowing expenditure to occur which is within the budgeted level. This involves the process of vetting decisions to engage employees or place purchase orders to ensure that by taking that course of action, actual expenditure will not as a result exceed the amount forecast.

In practice, items of expenditure which occur frequently, but where each transaction is of small value (e.g. travelling expenses and cutting tools) are best controlled by the first method, while those of high value but restricted incidence (e.g. advertising expenses and plant overhaul expenses) fit well into being essentially controlled by the second process.

While the mechanism for controlling expenditure within a budget is largely self-evident, the actual process of deciding what items the budget should include presents far greater problems. In this process, there can be no absolute set of rules or neat formula, but the following represents some of the approaches which are, or can be, applied:

1    It is possible that a commitment to incur certain specific expenditure has emerged as part of the strategic planning process, the result of which is that the question is one of 'when' rather than 'whether' the item is to be included in the budget.

2    Such items apart, the most obvious and powerful objective criterion for determining budgets is to require evidence that a particular item of expenditure can be expected to be offset by an even greater level of cost savings elsewhere, or will generate additional turnover which in turn will generate a greater level of profit.

Given that a business is often presented with a number of alternative propositions, each competing for limited cash resources or limited amounts of managerial time, such an approach enables the business to rank these propositions in order of priority.

There is a tendency where this approach is being adopted for those proposing that the expenditure should be made to take a somewhat optimistic view of the savings. To guard against this, it is important that, wherever possible, the expected savings are not only expressed in bald profit terms, but also in terms of some tangible and quantifiable change which will take place, e.g. numbers of employees on a particular activity to be reduced from $a$ to $b$, quantities sold to be increased from $c$ to $d$, machine breakdowns to be reduced from $d$ per cent to $e$ per cent.

To ensure that a proper discipline is maintained in these projections, it is necessary subsequently to review whether these anticipated changes were actually achieved. By the same process, if the budgeted item involves expenditure in a series of stages, it is desirable to specify review points at which it can be considered whether the results and costs of the item to date have been as projected, before any further monies are spent.

A further need where, say, staff are being engaged or assigned to undertake a particular, rather than an ongoing task or project, is to identify the likely duration of the task, so that as the scheduled completion date approaches, proper steps are taken to ensure that the staff are deployed on to the next potentially most productive activity.

This profit and loss approach to establishing budgets ought to be applied wherever possible, but it is suggested that in practice the number of areas in which it can sensibly be applied is limited, and thus other, less objective approaches also need to be considered.

3    A basis which is frequently adopted in preparing budgets is to establish what level of overhead expenditure the business can afford. This process involves establishing the gross margin which it is projected will be earned in the coming period, determining the net profit which ought to be earned, and thereby deducing what can be spent on overheads. Strictly speaking, such an approach inherently assumes that overheads are a non-productive luxury, rather than fundamental in enabling profit to be generated in the short or long term. This approach tends on the one hand to neglect the reality that overhead expenditure will almost inevitably become an increasing part of a thriving business enterprise, while on the other hand, it can result in an attitude of considerable complacency regarding overhead expenditure in times of plenty.

The approach does have some validity if the constraint on overhead expenditure is seen as being one of cash availability rather than profit. After all, what is declared as profit in the short term is largely a product of some fairly rigid accounting conventions regarding the capitalisation of expenditure, and a course of action which enables the maximum profits to be declared in one year may well be quite the wrong course of action to ensure the long-term prosperity and growth of the business. With cash, however, neglect of the short-term requirements can be extremely dangerous for the business.

While in theory the need to generate profit in a particular year need not be considered as a necessary constraint in establishing overhead budgets, in practice the performance of the management of virtually all businesses is judged by shareholders on the basis of the half-yearly figures; and this is a very sound pragmatic reason why this approach is so often adopted!

4    While the previous approach can set a limit on the total amount of the overhead budget, it is also normal for the individual managers of a

business to state the amount of money they need to have included in the budget for their particular area of responsibility. The initial result of this exercise usually reinforces the opinion of most financial managers that the only people in a business who believe in profit maximisation as a concept are themselves!

If the answers received from such a process are sometimes alarming, it can be because the right question is not being asked rather than because all the respondents are totally irresponsible or financially naive. The answers tend to be more logical if the managers at least are aware of the level of business activity which it is expected will arise in the period of the budget. It will be of even greater value if the individual manager and the business have clearly established what the objectives of that manager should be.

To take a crude example: the resources which a warehouse manager would feel he needs to ensure that he can dispatch all orders within 24 hours are likely to be very different from those he would consider he would need if his objective was set at despatching all orders within 14 days.

It is not proposed to consider the topic of 'management by objectives' in any greater depth, but simply to suggest that it can be rationally considered as integral to the budgetary control process.

5   Determining budgets simply on the basis of what managers ask for is a technique which relies on subjective valuations, and on the integrity and competence of the individual managers which unfortunately are qualities never possessed in equal measure by all human beings. There is a need to have other more objective measurements. The simplest and most commonly applied of these is to base the budget on what was spent in the previous year together with an appropriate provision for inflation. This historic approach can sometimes be made more sensitive by considering the criteria which determine the amount of overhead expenditure incurred on a particular activity. The number of people employed in a buying office might thus be considered as a function of the volume of productive materials purchased. The number of people and money budgeted for the buying department would, in this case, be varied according to the forecast increase or decrease in the value of production materials purchased in the coming year.

Such an approach has the obvious limitation that it is likely to perpetuate in the future inefficiencies which have arisen in the past. In practice most businesses have a vast range of incidental expenses for which this is the only practical basis on which to compute a budget.

An approach which can sometimes be effective, provided those involved are willing to be committed, is quite arbitrarily to set a low budget for a given year for a particular item or items, to centre people's attention on actually reducing costs to keep within the budget.

6   In circumstances where a budget cannot be established on a logical profit and loss basis, it can often be very revealing to consider what would happen if an activity were not undertaken at all, and then work up to the point where the budget will provide for the minimum possible service, but at the same time involve the least resources.

Another approach is to consider what would be the cost if an activity were performed in another way, e.g. renting rather than buying office equipment, despatching goods by passenger train rather than post. Individually, the examples given are deliberately some-what trivial, since the wider issues are areas which should receive exposure as part of the process of strategic planning. Cumulatively, consideration of a range of these smaller options can however lead to a significant improvement in operating costs.

The process of overhead cost control should not only be concerned with the establishment of budgets and containing expenditure within these budgets. Indeed, the budgets should be considered as guidelines, not tramlines.

It needs to be recognised that when the budget is being compiled, there may be only the sketchiest view of the justification of incurring expenditure which represents an investment (e.g. in a new computer system) as opposed to expenditure which is largely inevitable (such as rent and rates). In the case of investment expenditures, the control-ling management will not consider itself irrevocably committed to the expenditure simply because it has been included in the budget, but will formally review the case only when the fullest information has been assembled.

By the reverse process, during the period covered by a budget, it is quite likely that an opportunity to advance the prosperity of the business will emerge which had not been previously anticipated, but which would require overhead expenditure for which no provision had been made in the budget. It is important that the application of budgetary control does not result in a business operating in such an inflexible way that such opportunities are turned aside.

A further danger in operating budgetary control is that individuals feel committed to spending all money allocated in a budget in a given period (this is a particularly common problem when budgets are based on historic expenditures). This attitude tends to result in funds being simply squandered at the end of a budgetary period. The tendency seems to be particularly prevalent in local government but is by no means absent from many large commercial organisations.

In practice it is suggested that budgetary control is not, of itself, sufficient to minimise overhead costs. There is also a requirement for perpetual alertness to prevent unnecessary expense being incurred. In general, a second opinion as to whether money should be spent is helpful.

The attitude also needs to be developed within a business which considers overhead items in the same way as attention is traditionally concentrated on the production process, by regularly considering the value of a particular activity, considering whether it is being performed by the most effective means, and considering whether the least number of resources is being committed to that activity. It is suggested that business managers are traditionally orientated to think in this way about the direct production process, but often experience difficulty in adapting their thinking to the more abstract problem of overhead control, in spite of the fact that overheads are likely to increase while the direct costs of production are likely to contract.

## THE LOSSMAKER SITUATION

The techniques of cost and profit control which have been considered so far are really only appropriate when the circumstances in which a business finds itself are broadly as expected. In practice, even with the best planning and forecasting, every business will occasionally encounter situations which are substantially worse than they would have expected, affecting if not the business in its totality, at least individual product ranges. The types of problems which create these situations are: encountering greater difficulties in the production of a new product than was expected, encountering abnormal increases in the costs of one of the factors of production, finding that the demand for a new product was lower than expected, encountering a fall in demand due to the activity of competitors, or experiencing abnormal difficulties as a result of government fiscal policy.

The main difficulty is that although the problem may be perceived very quickly, it is often extremely difficult to know whether it represents a fundamental long-term problem which the business will be unable to overcome, or whether it is a short-term problem which will ultimately be resolved. To return to the nautical analogy used earlier in the chapter: should the storm be ridden out, or should the ship be abandoned?

It is suggested that, at this stage, the tactics of profit control should be for the business to remain as flexible as possible for as long as possible, so that either option can be pursued.

This is likely to require decisions to be made which on a straight profit and loss basis are not necessarily the most attractive propositions. For example, it may be preferable to incur high maintenance costs on old machinery rather than replace it with new equipment; it may be preferable to increase overtime working rather than to engage staff to fill vacancies; it will nearly always be preferable to rent than to buy; and investment decisions will be based on which option provides the shortest payback period rather than that which provides theoretically the best discounted cash flow.

A further commercial reality which will need to be recognised in these situations is that inadequate liquidity is more likely to sink the ship than simply the absence of profits as computed on the conventional accounting basis. Attention may thus need to be centred on minimising stock holdings, even at the expense of perhaps less than optimum production efficiency being achieved. It may well result in length of credit being a significant factor in the selection of suppliers and by the same process, payment terms will assume greater significance in the selling process. The liquidity requirement is also likely strongly to influence the rent or buy decision as much as the flexibility requirement.

A marginal cost approach to business decisions is likely to be far more appropriate in these circumstances than when the situation is close to that which had been expected.

So far as costs are concerned, making in is likely to be far more attractive than buying out if the problem is one of demand. It is also likely that in practice so-called direct labour will prove to be very much of a fixed overhead, and in these circumstances it may be appropriate to use direct workers on jobs which generate some revenue although not recovering their full hourly cost.

Perhaps the most significant area of cost and profit control is that of selling price. Businesses are far less certain of the demand curve of price against volume for their products than is implied in conventional economic theory. In practice, businesses tend to establish a price level for their product, find that this results in their earning a reasonable profit, and are then extremely nervous about departing radically from that level for fear of finding themselves in a less advantageous position.

If a business is in the position that relatively high proportions of its costs are fixed, but it can accommodate a substantial increase in volume without incurring any increase in these fixed costs, then it may well gamble on being on an elastic demand curve and reduce its prices. Conversely, if either variable costs constitute a high proportion of total costs, or a substantial increase in fixed costs would be required to provide additional capacity, the business may as well gamble on being on an inelastic demand curve, and increase prices.

If it is possible to take those gambles in an individual discrete market, rather than across the entire range of business, then this is likely to minimise the risks involved. Thus, the decision to change prices might be tested in a particular self-contained territory, or an individual product out of the range.

All these courses of action are only appropriate to employ as devices to play for time in the hope that the situation will take a turn for the better. What is absolutely fundamental is to make sure that if the situation does not improve, the ship is abandoned before it sinks.

To this end, it is imperative that the point of no return is clearly predicted. This is the time beyond which if the lossmaker continues to incur losses at its current rate it would put the total business in jeopardy. The business must be quite specific about the duration and/or extent of the losses it is prepared to incur before it cuts out a lossmaker, and it should establish these principles as soon as possible once the losses are perceived as occurring.

How the lossmaker will be cut out will depend on the cash flow it generates. If it is a net user of cash the cut needs to be made as soon as possible, but in other situations it can be allowed to fade out until it reaches the stage where it ceases to be a positive generator of cash.

It is suggested that the lossmaker situation is one of the few areas in which business decisions have to be considered as relatively intractable once made.

Concurrently with reaching a decision as to when to abandon a lossmaker, the business should also start to formulate its policies as to whether alternative ventures should be pursued, and tactically, how the minimum loss can be incurred in disposing of the lossmaker and its associated resources and assets. In this latter respect, a marginal costing approach is again likely to be highly relevant.

## CONCLUSION

It needs to be recognised that the majority of the techniques outlined previously are concerned with the process of analysis. They identify points of weakness and areas of opportunity. They do not stipulate the specific action which needs to be taken, nor do they, of themselves, result in action being taken. Costs and profits are actually controlled by people taking action, albeit in an informed manner. Unfortunately, human beings behave in complex and somewhat unpredictable ways. With a machine, the pressing of an appropriate button will automatically result in its performing a prescribed operation – provide a human being with a financial analysis, and a state of inertia is just as likely to result!

It thus needs to be recognised that a vital aspect of cost and profit control is getting people to react to the information provided. Clearly, this is an extremely complex subject, and arguably practical experience is of more relevance in solving the problem than academic theory. However, the factors which determine the way people react to financial data fall broadly into the following categories:

1 *Comprehension*

It is fairly self-evident that whoever receives financial data, and is expected to act on it, should understand its meaning and significance. At foreman level, this may amount to an understanding of the concept and significance of measuring labour utilisation and efficiency. At more senior levels, a more general appreciation of the derivation, construction and relevance of the profit and loss account, balance sheet and cash flow statement is probably called for. In a wider context, the overall performance of a business is dependent on the interrelated activities of the departments within it. However, the existence of a departmental structure presents a natural barrier to people perceiving this interrelationship, and encourages them to pursue narrow objectives associated only with the advancement of their particular specialism. There is thus a need for all managers to develop a general understanding of the problems and objectives of other functions in the business.

## 2  *Communication*

The clarity with which financial reports are presented is clearly important in the process of communication. In addition, as has been mentioned previously, it is essential that problems are identified as the responsibility of a specific individual to resolve, e.g. it is desirable that a problem of generally high tooling costs is identified as being specifically associated with the press shop, rather than simply the factory as a whole. However, the periodic formal report should represent only one level at which costs and profits are controlled. As a matter of normality, and on an informal basis, particular financial problems or opportunities should be perpetually in the process of being identified and discussed with a view to action being taken by those involved. It is essential for this process to take place if financial problems are to be avoided rather than tackled after the event.

It may be difficult for this process to occur in organisations with very rigidly defined structures, and clearly it requires a generally high level of comprehension, and an even greater degree of commitment from the parties involved.

## 3  *Commitment*

As a starting point, the more committed the employees of a business are to making it successful, the more readily are they likely to react to information on cost and profit control. The degree of this commitment will be determined by a combination of the financial rewards offered by the business, the significance of the threat of loss of security, the basic satisfaction which the job provides, and the sense of communion with fellow employees. While this general area is popularly regarded as the preserve of the personnel function, it is suggested that it would be naive of someone concerned with cost and profit control to ignore its relationship with profit maximisation.

On a more specific level, it is one thing to agree upon seeking to meet the objectives of a business, but is quite another to agree upon the means by which this objective should be reached. A budget or forecast which has been agreed will clearly receive a higher degree of personal commitment than one which has been imposed. Unfortunately, economic conditions are often such that the aspirations of all individuals in an organisation cannot be fulfilled in establishing such budgets. In those situations, it is imperative that at least the overall position of the business which has created these constraints is fully understood by all involved. In addition, if the strategy of the business is clearly defined, then individuals may well be prepared to modify their natural aspirations if they perceive them either as fundamentally inconsistent with the strategic objectives, or simply tactically unattainable in the short term, but realisable in the long term.

# 9

# Controlling the Funds

**R. Aitken-Davies**

*It is noteworthy that contributors to preceding chapters have emphasised not only the importance of the planning and control of profit, but also that of cash flow. This theme will recur frequently in subsequent chapters. The following contribution examines the subject of cash control from an essentially practical viewpoint and widens the discussion to embrace the idea of funds derived from the current assets. The author maintains that it is by the budgeting and monitoring of cash flow and funds flow that the financial controller exercises a major influence on the management of the business. Closely related to the general subject are the control of stock and debtors and the sourcing of finance.*

In considering the control of the funds of a business, we are led inevitably to question the management of that group of balance sheet items to which the unfortunate term 'working capital' is often applied. Working capital is defined customarily as current assets (stock, debtors, cash and short-term investments) less current liabilities (creditors and short-term funding).

The unfortunate aspect of the term 'working capital' is that there is a literal implication that other items of capital, usually referred to as 'fixed', do not work and thus, by deduction, do not pay their way. In a successful enterprise, such an interpretation would be patently erroneous and it is perhaps for this reason that some suggest that a more suitable rubric for current assets less current liabilities is 'circulating capital' or, more rarely, 'fluctuating capital'; accountants usually refer to 'net current assets'. Nevertheless, the term 'working capital' is employed throughout this chapter as it is the most commonly used in practice.

While on the subject of nomenclature, the distinction should be drawn between 'working capital' and 'liquid capital'. The latter is essentially a derivative of working capital from which the items not normally realisable in the short term have been excluded. Thus liquid capital is cash and cash equivalent (e.g. short-term investments) less current liabilities. It is generally regarded as being a sounder measure of a company's solvency than net working capital since it highlights the company's ability to meet short-term liabilities in simple cash terms.

In their favour, it can be said that these alternative terms at least indicate that notable feature of so-called working capital, which is its transience. And here lies a paradox; it is this very transient nature which renders the items of working capital particularly conducive to management by the financial controller. This is in contra-distinction to items of fixed capital over which his influence is commonly limited to the marginal aspects of investment planning and, even in this area, is usually kept within the confines of raising finance and application of mechanistic appraisal techniques. Questions concerning the existing fixed capital of a business will involve matters of wider commercial and operational policy in which, arguably, the financial controller does not have a decisive voice.

However, it seems to be the general rule that those involved in the major political and operational decision-making processes of a business venture are prepared to leave the control of working capital to their financial management. Such delegation and the accompanying lack of interest on the part of the executive may be deliberate, or merely an omission but, either way, the underlying cause will probably be their ignorance of the true significance of working capital to the successful management of the enterprise.

## THE ELEMENTS OF WORKING CAPITAL CONTROL

### The four ingredients

To justify the close attention of the financial controller to managing working capital, it is necessary to identify the need for and benefits of the exercise of such control, other than the fact that other managers eschew the responsibility.

There are four principal ingredients in managing current assets and liabilities:

1 Servicing the business
2 Cost
3 Security
4 Liquidity.

It will be immediately apparent to the critical eye that these elements are not mutually exclusive but overlap and vie with each other to create the nub of the control problem which is simply to find the optimum mixture conducive to and supportive of a successful business.

## Servicing the business

The items embraced by the term working capital sustain the business by bridging the time-lapse between the incurring of expenditure in the manufacture and supply of a product or service and the receipt of the consideration from the purchaser. In practical terms, this means simply that working capital provides materials and labour for stock and overhead activities to support the production and selling functions and, thereafter, finances the debtors from whom further funds will be obtained to pay for the organisation's everyday transactions. The service function can be seen as a progression of cash, through the other forms of current asset, back into cash, as illustrated in Figure 9.1.

This figure also symbolises the trading cycle and serves to highlight a critical test of the success of an enterprise – which is that the cash at the end of the working capital service cycle should exceed the input at the beginning, the difference being realised profit before capital charges.

Now, if the level of working capital were determined by the production or sales management, the function of servicing the business would inevitably become an overriding concern. The inclination of the business would be towards high production, lavish stocks and generous credit in almost certainly misguided attempts to maximise profits by maximising sales. The financial controller's duty would therefore seem to be clear. He must temper such inclinations by emphasising that it is the conversion of working capital back into cash which realises the profit to which most enterprises aspire, even in the current social and political climate, and that there are special costs

**Fig. 9.1 Working capital service cycle**

and dangers associated with working capital management which increase as the level and time-span increase.

## Cost

There is always a concomitant cost for any level of investment in working capital whether the funds are internally generated or are raised from external sources or, indeed, are a mixture of both. If the funds are internally generated, the cost can be regarded as the higher one of the rate of interest which could be obtained by investing in the external money market, and the return on the enterprise's marginal investment opportunity which has to be foregone because of the resources tied up in current assets. In the case of external funds, the cost is the higher one of the rewards they command by way of interest/dividend and, again, the return foregone from the marginal investment opportunity.

The facile conclusion which could be drawn from this is that working capital should always be minimised to save financing or opportunity costs but, it need hardly be said, this would be far too glib a deduction. Apart from the obvious risks of losing sales as a result of inadequate stocks or an unduly stringent credit policy, there will always be occasions when the potential savings from an otherwise unjustified increase in working capital exceed the marginal cost of the funds thus employed. Such conditions may obtain, for example, in bulk purchase opportunities, prior to a sales promotion campaign or in commodity future trading. The person controlling the funds must be as alive to these factors as he is conscious of the more straightforward costs of capital if cost minimisation is to be reconciled with profit maximisation.

## Security

A third element of working capital control is security of current assets and, in this sense, security embraces many areas of concern. For stock, the questions of theft, loss, deterioration and control of consumption must be considered. In relation to debtors, the integrity of the debtor, particularly his ability and inclination to pay and the adequacy of the organisation's credit control function are significant. The security problems of cash are self-evident.

Generally, one could expect the security problem to increase as the levels of current assets increased, although this is belied by the number of exceptions which can be found in specific circumstances. Hence, there may be no more security difficulties in holding £600,000 cash than there are in holding £500,000 in an appropriate safe, nor in storing 15 tons instead of 10 tons of copper in an adequately appointed building, nor of granting £50,000 rather than £40,000 credit to a solvent and reputable customer. Security assessments such as these depend on the particular position of the company concerned at any given time.

## Liquidity

The essence of the liquidity problem is simple, namely that an organisation must always be in a position to meet liabilities as they arise. Consequently, in this area, working capital control is especially concentrated on cash and the need to predict cash requirements so that potential surpluses and deficits are forecast well before they prove to be an embarrassment. In this way, the financial controller is given time to seek out extra sources of funds to meet predicted shortfalls or, alternatively, is forewarned of the generation of cash surpluses for which a profitable home (temporary or otherwise) must be found to avoid loss of income. The conditions in which cash is useful to have in quantities exceeding what is necessary to meet immediate liabilities must be very rare indeed and it could thus be contended that hard cash is one element of working capital which should consistently be minimised, even if this means merely that periodic surpluses are invested on short-term money markets.

## WORKING CAPITAL BUDGETING

It should be understood that a working capital budget cannot be prepared until all the other budgets are available since, by definition, it must be a quantification of the circulating assets and liabilities needed to service the levels of activity indicated by those other budgets. Thus the working capital budget forms the final stage in the compilation of the enterprise's master budget.

It is customary, for monitoring purposes, to phase budgets into review periods (usually of four weeks or a calendar month each) and this practice is of particular relevance to the working capital budget because of the transient nature of the items which it comprises. Indeed, in relation to the cash element of this budget, it may be desirable or even necessary to work on much shorter review periods (e.g. one week) for reasons of liquidity monitoring.

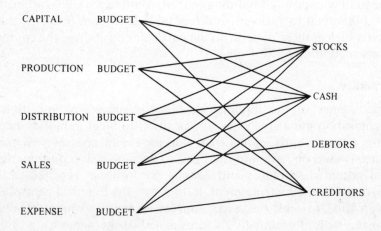

**Fig. 9.2   Interrelationship of working capital and other budgets**

The interrelationships of the different components of the master budget are rather complex and in no case is this more true than between capital and the other budgets, where the chicken or the egg argument is regularly encountered. Figure 9.2 illustrates the interdependence of working capital with the other main budget categories and highlights the consequent difficulties of determining soundly-based budgets for the elements of working capital.

## Stocks

Taking the term 'stocks' in the broadest sense, there are four categories with functions as shown:

| | | |
|---|---|---|
| 1 | Raw materials | — service production |
| 2 | Work-in-progress | — services production |
| 3 | Finished goods | — service sales |
| 4 | Stores | — service production, sales (e.g. bought-out components) and overhead activities (e.g. maintenance, administration) |

As has been pointed out earlier in this chapter, the service function is but one of the considerations in determining optimum working capital levels, the others being cost, security and liquidity. In practical terms, these competing elements give rise to a wide range of questions to which the financial controller should address himself in the budget compilation exercise (and, for that matter, in the monitoring process). These are shown in Table 9.1.

Many mathematical and statistical techniques are available to assist in stock control and associated problems but the author feels generally that these are more of academic interest than practical application. However, it is contended that the array of variables noted in the table does suggest the desirability for computerisation to assist the financial controller in his efforts to compile a stock budget based on optimum quantity levels for each of his company's raw material, product and stores lines.

In a larger company, this is the sort of modelling exercise which an enthusiastic and competent computer department should be delighted to tackle. For the smaller organisation, reference to the increasing number of specialist consultants in the field of commercial computer applications may be appropriate. This could lead to the

### Table 9.1
### Budgeting for stocks
(A list of factors to be taken into account in determining stock budget levels)

| Factor | Question |
|---|---|
| Activity | |
| 1 Sales/production/distribution/ expense budgets | Are increased/decreased stocks required to service expanding/contracting activity? |
| 2 Budget incidence | Are there any seasonal/other factors affecting levels required in particular review periods (e.g. Christmas, promotions, new product lines)? |
| 3 Sales mix Physical | How are sales broken down between individual product lines? |
| 4 Nature of products | How long and in what conditions can they be stored? |
| 5 Storage capability | What is the organisation's stocking capability from space and security viewpoints? |
| 6 Production lead time | What is the time-lapse between receipt of an order for an out-of-stock item to delivery to customer? What confidence levels of immediate delivery are acceptable? |
| 7 Distribution lead time Economic | What is the time-lapse between receipt of an order for an item not in stock locally to delivery to a customer? What confidence levels of immediate delivery are acceptable? |
| 8 Sensitivity of forecasts | What would be the effects of ±10% (say) error margin in sales, production, or other major forecasts? |

9 Contingencies

What, if any, buffers are desirable to cater for the effects of forecasting errors, industrial action and other unpredictable events?

10 Economic order quantities

What advantages/disadvantages are there from bulk discounts, small order surcharges and similar factors?

11 Economic batch quantities

What are the economics of producing differing batch sizes of the organisation's product lines? (e.g. overhead recovery on tooling costs v. stockholding costs).

12 Taxation

Is relief available for stock increases under S 37 Finance Act 1976?*

13 Cost of capital

What is the capital cost of holding the proposed level of stocks? Are other investment opportunities being foregone as a result of investment in stocks?

14 Other stockholding costs

What are the storage and associated costs? How do these compare with inflation in raw materials and labour inputs?

---

* The nature of the relief available is discussed in the section on 'stock' (p.206).

purchase of one of the advanced microprocessors now available together with the associated software technology (which, incidentally, is becoming increasingly accessible and intelligible to the layman) or, alternatively, to the use or increased use of computer time-sharing facilities.

## Debtors

Debtors are a function of credit sales, the incidence of those sales in the budget period and the organisation's credit policy. Inevitably the success of a credit control policy depends on the rigour with which it is applied. The degree of such rigour in turn depends upon the strength of the company's market as well as the motivation and direction of those concerned in selecting and applying the policy. But whatever the credit control policy and however effectively it is applied, there will always be an element of overdue debt unless the business is cash only (such as a supermarket). Anyone who has had experience of obtaining payment through a large organisation such as a nationalised industry or one of the blue chip giants should know of the delay mechanisms inherent in bureaucracy, to mention but one intractable factor.

Unless a change of policy is envisaged in the budget period (e.g. by introducing discounts for early payment), debtors' budgeting is best effected by reference to percentages of sales (phased by budget review period) gleaned from historical data.

The past record technique may appear to be over-facile to the scrupulous management accountant who believes that an assessment should be made of likely economic trends in the budget period and the effects of these on his company's customers so that changes in pressure for extended trade credit could be anticipated. For those intrepid forecasters who claim to be able to draw worthwhile conclusions from their scrutiny of the crystal ball, such an approach may conceivably be rewarding. Certainly in the absence of any historical information (for example, in a new market or for a new company) a forward-looking assessment will be required based on:

1  Credit policy
2  Type of custom (e.g. builders are notoriously slow payers)
3  Strength of the company's market position (e.g. a monopoly supplier of an essential product can exert considerable pressure for timely settlement).

## Creditors

Creditors' budgeting is, in many ways, the antithesis of debtors' budgeting. Instead of posing the questions as to what credit should be allowed and what pressures can be exerted to secure timely payment for sales, the financial controller must ask what credit periods he can get away with before settling his company's debts and, the corollary, what pressures his creditors can apply to minimise such credit.

In this connection, it may be helpful to categorise creditors along the following lines:

1 *Statutory* (e.g. tax, national insurance, licences) where legal sanctions may be applicable if payment is delayed.
2 *Essential* where any interruption of deliveries may affect the company's performance quickly and adversely.
3 *Dependent* where the suppliers rely on the company for a substantial proportion of their business and could not afford the loss of this. Extended credit may be negotiable with this category of supplier subject to their own liquidity and to any business ethics the company may wish to observe.
4 *Discount* where worthwhile financial advantages are offered in return for early settlement of invoices.

Such classification of creditors has a place particularly where liquidity problems are arising; this matter is further discussed in the section on cash budgeting.

However, for most budgetary purposes, it is sensible to assume, in the first instance, that payment of creditors will be effected by the due dates on the grounds that such an approach would be conducive to goodwill of suppliers, and, generally, to the reputation of the firm. On this basis, the creditors' budget can be related directly to the budgeted purchase of goods and services and the settlement terms required by the suppliers thereof. Calculations could be made under the headings as in Table 9.2.

In relation to creditors' budgeting (and consequently to cash budgeting), it is important to recognise the special problems associated with capital expenditure. Reference to the capital budget will be required to assess the timing and scale of settlement of capital creditors. In the case of existing commitments, this exercise should be a relatively straightforward one of extracting details from capital contracts: cruder measures will, however, be needed for the uncommitted element of the capital budget since detailed work programmes and contract terms covering items such as progress payments will not be available at the time of the budget compilation. Furthermore, provision must be made in the capital creditors' budget for the release of any retentions becoming due for payment against existing or completed contracts in accordance with the terms of those contracts.

## Table 9.2
## Calculating the creditors' budget

| Category | Source of information | Common settlement terms |
|---|---|---|
| Purchases for stock | Stock budget | Monthly |
| Direct costs | Expense budgets | Monthly or quarterly[1] |
| Capital investment | Capital budget | Subject to contract |
| Statutory (UK) | | |
|   Value added tax | Sales/creditors' budgets | Quarterly[2] |
|   Advance corporation tax/ income tax | P and L appropriation | Quarterly[3] |
|   Corporation tax | P and L appropriation | Annually[4] |
|   Social security contributions | Expense budgets (wages and salaries) | Monthly |
| Appropriations of profit | P and L appropriation | Bi-annually[5] |

[1] Direct costs in this sense implies that they are not charged through stores control procedures, e.g. services (electricity, gas, telephone), cleaning contracts, maintenance contracts.

[2] VAT represented by an excess of output tax (primarily on sales) over input tax (primarily on purchases) must be accounted for to the Customs and Excise on the fixed quarter days relevant to the particular company.

[3] Advance corporation tax on qualifying distributions (primarily dividends) and income tax retained on annual payments must be accounted for to the Inland Revenue on the calendar quarter days and, in addition, at the end of the company's accounting period if this does not fall on a quarter day.

[4] Corporation tax is normally payable 9 months from the end of the company's accounting period unless trading commenced before 1 April 1965, in which case the due date will be after the same interval from the end of the accounting period as there was between the end of the basis period for 1965/66 income tax and 1 January 1966.

[5] Appropriations of profit cover items such as dividends, capital distributions and financing costs (e.g. bank and debenture interest).

## Cash

There can surely be no doubt that cash forecasting is the most crucial aspect of working capital budgeting. Indeed, it can be argued that cash management should be the primary concern of the executive of any organisation on the grounds that, whatever the objectives of the organisation or its members, continued existence will be a pre-requisite to realising those objectives. The ultimate consequences of a dearth of cash are the collapse and dissolution of the organisation.

Yet, it is customary to lay the principal responsibility for cash management on the shoulders of that much-tried individual who is known variously as financial director, financial controller, chief accountant, treasurer or by one of the other modern euphemisms for the man in charge of the books of account. Fortunately for him, there is a good deal of job satisfaction to be had from cash management arising from that sense of relevance, reality and urgency which is perhaps not associated with the more mundane aspects of financial recording and statutory accounting. The fact is that a cash crisis can have a serious impact on the business, particularly when it is neither nationalised nor large and labour-intensive and thus probably not in the market for a timely injection of funds from the National Enter-prise Board or the Treasury.

Much of the information needed to construct the cash budget should be obtainable from the other elements of the working capital budget which must have been compiled before the start of the cash budgeting exercise. Receipts will be represented chiefly by realisa-tion of debtors and payments by the settlement of creditors. Nevertheless, there will be cash transactions which have been covered neither within those other sections of the working capital budget nor within the other main budget categories of which the master budget is composed. The financial controller must be very much aware of this problem, as a major cash requirement could otherwise easily be overlooked.

Such non-budgeted transactions should fall into one or more of the following main groups. The list may prove to be a useful aide-memoire during the compilation of the cash budget.

1 *Government grants and subsidies*, e.g. employment subsidies; development grants.
2 *Investments*, e.g. Sale/purchase of stocks and shares; short-term investment/realisation of funds.
3 *Non-trading income*, e.g. income from property; dividends received.
4 *Non-credit transactions*, e.g. payments received/paid on account (cash sales/purchases; wages and salaries should be obtainable through relevant budgets).
5 *Sales of assets*, e.g. motor vehicles; scrap.

6  *Rentals,* e.g. H.P./lease rentals not included in capital or revenue budgets.
7  *Appropriations,* e.g. dividends; taxation; financing costs.
8  *Extraordinary items,* e.g. legal damages received/paid.

At this stage, an initial cash budget should be extracted, a suggested format for which is given in Table 9.3. The purpose of this exercise is to foretoken any serious surpluses or deficits of cash in the budget review periods and thus to provide a basis for advice to Board members on financing policy. The object then is to establish a coherent funding policy for the administration of liquidity fluctuations in the budget period so that the financial controller can fulfil his customary treasury function with a relatively free hand. It may be that the company's objectives are changed as a direct result of the Board's financing deliberations (e.g. by means of modifying investment plans) and this will necessitate amendments to the other draft budgets. Alternatively, longer-term financing difficulties may have been identified which cannot be overcome merely by altering existing company policy (e.g. because the Board is unwilling to change that policy or because the financing problems are more fundamental) and, in these circumstances an investigation of longer-term solutions will be needed.

Notwithstanding the above, the stage must be reached eventually where policy is broadly settled and the financial controller is left with short-term operational surpluses and deficits in his draft cash budget. He will then wish to review the range of short-term financing sources available and/or to establish, in principle, where short-term surpluses can be deposited to the greatest advantage of his company. Here it may be worth reminding the reader of some of the principal methods of securing short-term finance.

### Bank accommodation

The most obvious means of avoiding temporary financial embarrassment are overdraft or loan arrangements with the company's bankers. Plainly, an approach to the local manager to discuss an anticipated short-term deficit a year or so in advance is going to leave him a good deal more impressed than a desperate telephone call a year later from a company on the verge of insolvency. Even if the deficit actually occurs sooner or later than the budget had indicated, the fact that the company is attempting to plan for its cash requirements must help to instil confidence in its bankers – at least to the

## Table 9.3
## Format for cash budget

CASH BUDGET 19—

(−) = Deficit (£000's)

| SOURCE/APPLICATION | Review period | 1 | 2 | 3 | 4 | 5 | 6 | 7 | 8 | 9 | 10 | 11 | 12 |
|---|---|---|---|---|---|---|---|---|---|---|---|---|---|
| OPENING BALANCE* | | | | | | | | | | | | | |
| RECEIPTS | | | | | | | | | | | | | |
| Debtors and cash sales | | | | | | | | | | | | | |
| Sales of assets | | | | | | | | | | | | | |
| Government grants | | | | | | | | | | | | | |
| Miscellaneous income | | | | | | | | | | | | | |
| Other | | | | | | | | | | | | | |
| SUB-TOTAL | | | | | | | | | | | | | |
| PAYMENTS | | | | | | | | | | | | | |
| Creditors and cash purchases | | | | | | | | | | | | | |
| Wages and salaries | | | | | | | | | | | | | |
| Capital investment | | | | | | | | | | | | | |
| Appropriations | | | | | | | | | | | | | |
| Other | | | | | | | | | | | | | |
| CLOSING BALANCE† | | | | | | | | | | | | | |

* Closing balance in previous review period.
† Estimated cash balance/amount overdrawn at end of review period.

BUDGET ACTION NOTES
Period 1
2
3
4
5
6
7
8
9
10
11
12

same degree as a round of golf between the financial controller and the local bank manager.

### Factoring

An increasingly popular source of short-term finance is to factor the company's debts. Such deals can vary from pure financing measures in which the factoring organisation advances cash against the security of sums invoiced for a fixed rate of interest, through several intermediate variations to a full takeover of the company's invoicing and credit control function, whereby the debts are actually purchased at a discount by the factoring organisation, invoiced and subsequently collected by them in their own fashion.

The advantages of a comprehensive factoring agreement are clear: immediate funds are released and relief is obtained from the administrative burden and frustration of invoicing and accounts collection. The disadvantages are, perhaps, equally obvious: the factors' discount will presumably exceed the bad debt, administration and financing costs normally experienced by the company, and a crucial link with customers will be relinquished with the attendant risk of sacrificing goodwill as a result of the more stringent methods of securing timely settlement likely to be employed by the factoring organisation.

### Hire purchase and leasing

For a more fundamental solution, the company could look to converting all or part of its capital investment programme from direct purchase to hire purchase or leasing arrangements. Leases can be either of the operational or finance varieties.

Finance leasing as a method of funding capital equipment has exploded in popularity since it was introduced into the UK in the 1960s, riding on the back of the substantial tax advantages which were conferred upon lessors with high profits and low equipment requirements, such as the commercial and merchant banks. In essence a bank, usually operating through a leasing subsidiary, provides funds to a lessee company to purchase its specific equipment requirements but then the bank reserves title to the assets so that 100 per cent first-year allowances are available for set-off against its other taxable banking profits. Meanwhile the lessees can set the lease rental payments against their profits subject to corporation tax as a proper revenue expense, provided those rents are commercial and reasonable in the relevant market circumstances.

As the term implies, finance leasing is merely an alternative method of funding capital requirements on the part of the lessee company. The lessors are unlikely to have expert knowledge of the equipment subject to lease and although they will retain title to the goods, the period of the lease agreement usually extends over the useful life of the asset and puts the onus for operation and maintenance entirely on the lessees.

On the other hand, an operational lease generally involves hiring plant and machinery from an acknowledged expert in the relevant field in much the same way as one would hire a car. In these cases, the period of the lease may be substantially less than the useful life of the asset and maintenance of the asset normally remains the responsibility of the lessor. The lessee loses the security of tenure and operational control associated with a finance-type lease but gains the advantages of a lower financial commitment to the asset concerned and the removal of the burden of responsibility for maintenance.

*Acceptance credits*

The acceptance credit method of raising funds in the short term (usually for three months) may appear unnecessarily intricate to the pragmatic accountant. The procedure is that the company must draw a bill of exchange (i.e. a promise to pay a sum of money at a fixed date in the future) which is then 'accepted' for payment by an 'acceptance house' (i.e. a merchant bank) at the expense of an 'acceptance commission' usually of 1–2 per cent. The bill is then sold for cash by the acceptance house to a 'discount house' (commonly a member of the London money market) for a discount charge related to the date the bill is to be honoured and the prevailing market conditions. Thus the company receives immediate cash from the acceptance house (value of the bill less acceptance commission and discount charge) and is not required to repay the acceptance house until it has honoured the bill at maturity in favour of the discount house. The overall cost of this method of finance usually equates to the cost of the more straightforward forms of bank accommodation.

*Creditors' control*

Reference was made earlier in this chapter to what is probably the least obviously scientific means of financing a short-term cash deficit, i.e. delaying payment of creditors either by agreement or by default depending on the nature and desperation of the shortfall problem. The classification of creditors as suggested above is most appropriate as there will be certain debts which absolutely must be settled by the due dates and then, in a gradual descent of priority, key creditors whose supplies are essential down to those creditors from whom the loss of supplies or goodwill would be least damaging to the company.

Having satisfied himself on the short-term cash management problems highlighted by the initial cash budget, the financial controller should be in a position to compile the final version of the cash forecast, incorporating any changes necessitated by proposed fundings/investment of cash deficits/surpluses. Deficits met by bank overdrafts and surpluses retained as cash deposits with the bank should be left as negative and positive balances respectively, whereas deficits met by loans or acceptances and surpluses invested are inflows and outflows of cash and should be reflected as such in the cash budget. Conversely, repayment of loans and realisation of investments should be shown as cash paid and received as appropriate in the final cash budget.

The form shown as Table 9.3 is also suitable for presentation of the final cash budget.

### The completed working capital budget

Consummation of the cash budget completes the detailed construction of the working capital budget, which can then be consolidated and presented in a suitable form. Such suitability will, of course, depend on the circumstances of the organisation concerned, but it is felt that the format illustrated in Table 9.4 should serve most purposes with the minimum of adaptation to individual requirements.

## WORKING CAPITAL MONITORING AND CONTROL

One feature of budget compilation at least is certain. Whatever the quality of the exercise, the effort will be worthless unless, first, there is a sound monitoring procedure to complement it and, second, the information available through that monitoring procedure is actually used by those in authority as a basis for making decisions pertaining (in our case) to the control of funds. Here, one might note an increasing tendency to confuse the words monitoring and control almost to the point of synonymity by many who should know better. Neither budgeting nor budget monitoring provides any control in

**Table 9.4**

**Format for working capital budget**

| ITEM | Review period | 1 | 2 | 3 | 4 | 5 | 6 | 7 | 8 | 9 | 10 | 11 | 12 |
|---|---|---|---|---|---|---|---|---|---|---|---|---|---|
| | | | | | | | | | | | | | |

WORKING CAPITAL BUDGET 19—

(+) = current asset
(−) = current liability
£000's

DEBTORS

STOCK
  Raw materials
  Work in progress
  Finished goods
  Stores

SHORT–TERM INVESTMENTS

CASH

CURRENT ASSETS

CREDITORS
  Trade
  Statutory
  Other

SHORT–TERM LIABILITIES

NET WORKING CAPITAL

BUDGET ACTION NOTES    Period   1
2
3
4
5
6
7
8
9
10
11
12

itself; the control is exercised by those with the power and perception to react competently to the messages thrown out by a budgetary control system and, thus, to influence to advantage the course steered by their organisations.

The aim of budgetary control is, of course, to assess the performance of a company by comparing various elements of that performance against a series of predetermined indicators (or budgets) which, taken together, represent a quantification of the company's short-term objectives. The working capital budget differs from most other indicators in only one major respect: its constituents fluctuate rather than accumulate. In this sense the phased working capital budgets can be regarded as being largely self-contained within individual review periods, in contrast to the other budgets where aggregation is necessary to reflect the company's progress towards its annual objectives.

This leads us to the matter of the presentation of monitoring data; the topic is essentially subjective, partly because of the predilections of suppliers and users of the information and partly because of the gamut of organisational types ranging from the corner shop to the multinational conglomerate. To presume to set any sort of standard format in such circumstances would be folly. Table 9.5 is therefore presented as one straightforward if unexciting approach to monitoring working capital.

Sceptics often claim that flexing is merely a cosmetic exercise designed to conceal management shortcomings by adjusting budgets to coincide more closely with actual performance, when the real need is for strenuous efforts to raise actual performance to meet the objectives intrinsic to the original budget. The power of cynicism lies in the grain of truth always present in its implications. Notwithstanding this, there is considerable merit in flexing the working capital budget to reflect changing circumstances and thereby to preserve its value as a front-ranking performance indicator. For example, a shortfall in sales should reduce both the debtors and the stock requirements of the company, not to mention the flow of cash. In any case, there is no reason why monitoring reports should not show comparisons between actual results and both the original and flexed budgets, as indeed the sample format in Table 9.5 seeks to do.

A further valuable refinement in working capital monitoring is the use of forecasting, by which means requirements can be regularly reviewed and updated independently of the budget. Such predictive

# Table 9.5
## Working Capital Monitoring Data

(−) = liability  
(£000's)

| Line | Component | Budget | | | Flexed Budget | | | Actual | | | Variation from Flexed Budget | | | Forecast --/--/-- | | | Note below | Line |
|---|---|---|---|---|---|---|---|---|---|---|---|---|---|---|---|---|---|---|
| | | 1 | 2 | 3 | 4 | 5 | 6 | 7 | 8 | 9 | 10 | 11 | 12 | 13 | 14 | 15 | 16 | |
| | **DEBTORS** | | | | | | | | | | | | | | | | | |
| 1 | Trade | X | | | X | | | X | | | X | | | X | | | | 1 |
| 2 | Other | | X | | | X | | | X | | | X | | | X | | | 2 |
| | **STOCK** | | | | | | | | | | | | | | | | | |
| 3 | Raw materials | X | | | X | | | X | | | X | | | X | | | | 3 |
| 4 | Work in progress | X | | | X | | | X | | | X | | | X | | | | 4 |
| 5 | Finished goods | X | | | X | | | X | | | X | | | X | | | | 5 |
| 6 | Stores | X− | | | X− | | | X− | | | X− | | | X− | | | | 6 |
| 7 | SHORT–TERM INVESTMENTS | | X | | | X | | | X | | | X | | | X | | | 7 |
| | **CASH** | | | | | | | | | | | | | | | | | |
| 8 | In hand | X | | | X | | | X | | | X | | | X | | | | 8 |
| 9 | At bank | X | | | X | | | X | | | X | | | X− | | | | 9 |
| 10 | CURRENT ASSETS | | | X | | | X | | | X | | | X | | | X | | 10 |
| | **CREDITORS** | | | | | | | | | | | | | | | | | |
| 11 | Trade | X | | | X | | | X | | | X | | | X | | | | 11 |
| 12 | Statutory | | X | | | X | | | X | | | X | | | X | | | 12 |
| 13 | Other | X− | | | X− | | | X− | | | X− | | | X− | | | | 13 |
| 14 | SHORT–TERM LIABILITIES | | X− | | | X− | | | X− | | | X− | | | X− | | | 14 |
| 15 | CURRENT LIABILITIES | | | X= | | | X= | | | X= | | | X= | | | X= | | 15 |
| 16 | NET WORKING CAPITAL | | | X= | | | X= | | | X= | | | X= | | | X= | | 16 |

Comments and Variance Analysis

*Note no.*  
Include in this section:
(a) main factors in flexing of original budget;
(b) explanations of major variances from flexed budget;
(c) significant features of forecast for next review period;
(d) action and recommended action notes.

reporting is particularly relevant in the shorter term when the level of reliability should be at its height and liquidity considerations at their most immediate. Again, provision is made for forecasts to be propounded in Table 9.5. It is suggested that such predictions should be for the end of the subsequent review period although there is no reason why a longer forecasting cycle cannot be used where appropriate.

In the remaining paragraphs of this chapter, a variety of points are raised in relation to the monitoring and control of the components of the fluctuating capital budget, many of which may seem obvious but are nonetheless worth mentioning if only as an aide-memoire to the financial controller.

## Stock

As intimated earlier in this chapter, the merit of a computerised stock control model is that any changes in the range of variables affecting stockholding optima (which should be evident from the budget monitoring process) can be introduced into the system and revised optima then computed at great speed. Thus, such factors as a drop in sales, change in sales mix, lengthening of delivery times or change in inflation rates can be assimilated rapidly to flex the original stock budget. In normal conditions, such a service must facilitate quick decisions on stocking policy and enable positive direction to be given to the personnel concerned in good time.

Where a model will not be quite so helpful is in the application of the entrepreneurial spirit, experience and intuition required, for example, in commodity deals such as spot purchases. Nor will it be of much help where obsolescent, slow-moving or deteriorating stores are building up, except perhaps by highlighting the items concerned. In these matters, commercial acumen is (somewhat reassuringly) required. The financial controller's role in such decisions may be limited to the provision of advice and, in this regard, he should be mindful of the following main factors:

1  Marginal storage costs
2  Net realisable values
3  Likely market trends for the stocks/stores concerned
4  Likely future consumption for the stocks/stores concerned
5  Cost of capital
6  Inflation and its effects on replacement costs where relevant.

The concepts of optimum stock and reorder levels and other such criteria were rather glibly inserted in the earlier discussion without any consideration of the difficulties of compilation of the data from scratch for hundreds or thousands of stock and stores items. Practically, this is a long-term exercise and it may be apposite here to apply the philosophy of the 80/20 rule. In this context, the rule says, quintessentially, that 80 per cent of the stock value will be represented by 20 per cent of stock items and vice versa. Given that the popularity of this rule appears to thrive on its exceptions, the principle of concentrating initially on high-value stocks and stores is not a bad one. From this point, one can work through the items gradually and develop subsequently a stock control cycle to ensure that the optimum levels for each line are reviewed on a regular basis. The length of the review cycle will depend upon the nature of the industry: engineering companies, for example, may find a 3-year cycle adequate, whereas an organisation involved in fashionable attire is unlikely to benefit from anything less regular than a quarterly review. Where the review is continuous in nature, regular updating of stockholding optima will be necessary together with appropriate flexing of the stock budgets. Here also advantages of a computer model are manifest.

In recent years, tax law has thrown an additional complication into the stock management question. Relief is at the time of writing available against a trading concern's taxable profits for increases in stock values. The system, put simply, is that the increase in stock value between the beginning and end of each accounting period, less 15 per cent of the profit as adjusted for tax purposes and net of capital allowances, is treated as an allowable charge against the taxable profits. There are converse provisions for recouping relief thus given by treating any reductions in stock value in an accounting period as a taxable addition to trading profits up to the level of unrecovered past relief. Her Majesty's Inspectors of Taxes have swingeing powers to preclude any spurious claims at their discretion, but subject to appeal. It would not be considered 'just and reasonable', for instance, to make a massive purchase immediately before the end of the company's financial year, only to sell the items on the first day of the next financial year, and to make a claim for stock relief on the strength of such a transaction.

The marginal tax saving achieved by a stock relief claim could be as much as 52 per cent of the stock increase in the case of corporate bodies and 60 per cent in the case of an individual's business and, clearly, this factor must be brought into the equation in assessing budget stockholdings. Two warning notes should be borne in mind. First, the relief is available once in respect of each increase and second, the benefit from relief is deferred in relation to cash flow to the date that any tax is due and payable – which could be anything from 9 to 22 months after the end of the relevant accounting period. In due course stock relief may be replaced by some form of inflation accounting for taxation.

## Debtors

The mechanics of credit control, the first stage of debtors' control, are fairly common to all organisations. There should be a procedure for obtaining credit references for each new customer and then establishing a credit limit based on the expected level of trade and the client's financial circumstances. Where, subsequently, the credit limit is on the verge of being exceeded, it is reviewed and an increase allowed or credit withdrawn pending payment against the existing debt, as deemed appropriate. Similarly, where debts are not settled within the laid-down credit terms, suitable steps must be taken, with the option available of withdrawing or extending credit facilities and/or taking legal action to recover amounts overdue.

How does all this fit into working capital monitoring? As has already been asserted, credit policy is a critical factor in debtors' budgeting and the company's market strength and accounts collection ability are correspondingly critical factors in determining the effectiveness of that credit policy. However, credit decisions are not purely mechanical matters: pragmatism is called for in the degree of control exercised in each case. For instance, if business is slow and the market weak, less stringent policies may be rewarded. Conversely, buoyant sales may support a more rigid policy although, even in this happy position, it may pay to think of the future in relation to goodwill won or lost during times of plenty.

The level of debtors has a direct yet deferred relationship to credit sales based on average credit permitted. An extremely useful measure of debtors' control is an 'age analysis' which can be compared with historic and budgeted trends to indicate the success or otherwise of current policy. This information can be incorporated into a regular debtors' monitoring report such as is illustrated in Table 9.6.

If the argument that debtors cannot be subject to the same scien-

## Table 9.6
## Debtors' Monitoring Report

| AGE ANALYSIS | | Review period ended — | | | | |
|---|---|---|---|---|---|---|
| | | Under 28 days | 28–56 days | 56–84 days | Over 84 days | Bad |
| 1 Current position | { (£) | X | X | X | X | X |
| | (%) | X | X | X | X | X |
| 2 Budget | (%) | X | X | X | X | X |
| 3 Historic trend | (%) | X | X | X | X | X |
| 4 Last review period | (%) | X | X | X | X | X |
| 5 Next review period (forecast) | { (£) | X | X | X | X | X |
| | (%) | | | | | |

ANALYSIS OVER 84 DAYS

| Customer | Credit limit | Salesman responsible | Amount outstanding | Over 84 days | Action |
|---|---|---|---|---|---|
| 1 | | | | | |
| 2 | | | | | |
| 3 | | | | | |
| 4 | | | | | |
| 5 | | | | | |
| 6 | | | | | |
| 7 | | | | | |
| 8 | | | | | |
| 9 | | | | | |
| 10 | | | | | |

tific assessment as, say, stocks is accepted, then there remains a gap in the budgetary control process. In practice, this gap will normally be filled by commercial and intuitive judgements on the part of the sales/marketing management. Experienced management accountants will know that these managers often exhibit a singular reluctance either to quantify themselves or to have quantified for them the ramifications of their business judgement. However, all is not lost. A most useful stratagem is to delegate responsibility for accounts collection to the salesman who secured the original purchase, once the debt becomes overdue. A further refinement of this policy is to reflect the degree of success in avoiding overdue debts in any schemes for calculating bonuses and commissions for the sales force – a concept fully vindicated by the fact that it is the payment for goods which produces profit rather than the sale. Apart from the financial stimulus to the salesmen, it is well accepted that personal contact is the most effective means of collecting accounts, where the customer is still solvent.

Cash discounts can be used to encourage early payment but anything less than $2\frac{1}{2}$ per cent is unlikely to have the desired impact, especially on larger organisations, and $2\frac{1}{2}$ per cent per month does, after all, represent an annual rate of 30 per cent. There has to be a fairly serious liquidity problem or, alternatively, a high-return investment opportunity available to justify such a cash discount.

## Cash

While a conscientious financial controller will wish to keep a daily watching brief on cash movements, the necessity for regular formal monitoring reports will depend on the organisation's financial circumstances or what may be described as its liquidity sensitivity. Where cash is tight a weekly or even daily report may be desirable. Also, in companies where large positive cash balances occur (e.g. retailing), it may be advantageous to have frequent monitoring data so that the surpluses can be identified quickly and made to work on short-term money markets. In 'normal' conditions, which could be defined as those where the organisation is neither on the threshold of classic liquidity crises nor enjoying regular cash surpluses, a monthly cash monitoring report should be more than adequate as far as the Board are concerned.

Included in the monitoring report should be a cash forecast which, in essence, is a short-term budget, updating, supplementing and,

## Table 9.7
## Cash monitoring and forecasting report

Review period ended –

(−) = cash outflow/deficit (£000's)

| | This review period | | Year to date | | Variations from budget | | Next period | Year |
|---|---|---|---|---|---|---|---|---|
| | Budget | Actual | Budget | Actual | Period | Year to date | | |
| OPENING BALANCE | | | | | | | | |
| RECEIPTS | | | | | | | | |
| Sales | | | | | | | | |
| Asset realisations | | | | | | | | |
| Government grants | | | | | | | | |
| Miscellaneous income | | | | | | | | |
| Other | | | | | | | | |
| PAYMENTS | | | | | | | | |
| Trade creditors | | | | | | | | |
| Cash purchases | | | | | | | | |
| Wages and salaries | | | | | | | | |
| Capital investment | | | | | | | | |
| Statutory creditors | | | | | | | | |
| Capital costs | | | | | | | | |
| Dividends | | | | | | | | |
| Other | | | | | | | | |
| CLOSING BALANCE | | | | | | | | |

*Commentary*

eventually, replacing the original cash budget. By reflecting changed circumstances since the compilation of the cash budget, the forecast is, in effect, a form of rolling budget. The financial controller will use the forecast to supplement or amend any financing arrangements made at the time of the original budget compilation.

Table 9.7 shows one method of presenting the cash monitoring and forecasting information.

## Creditors

Manipulation of credit facilities as a method of managing very short-term cash exigencies has already been suggested above, primarily in respect of trade creditors. There is also some scope for manoeuvre in the dividend policy adopted by the company, although the financial controller's options are limited by what is acceptable to the Board, and ultimately, to the shareholders. While it is usually most desirable that as much of the company's fixed and working capital requirement as possible is financed from retained profits, it is common to find deep-rooted prejudice amongst Board members in favour of recommending at least the maintenance of the previous level of dividend whatever the profit performance; what is more, this attitude is equally commonly reflected in the expectations of the shareholders. The financial controller may thus have to satisfy himself with persuading his Board to limit any proposed increase where cash is tight. Even here the benefits may be marginal as statutory restrictions on dividend increases may be applicable. It may be stated with some confidence, therefore, that the company will have to be in serious financial straits before the financial controller can look to adjusting the size of the dividend to help him in his battle for solvency.

However, apart from the size of the dividend, there is the possibility of synchronising the timing of payment with a good period in the company's cash flow profile. Thus, it may be an advantage for a retail company to pay its dividend in December when it should be enjoying the fruits of a seasonal upsurge in sales. In addition, it should be noted that, under UK tax law, advance corporation tax (ACT) is payable on dividends at a level equivalent to the basic rate of income tax on the amount distributed as if that were a sum net of basic rate income tax. Thus, if the dividend were £140,000 and basic rate of tax 30 per cent, ACT of £60,000 would be due (being 30 per cent of £140,000 + £60,000). ACT can be offset against the company's main corporation tax liability and, in addition, against equivalent ACT paid on any

## Table 9.8
## Statement of sources and applications of funds

| SOURCES | This year | | Next year | |
|---|---|---|---|---|
| | £k | £k | £k | £k |
| Profit before tax and extraordinary items | X | | X | |
| Extraordinary items[1] | X | | X | |
| Adjustments for items not involving movement of funds[2] | X | | X | |
| Total generated from operations | | X | | X |
| Funds from other sources[3] | | X | | X |
| | | X | | X |
| | | | | |
| APPLICATIONS | | | | |
| Dividends | X | | X | |
| Taxation | X | | X | |
| Purchase of fixed assets | X | | X | |
| Loans repaid | X | | X | |
| | | X | | X |
| | | X[4] | | X[4] |
| | | | | |
| CHANGES IN WORKING CAPITAL | | | | |
| Increase/decrease in stocks | X | | | |
| Increase/decrease in debtors | X | | | |
| Increase/decrease in creditors excluding dividends and taxation | X | | | |
| Increase/decrease in cash | X | | | |
| Increase/decrease in short-term investments | X | | | |
| | | X[4] | | X[4] |

*Notes*
[1] Extraordinary items would include, for example, profit on sale of investments.
[2] Adjustments would include, for example, depreciation.
[3] Other sources would include, for example, cash from issue of shares.
[4] These figures must equate.

dividends it may receive from UK companies but there may be substantial timing differences for cash budgeting purposes.

### Funds flow statements

The importance of a company's performance as measured by utilisation of funds was recognised by the accountancy professions in October 1975 with the publication of *Statement of Standard Account-*

*ing Practice (SSAP)* 10 entitled 'Statement of Sources and Applications of Funds'. This requires the inclusion of a funds flow statement with published accounts of enterprises with a turnover in excess of £25,000. The funds flow statement shows, as the name suggests, the sources of funds coming into the business and the use of funds by the business and the balance of these is reconciled to the change in net working capital in the period concerned. The form of this statement is given in Table 9.8.

While the *SSAP* is limited to the presentation of historical information which is readily available from the profit and loss account and balance sheet, there is no reason why the movement of funds cannot be budgeted and monitored in the same format as illustrated in Table 9.8. This represents an alternative approach to the simple cash budgeting and cash monitoring method which is discussed above and demonstrated in Tables 9.3 and 9.7.

## CONCLUSION

This chapter began with the strong if contentious view that working capital control is one of the few areas, nay the only area, of business management in which the financial controller has any real influence. This sentiment is by no means as damning as it may first appear since controlling the funds is probably the most critical factor in the successful management of an enterprise, as the preceding paragraphs have sought to demonstrate. Profit and the continued existence of a company largely depend on the efficient conversion of cash.

It could be assumed that the responsibility for the control of the funds is left to the financial specialist deliberately on the grounds that he is best equipped to handle it. The more cynical interpretation is that there is widespread ignorance of the implications of working capital control, and of the consequences of a lack of control, and that the responsibility falls to the finance man by default. Either way, the finance specialist can afford to be philosophical as he can benefit from the opportunity to make a real and significant contribution to the affairs of business in addition to his superficially prime function of keeping the financial records.

## REFERENCES AND ADDITIONAL READING

Accounting Standards Committee, *Statement of Standard Accounting Practice – SSAP 10 Statements of Source and Application of Funds,* 1975

Battersby, *A Guide to Stock Control,* Pitman, 1970.

Batty, *Management Accountancy,* McDonald & Evans, 1975.

Davidson and Weil, *Handbook of Modern Accounting,* McGraw-Hill, 1977.

Franks and Broyles, *Modern Managerial Finance,* John Wiley, 1979.

Franks and Scholefield, *Corporate Financial Management,* Gower Press, 1977.

Harvey and Young, *Tolley's Corporation Tax,* Tolley Publishing, annual.

Taha, *Operations Research – An Introduction,* Macmillan, New York, 1971.

Van Horne, *Financial Management and Policy,* Prentice-Hall, 1977.

# 10

# Internal Audit and Internal Control

**P.C. Chidgey and Heather Watts**

*The authors of this contribution argue that systems of management accounting, whilst fulfilling essential roles in providing information for management, have certain defects in respect of the completeness, the timeliness and the objectivity of the data produced. All businesses, as a result, need systems of internal control and most need internal audit functions, particularly those of any size and where branches are involved. Whatever changes of emphasis or direction may await the external audit, it may be widely agreed that the internal audit function is now well established and must develop in parallel with the growth of computerised information systems. The potential of the internal audit is examined in detail and in depth by the authors of this chapter, which covers not only the techniques and problems of the function but also defines the principles to be applied. The natural extension of the audit of records and systems towards an audit of management, and the difficulties associated with such an audit, are carefully analysed. The chapter is concluded with some interesting observations on possible developments in the scope of the external audit and the appearance of the audit committee.*

The idea of an audit is normally associated with the annual independent verification of a set of a company's accounts for the benefit of its shareholders, which in addition involves some responsibility for detecting frauds and errors. Large amounts of resources are devoted to this use of auditing because of the legal requirements for an audit of all companies in the UK (and of large companies in most other countries). From the managers' point of view such audits do not contribute greatly to their efforts to achieve business goals and objectives. Auditing, however, has uses in a much wider context than the verification of a set of final accounts. When fully employed it is a means of independent identification of departures from specified standards in any area and as a first stage in the initiation of improvements. In these wider terms auditing can aid the assessment of management practices both for management's own internal purposes and also for the purposes of external parties.

To be effective the audit process should consist of the following four stages:

1  Choice of standards in terms of which the subject of audit will be assessed, e.g. existence of effective controls, performance and reporting standards (including accounting standards).
2  Investigation, testing and collection of evidence about the actions, reports etc. which are subject to audit.
3  Report to independent interested parties of how statements, actions etc. measure up to standards.
4  Follow-up procedure which considers rectification of reported divergences from standards.

If these four stages are followed, auditing can be a useful means of identifying those problem areas where departures from specified standards have occurred and of impelling improvements.

In practice, most of the developments of auditing as a means of assessing management have occurred in the area of 'internal auditing' which is the use of auditing by management for their own purposes. This chapter will initially examine the roles filled by internal auditing which can be examined under two headings:

1  *Traditional purposes.* Internal auditing originally developed out of the external audit function. As organisations developed both in size and complexity, the reliability of the financial records which underlay the accounts became subject to the existence of adequate controls. In the largest companies internal auditing grew to secure compliance with these controls which ultimately came to serve two purposes,
(a) to ensure accuracy of the financial records; and
(b) to protect the company against fraud and misappropriation.
The use of internal audit for these purposes is of great importance, increasingly so because of the growth of computerised accounting systems and geographically decentralised companies.

2 *Developments from traditional purposes*. A later development was the extension of the audit examination to performance itself. It is possible, by means of audit, to examine all aspects of performance from areas such as organisational structure, information systems and planning methods to activities such as production and purchasing. This use also answered the needs of management for reliable information about events and potential problems in divisions beyond their day-to-day control, which was not provided by conventional accounting systems.

The chapter will, in conclusion, examine whether the benefits of auditing as practised internally can be extended to a wider group of external parties. Some suggestions for an extension of an audit in this way will be considered, particularly the question of whether the external auditor has a role to play.

## TRADITIONAL PURPOSES OF INTERNAL CONTROL

In any enterprise various controls have always been needed to secure maximum administrative and operational efficiency in both the financial and non-financial areas. A basic necessity for such efficiency is that all transactions are properly authorised and correctly recorded and all assets are adequately safeguarded. These aspects must be examined in order to appreciate fully their importance in this area.

### Credible accounting records

These are necessary for several reasons, one being that they form the basis of the annual published accounts. However, this in itself is not so important to management as the production of more frequent ad hoc reports for decision-making purposes. Such accounts should enable them to assess their company's present situation, analyse their past performance and aid the compilation of forecasts. They also need these records to compare the actual results with budgets and to ascertain the reasons for variances. Management may require specific reports, for example, a stock report may be needed to identify areas where effective purchasing may be improved; or as a basis to decide whether or not a large sales order may be accepted; or to identify slow-moving items. A work-in-progress report may be necessary to assess the stage reached on a contract, the costs to date, those still to be incurred and whether the total is within the estimated budget.

Another important reason for credible accounting records concerns businesses with geographically dispersed subsidiaries or branches. While local management may be making their own decisions, head office needs the information from all the respective areas to ascertain how effective these have proved. They need to assess the individual branches with regard to the others and also to the overall position of the group. In order to reach valid conclusions, the information studied must be accurate.

Hence, such reports are extremely important to management and they must all be accurate and timely to be of utmost use.

## Security of assets

The second main control objective is to ensure there is an effective system for protecting the company's assets. There are two security aspects – physical security of assets and control over transactions.

Physical security of assets covers such things as ensuring cash is always safely locked away and subsequently banked. It is unfortunate, however, that security often appears to be strongest where cash is involved, when in fact large sums are often lost through theft of stock or moveable capital assets. There should always be strict physical control over access to the warehouse. Even where individual units of stock are not of great value, a steady disappearance of 'cheap' items may eventually lead to substantial losses. Fixed assets which can be transported are continuously 'at risk', especially where they are constantly changing location due to the nature of the company's business. For example, a construction company will keep items of machinery and plant on site. Even here, however, with the obvious difficulties of maintaining continuous surveillance, there should be adequate effort made to secure the safety of the assets. Theft is not the only danger to be protected against; adequate physical precautions in addition to sufficient insurance cover should exist against such disasters as fire and floods.

In order to achieve adequate control over transactions, attention should be focused on those points where a loss may be incurred by the company. For example, credit sales orders should only be accepted from credit-worthy customers, otherwise assets may well prove to have been 'given away'; purchase invoices should only be settled after proof has been given that they were 'bona fide' purchases and the goods have been received, while overtime should only be paid if the work has been properly authorised. All these controls ensure the safeguarding of assets whether they be cash or kind.

Hence it may be seen why management are extremely concerned with minimising accounting errors and trying to prevent loss of assets either fraudulently or unintentionally. As enterprises expanded, however, management became aware of the need to set up a formalised procedure of control to achieve these basic objectives. The checks that they instituted are known as 'internal controls'.

## Internal control

Any effective system of internal control will incorporate certain fundamental principles. One is that the accounting responsibilities are divided amongst the employees in such a way that no single person is given complete control of a transaction. The guiding principle here is that those who authorise a transaction must not also be in charge of the relevant assets and that neither be responsible for recording the necessary details. Someone who prepares the payroll, for example, must not be allowed to make up the wage-packets and also deliver them to employees. If all was left in the hands of one person he would have ample opportunity to pay what he liked to whom he liked.

Another important principle is to make certain that, as far as possible, one person's work is checked by another without any unnecessary duplication of effort. For example, the cashier's work may be proved to a certain extent by the accountant reconciling the statement received from the bank (an independent third party) to the cash book. These two basic principles of internal control are often known as 'internal check'.

Such control systems may well be complex and to cope with this, management should draw up a plan of their organisation. This plan should set out clearly the responsibilities of the different offices, eliminating any intermediate areas which may otherwise have led to confusion. Without such clarity, the result may be that controls are either not exercised or are unnecessarily repeated. In addition to identifying the personnel responsible for the individual controls, a detailed plan of the organisation will also facilitate the identification of the flow of authority and instruction downwards through the hierarchy and the corresponding reverse flow of information. This is important for these communication flows are strongly interrelated; the most appropriate and effective management decisions will be based on prompt, reliable information.

Any efficient system of internal control will be one where the benefits arising from the controls exceed the cost of implementing them. However, regardless of how effective an internal control system appears in theory there is no guarantee that it will function as well in practice. Control systems depend very much on people and people are subject to many failings such as fatigue, boredom and lack of understanding. Furthermore, it is extremely difficult to institute controls that will effectively counteract any fraudulent collusion between employees. Any of these weaknesses may well cause the best control system to fail occasionally or even break down. Therefore, another control principle which management should implement is the regular examination of the systems to ascertain how well they are operating and to pinpoint and rectify weaknesses. In many of the larger businesses, however, management has found that due to the sheer size of the enterprise they were unable to devote sufficient time themselves to making adequate reviews. They realised that the potential benefits involved justified the costs of employing an internal auditor or even of setting up an internal audit department to perform this function.

When used for this purpose internal audit takes as a standard the existence of and compliance with controls sufficient to ensure adequate records and protection of assets.

The second stage of the internal audit process is the actual investigation needed to achieve this.

## Audit methods

With the traditional objectives in mind, the internal auditor will review the internal control systems as laid down, taking into account the various divisions of responsibility and other internal checks. After he has noted the theoretically weak areas he may then commence testing the system in practice. This he will do by employing a combination of techniques, the main ones being 'depth-testing', observation and reviews. 'Depth-testing' involves tracing a transaction from its inception to completion, noting at each stage the various recordings and authorisation required for effective control. Emphasis will be placed here on the recognised weak spots.

The growth of enterprises has meant that an enormous number of transactions takes place annually. Since it is practically impossible for the internal auditor to check every individual item, the practice of sampling has developed. The theory is that a number of transactions are selected at random from the whole population. Thus, when the auditor has thoroughly tested these items the conclusion he draws about them should indicate the total of similar transactions. The internal auditor can employ statistical techniques or rely on his own judgement to choose the sample. Whichever method is chosen, he should do sufficient sampling to form an opinion on whether the system works well in practice. Obviously if it does not, then the auditor must endeavour to pinpoint the weaknesses and recommend improvements. He should also attempt to quantify the effects of any deficiencies and ensure any errors are rectified.

Another method the internal auditor may employ is actually to observe procedures as they take place. For example, he may witness the opening of the mail to see if all receipts are pre-listed, before being passed to the cashier to enter into the records. He will then need to ascertain whether the control is fully implemented with the accountant checking that the cash book entries agree with the pre-lists. He may also physically observe the control procedures operated within the warehouse to check that no item is withdrawn without an authorised requisition note; all incoming goods are clearly identified and nothing is accepted unless the goods inward note corresponds to the actual goods. He should not omit to physically observe the presence of fixed assets.

One other technique that the internal auditor may use is to review certain items. For instance, he may closely scrutinise the debtors' ledger to obtain some indication of whether credit control is functioning as efficiently as it should. A large number of overdue balances may mean that there is no effective check of credit-worthiness.

In testing to ensure reliable records are kept and all assets are safeguarded the internal auditor will conduct very similar checks to those of the external auditor, because they are both very much concerned with this area. However, the external auditor at present looks at the audit from a narrower point of view – that of ensuring the records are sufficiently reliable to form the basis for true and fair year-end accounts. The internal auditor will be conducting his tests for the purposes of aiding management.

### Problems of computerised systems

In recent years the main problem which has faced the internal auditor when performing this function has been the growth of computerised systems. If an organisation has such a system, the internal auditor must audit it thoroughly, for a computer need only be criminally instructed by one man, to produce the criminal capabilities of thousands. It is exactly the same situation with errors, for if a master-file contains incorrect data, it may affect numerous transactions. For example, if the selling price of an item is incorrectly recorded, hundreds of invoices may be wrongly priced before the mistake is discovered.

The problem has been exacerbated with the introduction of data banks. The theory of data banks is that the same basic accounting information may be required for many different reasons. The sales figure may be needed to analyse the sales by products, by geographical or customer distribution and also for costing, stock-level, credit-control and forecasting purposes. This illustrates how often the same basic information is capable of reclassification and use for completely different purposes and by departments other than those who originated the data. Efficient computer data banks are those where the information is stored only once, but in a way that will allow all these later types of reclassification. A mistake in the original data can thus invalidate all the subsequent analyses, and this shows how vital it is that the initial input data is correct.

Here, the major problem facing the internal auditor is of ensuring that the input is complete and accurate – if not, the output will be of little use. Hence, he should scrutinise the procedures to make certain appropriate controls are instituted. One such control is to check that all sales despatch notes fed into the computer run in strict numerical sequence; so any omissions will be quickly noticed. Also, check digits can be incorporated into the system so that, for example, invalid account numbers would be rejected. A further problem here, however, is that he relies on the computer for some of these controls.

Once the data have been fed into the computer, another difficulty arises for the internal auditor – the 'loss of audit-trail'. This occurs when a vast amount of information is fed into the computer and is regurgitated in a completely different form with no trace of the build-up to this new appearance. This means that a comparison of input with output will not tell the auditor whether the data have been processed correctly. For example, a month's purchase invoices may be input to the computer with the resulting output merely consisting of a total figure for each type of purchase. The only way that the auditor is able to check completely that this is a correct analysis is to reproduce manually the computer process himself. This is obviously very time-consuming and in an attempt to overcome the problem, the internal auditor has to rely on procedural controls incorporated within each program. One method is the use of 'run-to-run' control totals, i.e. the sum of a number of items must reconcile with another total before the program will continue, for instance the sum of the analysed totals of purchase invoices must agree with the total figure of these invoices. However, the internal auditor should not allow total reliance to be placed on the computer's procedural controls. He should ensure there are sufficient manual procedures in an attempt to check the computer's work. One way is to total batches of data before they are fed into the computer and then check that the total output figure agrees. These batch totals may be in monetary or numerical terms or even be 'hash' totals which are meaningless sums of figures such as the total of account numbers. One drawback of these is that they do not ensure accurate processing, even though they ensure completeness.

It is also possible to use computers to apply controls which have previously been exercised manually. For example, if a customer's credit limit is exceeded, or if the amount of a purchase invoice is excessive, the computer can be programmed to show these particular items in an exception report. Once again, the internal auditor must check to ensure the computer is functioning correctly.

Hence the internal auditor has many problems when auditing the computer itself. He needs to ascertain whether the actual program is operating as it should (for instance, is there a correct analysis?); whether the procedural controls are functioning correctly (such as the run-to-run control totals) and also whether the exception/rejection reports are complete and accurate. One technique he may utilise in an attempt to overcome these difficulties is that of 'test packs'. These are designed to process artificial transactions with the company's operational program and the output is then compared with predetermined results calculated manually.

However, test packs on their own are insufficient. The ideal starting point for the internal auditor to test for the incorporation of controls is at the systems development stage. He should ascertain whether there is sufficient control over the development of the systems. There must be strict security procedures over the initial development; then over the ensuing testing for effectiveness through the use of 'desk-testing' and 'pilot-runs' and also over the subsequent amendments which must be authorised and then the whole system retested. It is obviously best for controls to be incorporated in the systems from their inception. However, it is a common failing for electronic data processing personnel to be more concerned with efficiency in their programs than with security. The internal auditor should accordingly provide this important security viewpoint and combine it with the efficiency aspect when the systems are in an embryonic form. To cause changes to be made when the systems are developed is extremely expensive and aggravating.

Security cannot be over-emphasised where computerised systems are concerned for the computer frauds that have been discovered show that the losses may be colossal. Hence as well as the procedural and systems development controls mentioned above, the internal auditor should also ensure that organisational controls are instituted. This is the division of functions so that, for instance, the systems development personnel do not actually operate the computer and also that operators do not develop the systems. It is undesirable to have personnel who know how to alter the program (systems development personnel) to operate them and vice versa. Thus, it is also important that access to files and programs should be restricted to the operators and librarians. These controls are very necessary, one reason being that computerised records may be changed and show no sign of alteration (unlike normal 'paper' records). Hence, dividing functions makes it extremely difficult for such alterations to be made. However, whenever amendments need to be carried out, there should always be full authorisation, and the internal auditor should check that this is complied with.

An inherent problem with any accounting system is that a major failure of such systems may have a disastrous effect on the company. Unfortunately, a computerised system is more susceptible to such hazards than a manual system. Fire is a fairly common occurrence in such a mechanised area and since it could practically eliminate a company's records sufficient safeguards must exist. Fire-fighting equipment should always be at hand, and copies of important files should be stored at another location, so that in the event of the destruction of the originals, these files may be used. Also, breakdowns in the computer are fairly common and so adequate stand-by facilities should be provided which the internal auditor must ensure are entirely satisfactory.

*Other problems*

As well as the problem of computerised systems, the internal auditor may be faced with another – that of a large number of widely located small subsidiaries. The difficulty here is the same as for all small entities – that of insufficient staff to allow the accepted theoretical division of duties. There will probably be little reliable documentary evidence for the internal auditor to use to check if a system is working. The control is very often centred in the hands of the individual in charge who, because of the size of the business, knows everything that is happening. In the smaller entities, this one man will be fulfilling the internal audit function. Due to the size, he is probably in full possession of the intricate details of his firm and thus will quickly see where things are wrong. However, for the larger companies the group internal auditor will have to satisfy himself that there is sufficient internal control within the small subsidiaries. It has been noted there may well be little documentary proof that any control systems are functioning, but the internal auditor should vouch the recorded transactions and he should make great use of comparisons either with budgets or past years' performance and then attempt to identify reasons for any significant variances.

Regardless of size restrictions, the auditor will require that certain controls still be present. For example cash and cheques should always be kept safely and banked promptly. In extreme cases where effective controls are impossible, it may be advisable to centralise certain procedures. Head office could be given charge of the sales ledger and credit control, with the subsidiary's responsibility finishing once the goods have been despatched. It could also control purchase orders, with area 'heads' only being allowed to place orders up to a stated amount. Any in excess of this should be approved by 'head office'. This may, however, prove to be an expensive way of instituting control.

## Conclusion of audit

Once the internal auditor has completed testing a particular area, he should make a full report on it. Regardless of how skilled and experienced the internal auditor may be, it is in management's hands to make the utmost use of his expertise. They should, therefore, never place him in the position of making a report to the person in charge of the area reviewed. If this does occur, especially where the report is critical, the full value of it is often not realised. Furthermore, management should always seriously consider the internal auditor's recommendations for improvement and implement those that meet with their approval. This should clearly demonstrate that he is not merely an 'interfering busybody' but that his work is deemed to be of real value. The internal auditor's function is to assess critically the internal control systems and it would be a waste of resources if his reasoned suggestions for improvements are not carried out.

Thus the traditional use of the internal audit, namely to ensure accuracy of financial records and to protect the company's assets, remains of great importance. This function continues to have a vital role to play in ensuring the efficient operating of any business.

## EXTENSION TOWARDS AUDITS OF MANAGEMENT

The potential of auditing has proved too useful to be restricted to traditional areas. In the post-war period there has been a movement in the USA towards using audits to identify problems arising not only in the application of controls within a company but also with the operations and performance of the company itself. The use of auditing for these purposes has been termed 'operational' or 'management' audit.

The aim of management is to achieve certain business objectives. This they attempt to do by a constant process of making plans, implementing them and adapting these plans and methods in the light of the results of their previous attempts and changes in their environment. Throughout this process of planning, implementing and adapting to changes, management need information about the outside world in which they operate, about the resources available to them, and about the results of previous efforts. To satisfy these needs management relies on information systems, one of the most important aspects of which is a management accounting system.

Auditing is of use in the management process on two levels. It can be used to assess the adequacy of the information systems as an aid for management. It can also be used in the assessment of the way that plans are made, the methods of implementing them and adaptation to changes.

Performance will suffer if management does not receive and act upon sufficient relevant information. An audit of the information systems will thus assess whether management is receiving as much useful information as is possible and how far this information is used. The audit of information systems has been a natural role into which audit has developed. The accounting systems, especially, have traditionally been the focal point for testing within the objectives of protection of assets and correctness of recording. Part of the assessment of information systems concentrates on the same records but with the emphasis instead in terms of the usefulness of information.

Audit fulfils two needs as far as examination of performance is concerned. It can provide an independent review of internal practices throughout the company, (and the performance resulting from their use) in terms of an overall standard of what practices should be followed. This has potential use at all levels of management, especially the highest.

It also fulfils the need caused by the inadequacies of management accounting systems to provide an adequate reflection of the results of performance. The traditional management accounting systems can be criticised in this respect for three reasons:

1   At best they only paint a partial picture of what has happened in the sense that a table of figures can never adequately describe a business.

2   The information provided about performance tends to be out of date on receipt due to the time taken to prepare reports. Management accordingly tends to obtain little information about the current position in remote departments and about likely developments such as imminent loss of control. The development of realtime computer applications may alleviate the first problem but can do little for the second.

3   They are liable to bias in the interests of those preparing and recording the information. This is particularly so in cases where the accountants are part of a local management team but are responsible for reporting to central management as well. It is also equally likely if large quantities of basic data come from production departments who will be paid bonuses on the basis of their results.

In small or medium-sized businesses these problems are not crucial as direct knowledge of the business from other sources can remedy any misleading impressions that accounting information gives. As a business expands, however, management can no longer have direct contact with all the areas for which they are ultimately responsible. They are therefore less able to complement the picture of the firm that the accounting systems give them and less able to identify those occasions when the accounting system is providing an erroneous or incomplete picture of what has happened.

The use of audit to assess the planning procedures and the manner in which the plans are implemented attempts to counteract these disadvantages. Here, the aim of auditing is to give the manager an independent view of events in the areas beyond his direct contact, by reporting to him actual or potential problems which the system would not usually report or report too late.

The appropriate scope of audit in the individual business, i.e. the decisions about whether to restrict to information systems or extend to performance and what levels of management to assess, must ultimately be decided by comparing the costs of the audit with the potential benefits which should flow from the assessments.

## Application

To be of use in this context, as in others, the audit must go through the four stages of establishment of standards, investigation, reporting and being part of a follow-up procedure, each of which is an important element in the success of an audit.

The adoption of standards becomes a far more difficult exercise with the audit of information systems or performance than with the traditional types of audit exercise. At the basic level of routine and repetitive tasks, set procedures can be used as a standard and the auditor will report on lack of compliance. However, many parts of management's function do not lend themselves easily to the issue of guidelines and in these cases some other standard must be used.

A general answer to this problem may be obtained by looking at different aspects of performance in the light of how they contribute to the company's objectives. This is obviously much easier in companies which adopt a 'management by objectives' style. It is far more difficult, however, where formal objectives are not stated. Indeed, one of the advantages of using auditing in the management area is that it frequently leads to a more formal examination of objectives. In some areas the auditor will need to use standards derived from apparent best practice outside the company or based on the performance of the functions under performance at an ideal level. This type of exercise will require knowledge and experience of the area under audit.

There are problems with most of the approaches. A too ready acceptance of internal standards may lead to their adoption even when they result in inefficiency. A standard set to promote efficiency of one function, e.g. purchasing, may damage efficiency in another area, e.g. production. Another problem is that management may be subject to controls from bodies outside the company. An example of this might be government controls over pollution levels which could prevent management from operating at peak efficiency. All these problems should be taken into account in choosing the most appropriate standard.

The investigation stage will use the methods and techniques which have been developed in the traditional field of auditing. The auditor will familiarise himself with the area under review and then by means of questionnaires, tracing of records and direct observation he will obtain evidence about performance in that area. A review of purchasing, for instance, may consist of questioning responsible officials about their methods, observing the methods in practice over several days and tracing records of past performance to check that what has been investigated is representative of what is normally done in the department.

The conclusiveness and reliability of evidence that an auditor can collect in respect of performance makes it much more difficult to measure than the correctness of accounting entries. When assessing the evidence the auditor will use much more subjective judgement than in the similar assessment during an external audit. Accordingly it is necessary for the auditor to be especially sceptical about the significance of the evidence that he has collected, when using it to come to a conclusion.

The report will be more detailed than for example the usual external audit report. It is necessary, here, for the auditor to state the standards used to assess performance and to describe the methods of investigation used during the audit. The auditor must also state the opinion he has come to on the area under review, indicating the degree of assurance he has in it. If the auditor's report is to be used as the basis for decisions then it should provide sufficient detail to allow these decisions to be taken properly.

The use of the audit findings to consider whether there should be any effort made in the area to improve performance is of vital importance to the usefulness of auditing in this context. If this is not done there will be little benefit from the audit. Ideally, it should provide the basis of decisions made by the managers of the departments concerned and their superiors about improvements in future performance. This can range from adjustments to routine procedures to the installation of new systems.

*Problems*

The application of auditing in this area is not without problems. The major ones centre around the questions of competence, scope of use and cost. The question of competence arises out of using auditors who are not skilled in the particular area that they are auditing. The development of an internal auditing department from the traditional protective and financial audits to a 'management' or 'operational' audit calls for a correspondingly greater breadth of vision from the auditors involved. The strongest internal audit departments will be those which include people who have specialised in certain areas and who can use a team approach to the audit. There will still, however, be advantages in an independent investigation even by someone not skilled in a particular area, so long as he can apply the evidence-gathering techniques of auditing properly. Techniques such as standardised questionnaires and checklists have proved very useful in ensuring that internal audits are of a high standard despite the lack of a specialist knowledge on the part of those carrying them out.

The problem of scope of use refers to the employment of auditors not only to discover problems but also to make recommendations and assist in the introduction of improvements. This is a dangerous course because the internal auditor will inevitably suffer a lack of independence in a subsequent review of the system that he is in part responsible for. There will be occasions, however, when just by stating the problem the remedy will become apparent and other occasions when the most cost-effective course will be for the auditor to recommend small changes. It is also normally accepted that an auditor should be consulted about the appropriate levels of control to be incorporated in, for example, a new information system. However, the subsequent loss of independence must always be recognised as a major disadvantage in using the internal audit department in anything but a small way outside its usual function.

There is an additional disadvantage in that the organisation will not be receiving as much benefit from the internal audit department as it should. This is because internal auditors are specialist auditors and are of most value to the organisation when performing that role. They are thus more likely to be economically employed in auditing further areas rather than implementing improvements to existing areas.

The problem of cost occurs at two levels. The first type of cost problem concerns companies who through lack of resources must choose between the traditional and 'protective' functions and the more modern 'management audit' functions. In this case the decision about where to direct internal audit must be made on a cost–benefit basis and normally those areas with the greatest effect on company performance and those least susceptible to management control should receive primary consideration.

The second type of cost problem is that many small or medium-sized companies will find that the cost of a permanent internal management audit department at an effective level exceeds the potential benefits. This is because in order to be effective each area which is audited must be visited on a regular basis. Depending on factors such as size of organisation and type of business this is commonly thought in practice to range from one to five years. This disadvantage can be offset in two ways. In the case of small and medium-sized companies the control problems which cause the need for internal audits can be overcome by informal management review. The other possible solution is for internal audits to be conducted by the external auditors or management consultants on a sub-contract basis. The proposal for 'management' or 'operational' audits by external auditors has the attraction of cost savings as the external auditor is involved in the company's systems anyway. There are however difficulties with this solution.

## The external audit

The role of the external auditor is to establish for the benefit of the shareholders of a company that a set of financial statements prepared by the management of that company give a true and fair reflection of company performance in the last accounting period and its position at the date to which the accounts are prepared. In this context the external auditors are acting as agents of the shareholders and should be independent of the management of the company.

This is not to imply that management will not benefit at all from the audit process, as the external auditor will want to see controls to protect the company from fraudulent practices and controls which ensure that information is correctly recorded. Management will be interested in the same controls (as will the internal auditor as an agent of management), but whereas the external auditor will examine them to provide assurance of accurate external reporting, management (and the internal auditor) will look at them more as a means of ensuring the attainment of company objectives.

Despite their different interests management can be greatly aided by the review of these controls performed by the external auditor, for often as a by-product of the external audit the auditors will make a report to management about the level of controls. However, this is only incidental to their main function which is to report to the shareholders.

To extend the external auditor's function to report to management on information systems and performance while still continuing to report to shareholders on the accounting statements would cause insurmountable conflicts of interest. The auditor here would be responsible to management and at the same time responsible to the shareholders to perform an audit of statements prepared by management.

There would also be problems of competence to resolve. Most external auditors at present are not particularly skilled in management audit and presumably this is a factor which management should take into account in deciding whether to employ them in this way.

In the final resort the most sensible solution in most cases will be to employ either sufficiently experienced management consultants or a firm of accountants other than the external auditors with access to a wide range of management skills.

Provided that these problems are recognised, 'internal audit' in the 'management' and 'operational' sense can prove a useful tool to aid management in the achievement of their objectives, but, as emphasised above, it should be judged in the same manner as all other management tools by means of frequent comparisons between its prospective benefits and costs.

## Audit as a means of extending third party control

In recent years it has been frequently argued that there is a need for more control over the managements of companies in the interests of both ownership groups, such as shareholders, and society as a whole, in matters such as pollution controls. Effective control depends on information and an audit is a useful source of such information. Accordingly there have been proposals from many sides to extend the audit function to provide more information about the company to external parties. While some of these calls have come from parties who required social assessments or audits of companies others have seen such an extension as a means of improving company profitability by providing information to interested parties who can pressure management towards more efficient practices.

Two particular suggestions can be considered for the practical implication of these ideas:

1  An extension of the present external audit report to cover internal controls, management information and performance, or
2  the preparation of reports on these areas, made by either the internal or external auditors, for consideration by an audit committee which would contain representatives of outside interests.

### Extension of external audit report

The publication of reports on company performance and systems by external auditors should have two advantages. The knowledge that such a report is to be prepared should induce more efficient behaviour among certain companies and the reports themselves should be a useful source of information for judging the relative efficiency of different managements. This would result in corrective pressures or decisions to re-allocate resources to more efficient areas.

There is, however, a major weakness with this suggestion and also several unresolved problems surrounding the implementation of such a proposal. The weakness is that it does not provide in itself an effective follow-up procedure. Publication of reports about inefficient management does not necessarily result in improved performance and without a channel through which effective pressure can be brought on inefficient management, many of the benefits of this extension of audit could be lost.

The problems are in the area of standards, competence, evidence and confidentiality.

### *Standards*

Auditing is a process during which the subject of audit is independently assessed and reported on, in terms of a standard. Information systems and performance are capable of being judged in accordance with many different standards each of which may be perfectly valid given the purpose for which the audit is undertaken, and none of which can lay claim to universal application. In the absence of a single well-defined standard, however, comparability between reports on different companies will be difficult to achieve and the reports could even be misleading if it is assumed that they are in terms of a common standard.

*Competence*

It is doubtful whether the external auditor, although presently qualified to undertake reviews of internal controls and possibly management information systems, would have the necessary skills to perform 'management' or 'operational' audits. Suitably qualified individuals would have to be employed to fulfil this role, and this would significantly increase the cost of these audits.

*Evidence*

Because of the subjective assessments which are required during a management audit, the final report may not be given with a level of assurance significant enough to be of much use to external users. An internal audit reports problems in departments which management can investigate further if they are unhappy with the degree of subjective judgement involved in identifying them. External parties would not have this option.

*Confidentiality*

The publication of certain details may harm individual companies. Competitors could take advantage of reports on weaknesses in different production areas or unscrupulous employees could take advantage of disclosed weak controls. Even in the context of a national requirement for such audits there would still be the problem of international competitors.

These problems will require careful consideration if an extension of audit is to result in improvements in performance.

**Consideration of reports by audit committees**

The idea of audit committees which has developed in the USA, to the extent that the Securities Exchange Commission has endorsed their establishment by all publicly held companies, overcomes the major weaknesses in the first proposal. It does this by providing a channel of communication between the recipients of the audit report and the management of the company.

The proposal involves the setting up of an audit committee composed of representatives from various external interest groups which would receive audit reports on all aspects of the company's affairs and would be able to commission further work if required. This would allow confidentiality to be maintained and also ease the problems relating to standards and evidence.

The use of audit committees in the UK has grown in recent years. W.H. Smith and British Petroleum are examples of companies which have adopted them. The proposal would however, result in a different role for the audit committee than is presently conceived in the UK where its chief purpose is seen as providing a link between external auditors and the company. Its proposed role would be as a body independent of management which could apply pressure on them to perform in an efficient manner, with the ultimate sanction of publication of the results of the auditors' investigation. Such a committee would provide a useful force for more efficient performance.

There are still problems with a proposal of this kind. The question of which auditors would report to the committee requires resolution. The external auditor would still suffer from the competence problems referred to above, while to use internal auditors would mean that they were no longer a tool which management could direct according to their objectives. This might encourage the setting up of two forces of internal auditors within a company with resulting additional costs and conflicts.

This proposal would also be costly and some consideration should be given to the question of whether the cost is justified if there is not a significant divergence between management and external parties, for example, in the case of owner managers or where loan creditors can appoint a director. Each enterprise considering the adoption of such a committee in the absence of a national requirement must weigh the costs against the anticipated benefits as in all other aspects of the use of audit for management purposes.

## CONCLUSION

Auditing can be of use in the assessment of all aspects of business. In practice it was initially restricted to ensuring compliance with internal controls which attempted to protect the business against loss of assets and incorrect financial records. It has however developed far beyond that into an assessment of the factors which affect performance itself. These uses have thus far been almost primarily for the benefit of management. The increasing demands for greater accountability within society, however, may in the future result in the use of audits for the benefit of a much wider range of external interested parties.

## REFERENCES AND ADDITIONAL READING

Bird, P., *Accountability: Standards of Financial Reporting,* Accounting Age Books, 1973.
Brink, Cashin and Witt, *Modern Internal Auditing,* Ronald Press, 1973.
Lindberg and Cohn, *Operations Auditing,* Amacom, 1972.
*The Internal Auditor* (Journal of Institute of Internal Auditors)

# PART III
# THE MANAGEMENT
# OF CHANGE

## PART III   THE MANAGEMENT OF CHANGE

The fact that we live in a world of change is particularly noticeable in the field of business. Change in itself is not a new phenomenon for businessmen and it is reasonable to suppose that throughout the ages they have had to learn by the hard way of experience that the essence of management lies in adaptation to change. What is new is the speed and the variety of the changes which have occurred in recent years, and there seems to be no reason to expect any slowing down in the pace of events; nor can we predict the precise nature and form of the changes which will occur.

The changes which affect business are classified by Avison Wormald in Chapter 11 as political, economic and technological, not omitting the large and complex movements which have been and are taking place in the value of the world's currencies. Price changes in the various elements of production pursue each other with varying momentum in a moving scenario with a velocity which it is difficult to forecast and equally difficult to rationalise. Change thus demands vision in planning, flexibility in budgeting and adaptability, if not opportunism, in control mechanisms.

This part contains an analysis of a necessarily limited selection of business activities, reflecting many of the categories of change outlined by Wormald. Thus technological change necessitates the financial control of research and development, the principles of which are expertly expounded by Alan Pearson of the Manchester Business School in Chapter 12. A further chapter by Avison Wormald deals with trading overseas, where the business is particularly vulnerable to political, economic and monetary movements, of which the incidence varies widely between one country and another.

The international theme is taken up by Professor Elwood Miller of Saint Louis University, Missouri, in his chapter on the multinational company. For those organisations special problems are posed for financial management in co-ordinating activities, consolidating the results, evaluating the performance and managing the finances.

The managerial function of planning and control in an environment of continual change has to be conducted against the background of a society which is itself changing fundamentally in its structure and attitudes. Searching questions are being raised as to the objectives and responsibilities of business. Aspects of what we call social accounting arising from changes in the structure of society are discussed from a balanced but uncompromising viewpoint in the final chapter of this part contributed by Richard Dobbins and David Fanning. These contributors analyse the implications of social change for financial objectives and the communication of results in financial terms.

# 11

# Financial Planning in Conditions of Change

**Avison Wormald**

*For most businesses of significance change is now the normal rather than the exceptional, and it follows that one of the most important responsibilities of management is to cope successfully with the various changes, predictable and unpredictable, which affect the fortunes of the business. The experienced contributor to the opening chapter of this part of the handbook classifies the changes which are most likely to affect business as: political change; change in money values, i.e. inflation; economic change and technological change.*

*Economic change embraces factors such as economic groupings, such as the EEC, trends in the domestic economy, changes in the distribution of wealth, and in raw material prices and supplies. All these factors have direct repercussions on financial planning and may effect fundamental, but sometimes unnoticed, changes in the nature of a business. For a management team which is prepared to cope with risk and uncertainty, change can lend a stimulus and an excitement to the function of management.*

*Avison Wormald has seen the pace of change rapidly accelerate and, for the purpose of controlling the situation, he echoes what R. J. Brown maintained in an earlier chapter — that conventional budgeting and planning techniques are often inadequate and that flexible budgets or alternative 'scenarios' may be most appropriate. He emphasises the need for an efficient information service to management, presumably computerised, and this would need an audit every two years. Much the same thought was expressed in the chapter on internal audit by Peter Chidgey and Heather Watts and will be further developed in a subsequent chapter on computerisation.*

*The author illustrates his analysis by a series of short, but pointed case histories which show that growth in business, as well as decline, will demand the highest qualities from the financial controller.*

In recent years, the pace of change has been rapidly accelerating. Equally important, the changes seem more violent and more unexpected. The term the 'age of discontinuity' (Drucker, 1969) has been used, which carries these connotations.

In no field have these factors been more evident than in finance, where inflation, monetary instability and enormous changes in the geographic distribution of the world's wealth have shaken the western world, and to some extent, the eastern, to a degree which can only be compared to the impact of world wars.

These changes imply risk and uncertainty, particularly for the financial manager. Risk, by definition, can be estimated and planned for; uncertainty, by definition, cannot, except in so far as general measures can be taken to strengthen the business.

The financial manager's criteria for planning are not uniform; they are to some extent subjective and they are influenced by his particular environment. It has been suggested, as a result of a survey, that three widely applied criteria are:

1   Impact on long-term consolidated earnings per share.
2   Impact on cash flow.
3   Impact on the firm's market value.

These criteria will be used implicitly at least in the subsequent discussion, since they subsume a number of others which might be suggested; e.g. the impact on long-term consolidated earnings per share obviously subsumes a number of criteria about earning power in relation to capital, while the impact on the firm's market value obviously concerns its earning power and asset value. Whether the company is private or public is not really important.

## MAJOR POLITICAL CHANGE

In more and more places there is a pervasive feeling that no country, even apparently the most secure, is immune from major political change. If the domestic country goes through a phase of political uncertainty the market value of most companies will suffer as will their share prices. The reply to this threat, especially in 'unstable' countries such as Italy, is to invest abroad, or at least to place substantial liquid funds and even ownership in countries such as Switzerland. Many companies now feel it wise to spread their interests widely, with the USA, in spite of its current difficulties, as a preferred haven.

## INFLATION

Inflation is a subject in itself, in its proximate or further consequences perhaps the most important with which the financial manager has to deal.

For nearly 50 years inflation has been present in virtually all market economies, sometimes at quite low and tolerable levels of 2 or 3 per cent, sometimes rising to 25 per cent in such 'stable' countries as the UK. It must not be supposed that deflation will never recur, but even if it does not the fluctuations in the rate of inflation pose serious problems for the financial manager. If he is obliged to borrow for any but the shortest periods at penal rates of around 20 per cent, clearly he is in serious trouble. The raising of capital, either loan or equity, must therefore be planned for periods when interest rates are tolerable, which in 1979 meant less than 10 per cent, a rate which historically looked high, and which may look high again in the future. We say 'tolerable' because at least it leaves some margin between a 'normal' or 'basic' rate of return of 15 per cent and the cost of servicing capital. Obviously the timing of capital raising is now even more important.

## MAJOR ECONOMIC CHANGE

The major economic changes which may affect the financial manager are: changes in economic groupings; major trends in GNP in the domestic economy; changes in the distribution of wealth; and prices of raw materials.

### Economic groupings

This is one of the major structural forces in the world today. Entry into the EEC has had profound effects on the UK economy creating greater competition in some areas, larger markets and different currency alignments. One of the directions in which this concerns the financial manager is the trend towards larger operating units. For a company to survive it has to have a strong financial position and good profitability, otherwise the probability is that it will be absorbed by a stronger company.

## Major trends in GNP

The relative position of countries in the GNP table is changing, the UK showing a constant trend towards a lower position, and France and Germany in the highest position. Such movements affect the desirability of different countries for investment, a poor market having obviously fewer attractions than a rich one. The trend of these changes may change, as has been the case with Spain and Italy to some extent, so that a long view has to be taken of say 10 years at least.

An offsetting factor may be lower costs of labour which if not accompanied by an equally low labour productivity may make the country desirable as an export base; this would be the case for example for some industries with Eire.

The USA has for some time shown low growth rates and declining labour productivity so that its attractiveness for investment may rest more on the size of the market and its political orientation than on its profitability.

## Changes in the distribution of wealth

Various factors have brought this about, especially the transferability of industrial skills and the ability to plan on a large scale. This, with native qualities and the existence of reserves of labour in agriculture, has led to the phenomenal growth of the Japanese and Korean economies, and to a lesser extent that of Brasil. The traditionally wealthy countries such as the USA have been affected by the urbanisation of the population and the declining raw material base. These changes as already mentioned greatly affect their desirability as sites for investment.

Rising energy prices have had a marked impact on growth trends in many countries especially the USA, Brasil and Japan, and this effect is likely to last 10–20 years unless there is a depression deep enough to restore competition amongst oil exporters.

## Raw material prices

Very high growth rates in industry and the entry of many new countries to the list have resulted in great pressure on many raw material supplies, of which oil is only one example. The consequences of this for the financial manager are several. In the first place new investment has to be scrutinised more closely to see if it will be affected by higher material prices; second, working capital may form a higher proportion of total investment in existing or new business areas.

In the short term, for many commodities there are of course the 'futures' markets, where cover can be obtained at a known price for at least six months ahead. Where there is a long lead time between manufacture and sales, and firm prices have to be fixed a long way ahead, the use of these markets, where they exist, is almost inevitable. The dangers are not few, however, and there have been many cases where prudent coverage of raw material requirements has led to wild gambling either to retrieve losses or to make adventitious profits. Any company which makes use of the futures markets should establish an extremely tight system of authority to purchase or make contracts, where not less than three senior people are involved.

For many raw materials forecasts are available from research organisations. They are obviously not entirely reliable, but repay study since in this way a knowledge of the factors affecting the market is obtained. One of the most important of these is the cost structure of the industry concerned, which frequently is the main factor governing prices and the creation of new capacity.

## MAJOR TECHNOLOGICAL CHANGE

Another group of factors is those concerned with technology. In many industries rates of obsolescence for processes and products have become very high, with a consequential need to take a conservative view of the profits over the longer term and to provide for fast write-offs of equipment. Nearly all advanced technology is an increasing risk with patent protection frequently inadequate, high launching costs, possible customer claims and short product lives. Growth industries have their drawbacks as well as advantages, since they tend to attract competition, and may require a 'critical mass' which is very large, as for example in main-frame computers. The financial manager has to consider whether his base is large enough to achieve this minimum economic scale. If not, and if a good estimate has not been made several years before, much money and effort will be wasted, as it was in the UK both in the computer and the aircraft industries in 1950–65.

The opposite case is almost as frequent, that is where an important product is marketed and a large organisation created which cannot be sustained once the product has passed its peak. The answer in some of these cases would have been to have licensed the product even though it might have meant less profit.

The problems of Rolls Royce in the 1970s epitomise those in high-technology industries; large investment in R and D leading to a technical breakthrough, the development cost of which however is many times the cost of the original discovery or invention. This has to be financed through perhaps years of disappointment and difficulties until sales can be made. In this kind of industry the financial manager has to develop a deep understanding of the underlying technical situation, and a healthy scepticism about the timescales of engineers and scientists. In the case of Rolls Royce the financial function did not have the status in the organisation which was necessary in order to plan adequately; where a ten-year plan is necessary, a system based on annual budgets will lead to disaster. The most successful companies are those where the chief executive, as in the case of English GEC, has a lifetime knowledge of the business and an acute financial sense. The problems then are more frequently a surplus of cash than a deficit.

## CAPITAL MARKETS

The financial manager has to juggle several variables in relation to the raising of capital:

1  The form of capital: basically equity or loan, with a large number of intervening variables.
2  Timing: the needs of the company; the state of the capital markets.
3  Location: in which financial centre, the number of which has constantly increased.
4  Denomination: in what currency.
5  Terms: rate of interest; if loan, repayment, etc.

The changing international economic structure briefly referred to above has had far-reaching effects on capital markets. New York disappeared for a long time, sterling ceased to be used as an international currency, Hong Kong and Tokyo became international financial centres, virtually new currencies, the Eurodollar, the Ecu and the SDR appeared all in the space of 20 years.

The result of these changes has been near disaster for some companies which for example borrowed in German marks for repayment in the same currency; as nearly all currencies declined in relation to the mark there was for most borrowers a substantial capital loss when it came to repayment. Not all the changes were foreseeable by even the most acute observers, and certainly beyond five years requires some superhuman ability.

This type of problem can be solved using a linear program model. A variety of variables can be introduced to test the effect of the more probable occurrences, such as exchange and interest rates.

If there is one guiding principle for the financial manager in this highly dynamic situation it is to anticipate the requirement for fresh capital well ahead of time so that he does not have to go to the market at an unfavourable point in one of the recurrent cycles. An immediate penalty has to be paid in that cash balances appear unnecessarily large, and even perhaps tempting to some cash stripping 'raider', but with a generally high level of interest rates in the short term earnings from interest may approximate to earnings from the normal activity of the business.

## STRUCTURAL ECONOMIC CHANGES

The return on all types of investment is not of course constant. The financial manager of institutional funds has to recognise this and remain alert to the trends. In the UK for a number of years the return on industrial investment has been declining, while banking and property have shown a more favourable trend. The service economy on the whole is growing faster than the industrial sector, and its rate of return in many cases is higher.

Relative movements such as these may be the result of government policy, particularly in regard to interest rates on mortgages and bank deposits; they may be due to fears regarding inflation or to declines in, for example, the international competitiveness of certain industries. That the overall trend is frequently not easy to discern from close up is shown by the extent to which well-established banks and institutions were over-invested in property in the brief English boom of 1973.

Of all the indicators the most important is that of interest rates; booms of this kind follow low interest rates, but where there is a likelihood of inflation, with consequential negative balance of payments, it is inevitable that interest rates should increase, and share and other prices fall.

## GENERAL PLANNING TECHNIQUE

The list of factors making for change is sufficiently long and varied for it to be clear that there can be no one method or technique for dealing with them. Every business has to analyse its economy to see what elements are most important and then study those deeply so that a background of knowledge and a feel for the situation are created. The financial manager should therefore examine:

1. Factors affecting working capital: raw material prices; wages and salaries; selling prices; credit conditions; volume.
2. Factors affecting profitability: the foregoing and taxation; foreign exchange; competition.
3. Factors affecting availability of capital, equity, or loan: inflation and government policy; interest rates; balance of payments; general demand for capital; institutional policies (e.g. property versus equity).

Conventional budgeting and planning techniques have not proved useful in all cases in such unstable conditions. They necessarily tend to give insufficient weight to external conditions. Increasingly 'scenarios' based on a number of different assumptions about the environment are being used as a flexible framework for planning. Planning however can never provide complete safety, the cost of which, if it is possible, is inevitably prohibitive. The story of the New York store group basing all its planning on the assumption of a post-war slump illustrates the point.

## THE INDIVIDUAL BUSINESS

Most businesses in their life cycles have periods of rapid change, frequently because of changes in their environment, at other times because of changes in management. All tend to throw a heavy burden of responsibility on the chief financial officer. These changes will be considered under the following headings: changes in the nature of the business; problems of growth; and problems of contraction.

## Changes in the nature of the business

Experience shows that this is commoner than generally realised. Some examples within the experience of the writer have been:

1 A commodity trading business became a consumer goods producer.
2 A low-technology business became involved in high technology.
3 A capital-intensive business became involved in a business requiring high working capital.
4 A business trading principally in the domestic market became heavily involved in foreign operations.
5 A financial investment business became involved in manufacturing operations.
6 A large basically unprofitable business acquired a small very profitable activity.

Any reader of *Management Today* (in the UK) or *Fortune* (in the USA) will have seen examples, with their stories of success or failure, of these and similar situations. A rapid analysis will cover most changes of this kind that the financial manager has to contend with.

### A commodity trading business

In this case the business concerned was a world-famous cocoa and chocolate company whose primary business had been for many years trading in raw materials, i.e. cocoa powder and cocoa butter. In order to provide more stability (and for historical reasons) the business had been steadily increasing its operations in manufacturing proprietary chocolate goods.

The management of the business, including the financial management, was however heavily oriented to speculative transactions in the 'futures' markets, which they understood very well. The result was that cost information regarding the more recent manufacturing activities was entirely inadequate, as was budgeting and detailed financial control generally. The change in the nature of the operations and the management and financial control requirements were not realised until the company was acquired by an American industrial group.

## A low-technology business

The essential characteristics from a financial standpoint of the low-technology business (fertilisers) were:

1 Low rate of change.
2 Requirements for very large seasonal finance to carry stocks and finance customer credit.
3 'Lumpy' nature of capital investment with large producing units.
4 High cash generation due to capital-intensive nature of the activities.

The financial management had great difficulty in adapting its methods and standpoint to fast-moving, high-risk advanced-technology business, and was consequently very critical of a policy of employing highly paid executives, spending on speculative research and building plants for products for which no demand yet existed. The result was that a new department dealing with forecasting and financial appraisal had to be created parallel to the finance department to provide for the requirements of the high-technology business acquired and created.

## A capital-intensive business

The basic business was a well-known fishing organisation which was characterised by large fixed investment in ships (largely financed by government however), low working capital and high cash flow. When the business became involved in service businesses, particularly popular restaurants, it was not appreciated that much higher rates of return were required because of higher risk and low depreciation (with a consequential low cash flow). Without high rates of profit it was impossible to justify investment on a DCF basis.

## A business oriented to the domestic market

The business concerned, one of the best-known in the UK, embarked on an ambitious programme of overseas expansion, largely through acquisition. Its basic business was relatively slow-moving and the company had ample cash requirements for its normal business. The new overseas business was largely financed by loans, some of which were in foreign currencies. The acquisition programme did not produce sufficient profits, some loans had to be repaid in depreciated sterling, with heavy capital loss, and the group found itself in a major financial crisis. The financial management had little experience of conditions overseas, of making acquisitions or of the foreign loan market. Its financial control in its domestic business was excellent, but the skills required for the new policy were of a different kind, and the deficiencies could not be made good until too late.

*A financial investment company*

In this case, a large international group, the primary business was the acquisition of companies, the application of rigorous financial controls, and investment or divestment according to the subsequent results. There was little skill in industrial management and virtually no ability to turn unsatisfactory situations around. In this case, however, the higher management of the business had an excellent understanding of its own strengths and weaknesses, and sought in every case to underpin the situation by requiring a strong asset base. If the business was subsequently found to be less profitable than had been hoped, the policy was to sell the assets or the business as a going concern to someone better qualified to manage it.

*A basically unprofitable business*

Here the basic business was in a traditional conservative low-profit area, with a tendency for profits to decline over the longer term. The business, however, acquired more or less fortuitously a small subsidiary which was highly profitable and whose profits regularly 'topped' up the profits of the main business. The financial management was quite happy with this situation since the company regularly paid a satisfactory dividend. The financial control of the basic business was not sufficiently sophisticated to show that the rate of return, when corrected for inflation, was steadily declining, and that the correct policy was to withdraw progressively from the main business and concentrate on the profitable one. The day of reckoning came when the situation came to the notice of a well-known take-over group, who made a successful bid for the company, sold the assets of the main business, and rapidly expanded the business of the successful small subsidiary.

The basic lesson of these brief real-life cases is 'know your business'. The only real success story among these is that of the financial investment company whose management had an exceptionally clear understanding of what their expertise was. Since their ability to change businesses radically was very limited, other than in the area of financial control, they took exceptional care with the appraisal of the business to be acquired, and laid down extremely explicit conditions which the business had to satisfy, one of which was, as stated, a strong asset base. This policy was very coherent, its only weakness being that since its outlook was essentially financial, the industrial and commercial make-up of the group was very heterogeneous, with the result that the stock market, and particularly financial analysts, had difficulty in classifying it. This tended towards a rather low share price.

*Strengths and weaknesses*

In order that a business should avoid the kind of difficulties exemplified by the cases mentioned, what should it do? There is no short answer to this question as to how a business should come to know itself. At present the most powerful tool, in skilful hands, is strengths and weaknesses analysis, proposed by the Stanford Research Institute a good many years ago. However, this does not specify what key questions to ask in the financial area, or indeed in any other. First the basics of the problem have to be understood.[1] What kinds of business are there – what is the taxonomia of the genus? There are obviously fast-moving and slow-moving, market-oriented and production-oriented, high- and low-technology, capital-intensive and the reverse, and many other categories. For the financial manager a possible general form of profile would be as in Table 11.1 adding any special categories necessary in the case of his particular business.

Then a five or ten-year history, preferably in graph form, of the key ratios of the business: liquidity, 'quick' assets, stock-turn, sales/assets, return on investment, shareholders' funds/total capital employed etc.

But in fact most businesses are multi-faceted so that they have to be analysed as matrices (see Table 11.2).

The particular characteristics, as regards financial requirements and control, have to be studied for each product group or each 'business' – in effect here, a precision manufacturing and industrial 'business', a mass production industrial 'business' and so on. It is not enough to analyse the overall business from one standpoint.

---

[1] For this there is no better authority than the late Joel Dean whose *Managerial Economics* and other works are full of valuable insights.

**Table 11.1**
**Knowing your business – a profile**

| Fixed capital | Working capital | Profit-ability Earnings ─── Investment | Risk | Leverage (gearing) | Cash flow |
|---|---|---|---|---|---|

High
Low

In the absence of an explicit statement of strategy, obsolete patterns of corporate behaviour are extraordinarily difficult to modify. Where there is no clear concept of what current strategy is, the determination of what might be changed and why, must rest on either subjective or intuitive assessment. This becomes increasingly unreliable as the pace of change accelerates (Tilles, 1979).

(Part of the 'statement of strategy' is obviously the analysis of what the business is now.)

*The importance of trends*

For many financial managers there is a radical and difficult change in outlook which has to be made, namely to pay more attention to the

**Table 11.2**
**Analysis of business as a matrix**

| | | Production techniques | | |
|---|---|---|---|---|
| | | Precision manufacture | Mass production | Labour-intensive |
| | Durable consumer | | X | |
| Markets | Non-durable consumer | | | X |
| | Industrial | X | X | |

255

trends over the significant period than to short-term results – the current quarter or year. In this way structural changes can be recognised and if necessary changed; changes for example in fixed or working capital intensivity, return on assets (real, not inflationary), periodicity of earnings, and many other. The head of the successful business referred to above (who is himself a brilliant financial man) spent hours a day poring over just such statistics from the many businesses controlled.

*Information requirements*

Another lesson of these mini-cases is that different businesses require different types of financial control; some require rapid information, not necessarily extremely accurate, some, broad operating ratios, some, detailed product information. The financial manager, who is frequently the DP manager as well, has a great responsibility to keep the information available relevant to the particular business situation of the company.

In any substantial business there should be an audit not less frequently than every two years (small businesses have quicker reactions) of the whole computerised information system. The IBM information format can be used and a semi-permanent working party should be required to produce a detailed report on necessary changes. If the financial manager can give them detailed directions about any possible structural changes which may be needed, so much the better. Information which is not based on the real nature of the business can actually mask changes which are occurring, as for example changes in product mix, profitability etc.; information that is not regularly reviewed will be too detailed in some aspects, insufficiently detailed in others.

The importance of information in rapidly changing conditions cannot be over-emphasised. In a business of any size, without accurate, well structured information relating to current and future conditions, there will be a failure to take concerted action, since different parts of the business will be using different information, mostly relating to what are now irrelevant conditions.

The rapidity of change has brought so-called long-range planning into some disrepute because it gives more attention to internal factors, which are more controllable, than to the rapidly changing environment, which is more difficult to forecast. What is more appropriate to changing conditions is to analyse the key features of the business and to consider how each one may be affected by possible changes beyond the control of the business itself. It is not necessary that an elaborate econometric model of the business should be constructed. Since this is a highly sophisticated task where experts have to be used, it may actually interfere with the more important aspect, which is for everyone in the business to reach a consensus about what the business is and what strategy it should pursue.

The most important probable changes are used as the basis for several 'scenarios', each of which gives a picture of what may be the situation in several years' time. It cannot take account of all the possible variables, nor all possible combinations of them but, for example, a series of three or four financial scenarios developed from the opinions of a cross-section of management will give a better 'feel' of what might happen than a static five-year forecast. This method is increasingly used by companies which feel the impact of major environmental changes. Shell is one company that uses the approach.

## Problems of growth

The problems of growth, as far as they affect the financial manager, are generally more apparent than those just considered. They are not necessarily easier to deal with. In the first section of this chapter we have referred to the problems of high-technology business, such as Rolls Royce.[1]

In this kind of situation, the financial manager will frequently find himself fighting a trend of over-optimism on the one hand and a reluctance to provide specific estimates on the other. Dr Eberhard Rees of NASA has this to say: 'It is a strange fact that so few otherwise gifted managers don't see the significance and great importance of proper planning', (Rees, 1976).

In the pharmaceutical, computing or space business, to take a few examples, one product breakthrough can bring an enormous increase in the rate of growth of the business, and much less exciting businesses can have their periods of rapid growth, which we might define as more than 15 per cent per annum. The problem will be financing initially working capital and then probably fixed investment. There will be a variety of different cases.

1   Large increases in sales but low profitability due to write-offs or development costs. In this case the need for working capital

---

[1] This case is amply documented in published sources. See for example various British government publications 1969–70.

will further depress profits, so that the prospect of raising permanent capital will be endangered.

2 Increases in sales and profitability but with a high rate of working capital to sales so that after tax cash flow is insufficient to finance working capital. If the business is in the service area the asset base will probably be small, and the conditions as regards bank loans will probably be stringent.

3 'Lumpy' capital investment, i.e. due to technical factors increments of productive capacity will be very large. The construction and commissioning period will probably be rather long (in the UK 3–5 years) and output low in the first few years of production. In this case the difficulties may be very serious and only capable of solution by treating the venture as virtually a new one to be financed as such; by placing the plant in a highly subsidised development area, or by securing favourable credit terms from the suppliers of the plant and equipment.

4 In high-technology businesses, it is often not realised that the cost of inventing a new product is frequently only a fraction of the cost of developing it to a marketable stage and then subsequently marketing it. In the case of a new drug or pesticide, the cost of actually getting the product accepted by the FDA can easily be $5 million, before any of the product is sold.

5 The pursuit of volume irrespective of profit margins is also a frequent cause of trouble in conditions of rapid growth. If 'direct' costing is used there will be a tendency to think in terms of 'contribution' rather than actual profit, forgetting that if products give an inadequate 'contribution' to overhead and profit, the result must inevitably be an overall loss.

In this case there will be a definite maximum to the amount which can be financed at any one time, which will be a function of the working capital/sales relationship, the net cash flow and the assets base.

In virtually all cases of rapid growth, finance is a major problem requiring a mixture of sources:

1 Supplier credits – capital or raw material supplies.
2 Customer credits or advances (virtually bringing in the customer as a partner).
3 Government support, direct or indirect.
4 Medium-term bank credit, perhaps in the form of syndicated loans if the amount is large.

*Control in rapid growth*

It is extremely difficult to maintain tight financial control in times of rapid growth. Even seasoned executives may take the view that growth tomorrow will take care of all the problems of today.

Where capital construction is involved, if the production or engineering department does not maintain a PERT chart, then the financial manager will have to do so. This will show him not only the progress of the venture towards revenue earning but also the incidence of payments to suppliers. It is quite common to have revenue earning delayed because construction is out of phase, but payments to suppliers and contractors actually ahead of schedule.

On the revenue side, rapid growth also tends to weaken cost discipline; more overtime is worked than budgeted, raw materials are bought at higher prices and control of accounts receivable is relaxed; the result may be, and frequently is, an impairment of profit margins.

In these conditions, where optimism is too prevalent, flexible budgeting is extremely useful in showing the effects of failure to reach forecast sales, costs or margins. It is also very important to budget for the whole of the development phase, so that the development and marketing people have to make a definite commitment as to when the situation will show a profit – two or three years or whatever – and then how much.

## Problems of contraction

A business may find itself on a declining sales or profit trend for a variety of reasons – financial, technological, commercial or managerial. Financial management is not generally in a position to make major policy changes, although it should propose them if they are required. The major problem areas for financial management are:

1   The provision of information which highlights the areas where action is needed: sales, profit margins, costs, etc. Detailed analysis by products and departments will generally be necessary. Ratio analysis will always be useful.
2   The improvements of profits by: (a) cost and expense control; (b) The reduction of capital employed – this is frequently the more neglected term of the ratio profit/capital employed. Redundant assets may be sold, working capital squeezed; (c) Reduction in financial charges (a) and (b) will reduce the amount needed; there remains the possibility of reducing the

servicing cost by loans instead of overdraft, etc.

3 Increasing liquidity: reduced investment and release of both fixed and working capital may lead to a highly liquid position in spite of low real profits. Such a position invites bids from cash stripping companies.

4 The undervaluation of the balance sheet, which may include valuable properties and tax losses (credits); management will frequently be reluctant to revalue assets because it will make a low profit position appear even worse.

5 Possible repayment of capital to shareholders: normally there is a *prima facie* case for returning capital to investors when it cannot be profitably used for the purpose for which the company was constituted.

## THE FINANCIAL MANAGER'S ROLE

The financial manager has a dual role:

1 He is the manager of a service department which, like the personnel department, covers the whole business.

2 He is chiefly responsible for a vital technical function, on which everyone will have views but where he has the final responsibility, subject to the Board.

The case studies show failures in both roles, not necessarily exclusively or principally the fault of the financial manager; he may have informed management of the needs of the business. In some cases there was the failure to generate vital information, on costs for example, in others to appreciate the implications of changes in the type of business, in different types of business economy. In financial terms there is a very great difference between a high-technology and a low-technology business, and the principles that apply to one will bring disaster in the other.

It is likely that top management will tend to view the business in terms of marketing or production, relying on the finance manager to interpret the policy himself in terms of accounting requirements, financial reporting to management and, frequently, capital requirements. He will arrange for the financial implications of policies to be brought out in the annual budget, supplemented perhaps by a three- or five-year financial plan, with a forecast of cash requirements and a budget of capital expenditure.

These estimates and forecasts will all be produced on a basis of sales, production and other departmental estimates, and so will tend to be static. As has been emphasised, and also to place one year's figures in a larger framework of three to five years so that the general trend of the business can be appreciated, the financial manager will need to bring some flexibility into the picture by showing what the implications of higher or lower figures may mean – a 5 per cent increase in sales, ten days increase in accounts receivable etc.

## CONCLUSION

Change of whatever kind – in the environment of the business, in the nature of its operations, of growth or decline – are all challenges for the financial manager. He is increasingly required to be a competent economist and acute businessman as well as a highly qualified accountant.

## REFERENCES AND ADDITIONAL READING

Drucker, P., *The Age of Discontinuity,* Heinemann and Pan, 1969.
Rees, E., paper on the 'Apollo Program' submitted to the 1976 CIOS Congress, Munich, Germany.
Tilles, S., 'Making Strategy Explicit', quoted in Ansoff, Igor (ed.), Business Strategy, Penguin Modern Management Readings, 1979.

# 12

# Planning and Control of Research and Development

**A. W. Pearson**

*As pointed out by Avison Wormald in the preceding chapter, a significant aspect of the change which is continually affecting business operations lies in changes in technology. In the following chapter Alan Pearson, of the Manchester Business School, who has specialised for many years in the problems associated with research and development, examines the factors involved in the successful planning and control of this business expense.*

*He insists that, as with any other business investment, the benefits derived from research and development should exceed the costs. The obvious problem in the case of this kind of expense is that the benefits likely to be derived from a particular project, or of a number of associated projects, are uncertain, and may not materialise at all. For this reason monitoring and control processes must quickly recognise when significant changes occur and point to the necessary corrective action, which might, in the extreme case, be the cancellation of the project.*

*In monitoring the expenditure the major need is to control the timescale of the work in relation to the output; the cost will be largely controlled by the number of people assigned to the work. The total funds to be allocated to R and D need to be based on identified organisational requirements as a result of 'top-down planning'; while at the same time the planning and control of individual projects will be based on 'bottom-up planning', for which the charting of key decision points or milestones will be helpful. The communication of information will be immensely aided by the computer, and it is noteworthy that most writers in this handbook refer to the immense potential available to business in the modern developments of electronic data processing.*

*The author of this chapter reiterates the warnings of other contributors of the danger of incurring large cash outflows with benefits far into the future but the inevitable long time period involved in many projects emphasises the need for close monitoring of progress. His long experience of the research and development area leads him to conclude that 'most attempts to impose standardised systems seem to have met with little success', and this thought again reflects the opinion of other writers dealing with other aspects of business expense. So far as R and D is concerned Alan Pearson suggests that financial planning and control should be motivational rather than penalising and the process should secure the involvement of the research teams.*

Investment in research and development must be looked at in the same way as any other investment in the business – the benefits it produces must exceed the costs. However, it is by no means easy to ensure that the practice lines up with the theory. The available evidence from a wide range of companies suggests that the costs incurred in the R and D phase of well-managed projects can be reasonably controlled, but that the time to completion is often significantly underestimated. Problems are also frequently encountered in the implementation phase and this causes further delays. Lengthening of the timescale to completion can have adverse effects upon the benefit stream which may not only be delayed but may be significantly altered due to external influences, for example, competitive activity and changes in economic, social, political and environmental factors.

Financial planning of R and D expenditures must recognise these uncertainties, particularly with respect to longer-term work, and any monitoring or control procedure must be capable of recognising significant changes and indicating corrective action as early as possible.

In examining ways and means by which this might be done, it is useful to approach the problem from two directions: first, to consider the overall allocation of funds to R and D based on identified organisational needs, and second, to consider the planning and monitoring of individual projects. The evidence is that attention to the former has a significant influence upon the success of the latter, allowing individual initiatives to be encouraged and managed within an agreed overall framework. The two approaches are complementary and in most organisations both will be used as starting points, with links becoming apparent at a very early stage, as the next two sections aim to show.

## TOP-DOWN PLANNING

In the late 1960s the word 'relevance' was frequently heard in discussions about the allocation of funds to R and D. Very simply this was meant to direct attention to the need to support R and D work which if successful would be put to effective use by the organisation. In the late 1970s the phrase 'top-down planning' was used very frequently. This refers to an approach which systematically questions where the organisation is going, and examines the structure of the organisation in terms of its size, the nature of the component parts, their growth, profitability and their strengths and weaknesses in relation to competitive and other environmental forces. The purpose of this exercise is to identify where the organisation is likely to end up if it continues in the way it has done in the past, and where it may need to change in order to improve its viability in the future.

Such an analysis will usually be undertaken by individuals or groups of people who are responsible for, and knowledgeable about, a specific area of activity and will often follow organisational lines, for example, focused on products or areas of like characteristics. Within the analysis a 'technological audit' should be undertaken and this will reveal both the level and type of R and D activity which can be directly related to the support of specific areas of the organisation. Such information then forms the necessary background to detailed discussion about the relationship (or 'relevance') of the R and D expenditures to the needs of the organisation, with emphasis being placed on the longer- as well as the short-term needs.

The time orientation of the people involved in such discussions may be different, with R and D tending to look further ahead than, say, production or marketing people. This must be accepted. The purpose of top-down planning is to focus attention on the organisation needs and each function should have an opportunity to make its view clear about these needs, bearing in mind the specialist knowledge it can contribute to the discussion. Differences of opinion are best brought out into the open at this stage, and it must be accepted that there is no certainty about the future. All opinions must be listened to. Where wide differences arise more information may need to be collected, and more views canvassed. However, it may well be that such differences still persist, and in this case it may be necessary to consider the variation of views as being a good representation of the actual situation, i.e. to accept that a high level of uncertainty exists about the future. In this case a decision may have to be taken to authorise a programme of work which will cover the different views and hence allow flexibility. This will almost certainly require the allocation of more resources to the area, with a consequent reduction in the risk. If this is the accepted strategy efforts must be focused on identifying those features of the situation which can be monitored to indicate at the earliest possible time where most needs to be done.

Top-down planning is therefore a way of focusing senior management attention on the needs of the organisation. It forces people to ask questions about the relationship between the expenditures on the different functional areas and the alternative futures which the organisation may encounter. In this process the R and D people should have every opportunity to put their own views forward and to make a significant contribution in respect of, for example, potential new technologies which may be seen as threats or opportunities. A thorough discussion of all these issues will reveal areas for attention and will generate commitment to a project, by the organisation and by the project leader and the team. Such a commitment is a necessary condition for success.

It is not, however, also a sufficient condition, as many champions of 'non-successful' projects know to their disappointment. Many other factors need to be taken into account and as some of these change over time, for example legislation, it is important to have a planning and monitoring procedure which will provide useful information to all parties. Such a procedure can form an important part of the 'bottom-up' form of planning.

## BOTTOM-UP PLANNING

This approach implies that individual activities or projects are the starting point for analysis. In many areas this is indeed the case. Ideas arise in a variety of ways: from discussions, casual meetings, problems, etc., and they often form the basis for a request for funds to develop the idea into a proposal backing a request for a larger allocation of resources. Requests for small amounts of funds for developing ideas should always be encouraged and seriously considered. In general such ideas will lie within areas which will be of potential relevance, simply because they will utilise the skills of people who have been recruited in line with the organisation's needs. The major cost of encouraging such requests is in fact the 'opportunity' one of not applying the same resources to other ongoing or preselected projects. However, the positive side of this is the increased motivation which can be generated by allowing some freedom for individuals to pursue their own ideas, and to convert them into projects which they can 'champion'. In most organisations the decision as to how much of this type of activity to encourage, and in which direction, is left to the R and D director, whose responsibility it is to develop and maintain an exciting and creative environment which will be a positive asset to the organisation. Many R and D directors report a lack of initiative on the part of their scientists and technologists in bringing forward new ideas, rather than any excessive demand. In some organisations this is partly due to pressure from projects of a more immediate concern to the organisation's needs, which itself can be due to lack of an adequate planning and monitoring system.

The important point about the bottom-up planning approach is that it focuses attention on the level of resources which will be required to service all the projects which have been accepted into the R and D portfolio. If these projects are to be progressed well they cannot command in total more resources than are available, at any one time. This may sound an obvious statement, but the evidence is that many organisations consistently fail to complete projects on time due to the pressure on resources. If this is the case, corrective action must be taken either to reduce the number of projects which are being progressed simultaneously, or to bring in assistance from outside agencies, for example contract research organisations. Both of these are essentially short-term measures. In the long term serious consideration needs to be given either to reducing the number of projects which are accepted into the portfolio or to increasing the level of in-house resources in particular areas subject to delays. If the first of these alternatives is chosen it will be necessary to examine carefully all the projects and to assess their relative importance to the organisation, so that any trimming down can be done in areas which are likely to have less significant effects. This can only be done after due consideration of the plans produced by the approach discussed in the previous section, and hence the top-down and bottom-up approach will come together when questions of direction and priority are raised. An important point to note is that unless this trimming down is well managed there will be a continuing scramble for resources which will lead to the not uncommon situation in which progress meetings end up as being primarily concerned with establishing priorities. The inevitable consequence is a lowering of motivation of the people involved in low-priority projects and a reduction in financial return when compared with that planned.

## PLANNING AND MONITORING

The success of the approaches outlined in the previous two sections will depend upon the degree to which the performance on individual projects matches up to the expectations. The purpose of a good planning and monitoring procedure is to ensure that any differences can be quickly identified and appropriate action taken. Those which have been found to be successful in practice are designed to monitor future expectations as well as past achievements. A number of methods is available for doing this, and the choice should be made in the light of the organisation's needs, with one point being emphasised – the simplest and most flexible approach should be adopted. Many people still consider that the introduction of formal planning and control procedures into R and D will stifle creativity and initiative. Most attempts to impose standardised systems seem to have met with little success. It is comparatively easy for an individual or group to get around a system they do not see as useful and which takes up time they feel could be better allocated to their scientific and technical activities.

Planning and monitoring must be seen as a positive aid to the individual, the project group and the organisation. It must place emphasis on obtaining and presenting information in a form which is useful for management purposes. This leads to a variety of methods being used for the planning of individual projects, the choice depending upon the type of work and the management style of the project leader. However, there is a need for a reporting and monitoring procedure which will provide common information across the whole of an R and D establishment. These two are not incompatible, and approaches which have been found useful in practice are discussed in the following sections.

## Project planning

Several methods have been described in the literature and further information can be obtained from the articles listed in the bibliography. Briefly they fall into the following categories.

### The bar chart

This is probably the oldest and yet still the most used method in many R and D establishments. The chart is really a calendar planner on which individual activities are identified and the time over which they are expected to be progressed indicated by a bar. The degree to which a particular activity has been completed is often indicated by a dotted line under the main bar. The advantages of this approach are its simplicity and its visual impact. It is not, however, always easy to update it, and not so easy to show dependencies between activities. Although both these disadvantages can be overcome, more complicated projects are often planned using a form of network diagram.

### The network diagram

This can take a variety of forms. Until recently the most commonly met was the simple form of PERT or activity on arrow diagram. Standard computer programs are available which allow easy presentation and analysis of such networks and also easy updating. In most cases the same programmes allow for the printing out of a standard bar chart for any section or all of the network. They also include facilities for multi-project scheduling and for resource levelling. These can be very useful. Networks of this type are most commonly encountered in larger projects of a more development type and particularly where external inputs are required, and external deadlines have to be met. They are used also where standard practices must be followed to satisfy, for example, government and legislative requirements.

Alternative forms of network diagrams are available, notably the activity on node, or activity in box method sometimes referred to as the metra potential method (MPM). As the name implies, the activities are written inside the boxes or nodes and these are linked by arrows which show the dependencies. This variation is claimed to provide more flexibility at the initial project design stage and is more closely related to the engineering flow diagrams with which many scientists and technologists are already familiar.

Arguments against the use of networks have, however, been put forward by many people who believe they are too structured and inflexible and not capable of handling the uncertainties associated with R and D projects. Some of these arguments have been countered by the further development of the methods, for example, to allow alternative outcomes to be considered at any node or activity completion point. At such points allowance can also be made for recycling by incorporating feedback loops into the diagram.

### Research planning diagrams (RPDs)

A further development of the network diagram, essentially following on from the activity in box approach, specifically calls for the incorporation of decision nodes. This is a very valuable addition in an area like R and D and the approach has been generally found most useful. Another point in its favour is the similarity to the commonly accepted logic or flow diagram which is used in other areas of business activity.

### The milestone chart

This is perhaps the simplest of all approaches and is generally used to provide a summary of the information which has been spelled out in more detail using one or more of the previously outlined methods. As will be seen later, it can form the basis of a very effective reporting and monitoring system. The basic characteristic of the approach is the identification of milestones, or key events, which can be readily identified in advance and recognised when they occur in time. In the case of R and D projects these may be defined in terms of, for example, technical specifications which have to be met, tests which must be completed, pilot plants built, production facilities designed, or specific market research information gathered, etc. The dates by which these activities should be completed then become the milestones. These will often be associated with specific review meetings.

The milestone chart is used in many organisations and expanded versions often include a breakdown of the activities by function or by individual, so that the responsibility for actions can be clearly identified. For this reason the name 'activity matrix' has been used to describe this form of presentation.

## Monitoring

The purpose of outlining some of the approaches to planning individual projects was to illustrate the variety. As stated earlier, the preference for a particular method will depend upon the type of project, and the management style of the team leader. Any method must be seen as an aid to, and not as a substitute for, management.

The project leader is responsible for planning, or agreeing the plans, and for progressing the project. However, it must be accepted that many things can change during the course of the work, and corrective action may need to be taken during the life of a project. The first person to recognise this is likely to be the project leader, and in general it is he who will be responsible for taking the necessary initiatives. The purpose of a good monitoring procedure is to record progress and to report actions which have been taken which were not originally planned and which might have consequences for the organisation. In addition it should highlight, if necessary, where actions are not being taken at the correct time.

The monitoring procedure should be essentially a communication system which adds to, but does not replace, the direct contact which is always necessary between the various parties interested in a particular project. It will almost certainly provide some historical information, but its value will be significantly increased if it also focuses attention on future expectations.

*Historical analysis*

Most organisations require all people involved in project work to record on a standard form information about the allocation of their time on different activities. Such forms are usually completed weekly and relate to the actual expenditure of time over the immediately preceding time period. Breakdown of time may be in half-hour intervals, half or whole days. This is converted into cost information by the use of simple factors based on the salaries of different categories of individuals with overheads being added in many cases. Sometimes the accumulated costs form the basis for direct charging to customers or departments within the organisation. In most cases they are presented so as to show the actual expenditure on the project alongside that originally agreed. Such information may be given in the form of a cumulative expenditure chart, but it is obvious that such information is of little value unless one can be clear about how much progress has actually been made on the scientific and technical work. That is why it is essential to have some form of plan, along the lines discussed earlier, set out in such a way that the actual work progress can be assessed at regular intervals against identifiable and agreed criteria.

An important point to note is that it is the exception rather than the rule for individuals to be working on only one project at any given time. If this is the case, it must be accepted that information about time, and hence cost, allocation to individual projects cannot be accurately assessed. Experience therefore suggests that although it is usually thought necessary to collect historical information on project costs it is not of very great practical use for management purposes. Clearly it can be used as an indicator of how much effort is being applied to a project, but its value is diminished if it cannot be directly related to the expected technical progress as set out in the original plan. One way of doing this is through the milestone chart. As defined earlier, a milestone is a point at which agreed and recognisable criteria have to be met. The actual cost of reaching a given milestone can therefore be compared with the original estimate and a simple chart can be used to illustrate progress (see Figure 12.1).

This figure shows that milestone 1 was reached on time, but at lower cost, 2 on time but at higher cost, and 3 again on time, but with cost exceeding expectation. Delays in time to reach any given milestone would be shown on such a chart as movement of the numbers to the right of the vertical line through the original estimates. However, such a chart only indicates actual achievement against milestones and information about progress between these key points cannot be easily gained without a more detailed breakdown of the project into smaller

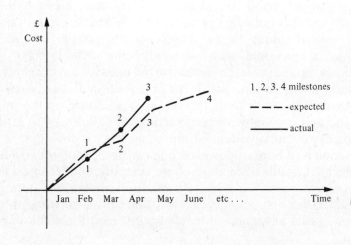

**Fig. 12.1   Progress illustrated by milestone chart**

activities. It is possible to do this and at the extreme every activity can be individually monitored and progress of cost and time against expectation almost continuously assessed. In this case computer analysis of a network-based plan is useful, but in general the amount of information required and generated becomes too much to handle effectively, and it often leads to an anti-reaction from scientists and technologists who think too much of their time is taken up in what they see as unnecessary administration. This is particularly so in projects with a relatively high degree of uncertainty, where they feel they may require to take initiatives which were not specifically planned but which will ultimately be of advantage in steering the project to a successful conclusion. Such initiatives should be encouraged in R and D and it has been found possible to allow a reasonable degree of flexibility by staying with the broad milestone approach but calling for information about future expectations as well as accounting for past expenditures as outlined in the following section.

*Progress charts*

When a project is selected and a project leader identified a plan is drawn up and agreed. This plan may be based on one of the approaches outlined earlier, but the key point is that it should highlight important decision points or milestones. The number of these will depend upon the type and size of project. They need not be very close together, but they should not be so far apart that the opportunity for taking corrective action is delayed too long. They may coincide with review points, and estimates of both time and cost to reach them should be made however uncertain these may appear to be at the outset. Such estimates can be updated as more information becomes available and as such the learning of the project is more clearly indicated.

This information could be added to the simple historical analysis chart described earlier, but this would very quickly become confusing if many changes occurred in the estimates of the time and cost required to reach future milestones. An alternative is to consider the time and cost variables separately and it has proved to be most useful to emphasise the time variable in the first instance partly because this can be more accurately monitored but also because time delays usually indicate the need for corrective action which if not taken is likely to reduce considerably the financial return on a project.

The simplest of the time-based charts in use has been referred to as a 'slip' chart, because it very clearly shows when progress is slipping (see Table 12.1).

**Table 12.1**
**Example of a slip chart**

|  |  | Calendar time | | | | | |
|---|---|---|---|---|---|---|---|
|  |  | Jan | Feb | Mar | Apr | May | June | etc. |
|  | Jan |  | 1 | 2 | 3 | 4 | 5 | 6 |
|  | Feb |  | 1 | 2 | 3 | 4 | 5 |  |
| Review | Mar |  | 1 | 2 |  | 3 | 4 | 5 |
| time | Apr |  | 1 | 2 |  | 3 | 4 |  |
|  | May |  | 1 | 2 |  | 3 |  | 4 |
|  | Jun |  |  |  |  |  |  |  |
|  | etc. |  |  |  |  |  |  |  |

The numbers refer to key stages or milestones in the project, and the chart acts as a historical record of how the estimates of the time required to reach a particular stage have changed as the project is progressed. In this respect it provides future-oriented information which is extremely valuable for planning purposes. Anticipated slippage is clearly shown as a movement to the right in the number associated with the milestone, and commands the attention of all interested parties. The chart therefore acts as an extremely powerful communication device. The information contained in the graphical presentation can quite easily be put on to a computer. Print-outs can then be obtained as required of the progress of any individual project or of groups of projects associated, for example, with one area of activity or under a single management, or relevant to and perhaps supported by a particular client.

Other forms of presentation can also be of value. For example, progress against expectations for an individual project can be portrayed graphically (see Figure 12.2).

A plot of the progress of a project on these two dimensions will show up deviations from plans as overruns above the line and ahead of schedule below the line. Both these methods are simple to use and are visually very easy to understand. They clearly indicate deviations from plan, not only those that have occurred, but also any that are expected in future periods. This is most important if corrective action is to be taken.

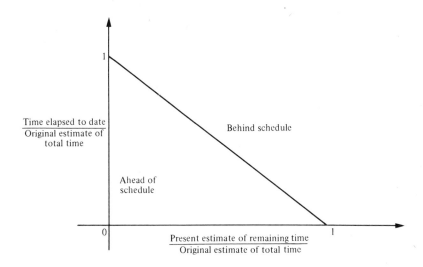

**Fig. 12.2  Progress against expectations for an individual project using time dimensions**

The reason for choosing time as the major variable on which to focus was discussed earlier. Overruns on time are more frequent and often much larger in many projects.

The effects of such overruns on the financial return can be very large. However, this does not mean that cost can be ignored. Historical methods of accounting were discussed earlier, and these can be extended to include future projections in a number of ways. Using the same format as one of the progress charts described earlier leads to the presentation in Fig. 12.3.

An organisation may choose to emphasise time or cost reporting as its needs dictate. However, it is obvious that both can provide useful information and taken together will often provide additional information. For example, keeping time and cost progress charts side-by-side will enable slippage in either or both of these parameters to be considered at the same time. Some conclusions which might then be drawn are as follows:

1 Time overruns but not cost overruns suggest a lack of effort on the project.

2 Cost overruns but not time overruns suggest problems are

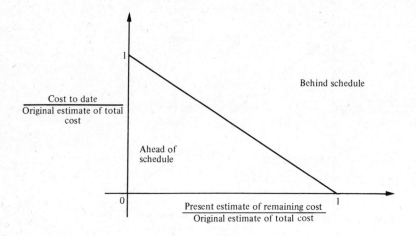

**Fig. 12.3  Progress against expectations for an individual project using cost dimensions**

> being encountered but extra effort is being allocated which looks like overcoming them.
> 3  Cost overruns and time overruns suggest there are problems which are proving more difficult to handle.

These three alternatives will require different types of management action and the value of the reporting system is the simple indication which is given of the possible area for attention.

## PORTFOLIO ANALYSIS

The approaches described above are essentially designed for assisting in the management of individual projects. The project leader and his team are the people who supply the information and as such are the first people to identify deviations from the plan. They are therefore able to take corrective action if this is within their terms of reference, or to suggest alternative courses of action if they require additional resources and/or support from other key people in the organisation. The value of the approaches must therefore be that they do not take away the responsibility for managing a project from those most closely concerned with its progress. Essentially what they do is recognise the uncertainty associated with research and development and encourage project leaders to provide regular position reports in the light of the progress made.

The individual planning methods focus attention on key decision points, milestones or review points. At these times the project leader will be expected to make a more detailed report on the project. Such review points will normally be agreed in advance. The progress chart, by its very nature, provides much more up-to-date information about the state of a project but without requiring this information in a detailed form. If milestones are not going to be met then the sooner this is recognised the better. In some cases this can lead to more rapid corrective action being taken; in others it may lead to an earlier decision to terminate a project which would otherwise become a cash drain with little prospect of providing an adequate financial return.

An important point about the progress chart approach is that it is clearly first and foremost an information system, with the project leader at the centre of the information network and primarily responsible for any necessary actions. It is possible to go further than this and provide some information to management on a more general basis. This can be done by presenting the information from the progress charts in an alternative form. Simple ratios can be calculated from the basic information already provided for the progress charts in a number of ways. For example

$$\frac{1 - \dfrac{\text{Cost to date}}{\text{Original estimate of total cost}}}{\dfrac{\text{Present estimate of remaining cost}}{\text{Original estimate of total cost}}}$$

becomes $\dfrac{\text{Original estimate of total cost} - \text{cost to date}}{\text{Present estimate of remaining cost}}$

A ratio of

    1 indicates a project on schedule for cost (but not necessarily time)

    $<1$ indicates a project on which overspending is likely

They can be used in conjunction with other information, e.g. expenditure to date, but they must be treated with some caution. They can clearly form part of a management by exception system but here there is a danger that they will take away the main feature of the progress chart which is its value as a communication device. Management by exception systems can too easily become the tools of people who know little about either the technical side of the work or the needs of the organisation in respect of the output. Some projects may need urgent attention when only very small exceptions are reported; others can tolerate much larger variations without causing undue alarm. The people who should be most concerned are those closely concerned with the project and outside interference should only be required if they are not taking the necessary actions. The use of ratios must therefore be seen essentially as a back-up mechanism, used mostly for senior management to monitor key projects. Their value will be diminished if an attempt is made to use them as the main control mechanism.

However, it is useful to consider whether additional information of a more general nature might be obtained about the overall performance of an R and D establishment which could be put to good use. There are two particular approaches which should be given serious consideration. The first focuses on the factors which cause delays to projects and the second on the outputs from projects in relation to the expectations. Obviously these two are interrelated, but can be usefully examined separately.

## Constraints on individual projects

The progress chart is built up from information supplied by the project leader. Deviations from the original plan will be due to a variety of causes. A simple request for information about the nature of factors causing delays can be very illuminating. In practice these usually fall into a few categories, for example lack of resources, external factors, technical problems.

An analysis of all the projects in the R and D establishment may also reveal a significant number of delays due to the same factor. If so, corrective action should be taken, which will reinforce the value of the planning and monitoring system, as people will see that the information they are providing is being used to their advantage. For example, if lack of resources is a common constraint then action to increase the level of resources or to reduce the number of projects will be much appreciated. It will also be of considerable motivational value to project leaders who will have to spend less of their time fighting for priority and working with inadequate support facilities.

The advantage of the progress chart is that it focuses attention on any likely changes in future resource requirements on individual projects due to changes in expectations about the achievement of particular milestones. Taken over the R and D establishment as a whole this information is of great value from the resource allocation point of view.

## Output assessment

At the beginning of the chapter the potential value of top-down planning was discussed. The actual value of this approach will be partly determined by the ability of the R and D establishment to complete the projects which are agreed to be relevant to the different needs of the organisation. A coding system can be developed which shows the relationship of an individual project to a particular need, e.g. business area, short or long term, product or process development, etc. Projects can then be identified readily and at appropriate intervals, say quarterly or annually; all projects related to a given need can be examined and their progress noted. This analysis may well reveal areas for concern, for example, that short-term projects are being progressed more effectively than long-term ones, etc. From the financial planning point of view, it will provide a simple breakdown of the expenditures and the progress which has been made against the expectation in each area. Deviations between these two can then be examined to see whether corrective action needs to be taken.

It must also be remembered that an R and D establishment will have activities which cover a wide range of uncertainties. The proportion of low to high probability of success projects will depend upon the needs of the organisation at a particular point in time as well as the attitudes to risk of the key decision makers. This balance must be reviewed at regular intervals and the monitoring procedure should highlight those projects in which the uncertainty is not decreasing over time at the expected rate. Again, the project leader will be the first to recognise the lack of uncertainty reduction, but this will also be highlighted through the lack of progress towards meeting defined milestones within the agreed timescales and cost. Decisions on whether to continue with such projects are not easy to make, as many major innovations have come about after sustained effort over many years with success always looking possible but always appearing to be just out of reach. In such cases the size of the potential benefits will usually be the deciding factor in obtaining further backing, but this must be balanced against the potential losses of not being successful, or of being beaten by competitive activity. There are many examples of organisations falling into difficulties through backing innovations requiring excessively large cash outflows with benefits appearing very far in the future.

## CONCLUSIONS

A financial planning and control system is just as necessary in research and development as in any other area. However, it must take into account the uncertainty surrounding the activity. It must be flexible and it does not need to be complicated. It must be motivational rather than penalising and the responsibility for management has to remain at the level at which the work is being done.

There is considerable evidence that the internal evaluation of projects is very compatible with external evaluations where the goals are agreed and accepted. The aim therefore is to provide the right environment in which the project leader and his team are motivated to be honest with themselves and with the organisation in the reporting of progress. The monitoring system can then be oriented towards signalling deviations about which other people might express different concerns than those most closely connected with the work. Such signals will encourage communication and agreement on actions which will be of benefit to all interested parties. The emphasis is on the positive aspects of monitoring which are too often hidden by disagreements about the reasons for deviations and the implied blame which often leads to the adoption of defensive positions by the different parties.

Planning methods can be allowed to vary within the organisation, although there may be some advantage in agreeing the type of approach which is likely to be most suitable for different types of projects. Monitoring is more useful if there is a high degree of standardisation, so that comparative analysis can be done and attention paid to those factors which will improve the overall management of the R and D establishment.

In looking at possible approaches more emphasis is placed on forward than on historical analysis, with time being considered of prime importance. It must be remembered that the largest part of the cost of an R and D establishment is in the people, and unless significant amounts of outside work can be rapidly commissioned it is not easy to overspend significantly on the overall budget. The evidence is that many organisations fail to live up to their expectations in respect of completed projects in any given time period. It must therefore be more sensible to develop a monitoring system which focuses on outputs and the approaches outlined in the previous sections are of assistance in this respect.

The basic characteristics of the suggested approaches should be carefully examined before any new system is considered, as experience suggests that the imposition of formal planning and control systems on R and D has not met with a great deal of success. Any system which is likely to be accepted and effectively used will be one which can be seen to be helpful to all parties. In this respect a monitoring of the system itself is also necessary, so that adaptations can be made in the light of experience, to ensure that the maximum use continues to be made of the information generated.

## REFERENCES AND ADDITIONAL READING

Beastall, H., 'The relevance tree in Post Office R & D', *R & D Management,* vol. 1, no. 2, February 1971.

Bergen, S. A., 'The new product matrix', *R & D Management,* vol. 5, no. 2, February 1975.

Brooke, D. G., 'The use of slip charts to review research projects', *R & D Management,* vol. 4, no. 1, October 1973.

Davies, D. G. S., 'Research planning diagrams', *R & D Management,* vol. 1, no. 1, October 1970.

Fishlock, D., *The Business of Science,* Associated Business Programmes, London, 1975.

Hardingham, R. P., 'A simple model approach to multi-project monitoring', *R & D Management,* vol. 1, no. 1, October 1970.

Longbottom, D. A. and Hay, S. J. D., 'Experience in the use of research planning diagrams in a synthetic fibres R & D unit', *R & D Management,* vol. 7, no. 3, June 1977.

Parker, R. C. and Sabberwal, A. J. P., 'Controlling R & D projects by networks', *R & D Management,* vol. 1, no. 3, June 1971.

# 13

# Development Overseas

**Avison Wormald**

*What is the justification for the inclusion of a chapter on development overseas under the generic title of 'change' which is the subject of this part? A number of concerns are multinational in their operations and, as Elwood Miller points out in the next chapter, this category in strictness covers both a few large and many small businesses. Others which do not fall within the generally accepted notion of 'multinational' engage as a matter of course in worldwide activities through branches, subsidiaries and associate companies; and for an even larger number exporting is an integral part of the business. However, it is when a company first extends its operations into overseas markets that a fundamental change occurs in the nature of the business. Furthermore, as the author of this chapter points out, any form of international activity is fraught with continual change, much of it unpredictable, in political, economic and monetary aspects.*

*The author, who has held top level appointments in international companies, lists the main problems of development overseas as: communications, complexity and risk. These factors are especially prominent in connection with questions of credit, foreign exchange and finance. The chapter contains a great deal of practical advice for dealing with these questions and also refers to the vexed problems associated with transfer pricing and the minimisation of taxation. The chapter ends with a reference to the different bases available for consolidating the accounts of parent and subsidiary where different currencies are involved. Many of the specialised accounting problems introduced by the author are developed in the next chapter in relation to multinational companies.*

Since the time of Adam Smith and the publication of *The Wealth of Nations* it had been increasingly accepted that international trade was advantageous to most countries. Then rather more than a century ago Ricardo showed that even when nations could be self-sufficient, there was generally an advantage in exchanging goods where there was a comparative advantage in the production of the same goods. If the advanced countries have sometimes retreated into protectionism it has not been so much from conviction as from disequilibria and pressures.

The individual businessman or company follows this trend perhaps not because of economic conviction but because it offers him an opportunity which his government encourages him to take. For him, however, it offers special problems in three main areas, namely communication, complexity and risk (Wormald, 1973). These problems affect all aspects of his business, and perhaps the financial area more than most.

## THE ROLE OF THE CHIEF FINANCIAL OFFICER

To a very large extent it depends on the chief financial officer whether business can be done at all in the international field, and if it is done, whether it is continuously and consistently profitable.

In the first place, the ability and willingness to extend credit to the overseas buyer is often critical in making a sale. There is, particularly in major capital equipment transactions, a good deal of open or disguised credit competition, although attempts are constantly made to limit some features of it by international agreement.

Credit has to be financed, so that the ability to finance it in the cheapest way is crucial. Moreover, credit represents risk, of payment and frequently of exchange, so that the ability to assess the risk and to use the most appropriate means to limit it is also very important. Both these factors are reflected in some form in price, so that financial decisions are those which determine whether the business is profitable or not at prices which are competitive enough to obtain it.

The raising of local capital, the protection of the company's assets in foreign countries, taxation and the remittance of profits are further areas where the chief financial officer has a key role to play.

For every country its currency is one of the most important manifestations of its sovereignty and every country has its own fiscal and economic policies. Even where these are liberal and even favourable to the foreign business, they have to be studied and taken into account.

## FOREIGN EXCHANGE

The simplest external transaction leads to problems of pricing and payment where the financial manager is involved. The price to the foreign buyer can be in the seller's currency, the buyer's or a third 'international' currency such as the US dollar. For the seller, his own currency has the advantage that he knows exactly how much he is going to receive, although he (or his government) may prefer another currency if his own is depreciating rapidly in value or if he wishes to make payments abroad, where another currency may be more acceptable.

The buyer, on the other hand, will have to purchase the necessary foreign currency, and in most cases the rate of exchange between his own currency and the foreign currency will not be fixed. So at least between the time of the quotation and the acceptance there may be a change, favourable or unfavourable. He therefore may well prefer a quotation in his own currency or in a third, such as the US dollar, which may be more familiar to him than the seller's.

The fact that the foreign exchange transaction offers both sides the opportunity for gain as well as loss is generally immaterial, since the businessman, either buyer or seller, will generally prefer not to have to bother about the speculative element. That is for the professional risk taker in currencies.

In the first place, the buyer can merely purchase the necessary foreign exchange to pay for the goods when he decides to accept the offer made. In this way he knows exactly how much the goods cost him. The foreign exchange can be deposited in a bank and will earn interest. The rate of interest, however, even on a time deposit, will frequently be below that obtainable by some alternative use of the funds. But in this way virtually all the risk has been covered, although if the exchange rate moves in favour of his own currency there will obviously have been a *'manque à gagner'* or a lost opportunity, since he would now be able to buy the currency cheaper.

It will not always be convenient to immobilise funds in this way, a long time ahead perhaps of the payment which has to be made, or the rate of interest which can be earned may not be considered sufficient. In this case there exists the alternative of the forward exchange market. This may be of advantage to the seller also, in the contrary case where he has quoted in the buyer's currency, or in a third currency; he may wish to know at the time of concluding the transaction how much he will receive in his own currency.

The forward exchange market, to which access may be obtained through any major commercial bank, will provide a quotation for a contract to buy or sell a wide range of currencies for delivery up to normally six months ahead. Contracts for longer periods are possible but can be very expensive.

According to the view the international money market takes of the two currencies involved, the price of the currency purchased may be higher or lower than the present price. Equally, when the contract matures and the currency is delivered it may be found that the contract price may be higher or lower than the then prevailing price. The rates for the principal currencies against the pound sterling are quoted daily in the London *Financial Times* for one month and three months.

If the forward exchange contract is made through the buyer's normal bank it may involve no down-payment at all, and therefore the funds are available for different uses. In other cases it may involve the payment of 5–10 per cent of the value, according to the credit status of the buyer and the risk involved in the particular currency. The buyer of the 'forward exchange' now knows exactly how much he will eventually have to pay, if he is the buyer of the goods, or receive if he is the seller. He will not have tied up his funds, but he will have preferred the judgement of the market to his own as regards the future relationship between the two currencies concerned.

These two arrangements can be combined in some cases (and dependent on exchange control regulations that may be in force) to produce a *foreign currency swap*. In this case the foreign currency is purchased in the 'spot' market and simultaneously a forward contract is arranged to sell the same amount of the currency at a future specified date. This is to cover the case when, for example, funds have to be advanced but will later be repaid in the same currency. There are also credit 'swaps' available in some countries: a bank in the foreign country makes a loan to a local borrower, for example a subsidiary of a foreign multinational, accepting the foreign exchange risk but of course charging interest on this loan. The foreign company then grants a loan to the bank outside the country, and normally this loan will be larger than the first so that the bank is compensated for the exchange risk and expenses.

All the foregoing arrangements are 'hedging' or safety devices to limit the risks implied in handling transactions involving foreign currencies. (In the strictly technical sense these measures are used to eliminate or reduce 'uncertainty', which is distinct from 'risk' in that it is possible to assign probability values to the latter.) It should be noted that normally it will be considered that the domestic currency is 'safer' than the foreign currency, since in effect the main part of the business of the buyer or seller is in any case inextricably involved in its own currency, good or bad. To take a 'bear' view of one's own currency and to hold funds in foreign currencies is normally considered to be speculative and, of course, may even be illegal.

This discussion was predicated on the requirements arising from the purchase and sale of goods but of course the arrangements mentioned are widely used in other cases where there has to be a transfer of funds across the exchanges.

## PAYMENT AND CREDIT

The question of payment arises in the simplest international transaction and it is therefore natural that there should be a wide range of instruments to deal with it and the related problem of credit. These arrangements also cover the important aspect of 'bridging' finance, that is to say financing the exporter's outlay over the frequently long period between the despatch of the goods and the receipt of payment.

### The letter of credit

The normal risks of commercial transactions are greatly increased in international trading, frequently because there is less knowledge on the part of one or both parties to a transaction about the other. Commercial practices differ greatly from country to country and there may be difficulties, imaginary as well as real, in obtaining recourse in the courts against one of the parties. The exchange risks already discussed also affect the arrangements in most cases.

The letter of credit has an important place in the list of arrangements designed to reduce risk. It consists essentially of an undertaking given by a bank, on behalf of its client, to a third party to the effect that it will honour its drafts on it provided that they comply in every respect with the requirements specified in the letter itself.

Since it constitutes an obligation to pay, the bank will require that it be backed by the necessary funds or that the bank should have control, partial or complete, over the goods involved in the transaction. Normally the credit will be irrevocable; if it is 'revocable' in very rare instances, then the conditions under which it can be revoked will obviously have to be very precisely spelled out, otherwise the credit is valueless as a guarantee.

Letters of credit have value to both buyer and seller and the initiative to use them may come from either party to a transaction. To the seller it guarantees that the funds for payment are available; if it provides that payment may be made in his own currency it eliminates the exchange risk. If the credit is 'confirmed' through a branch or correspondent bank in the seller's country the guarantee obviously extends to payment as distinct from the availability of funds and then becomes virtually total. To the buyer also the letter of credit may have value since it immediately establishes, normally at very little cost, that his creditworthiness is unimpeachable, while it removes any risk there might have been in advance payment, if such were required by the seller.

The form of letters of credit, the legal situation, the costs and extent of discounting facilities differ from country to country so that both sides should obtain detailed information from their banks on these points.

## The choice of payment method

Briefly the choices are between an irrevocable credit opened by the buyer in a bank in the name of the supplier and other methods mentioned above. The irrevocable letter of credit gives total security of payment, as far as both buyer and seller at least are concerned, but the seller may not obtain the funds until the goods are delivered. It is also mainly used where the seller has some doubt at least about the creditworthiness of the buyer.

Broadly speaking the choice of other methods will be between bank loans, or overdraft facilities (especially in the UK), and commercial paper which can be discounted or sold outright in the bill market. The value of commercial paper depends essentially on the credit standing of the parties concerned, and on whether it has been 'accepted' (see below) by a recognised financial institution, in the UK a major commercial bank or an 'accepting house' or merchant banker. When the paper is graded first-class it is the cheapest available source of funds, normally being at least 0.25 per cent cheaper than bank loans, and in times of tight money this spread can be up to 2.0 per cent. This method also has the advantage that it does not affect the general debt structure of the business, since it is self-liquidating. It should be clear that it can be used independently of shipping documents; in other words the sale can be on 'open account' if the relations between buyer and seller make this preferable, while the financing arrangements are made in parallel but independently of particular shipments.

Documentary credits, in the form of bills of exchange payable for example at 30, 60 or 90 days are generally preferred since they can be discounted in the bill market through the seller's bank and enable him to obtain his money much earlier. In most countries banks themselves will advance loans on bills of exchange, where the credit of the supplier is sufficiently good. A frequently used form of bank credit is the time draft which is drawn on the bank at the same time as the bill of exchange. Whichever method is used depends on the credit standing of buyer and seller, which in turn will affect the cost of the transaction, and the extent to which the seller at least can finance the transaction himself.

The residual risk in these transactions is covered partially at least as far as the bank is concerned by insurance of the goods, sometimes material proof that the goods exist in the form of warehouse receipts, frequently stipulations as to the nature of the goods, e.g. that they should be readily saleable in the event of default, and finally credit insurance.

### Use of statistical methods

With a variety of sources of finance available statistical methods may be used to determine the lowest-cost 'mix'. If the sums are large and there are several methods available it may justify the use of linear-programming techniques, the uses and limitations of which are explained in the standard treatises on mathematical techniques applied to financial problems.[1]

---

[1] For example, Van Horne, (1977).

## Credit insurance

This originated some sixty years ago and has increased steadily in volume and scope. It can confidently be said that the bulk of trade with the communist countries would not have been possible without it because of the lack of experience of most firms in the West in dealing with these countries, the very stringent requirements laid upon them by the buyers and the long credit terms frequently required.

The manner of operation of the British Export Credits Guarantee Department (ECGD) is typical of the many institutions, governmental and private, which now provide these services in all the principal trading countries of the West.

## Medium- and long-term financing

The problems of medium- and long-term financing are different from those of ordinary commercial transactions, financed largely by documentary credits and discounting. They arise in connection with the sale of capital equipment or with the financing of direct investment in the foreign country. Whereas the terms of everyday commercial transactions do not normally involve complex financial packages, this is more likely than not to be the case with capital equipment sales. Medium-term finance is generally taken to be six months to five years, and long-term from about this period to very long periods indeed, perhaps exceeding 20 years.

The possibilities here are chiefly: loans to the buyer, which may be quite separate from payment for the goods; loans raised by the seller to allow credit to be given and payment in kind from production facilities to be established.

In most countries the commercial banks remain the major providers of funds, but their attitudes vary widely from country to country, and are constantly evolving within the country. British banks have traditionally regarded themselves as providers of working capital, either for seasonal peaks or to bridge periods of expanding business before more permanent arrangements could be made. This attitude has now virtually disappeared, although many bankers would agree that it colours their basic thinking. German banks on the other hand have made little difference between short- and long-term finance providing that the terms were satisfactory.

In the UK, the ECGD has proved indispensable in bridging the middle-term gap, by insuring the credit risk and thereby enabling the debt itself to be used as collateral, rather than the assets of the company making the sale.

The ECGD operates normally by a comprehensive cover of the seller's business, not merely the more doubtful areas. There are also 'tailor-made' policies for large capital goods, and similar transactions. The ECGD guarantees can be used as security against bank loans and thus greatly facilitate the financing of longer-term projects. Normally of course a proportion of the risk, sometimes quite small, must be assumed by the seller.

These facilities, although increasingly used, are likely to be rather expensive so that other alternatives may be considered. Either the seller or the buyer, for example, can raise money through an issue of debt either in the national or the international money market, the terms being geared to the length of the repayment period, long-term rates tending to be higher than short-term.

Both the buyer and the seller may also seek funds from official sources, particularly the World Bank or its affiliates. Such loans are available for major projects which contribute to the economy of the country concerned, generally a less developed one. In the case of the UK there may also be the possibility of a government-to-government loan for a particular project, while in the USA the Agency for International Development (AID) is the main official channel for such loans.

## The European Investment Bank

In the EEC the European Investment Bank, founded in 1958, has become a major supplier of long-term funds for large projects, particularly those concerned with the restructuring of industry and problems created by the integration of markets. It administers the resources of the European Development Fund and has therefore a special role in connection with the associated territories of the EEC.

Like a number of development institutions it seeks to avoid propositions which can be financed through ordinary private channels, although this is of course not a clearly defined concept; it depends a good deal on circumstances. It does not take equity positions and the project for which funds are required must be approved, though not necessarily guaranteed, by the government of the country concerned. Typically loans are for a period of around ten years, with a grace period of at least two years during which interest is not payable.

In general, in the case of large projects, there is great advantage in close collaboration between buyer and seller in regard to finance, thereby taking advantage of the credit status of both parties and the financial resources which may be available to one side and not the other. In particular, the exchange risk is something of major importance in regard to which close collaboration may be essential. There have been many cases of loans raised in foreign currencies which have had to be repaid at very unfavourable exchange rates (e.g. in the worst days of the pound sterling).

Finally, the Japanese have assisted the buyers of complete plants by offering to take at least part-payment in the form of the product, fertilisers or plastics, for example. Of course such arrangements have been facilitated by the fact that in the majority of these cases the plant contractor concerned has been associated with one of the great banking and trading houses and has been able to use their international selling organisation to dispose of the product. Such arrangements can be very attractive to the buyer since it may take him some time to absorb the full production from the plant.

## CAPITAL INVESTMENT ABROAD

So far the subject has been chiefly the payment and financing of commercial transactions, including large and long-term ones. Many of the considerations apply to the most long-term and hazardous transactions of all, that is to say where investment in a foreign country is made in fixed assets and the associated working capital.

The decision to invest in a foreign country may arise from a variety of reasons: exports may have attained a level where they justify local manufacture; there may be pressure from the local government, who may eventually close the market to imports; there may be resources to exploit of labour, materials, or geographic position, so that local investment appears attractive in itself. These are largely commercial and manufacturing decisions, but at many points in the feasibility study and inevitably before a decision to proceed is taken, a variety of financial considerations has to be taken into account. These are, principally, the financial climate of the country concerned; its relations with the investor's country; the availability of capital; taxation; the ability to remit funds in either direction, including dividends; the financial structure of a local company; requirements as to local participation; detailed capital and operating budgets. Direct foreign investment may take several forms, that is to say investment in a foreign company, acquisition of such a company, or a 'grass-roots' project to trade and manufacture. In all these situations, all or most of the foregoing considerations apply.

## The financial climate

At the very outset of any economic feasibility study a view will be taken about the desirability of the prospective host country as a place for long-term investment, if only to screen it out in favour of more promising candidates. Such studies are expensive in money and manpower.

The criteria most used relate to political and economic stability and a number of other factors which may be subsumed under the heading of 'integration in the international economic and financial community'.

Although a great deal has been written about this subject in general, something like second sight is needed to be right over the long term (Wormald, 1973, p. 1). Purely impressionistic judgements are however greatly to be deprecated; they have for example excluded from the purview of many British companies countries which have an excellent record and most promising future, such as Venezuela. The best that can be said about this immense topic is that a detailed checklist of points for investigation should be made, using inter alia material published in the standard works and periodicals such as the *Columbia Journal of World Business* and the *Economist*. There should then be exhaustive on-the-spot interviews with local politicians, businessmen and notables. The views of the local embassy are always valuable but it has to be remembered that all the senior staff are changed every few years, many of them have no detailed knowledge of the country and draw their information from quite restricted sources. The value of their views is largely that they are able to bring a wide perspective and experience, as well as trained judgement, to bear on the problem. What they certainly will know is the attitude of the country concerned to the UK or the USA, for example, which may be reflected in such matters as reciprocal tax treaties and trade agreements.

In discussions on the desirability of countries as places to invest the security of capital against expropriation is generally prominent. Expropriation is rather rare (although the case of Peru is fairly recent); what is more to be feared is nationalisation or the forced sale of a majority interest. Looked at in this way few countries have been guiltless. The target for this type of action is more likely to be basic industry, such as has been nationalised in the UK, so that it has been the policy of some major companies, such as the RTZ Corporation, to bring in local capital from the outset. This is indeed now mandatory in certain countries, such as those of the Andean Pact (Venezuela, Colombia, Peru, Ecuador and Bolivia) and in most other countries the extractive industries, for example, will be reserved at least partially to the state. If therefore the project concerned is of the basic type, the most careful soundings will have to be taken in official circles. Of course, in many cases foreign companies have enjoyed freedom for sufficiently long to make the venture financially attractive, even though this freedom may have been curtailed later. A writer has aptly referred to capital investment of this kind as 'an investment with a fixed maturity'.

The other major risk factor, of a general character, is inflation. With rising levels of inflation in both the UK and the USA the nature and importance of this factor is better appreciated. Inflation may affect the proposed investment in several ways: by erosion of working capital; by erosion of fixed assets, unless depreciation is allowed on a 'present-value' basis; indirectly, by price control which will probably be used by government in an attempt to restrain inflation. On the other hand, an attempt has to be made to assess what are considered as 'normal' profit margins, and in some cases it will be found that these offset the factors mentioned. The propensity to inflation in a given country is a factor which can be forecast, at least in a general way, for quite long periods ahead, since it depends largely on deep-seated structural and social factors; Brasil, for example, uses controlled inflation as an instrument of policy; Venezuela has historically a low rate of inflation; US foreign political and economic policy made inflation virtually inevitable.

## Availability of capital

It will only be in very rare cases that the investor will wish to provide all the capital, both fixed and working, himself. Apart from offering a participation to local investors and using credit from commercial banks, he can frequently obtain grants and aid in kind from national and local authorities anxious to attract investment (not necessarily foreign) and in addition in many countries he will find an industrial development bank using government funds and frequently acting as an executive agent to promote enterprises identified as desirable by government planners. These frequently make available long-term loan capital at lower than commercial rates, with a grace period of several years before interest or repayment starts. In some cases there may even be equity participation. The fact that the Development Bank is involved may also help in getting tax concessions. External development agencies, such as the World Bank or the European Investment Bank, already mentioned, may also be sources of funds for major projects.

It may be the policy of the foreign investor to make the minimum possible fixed investment, deriving his profit from the sale of goods and services to the company, and in this case he may provide funds through the current account, supplying on extended credit, so that in effect they are part of the capital of the business. This has two advantages: the interest and profit on the investment is self-liquidating; and the capital itself can be increased or reduced according to the view which is taken of the situation at any one time.

This policy raises the difficult question of 'transfer' prices. In many cases a foreign subsidiary will be looked on by the parent as a vehicle for selling goods produced elsewhere by the same company or group. The fact that a commercial relationship of this kind exists obviously provides tempting opportunities for extracting profits, and thus avoiding or evading local taxation and perhaps also exchange control, where it exists. This subject has become in recent years one of the principal arguments used against the multinational corporation. Undoubtedly it is possible to transfer profits by this means to areas of lower taxation and, by obvious subterfuges such as invoicing through an address of convenience in a tax haven, to avoid (or evade) taxation in *any* country, including the domicile of the parent company. The legality and advisability of any such arrangement is a matter on which expert advice should be taken in each case, but it should be remembered that in many countries the price of goods will be closely scrutinised to see whether there is a likelihood of such methods being used, and inter-company transactions may be scrutinised by the tax authorities.

## Taxation

The case mentioned is one important aspect of taxation in foreign markets. In this case it is a potential advantage enjoyed by foreign companies. There are disadvantages also. In particular, the foreign company will generally consider that it should conform to the law, even if it takes advantage of legitimate loopholes. In many countries the native company will not feel this compulsion, and may only pay a fraction of the taxes it should. This may give it a strong commercial advantage, and this aspect should be looked at closely when setting up the foreign operation, to see whether a company paying taxes as prescribed can compete pricewise with others who do not.

The most serious concern of foreign companies is generally double taxation, that is to say taxation at the source and taxation where the profits are received. In a large number of cases both the UK and the USA have tax treaties, or double taxation agreements, which provide for the offsetting of the foreign tax against domestic tax. However, if the foreign tax is higher, then the effective rate will be the higher of the two.

By no means all countries are included in these arrangements, and then it is likely that profits remitted will be taxed in two places. It is these cases which give rise to many arrangements involving tax havens. It should be borne in mind that even the non-remittance of dividends may not exempt the parent company from taxation in all cases, and dividend policy in the subsidiary should be carefully considered from this angle. It may also be possible to remit some profits in the form of management fees or royalties, which may be allowed as business expenses in the foreign company.

Many countries have adopted withholding taxes on the remittance of dividends and profits, additional to the local income taxes. This of course makes it even more desirable to find other means of transferring funds. In some countries which have no tax treaty, the parent company may have to make a tax declaration on its local earnings, and in this case the withholding tax will be offset against any tax held to be due. In these cases the expenses of visiting directors and personnel can be included as business expenses. This form of treatment arises where the country concerned takes no cognisance of the fact that the local company has a foreign parent or shareholder.

The financial structure of the affiliate will also be affected by the taxation question, since it may be considered preferable to provide a substantial part of the capital as a loan. In all probability the interest on this loan will be allowable as a business expense, and therefore taxable only in the hands of the recipient. The repayment of the loan itself will not be taxable in the hands of the recipient, although in this case it may have to be made out of taxed profits. If depreciation allowances are generous, it may of course be repaid from *untaxed* profits in this way.

In each case, consideration should be given to all these possibilities, namely transfer pricing, royalties and management fees and loan capital, and the optimum mix chosen with a view to the present and future tax liability. Few companies, it may safely be said, give sufficient thought to this aspect; frequently however it is a key factor in the profitability of the operation

## Transfer of funds

The number of countries where there is complete freedom to remit funds is very few, although the trend towards the creation of larger economic units, such as the EEC, the Andean Pact and the Latin America Free Trade area is providing a partial solution.

Difficulties in remitting funds may affect the ability to pay for essential raw materials as well as dividends and repayment of debt. The difficulties may be of two kinds: the need for permits, and the exchange rate at which funds can be officially transferred. The situation will obviously be affected by the view taken by the government of the country as to the essential nature of the operations, so that if they are of any considerable size a specific commitment should be sought from the government. It will not amount to a guarantee but will establish a negotiating base at the least.

Equally it should be borne in mind that there are frequently restrictions on local borrowing by foreign companies, so that it is not always possible to respond to a policy of control of remittances by borrowing locally. There may well be a situation where owing to the growth of the business and or inflation, a continuous flow of capital will be required from the parent company, without always the assurance that it can be repatriated.

It may be noted that in some countries, including the UK and the USA, it is possible to insure at least against the ability to repatriate capital owing to political action.

Frequently legislation will include a requirement to have local capital and also directors and staff. In this case the freedom of manoeuvre in regard to remittances may well be affected, as the nationals of the country concerned may not identify their interests with those of the foreign company.

## Financial reporting

Since different currencies are involved the question of the consolidation of subsidiary companies' overseas earnings is extremely complex. Should the parent company's accounts show what is believed to be the real business situation (sometimes called the 'economic' position), that is taking into account the longer-term earnings position, exchange and remittances, or merely translate into the national currency the performance of the subsidiary, using the most convenient rate of exchange? In some countries there are mandatory requirements, while in the UK the public accounting bodies have made recommendations, which however are not binding on the company.

Where earnings are not consolidated the problem also exists, and there may be a temptation to present the situation in the best light, changing the basis of reporting accordingly. For example, where the foreign currency has not actually been converted into the domestic currency, there may nevertheless be an 'unrealised' exchange loss. This need not necessarily be reported but, of course, unless the situation improves it will eventually have to be reported when the loss is actually 'realised'. Even more than in domestic accounting it is important to take a conservative view of earnings, asset values and potential tax liabilities in overseas operations.

## REFERENCES AND ADDITIONAL READING

Eiteman, D. K. and Stonehill, A. I., *Multinational Business Finance,* 2nd edition, Addison Wesley, 1979.

Van Horne, *Financial Management and Policy*, 4th edition, Prentice-Hall, 1977.

Wormald, A., *International Business,* Pan Books, 1973.

# 14

# Accounting Problems of Multinational Businesses

**Elwood L. Miller**

*In this chapter Elwood Miller extends the theme of overseas develop-
ment, introduced by Avison Wormald in the preceding chapter, by
considering the specific problems of the multinational corporation
from a financial viewpoint.*

*The difficulty of defining a multinational business is solved by the
adoption of the simple description of an enterprise that conducts
operations in more than one country. The author acknowledges the
fact that such a definition embraces very small companies as well as the
immensely large organisations with which he is principally concerned.
He demonstrates that the turnover of any one of the few largest multinational companies exceeds the gross national product of many individual nations. In spite of, or perhaps because of, their size, power and
resources, there is evidence that these companies can have a beneficial
influence on competition, consumer choice and the flow of capital.
'Multinational businesses', according to the author, 'accept the
environmental challenge as problems waiting to be converted into
opportunities'.*

*The central problem of the multinationals is one of co-ordination of
operations, and the heart of the process of co-ordination lies in the
accounting information systems. These systems can be greatly aided by
developments in computerisation, provided that the computerised system is installed with the direct participation of management. This
advice is strongly supported by P. V. Jones in his chapter on Computerisation. However, financial reporting is complicated by the need
for it to fulfil both local and parent company purposes. Another*

*accounting problem, particularly related to the consolidation of the results of all the member companies of the group, is to decide whether the company is represented by the proprietary entity or the parent company concept. In this connection the author holds that 'reporting all transactions as if they were conducted in the parent company domain can only produce economic nonsense'. The only present remedy is the use of supplemental data to the accounts.*

*Reiterating the message of Avison Wormald in previous chapters, the author says: 'Since economic conditions are not static, the ability to adapt and respond to change . . . is of major importance' (thus justifying the inclusion of this chapter in the part of the handbook devoted to change). The quoted statement is made in particular relation to the need for multinationals to 'manage and co-ordinate resources on a global scale'.*

*The problem of establishing 'fair' transfer pricing policies is examined in relation to the interests of the business and to those of the countries concerned, with the conclusion that multinationals must not be too greedy. The author also discusses the need for performance evaluation by units and within units. This activity should be the product of forms of responsibility accounting which should 'prohibit the arbitrary allocation of expenses among units'. The much used measure of the return on investment is regarded with considerable qualifications as an evaluator of performance or as a motivator. The author ends with a plea for commonsense explanations in multinational accounts.*

For simplicity, a multinational business or company (MNC) may be defined as an enterprise that conducts operations in more than one country. This definition includes tiny companies as well as industrial giants. Each faces similar accounting problems; the differences are mainly in degree.

Multinational companies have begun to outgrow countries. If the 100 largest economic entities in the world were listed – countries, by gross national products, and industrial companies, by annual sales – the listing would contain 50 countries and 50 companies. Annual sales of the world's *largest* industrial company (either Exxon or General Motors in recent years) exceed the individual GNPs of 87 per cent of the free-world nations (106 out of 122) and are larger than the GNPs of the smallest 54 nations combined. The *smallest* MNC on the list will have generated sales in excess of $5 thousand million –

larger than the GNPs of 72 individual countries and larger than the GNP of the smallest 18 nations combined (Miller, 1979).

Virtually all the attributes of MNCs are a function of size. MNCs are considered to be: efficient, powerful, stable, oligopolistic, dynamic, and flexible. Although these characteristics are relative, the larger MNCs face only two effective challenges: a government (either home or host) and another competing MNC.

Multinational businesses are the first economic organisms engaged in the management of resources on a global scale. While feared in some quarters because of the options they have available, MNCs are reported to have, on balance: (a) increased competition; (b) increased consumer choice; and (c) directed capital and other resources where needs and opportunities existed.[1]

Most of the MNCs (95 per cent) are headquartered in eight countries: France, West Germany, Japan, the Netherlands, Sweden, Switzerland, the UK and the USA. Lacking an effective system of international law, MNCs must depend upon themselves to exist and function in a host of different environments: social, cultural, legal, and economic. Multinational businesses accept the environmental challenges as problems awaiting to be converted into opportunities. Most MNCs strive to purchase, produce, and assemble wherever they can at the lowest net costs, and to market their outputs where they command the most attractive prices. The central problem, then, is coordination of operations. Accounting and information systems constitute the heart of the coordination process.

At the risk of perpetuating the mythical dichotomy of accounting, this chapter will be divided into financial and managerial segments, followed by some concluding remarks on the states of the international accounting arts.

## FINANCIAL ACCOUNTING PROBLEMS

Financial accounting is considered to represent that portion of management information shared with external users. Two financial accounting dilemmas are unique to multinational businesses: multiple accountings and foreign currency translations. For each topic, the

---

[1] Summary results of the Multinational Enterprise Project (a large-scale, ongoing study begun by Harvard University in 1965) as presented by the project director, Frederick T. Knickerbocker (1975).

backgrounds, available alternatives, and the approaches suggested will be addressed.

## Multiple accountings, reportings, and disclosures

Accounting is said to be the language of business. Unfortunately, there is no international language of business as yet. Multinational operations are conducted in many dialects, both in the languages of people and of business.

In many instances, the first 'foreign' operations of multinational businesses were established as branches. Accounting and reporting systems represented duplications, in miniature, of those used by the headquarters supplemented by whatever reporting requirements (usually minor) were imposed by the host governments. In effect, these fledgling activities were not considered as foreign but were operated as if they existed in Liverpool or Manchester (for a London company) or in Chicago or New Orleans (for a New York firm).

Over time, branches and agencies were supplanted by subsidiaries and affiliates. Home-country oriented (ethnocentric) attitudes and systems were no longer feasible. Instead of mere appendages of the parent, foreign operations assumed the roles of strategic linkages in a transnational network (or TNN). Stockholders evolved into 'stakeholders', including influential interests such as trade unions and governments (Perlmutter, 1969a and 1969b).

Accounting systems also evolved. Differences in statutory and other reporting requirements of parent and host countries were usually overcome by the maintenance of multiple records. It is not at all uncommon today to find: (a) the official set required by the host country; (b) the set specified by the parent; (c) a set maintained to satisfy local tax regulations; and (d) a mini-set devised by local management for decision-making purposes.

MNCs place priority upon accounting information needed to operate. External financial reportings are (and have been) a nuisance – compliance reports bearing costs but few real benefits. Consequently, managements often regard external financial reportings as appendages of their internal information networks.

## Consolidated reports

In less than three decades, consolidated financial reports of large multinational companies have completed their full circle of usefulness as far as most external users are concerned. Complexities inherent in modern business, aided by myopic accounting approaches (particularly in the USA and Canada), have enabled consolidated statements to conceal more than they reveal. In the two countries cited above, consolidated statements have evolved from general-purpose to single-purpose reportings having limited usefulness, and then only to shareholders of the parent company. There are several underlying problems and causes.

Preparers of consolidated reports are faced with several dilemmas:

1 How should the structure of the business be reflected?
2 How should the differences in accounting standards and tax regulations of the several component legal entities be reconciled?
3 How are the various national currencies to be translated into a common denominator?
4 Are the relative inflation rates between and among various host countries represented by differences in exchange rates? If not, what other means can be employed without double-counting the effects?

The answer, it seems, to each question is 'it all depends'.

## Company structures

In most countries, the structure of the business may be represented by the proprietary, entity, or parent-company concepts, alone or in combination.

The *proprietary* concept does not commingle parent-company and minority interests. The investor takes up only the proportion of the assets of the investee that are owned; the assets may either be combined or reported as a one-liner investment, depending on the compatibility of the operations of the businesses. Historically, the advent of the conglomerate company rendered proprietary theory obsolete. Today, proprietary concepts are usually employed only in those cases in which no single investor company has ownership control.

Under the *entity* concept, both parent and minority shareholders are credited with their proportionate equities in the combined assets, tangible and intangible (including any differential or goodwill).

The *parent-company* concept emphasises the ownership interest of the dominant or parent company; the minority interest in net assets (excluding goodwill) is disclosed almost as an 'outsider' interest rather than as a segment of equity.

Although the problem of structure also confronts domestic consolidations, considerations are more complicated for transnational businesses that operate within multiple legal and tax environments. In such cases, attempts to combine legal entities into a single economic entity, however it may be structured, face many conceptual hurdles in an effort to present economic reality fairly. While generalisations are always difficult, some can be offered. Practices in the USA, UK, and the Netherlands generally[1] follow the parent-company approach for controlled subsidiaries, and the entity concept for associated companies (those in which 'significant influence', but less than majority control, exists).

Company law in West Germany treats a group of companies as a legal entity, thus adhering to the entity concept and mandating total elimination of intercompany profits. Since consolidations are not yet required in France, time, habit, and the nature of business firms continue to emphasise the proprietary approach; parent-company and proportional consolidations (the latter reflecting a gamut of ownership levels) are generally limited to the larger open companies. Among industrial nations, Japan is a relative newcomer as far as consolidated reportings are concerned (required only since April 1977); practices tend to follow the Anglo-American preferences for the parent-company and equity concepts. These same preferences seem to predominate in the EEC proposal for its seventh directive.

In this writer's opinion, the consolidation problems concerning company structures – like most accounting issues – cannot be resolved by specifying the use of any single, normative method. Standard-setting bodies, it seems, might be well advised to specify what methods are to be used in what circumstances, and require appropriate disclosures of the methods employed.

## Accounting standards and tax laws

The labyrinth of various accounting standards and tax regulations poses particular consolidation problems for multinational businesses.

As mentioned earlier, consolidated statements have become single-purpose reports furnishing a macro view of a multinational

---

[1] Except for 100 per cent elimination of intercompany profits (an entity concept) as a matter of convenience.

business to its parent shareholders. Consequently, it has become standard practice to adjust all transactions that occurred in different host country environments to conform with the accounting standards and tax laws of the parent's country. Naturally, these adjustments are well-intentioned; i.e. to report all transactions within accounting and tax frameworks familiar to the parent stock holders. Nonetheless, reporting all transactions as if they were conducted in the parent domain produces economic nonsense more often than not. Many multinationals are induced to operate in other economic environments because of business and tax incentives that are more favourable than those afforded by the parent country. To repudiate these benefits in the consolidation process is to ignore economic reality, particularly for those multinationals that consider foreign operations as long-run growth areas and that deploy and redeploy foreign assets at will, rather than seek a one-way flow of profit repatriations. For such companies, the home-country domicile of the parent is largely incidental. The tax incentives are, of course, much more of a problem for parent companies in countries, such as the USA, that function within worldwide, rather than territorial, frameworks of taxation.

As the process of harmonisation of accounting standards and tax laws moves forward gradually (such as in the EEC), some of the problems mentioned (as well as many of the existing incentives) will be removed. In the interim, however, managements can only adopt a situational approach in order to assure that financial reports, taken as a whole, coincide with economic reality. Given the inflexibility of the financial statements themselves, management must resort to devices such as supplemental data sections and president's or directors' messages in order to provide fair and useful information. Such approaches should be encouraged.

## Segmented disclosures

In October 1975, Price Waterhouse International issued its revised (and expanded)[1] edition of *A Survey in 46 Countries: Accounting Principles and Reporting Practices.* Of the 246 topics in the survey, nearly 40 were related to consolidated and/or segmented reportings. The survey included 14 leading industrial countries and 32 developing and/or emerging nations. An interesting continuum was dis-

---

[1] The previous 1973 *Survey* covered 38 countries and 233 topics.

covered. In 6 of the 46 nations surveyed, only consolidated statements were issued to shareholders (Canada and the USA were the only industrial countries in this group; 10 others had prohibited this practice). At the other end of the reporting continuum, in 18 countries (including 5 industrial nations) only parent-company statements were supplied to users.

A two-dimensional problem was depicted. Some countries were still moving toward consolidated statements. Others provided nothing else. Still others (such as the UK) required firms to file financial statements of all companies (subsidiaries, parent, and consolidated) with a government agency or registrar.

Consolidated statements provide a macro glimpse of the total economic entity – and this still picture of a moving scene is necessary. However, consolidated reports are threaded with aggregate information and can conceal more than they reveal. Adequate micro (segmented) disclosures by multinationals (as well as domestic conglomerates) are necessary to enable users to examine the weft and warp as well as the entire fabric.

Small wonder, then, that the OECD specified essential segmented data, as well as information for the enterprise as a whole, in the disclosure guidelines for multinationals contained in its 'Declaration on International Investment and Multinational Enterprises' adopted on 21 June 1976 (see Figure 14.1). On the heels of the OECD guideline, the European Parliament called for 'binding rules' to give the weight of law to the guideline. Instead, the fourth company law directive of the EEC implemented the segmented requirements – notes analysing turnover by category of activity and geographical market.[1] Consolidated reportings are the topic of the seventh directive now in its advanced stages of review.

Both directives, like most laws, specify only minimum reporting standards. For fair presentations, product or category-of-activity reports should be carried to segment margins, sales or turnover, less all directly traceable expenses (without any arbitrary allocations of home office expenses or income taxes). Geographical area results should also reflect segment margins but, where practicable, also

---

[1] The OECD *Declaration* was implemented by the US government in Public Law 94–472 (International Investment Survey Act), and by the Financial Accounting Standards Board in its *Statement of Financial Accounting Standards No. 14,* 'Financial Reporting for Segments of a Business Enterprise', December 1976.

# OECD Guidelines for Disclosure of Information

**Annex to the Declaration of 21st June 1976 by Governments of OECD Member Countries on International Investment and Multinational Enterprises**

GUIDELINES FOR MULTINATIONAL ENTERPRISES

*Disclosure of Information*

Enterprises should, having due regard to their nature and relative size in the economic context of their operations and to requirements of business confidentiality and to cost, publish in a form suited to improve public understanding a sufficient body of factual information on the structure, activities and policies of the enterprise as a whole, as a supplement, insofar as necessary for this purpose, to information to be disclosed under the national law of the individual countries in which they operate. To this end, they should publish within reasonable time limits, on a regular basis, but at least annually, financial statements, and other pertinent information relating to the enterprise as a whole, comprising in particular:

- i) the structure of the enterprise, showing the name and location of the parent company, its main affiliates, its percentage ownership, direct and indirect, in these affiliates, including shareholdings between them;
- ii) the geographical areas* where operations are carried out and the principal activities carried on therein by the parent company and the main affiliates;
- iii) the operating results and sales by geographical area and the sales in the major lines of business for the enterprise as a whole;
- iv) significant new capital investment by geographical area and, as far as practicable, by major lines of business for the enterprise as a whole;
- v) a statement of the sources and uses of funds by the enterprise as a whole;
- vi) the average number of employees in each geographical area;
- vii) research and development expenditure for the enterprise as a whole;
- viii) the policies followed in respect of intra-group pricing;
- ix) the accounting policies, including those on consolidation, observed in compiling the published information.

---

* For the purposes of the guidelines on disclosure of information the term "geographical area" means groups of countries or individual countries as each enterprise determines is appropriate in its particular circumstances.

**Fig. 14.1 Reproduction of disclosure guidelines**

reflect estimates of local income taxes. Together with disclosures of assets employed in each of the segmentations, users will at long last be able to glean some idea of the relative risks and profitabilities of the important parts of complex organisations. Managements of most well-managed companies have these data at hand and work with them regularly – segmented reporting merely stipulates that the data, in a condensed format, be shared with interested stakeholders.

## Foreign currency translations

The translation of foreign currency transactions is as old as record-keeping itself, and was cited in the works of Pacioli (see Brown, 1905). Modern theorists hold that a transaction is *measured* in a foreign currency if it is expressed in a monetary unit other than that of the local domicile. A transaction is *denominated* in a foreign currency if settlement is to be made by a specific sum in a foreign currency, regardless of the exchange rate existing at the time of settlement. In the course of trade, one participant will face neither problem; the other will be confronted by both.

The affected firm can treat the transaction and settlement as one event or two. If one event, the purchase (or selling) price would simply be adjusted for any difference (the conversion gain or loss) upon settlement. If the purchase (or sale) and subsequent settlement are considered to be two transactions, the conversion gain or loss would be treated as a separate, interim event – the result of a change in money prices. Naturally, the net result is the same regardless of treatment. Those who have engaged in international trade have learned to reckon with and accept changes in money prices as one of the costs of doing business. However, the transaction described assumed two separate entities – legal and economic. The advent of multinational businesses complicated otherwise simple events.

Suppose, now, a different circumstance in which a US parent firm has a wholly-owned subsidiary in the UK. The subsidiary obtains a long-lived asset here by means of a long-term debt denominated in pounds sterling. The subsidiary has no problem since the transaction is measured and denominated in its local currency. The parent, however, will report different results upon translation and consolidation of the subsidiary statements, depending upon whether the event is considered to be one or two transactions. If one transaction, the exchange rate at acquisition of the asset would also be applied to translate the debt over time. No imbalances (gains or losses) would be reported while the debt was held or upon payment in sterling by the subsidiary. Translation would simply express the amounts in their dollar equivalents at the time of acquisition. If two transactions are assumed, the acquisition would be translated at the rate existing on the date acquired (at a point in time), but the outstanding debt would be translated at the current rates (over a period of time). The imbalances would be reported as translation gains/losses (while the debt was held) and conversion gains/losses (upon settlement). This method measures and denominates the transaction in the parent's currency, as if the transaction were conducted by the parent, in the USA, and in dollars. Unfortunately, this unrealistic, if not mythical, approach was adopted by the American FASB (1975).

Typically, today, operations are undertaken in other domiciles in response to existing inducements, whether strategic, legal, tax, financial, etc. Methods of consolidating financial statements (as used in the USA) that: (a) recast foreign transactions to conform with US accounting standards, and then (b) translate them as if they occurred in the USA, are worse than useless. The resulting reports were not only unrealistic and far cries from fair presentations, they were misleading to the extent that users (external and internal) were induced to take uneconomic actions. Internally, managements were induced to incur the real, economic costs of hedgings in order to protect against paper, translation 'losses'. Multilateral netting pools were established at considerable cost by large companies, yet the operating costs involved were not related to the real savings alone (the conversion expenses saved), the mythical translation gains and losses were considered as well. The economic benefits of profitable foreign investments were commingled with those of other operations; only the translation effects were separately disclosed for all to see. Consequently, some otherwise desirable undertakings may well have been foregone, for who keeps an account of opportunity costs? Externally, investors may well be encouraged to change their portfolios in face of the 'yo-yo' earnings effects upon reporting companies.

Attempts to seek out and document the uneconomic actions mentioned are futile and irrelevant. The fact that an accounting practice induces such uneconomic action is *prima facie* cause for concern.

Economic sense can only be portrayed by retaining the essence of transactions as made in foreign domiciles, then translating them using the current rate (that existing on the balance sheet date) – often called the European method. Imbalances would still occur wherever foreign investments are accounted for by use of the equity method. Such temporary imbalances should be recognised for what they are – translation differences – and recorded simply as deferrals or reserves. Gains and losses on foreign exchange should be recorded only when realised through the process of conversion – the actual exchange of one currency for another.

## MANAGERIAL ASPECTS

The preceding accounting problems of multinationals pertain to external financial reporting and, as a consequence, arise primarily because reporting practices must conform with standards devised to protect external users. Managerial, or internal, accounting is not governed by externally imposed constraints. Managements are free to develop and use data internally as they see fit. As a result, managerial accounting or information problems arise from the scope and complexity related to the coordination of widespread operations.

Decentralisation – the process of delegating decision-making authority as far down the managerial hierarchy as possible – has been credited with the creation of domestic industrial giants, such as General Motors. Hindsight indicates that decentralisation was appropriate for the efficient management of business segments that were, in fact, miniature businesses having acquired unique niches in the economy as well as the requisite economies of scale. Multinationals, on the other hand, must manage and coordinate resources on a global scale – buying, producing, marketing, and financing wherever the most favourable conditions exist. Since economic conditions are not static, the ability to adapt and respond to change (or to manage change) is of major importance. Decentralisation is the antithesis of multinational operations; instead, coordination has become the theme.

Coordination explicitly requires centralised information and control of the major aspects of multinational operations. Four of the most troublesome aspects will be mentioned briefly and separately, although all are interdependent.

### Information systems

In a business context, an information system should furnish the right information, to the right people, at the right time. A good information system is one that does this at the lowest possible cost. Consequently, much as resources are viewed by economists, good information systems do not exist but are 'becoming'. As a result, managements must be content to make do.

Information systems of most multinationals evolved much as the companies themselves. Domestic systems were transplanted, then adjusted for local differences. Over time, a rather disjointed network of different components had grown in a random manner. Today, many multinationals are attempting to integrate the collage of systems one function at a time in order to disrupt operations as little as possible.

Multinationals might have evolved without information networks. However, they would certainly have been less efficient.

As with domestic networks, information systems of multinationals are constructed upon and around the accounting system in order to comply with legal and tax requirements. Problems of volume have been tempered by the use of computers and standardised reporting formats. Timeframes and privacy have been aided by the use of coded Telex transmissions and satellite telecommunications.

The remaining hurdles are people-oriented (political, social, economic, and cultural) and not easily resolved. Experience indicates that a single monolithic information system cannot serve the diverse needs of local managers and the coordination needs of central management. At best, multinational systems can attempt to supply the information needed by local managers to make decisions within their scope of authority, and to transmit the parallel but different information needed laterally (by sister units) and vertically (by the headquarters for centralised planning and coordination). The connecting loop, of course, relates to downward feedback from the headquarters. Most of this information is quantitative and structured; it is often called the formal information network.

Of at least equal import for global operations is the informal or strategic information system involving changes, actual or anticipated, in the local environments, e.g. laws, regulations, government policies, labour relations, consumer tastes, and the like. Such information does not lend itself to structuring in content or timing but, instead, depends upon the astuteness of management.

Two generalisations can be made. First, monies wasted on false starts have convinced managements that the computer is no more a system, in itself, than is an adding machine. Companies increasingly will not consider computerised systems without the direct participation of management in order to preclude the systems serving the whims of computer departments instead of the needs of managements. Second, effective information systems can only be developed over time, based upon the considered needs and inputs of all levels of management.

## Transfer prices

There is a consensus that, within the domestic milieu, the function of transfer prices strives to assure equity and goal congruence among the segments of decentralised firms. There is also a growing (yet long overdue) consensus that, in the international sphere, transfer prices are used to achieve a great diversity of goals and purposes, often interrelated and/or conflicting (see, for example, Sharav, 1974). Examples abound, as well as allegations, indicating that transfer prices can be (and have been) used to circumvent almost any type of control imposed by a host government.

As mentioned earlier, multinational businesses attempt to deploy and redeploy resources wherever they can be used to best advantage. Transfer prices are those amounts assigned to the movements of goods and services between and among related sub-units of an organisation. In the realm of international business, the organisation considers itself a single, economic entity: the transfers are often viewed as internal transactions to be priced as management sees fit. The sub-units, however, are considered as separate, legal entities by the host governments concerned; the transfers across national boundaries represent external transactions subject to valuation by 'arm's-length' criteria – as if the transactions were consummated by unrelated parties.

These two concepts of transfer prices represent the extremes of a continuum of methods found in practice. Arm's-length prices tend to be inoperable for a variety of reasons. On the other hand, multinational manipulators soon find themselves confronted by a maze of variables, often conflicting and posing a myriad of trade-offs. Unsuccessful manipulators soon learn to compromise; those that are successful are soon branded as undesirable citizens by host (and often home) governments and sanctioned accordingly.

Because of the need to adapt to changing events, multinationals cannot be expected to employ a uniform 'policy' of transfer pricing.

Neither can multinationals be expected to transfer the same good to a single recipient from various sources at the same price – that expectation conflicts with economic reality. Transfers will be expected to be made at fair prices, with 'fair' being determined *ex post* by the host government and the multinational. Since fair prices connote amounts in excess of cost, most multinationals have developed dual systems of transfer prices: the fair price, for external use; a cost-based price for internal decision making. In sum, multinational businesses should avoid becoming too greedy. Host governments will tend to be satisfied with a reasonable share of tax and other economic benefits.

## Performance evaluations

Responsibility accounting is the process that attempts to trace and compare the inputs and outputs of definable segments of an enterprise, whether domestic or multinational. Over time, these segments or responsibility centres have been labelled as cost, expense, revenue, profit, and investment centres, dependent upon the inputs and outputs controllable by the segment. Much like transfer prices, responsibility accounting concepts were products of decentralisation. Delegations of authority carried with them the responsibility to make periodic reckonings of accomplishments. These periodic reckonings are called performance evaluations.

Unfortunately, while performance evaluations are widely used, they are not as widely understood and often are misused. Domestic ramifications will be examined first, since they are transferred to and permeate international practices; then the peculiar aspects affecting foreign operations will be addressed.

### Domestic operations

In the domestic context, insufficient attention is directed to what is being measured, the meanings of the measurements themselves, and the controllability of the inputs and outputs by the levels being evaluated. Frequently, activities that produce entirely for distribution to affiliated units are converted into profit centres. Pseudo-profits are added to the prices of internal transfers, thus obscuring realities. Production activities are basically cost centres. Attention should be directed primarily towards the control and use of resources employed, usually by means of standard cost and budget systems. This cardinal error stems from the recognition that profit is an inclusive denominator and a powerful motivator. However, few levels below the top executive echelon are really responsible for profits. Consideration must be applied to the meanings of measurements (Wilkinson, 1975) as well as the attributes measured. For example, monetary measures are products of units and prices. In times of rising prices, monetary measures used alone often confuse accomplishments and circumstances. Focusing upon quantities of units (goods or services) is an excellent way of eliminating the uncontrollable effects of changing price levels. In all cases, evaluations should focus upon those operating aspects that are controllable at the particular levels. This last observation prohibits the arbitrary allocations of expenses among units. The above tenets are so frequently violated in practice that one can only believe that they have come to be ignored completely.

Two additional fallacies are interrelated. First, the duality of performance evaluations is often not recognised. Rarely can the same criteria and measurements be applied to operations and the personnel involved – overall functions and responsibilities seldom coincide. A second common fallacy is the misplaced reliance upon the data in routine, financial accounting reports as the basis for performance evaluations. Financial accounting reports are designed to, at best, report on the accountability or stewardship of the company as a whole (a macro viewpoint). Applications to segments are unwise.

The ill-placed emphases upon profit as an evaluator are common to other profit-based criteria, such as return-on-investment and residual-income measures. Return on investment (often termed the 'DuPont formula') is prized for its ability to:

1 reflect all important factors in a single measure – operating incomes and resources employed;
2 be computed from routine financial statements;
3 serve as a comparative measure, internally (among segments) and externally (among firms and industries); and
4 to motivate as well as evaluate.

Shortcomings are either not considered or simply ignored. As mentioned earlier, accounting profit is rarely synonymous with accomplishment. Relating profits with resources can be, at least conceptually, superior to looking at profit alone. However, extreme care must be taken to:

1 identify controllable resources;

2    determine the measurement basis to be used (gross historical/
current costs or costs net of depreciation, and, if the latter, the
depreciation method to be employed);

3    decide whether the asset base will be determined at the beginning or the end of the year, or by means of a simple, moving, or
weighted average; and

4    assure that the methods selected are applied uniformly to all
segments if ROI is to be used as a comparative device.

Even if the obstacles mentioned are overcome, others may persist.
Operating conditions must be comparable, or allowances made for
differences, otherwise the results of achievement will be commingled
with those of circumstance. As a macro measure, ROI attaches the
same risk to all assets employed – this may neither be appropriate nor
desired. Finally, someone must establish a benchmark ROI to serve
as a reasonably attainable benchmark.

While ROI has defects as an evaluator, it may be even more suspect
as a motivator – and for the most profitable segments. For example,
the manager of a segment reflecting an ROI of, say, 30 per cent would
not be motivated to undertake a venture expected to yield 20 per
cent, thereby lowering his performance (and bonus). However, if the
other segments of the company are earning returns of only 10 to 15
per cent, the company as a whole will have missed a desirable opportunity. This defect may be remedied by a refinement of the ROI
method – residual income – that considers returns in monetary terms
as well as percentages. Here a threshold rate of return is applied to
the resources employed and the resultant amount is deducted from
reported profits reflecting a residual (or deficiency) amount. Also,
various threshold rates can be applied to different resources (or
operations) bearing different degrees of risk. Thus, the refinements
mentioned make residual income a more flexible and logical
approach than ROI. Nonetheless, both methods suffer from the
remaining defects cited and should be approached with due caution.

*Foreign operations*

The foregoing problems are common to evaluations of domestic
operations and managers. Evaluations of foreign activities are
fraught with all those mentioned plus several others. Domestic operations benefit from a common set of environmental factors, whereas
foreign operations are often conducted in circumstances that defy
standardised measurements. Furthermore, it is common for some

overseas activities to perform strategic roles that are not profit producing at all. Headquarters' decisions concerning coordination and
deployment of resources (including the multiple approaches to transfer pricing) directly impact the operating results of individual units.
Whose decisions are being evaluated? Should the evaluations be
made in the currency of the parent or of those of the foreign
domiciles? How are relative inflations and exchange-rate fluctuations
(two related but dissimilar matters) to be taken into account? Such
questions do not lend themselves to simple solutions.

Regardless of the defects related with profit-based measures,
studies recurringly indicate that ROI (or some variant method) is
employed almost universally (Robbins and Stobaugh, 1973).[1] Executives acknowledge the weaknesses mentioned yet contend that ROI is
the best method available. That borders on nonsense.

Most executives will also admit that ROI and similar measurements based on financial accounting reports are used because they
are routinely available and are easy to calculate and compare.
Moreover, top executives are evaluated by ROI methods, why should
it not be applicable to others? While the demands on executive time
are often tremendous, it should be recognised that the results being
evaluated usually represent the fruits of a year's efforts by other
parties. Surely performance evaluations warrant more time and
thought than perusal of lines on a graph or an array of numbers on a
list.

Realism and equity suggest a process similar to the following:

1  Define the purposes of the various units.
2  Determine the roles of the units and their managers.
3  Select appropriate criteria to measure efficiency (doing something right) and effectiveness (doing the right something).
4  Establish standards to evaluate the above performances.
5  Select the timings of evaluations.
6  Establish a process to communicate the results.

If nothing else, the above process will tend to create a better
understanding of the company as a whole as well as the interrelationships between and among segments, domestic and foreign. Past
results and future prospects will, more often than not, be seen as the

---

[1] John Dearden, Professor at Harvard Business School, has dissected and
criticised use of the ROI approach perennially in a series of articles in the
Harvard Business Review between 1960 and 1969.

products of a melange of factors: past decisions made by managers at the headquarters and unit levels, the effects of subsequent events (planned and otherwise), all coloured by future expectations.

Normative measures will be found difficult to construct. Subjectivity will be found equally difficult to avoid. Such tends to be the nature (as well as the source of the challenge and satisfaction) of the multidimensional art of multinational business.

## Taxation

The intricacies of international taxation are addressed elsewhere in this *Handbook*. This section will examine briefly some of the aspects of accounting for the infinite forms of international taxation that vex most businessmen (and accountants as well). Some cautions are in order. Few accountants can lift, much less comprehend, the more than 50,000 pages comprising the current manuals of the US Internal Revenue Service alone, not to mention the directives employed in other countries. Also, the US system of taxation is without parallel as far as complexity is concerned – it is unwieldy, to be precise. Unfortunately, more countries seem to be gravitating toward US methods and the problems of tax accounting will tend to become even more complex.

Tax accounting procedures should serve three needs of managers of headquarters and foreign companies:

1  To comply with statutory requirements.
2  To reflect fairly the amount of taxes paid or payable.
3  To assist in tax planning.

Compliance with statutory requirements is simplified in those countries (such as France and Sweden) which require conformity between financial and tax accountings. Most countries, however, recognise that tax accounting (serving a macro purpose) should be separated from financial accounting (serving the needs of micro units or firms). In the latter cases, supplementary tax records must be maintained, the accountant's function being to reduce redundancy and cost as much as possible.

Difficulties in accounting for some local taxes paid usually concern the volumes of transactions, such as those related to border, sales, and value-added taxes. These are best resolved by standardised or computerised handling. Documentation supporting other local taxes paid, such as on business incomes, is typically a non-recurring yet important matter. The standard advice encourages firms to understand the statutes and, where interpretations can vary, take the most favourable avenue that can be supported by documentary evidence.

At the headquarters level, accounting for taxes paid by foreign units is relatively straightforward if the headquarters' domicile taxes incomes earned solely within its borders (the territorial principle of tax domain).

On the other hand, if the headquarters is located in a country (such as the USA) that exercises taxing authority on incomes wherever earned (the worldwide principle), significant accounting problems result. To avoid double taxation of foreign-based company incomes, the USA employs complex systems of tax treaties and foreign tax credits. Both systems mandate accurate, supplementary accountings be maintained that reflect, by country and by year:

1  foreign earnings and profits, recast to conform with US tax-accounting standards;
2  the amounts of taxes paid (or deemed paid by second and third tiers of related companies) on incomes to foreign governments (national and sub-national), supported by foreign tax receipts and copies of foreign tax returns (translated into English);
3  foreign earnings and profits classified by nature (generally, operating profits are deferred until received by the US parent, whereas passive incomes, such as inter-unit dividends, interests, fees, and similar distributions are taxed concurrently to the parent as constructively received); and
4  dividend distributions received by the parent.

In short, foreign earnings and profits must be calculated each year for each foreign location and maintained in a sort of LIFO layer-cake fashion. Dividend distributions to the US parent, foreign taxes paid, and potential US tax liabilities must be identified with earnings and profits of a specific year (or years), using the LIFO basis, in order to compute foreign tax credits and any residual US taxes due.

This illustration, although highly oversimplified, indicates the need for close cooperation between accounting and tax departments, as well as mutual understanding of the peculiar needs of each. For instance, tax departments need detailed operating statements for each foreign location – consolidated statements are of no value at all. Natures and sources of revenues and expenses must be clearly described. Foreign tax receipts, translated copies of returns, and detailed information often prove to be difficult to obtain where there is no control of foreign entities.

International tax planning is a process that draws on accounting, tax, and other projections of data to determine whether, where, how, and with whom to conduct operations in order to achieve the desired business objectives with the minimum total tax burden. Considerations of proposed new ventures offer a wide range of alternatives. Tax planning of ongoing foreign operations soon becomes a maze of trade-offs resulting from change, both in frequency and magnitude. Experience indicates that, on an ongoing basis, planning of the sources and timing of dividend repatriations furnish the greatest benefits. Tax planning, much like all forms of forward thinking, also provides a better understanding of the complex multinational organism. Manipulations of other tax trade-offs, while important, should not be allowed to relegate otherwise sound business strategies to minor roles.

## ACCOUNTING FULL CIRCLE

Accounting enjoyed an international genesis or birthright. The Babylonians, Greeks, Romans, Turks, and Italians contributed and synergised ideas and practices that led to the invention of bookkeeping. The invention of movable type by Gutenberg, a German, enabled a Franciscan monk to describe double-entry bookkeeping for use by the rest of the existing world.

In the exodus that followed, bookkeeping travelled in the wake of business to Holland, Scotland, England and eventually, to America. In the process, bookkeeping was transformed into a profession known as accountancy, or the language of business.

Over time, the influences of different environments led to the crystallisation of national accounting practices. Today, there is US accounting, UK accounting, German accounting, and so on. The result is a language of business comprised of many dialects.

The present situation is also something of a paradox. International accounting organisations are pressing for greater uniformity of national accounting and reporting standards. On the other hand, multinational and other complex companies are being required to employ situational approaches to accountings of international operations. The solution, of course, lies in the middle ground in the nature of harmonisation, initially by regions or spheres of influence, eventually worldwide. In the process, international accounting will develop and mature while serving the needs of an interdependent world community. Accounting will have come full circle.

During the interim, standard-setting bodies must realise that time and circumstance have precluded reliance on normative applications if economic sense is to be reflected in financial reports. The situational approach must be recognised. This means that standard setters should seek to identify those cases that are alike, then prescribe the accounting practices most appropriate. More responsibility and reliance will need be placed upon the judgements of managements and auditors: the former to match situations and accountings, as well as to explain the methods used; the latter to attest to the appropriateness of the methods selected as well as the fairness of the reported results.

Examples of useful management explanations are:

1 The structure of the firm – organisationally and geographically.
2 Major differences between the home and host environments – economic, legal, tax, and accounting.
3 The effects, good and bad, of the above differences upon the financial reports.
4 The effects, good and bad, of changing price levels and how management is planning to keep the stockholder whole (Miller, 1978).
5 The nature of foreign operations: whether they are short- or long-run ventures, considered as dependent or independent activities and, consequently, the perceived extents and effects of foreign exchange exposure, segmented as considered necessary.

These examples may seem to be radical suggestions. Nonetheless, they are compatible with the fact that accounting, financial reporting, and auditing are adaptive arts, rather than rigid sciences.

Furthermore, the suggestions for commonsense explanations threaded throughout this chapter can be implemented internationally today, regardless of the differences existing in the languages of people or the languages of business. We should get on with it.

## REFERENCES AND ADDITIONAL READING

Brown, R. (ed.), *A History of Accounting and Accountants,* Jack, 1905.

Financial Accounting Standards Board, *Statement of Financial Accounting Standards No. 8,* 'Accounting for the Translation of Foreign Currency Transactions and Foreign Currency Financial Statements', FASB, October 1975.

Knickerbocker, Frederick T., *Proceedings: First Annual International Business Conference,* Saint Louis University, 1 December 1975.

Miller, E. L., 'What's Wrong with Price-Level Accounting', *Harvard Business Review,* November–December 1978.

Miller, E. L., *Accounting Problems of Multinational Enterprises,* Lexington Books D. C. Heath, 1979.

Miller, E. L., *Inflation Accounting,* Van Nostrand Reinhold, 1980.

Perlmutter, Howard V., 'The Tortuous Evolution of the Multinational Corporation', *Columbia Journal of World Business,* January–February, 1969(a).

Perlmutter, Howard V., 'Alternative Futures for the Multinational', *Proceedings: Second Annual International Business Conference,* Saint Louis University, 16 December 1976(b).

Robbins, S. M. and Stobaugh, R. B., 'The Bent Measuring Stick for Foreign Subsidiaries', *Harvard Business Review,* September–October 1973.

Sharav, I., 'Transfer Pricing – Diversity of Goals and Practices', *Journal of Accountancy,* April 1974.

Wilkinson, J. W., 'The Meanings of Measurements', *Management Accounting,* July 1975.

# 15

# Social Accounting

**Richard Dobbins and David Fanning**


*There can be little doubt that one of the significant aspects of change in business is the widening awareness of the social responsibility of companies, especially large companies. As a result, a natural transition of thought leads from the subject matter of the preceding chapter, that of the powerful and influential multinational company, to the more generalised topic of social accounting.*

*The authors of the present chapter point out that although financial texts often postulate that the objective of the firm is to maximise its market value, that is not a view which is universally accepted. It is considered that a company has many obligations to the community and to the environment, and even the traditional profit and loss account reflects in some degree the interests of various groups other than investors.*

*Social accounting is defined in the chapter as 'the measurement and reporting of information concerning the impact of an entity and its activities on society'. The chapter specifically categorises the activities which are covered by this definition and the authors maintain that what has become known as human resource accounting is also embraced by the general subject.*

*The quantification in monetary terms of the social responsibilities of business is difficult and rarely attempted; it involves experimentation and adaptability to the business concerned; but it has promise of considerable value to those interested in the industrial and commercial world. 'The traditional leavening of discretion exercised in conventional financial accounts', the authors consider, 'may be successfully transferred to social accounting'. They provide examples and a model of how this can be done.*

*The authors also echo the thought expressed by other contributors in connection with different topics by referring to 'the growing disenchantment with the parameters and conventions of traditional financial accounts'.*

Modern financial texts postulate that the objective of the firm is to maximise its market. Acceptance of this single objective should lead managers to maximise the anticipated level of net operational cash flows and minimise the perceived level of risk associated with those cash flows. The value of the firm is its discounted anticipated net operational cash flows. Acceptance of projects with positive net present values will increase the market value of the firm. The aggregate market value of the firm can therefore be expressed as follows:

$$V = \sum_{t=1}^{n} \frac{1}{1+r}[R - W - I]_t = \frac{\bar{x}}{pk} = \sum_{t=1}^{n} \frac{A_t}{(1+k)t}$$

where $V$ =     the market value of the firm,
     $r$ =     the overall cost of capital,
     $R$ =     the firm's anticipated operational receipts,
     $W$ =     the firm's anticipated operational expenditure,
     $I$ =     the anticipated level of new investment,
     $\bar{x}$ =     the firm's net operational cash flows, i.e. $R - W - I$,
     $pk$ =     the overall market capitalisation rate depending upon the firm's operational risk class, i.e. $k$, and
     $A_t$ =     the firm's anticipated net operational cash flows in future time periods, i.e. $R - W - I$ or $\bar{x}$.

The above equations demonstrate the equivalence of modern approaches to the value of the firm which is the discounted future operational receipts less operational expenditure and new investment, or the capitalised future net operational cash flows, or the discounted net operational cash flows receivable in all future periods. In operational terms the objective of the firm is to maximise anticipated cash flows, $\bar{x}$, and minimise risk which results in a lower discount rate, $k$, or lower capitalisation rate, $pk$. The trade-off between risk and return ensures that two companies with the same anticipated cash flows will have different market values, depending upon their overall risk classes – the greater the risk, the higher the discount rate and the lower the market value.

**Table 15.1**
**Companies' responsibilities to various**
**interest groups**

Profit and loss account for the year ended 31 December

| Conventional | | | Interest groups |
|---|---|---|---|
| UK sales | 100 | | UK consumers |
| Export sales | 60 | 160 | Foreign states, treasury |
| Less: cost of sales | | 40 | Suppliers |
| | | 120 | |
| Less: wages | 70 | | Employees |
| salaries | 20 | | Directors, managers |
| expenses | 10 | 100 | Local community |
| | | 20 | |
| Less: interest payments | | 4 | Debenture holders, bank |
| | | 16 | |
| Less: taxation | | 6 | UK government |
| | | 10 | |
| Less: dividend | | 5 | Shareholders |
| Retentions | | 5 | Shareholders, managers, employees, government |

The single financial objective of maximisation of the market value of the firm has not been universally accepted. Even a cursory glance at the conventional profit and loss account suggests that companies have responsibilities to various interest groups, in addition to the providers of funds. Table 15.1 can be interpreted as suggesting that corporate managers have responsibilities to consumers, managers of international payments, suppliers, employees including managers, local communities, and managers of government finances as well as shareholders and providers of loan capital. Other interest groups might include competitors, females, non-whites, the disabled, sports and charity sponsors, and all those concerned with conservation of the environment.

Managers of industrial enterprises have been called upon both to recognise the interests of various groups when making decisions and to make periodic reports to interested parties, in addition to the providers of funds who have rights to receive information under the Companies Acts. The provision of information for interest groups other than that information regarded as being of considerable importance to the providers of funds, is generally referred to as social accounting. Applied social accounting therefore tends to be little more than additional corporate reporting whereby information relating to employment, energy utilisation, charitable donations, exports and product safety is disclosed. Social accounting is not cost–benefit analysis. Many advocates of social responsibility would like corporate managers to take social costs and social benefits into account when making decisions, and indeed the net present value formula can be adjusted for social costs and benefits, although the monetary measurement of these items is extremely difficult. However, although company directors may well consider social aspects of decisions, social accounting as evidenced to date amounts to little more than a supplement to financial reporting.

'You can't actually see fresh air. Or peace and quiet, or water purity. But a decent environment is an asset which everyone values: an invisible asset.' This introduction to a newspaper advertisement by Mobil proclaims the fact that the company is spending around £12 million – the cost of equipment to curb air, water and noise pollution – at its new refinery development on the Thames estuary. According to Mobil's corporate advertising, the cash is well spent. Mobil's response to what it sees as its corporate social responsibility is typical of the reaction of modern business to political and societal pressure for companies and other institutions to respond to issues beyond their traditional task of producing goods or services at a profit. The traditional corporate objective of wealth maximisation has been transmuted to the more recent objective of ameliorating the impact of an undertaking on the community in which it operates. There has developed a strong feeling that business must forgo some of its profits in order to serve social goals, although economists of a conservative inclination (such as Milton Friedman) hold firmly that the social responsibility of business is to increase profits (and sophisticated liberal economists believe equally firmly that there are not enough profits to forgo to make much difference).

This view of social responsibility – the special programme or one-off action which a firm may undertake out of forgone profits – diverts attention away from the social impact of what a firm does in its main line of everyday business. It is the overall social impact of business that is the issue. The measurement of the extent of that social impact and the identification and attainment of social objectives are central to any discussion of corporate social responsibility.

As pressure has mounted for corporations to report their social performance, so there has developed the concept of social accounting, which may be defined as the measurement and reporting, to management, investors, and a firm's public, of information concerning the impact of an entity and its activities on society. To date the greatest response in this area has been from US and German companies, with significant contributions being made by French and UK corporations, although the latter have responded only slowly and in isolated instances. In many countries, of course, the response of business firms to the demand for social accounting has been directly related to the strength of special interest groups and the vociferousness of their demands. By and large, the individual investor has not been an ardent supporter of social responsibility statements and their concomitant costs. As many an investor has told many a board of directors, the ordinary shareholder would prefer a little less social accounting which makes the executives feel good and a little more in the way of dividends and capital gains which would make the shareholders feel good. Nevertheless, while there are debates about the usefulness and relevance of some of the social impact information demanded by special interest or pressure groups, this chapter outlines a set of approaches to social accounting and, by drawing on the published social reports of US and UK companies, proposes a standardised social accounting model. As a preliminary step along this path there will be a brief examination of the major areas of corporate social performance in which companies may wish to: establish goals, objectives and priorities; plan the use of monetary, physical and human resources; and measure progress.

It is worthwhile emphasising the relationship between social accounting and conventional accounting measures. While many of the social effects and impacts of a modern corporation cannot be assessed by the financial and economic mechanisms of traditional accounting information, social accounting not only includes but extends many of the procedures and statements present in established financial accounting practices. The social significance of profit and its distribution, of capital investment, of employment opportunities, and so on, have to be considered before dealing with other categories of social performance. In many ways, advocates of social accounting tend to eschew traditional financial accounting measures and to concentrate on descriptive and qualitative statements of corporate social responsiveness. The majority of writers on social accounting (or socio-economic accounting or social audit or social responsibility accounting or any other of the variety of names by which this information disclosure has been called) do not include within their remit the mechanism of human resource accounting, which they see as a mere modification of traditional financial accounting. Since quantification of social performance achievements is a prerequisite for informed comparison of companies' social contributions, such an omission is regrettable. Despite the dangers inherent in such a proprietorial approach to the human resources employed in an organisation, it can have beneficial and valuable attributes as an effective component in a company's overall social accounting machinery.

## MAJOR AREAS OF SOCIAL PERFORMANCE

The most useful categorisation of the variables present in social accounting measurement has been advanced by the Canadian National Association of Accountants. Social concerns are divided into the following four major components:

1 community involvement;
2 human resources stewardship;
3 physical resources and environmental stewardship;
4 product or service contributions.

Community involvement includes those socially oriented activities which tend primarily to benefit (or disadvantage in some cases) the general public, e.g. philanthropic programmes, community involvement by employees, corporate community services. 'Community' in this sense means more than just the specific geographical location of company offices and plants. Human resources stewardship covers activities directed to the wellbeing of employees, e.g. hiring practices, pension and retirement benefits, working conditions, training and promotion policies, job enrichment and satisfaction. Physical resources and environment stewardship includes corporate activities directed towards the conservation of resources and the protection of the environment. Product or service contributions of a social nature deal with the impact of a company's products and services on society and its relations with consumers, e.g. product quality and innovation, advertising and packaging, product safety, guarantees and warranties, customer satisfaction and consumerism.

The checklist of items under each of these four major headings (Table 15.2) identifies typical examples of social performance. The list is neither all-inclusive nor ranked by importance, but it serves as a beginning framework for social reporting by providing divisions which are reasonably clear and logical.

**Table 15.2**
**Categories of social concern**

| Community involvement | Human resources stewardship |
|---|---|
| 1 General philanthropy | 1 Employment practices |
| 2 Transportation | 2 Training programmes |
| 3 Health services | 3 Promotion policies |
| 4 Housing | 4 Employment security |
| 5 Aid in personal and business problems | 5 Remuneration and retirement benefits |
| 6 Community planning and improvement | 6 Working conditions |
| 7 Volunteer community activities | 7 Health and safety |
| 8 Specialised food and welfare programmes | 8 Job satisfaction |
| 9 Education | 9 Communications and participation |

| Physical resources and environmental stewardship | Product or service contributions |
|---|---|
| 1 Air | 1 Labelling and packaging |
| 2 Water | 2 Marketing representations and product claims |
| 3 Sound | 3 Guarantee and warranty provisions |
| 4 Waste creation and disposal | 4 Consumer satisfaction and complaints procedures |
| 5 Scarce resources usage | |
| 4 and conservation | 5 Consumer education |
| 6 Aesthetic considerations of design and presence | 6 Product quality and suitability |
| | 7 Product safety |
| | 8 Constructive research and development |
| | 9 Advertising and promotion |

Within these areas, the modern corporation will identify standards and objectives, whether from governmental legislation and regulation or from societal pressure and demand or from internally perceived norms of 'good behaviour'.

## REPORTING PROGRESS

Even when an organisation has developed a presentation format for its social accounting report, there are two other basic dimensions which will affect the final published report: specificity of disclosure, and focus of disclosure.

Current social reports employ at least three different degrees of specificity. The descriptive format provides purely qualitative commentary on the firm's social activities. For example, in the De Beers Consolidated Mines 1978 Report: 'Close attention is being paid to the training and development of employees on all of the mines and good progress has been achieved. . . .'

The quantitative format depends on the use of specific data to summarise performance. For example, in the Rio Tinto-Zinc 1978 Report, we read 'The Group's environmental expenditure in 1978 was some £27 million. This figure includes grants to universities and other learned institutions undertaking research on subjects of importance to Group companies. From 1970 to 1978 inclusive the Group spent some £152 million on environmental controls, an average approaching £17 million a year.'

The monetary format requires the conversion of activities to monetary amounts and accounting statements reflecting the social costs and benefits of a company's activities. For example, the social balance sheet and income statement of Abt Associates, an American pioneer of social accounting, quantifies such social costs as pollution from automobile commuting by its employees and inequality of opportunity.

On current performance, the descriptive format is the most commonly used, often supplemented by illustrations and sporadic quantitative data. The monetary format is a rare and still experimental phenomenon. The overriding problem, of course, is that of quantification. As Michael Shanks of BOC International has commented:

> Objectives of a social nature can be set, and some . . . can be
> quantified, particularly those that deal with relationships with

employees. But they do not have the beauty, the precision and the clarity of the traditional numerate objectives of financial marketing, and production targeting, and it is very hard to see that this will ever change. It seems that this area of social responsibility will always be a much fuzzier area than that of financial, marketing or production accounting (Shanks, 1978).

There is the additional factor of the focus of social performance reports. While sophisticated analysis and reporting exists within organisations for *internal* social accounting purposes, it will be some considerable time before externally directed reports are similarly sophisticated. Companies tend surely to experiment with social performance accounting before publicly disclosing the results, and disclosure usually follows a non-objective pattern. The focus of disclosure will be either input-oriented, in which case the report will concentrate on the firm's efforts and expenditures in specific areas, or performance-oriented, in which case it will attempt to measure the output of social activities and their impact on society. Comparison with explicit defined company objectives is obviously easier than comparison with general societal goals, and most social accounting statements issued so far have generally taken the easier alternative.

However, even though there may be a conformity of practice there is no consensus as to the right format and a number of options is available in each of the three dimensions: categorisation, specificity, and focus. This chapter proposes a standard format for social reports, accompanied by an examination of existing efforts by public companies. Before that, it will outline and discuss two related topics: the preparation of social accounts in monetary terms, and human resource accounting.

## MONEY VALUES IN SOCIAL ACCOUNTING REPORTS

As intimated above, there are considerable difficulties involved in the quantification of social objectives, but as emphasised by Seidler (1975) and others, accountants and financial managers do possess the necessary skills for the task, even though they display little interest in the subject. Seidler reports the most common objection as being that it is not possible to make valid social accounting calculations – there are too many problems involved. However, the measurement of the net profit of a major industrial undertaking calls for many calculations relating to stock valuation, cost of research and development, depreciation charges, etc. Accountants have faced many of the problems of income measurement for many years. As Seidler (1975) points out: 'Certainly, the complexities of social measurements do not appear much more foreboding than those of an international oil company; practice should yield some reasonably accepted results' (p. 12). He recognises, of course, that there are some rather awesome problems associated with social accounting measurements. How, for example, does one assign a monetary value to the increase in human self-esteem and dignity resulting from job creation or training programmes? It is virtually impossible to quantify attitude changes, especially socially significant ones. Nevertheless, the traditional leavening of discretion exercised in conventional financial accounts when valuing mineral reserves or goodwill may be transferred successfully to social accounting.

If it is decided that the process of assigning monetary values to social inputs and outputs, however difficult it may prove in practice, is capable of being carried out in some meaningful way, it is then possible to move to a comparison of a conventional income statement and a social accounting income statement. The following example and discussion is derived from Seidler's paper.

Take the case of a university of medium size, regularly in a position of operating deficit – its costs regularly exceed its income. Matching income and outgoings on a conventional basis produces a deficit and gives rise to any number of financial difficulties. The university can, however, be seen in a social context. What benefits does it produce for society, and what are the associated costs to society? If a fairly simplistic approach is adopted, the two income statements might appear as shown in Table 15.3.

In the conventional statement, there is not much dispute about the valuation of the individual categories. The preparation of the social statement will be a matter for wider disagreement. However it is possible to start from simple principles. It is generally accepted that graduates usually command higher salaries than non-graduates. From that premise, it is possible to calculate a net present value for the increased salary attracted by graduates. Similarly, it would be possible to attribute net present values to the savings or incremental income occasioned by the implementation of research findings or innovations. The judgemental valuation of both these income or benefit categories will, of course, be a contentious matter, open to all manner of interpretation. On the cost side, the problem is essentially less difficult. Tuition fees, research grants and government aids are all denominated in money terms and are a direct cost to society, but there are also opportunity costs to be considered – again a contentious business.

Overshadowing both sides of the social accounting equation will be the question of 'society'. Which society benefits? Which pays the cost? Is it the local community? Is it the professional community? Is it the nation as a whole? In this simple analysis, it is possible to regard society as a whole. For while it is the individual student or the company which employs him which will benefit and derive an immediate advantage from his tuition, it is equally true that the nation will benefit from increased productivity and increased tax revenues. On the research side, the nation as a whole will benefit from increased productivity, higher trading levels, or greater product competitiveness, and from such slightly less tangible benefits as better working conditions, increased health and safety, and so on. From a practical point of view, the construction of a social accounting statement for an institution such as a university would have wider

**Table 15.3**
**Alternative income statements**

| Conventional | | Social accounting | |
|---|---|---|---|
| | £ | | £ |
| Income: | | Benefits: | |
| Tuition fees | XXX | Increased value of students | XXX |
| Research grants | XXX | Value of research | XXX |
| Government aid | XXX | | |
| | XXX | | XXX |
| Outgoings: | | Costs: | |
| Teaching costs | (XXX) | Tuition fees | (XXX) |
| Research costs | (XXX) | Research grants | (XXX) |
| Student costs | (XXX) | Government aid | (XXX) |
| Administration costs | (XXX) | Other | (XXX) |
| Deficit | (XXX) | Social profit | XXX |

uses than the simple gratification of those responsible for the increased social value. Such a statement, showing a substantial 'social profit', would make a powerful bargaining tool when seeking extra funds from government or raising funds from philanthropic or research-supporting bodies.

The example of a university is probably easier to sustain than that of a commercial enterprise, but it is equally possible to construct a social income statement for a profit-making (or seeking) entity. If the reasonable convention that all production is socially desirable is adopted, *ceteris paribus*, then it is possible to arrive at the form of social income statement shown in Table 15.4. This form of social value-added statement would, it is argued, contain far more useful information than conventional value-added analyses. The category 'socially desirable outputs not sold' would include such items as job training, minority employment, health and safety at work, and leisure and environmental contributions. On the 'socially undesirable effects not paid for' register might be entered such items as air and water pollution, increased demands on public transportation systems, and usage of dwindling resources. The resultant social 'profit' or 'loss' might well be a more potent measure of an enterprise's role and effect in society than conventional financial accounting measures of value added.

However desirable social accounting in money terms may be, there is the obvious difficulty of attributing money values to some of the essential constituents of a social statement. Money measurements are a common language of most people, and it is to 'most people' rather than a sophisticated handful of professionals that social accounting information needs to be made available. That being the case, the introduction of ranking scales or esoteric grading systems would only serve to confuse the issue. However difficult the assignment of monetary values may be in practice, any attempt at a social accounting statement in quantified money terms may be better than no attempt at all.

## HUMAN RESOURCE ACCOUNTING

Advocates of human resource accounting stress the importance of the human element in organisations and the failure of conventional accounting in dealing with it as an asset. In its simplest form HRA involves the identification of the costs of recruitment, training, and maintenance of an entity's human assets. There is now a substantial body of literature on the subject of HRA (see, for example, Flamholtz, 1974; Likert, 1967; McRae, 1974). This growth of interest has been accompanied by the development of strong factionalism as to the merits and demerits of accounting for an organisation's human assets. To some, HRA is degrading to the individual, implying as it does 'ownership' and even 'slavery'. Furthermore, the techniques are almost as numerous as the articles on HRA. Accountants have proposed several methods for calculating the value of human assets, and the associated calculation of writing-off or amortisation instalments (see Brummet, 1977). For the purposes of this chapter, in outlining the approach to be followed in principle rather than detailing a specific method of calculation, five widely documented methods of valuation can be identified – historical cost, replacement cost, opportunity cost, value measurement, and non-monetary measurement (Dobbins and Trussell, 1975).

### Historical cost

The total cost of the investment includes those quantifiable expenditures associated with recruitment, selection, hiring, training, placement, familiarisation and development. This method simply capitalises human resource costs and does not seek to value people. It is similar to the approach followed when valuing fixed assets and writing off their cost over their useful life. The cost is capitalised, not being charged against current income, and a deferred taxation charge is made on the notional increase in profit.

### Table 15.4
### Social value-added statement

|  | £ |
| --- | --- |
| 'Conventional' value added | XXX |
| Socially desirable outputs not sold | XXX |
|  | XXX |
| Socially undesirable effects not paid for | (XXX) |
| Net social profit | XXX |

## Replacement cost

This method is based on current value or replacement cost. Under this system, an organisation values an employee at the estimated cost of replacement with a new employee of equivalent ability. The application of such a method, however, is made difficult by the problems of defining and measuring replacement costs.

## Opportunity cost

This is a largely artificial method involving the concept of the competitive bidding process. Under this system, profit-centre managers are encouraged to bid for scarce employees, the successful bid being included in the organisation's human investment calculations. Employee abilities are related to profit generation, and may lead to a more efficient allocation of human resources.

## Value measurement

Under this method, established capital budgeting techniques are applied to people, the argument being that the value of a firm's employees is their discounted future earnings. Value methods try to measure economic value rather than simply record investment in human resources at historic or replacement cost. An alternative approach to value measurement is that of estimating the contribution of human resources to the economic value of the firm. Valuation is determined by allocating to human resources a portion of the firm's present value (this being defined as discounted future earnings).

## Non-monetary measurement

This method is fundamentally different from the other four. Basically, the alternative approaches proposed by a number of writers have centred on social and psychological determinants or what have been labelled causal and intervening variables which combine to affect end result variables. Briefly, leadership skills and policies influence employee attitudes, motivations, behaviour and goals, which in turn affect sales, costs, cash flow and profit.

A simple example of the application of the first three methods is given in Table 15.5 which demonstrates the effect on balance sheet totals of implementing HRA in very basic terms.

The benefits of HRA include the important influence on management's attitudes towards employees and the proper consideration of human assets when preparing strategic and budgetary plans. The influence of human variables on a firm's performance and profitability may be better understood, and human resources may be allocated more efficiently. From a cosmetic viewpoint, the realisation by a firm's public of its strong commitment to its employees may enhance its image and standing. Against this must be set the reluctance of financial accountants to bring the process of valuation on the basis of future earnings into records of accounting transactions. Additionally, there is a widespread antipathy amongst employees and others to the whole concept of human resources being either owned by or even made profitable use of by firms. Not to be overlooked is the fact that an increase in the firm's capital base and reported profit will lead to changes in the rate of return on capital employed and other financial ratios.

On balance, however, HRA is potentially a most valuable aid to managerial decision making. Even though it may be many years before HRA statements appear in conventional financial accounts, the use of human resource accounting information for internal management accounting purposes is already fairly well established.

**Table 15.5**
**Human resource accounting balance sheets**

| (£ millions) | A | B | C | D |
| --- | --- | --- | --- | --- |
| Sources of funds | | | | |
| Conventional sources | 1.0 | 1.0 | 1.0 | 1.0 |
| Human resource reserve | – | 0.5 | 1.5 | 3.5 |
| Deferred taxation (increase) | – | 0.5 | 1.5 | 3.5 |
| Total sources | 1.0 | 2.0 | 4.0 | 8.0 |
| Employment of funds | | | | |
| Conventional assets | 1.0 | 1.0 | 1.0 | 1.0 |
| Human assets | – | 1.0 | 3.0 | 7.0 |
| Total assets | 1.0 | 2.0 | 4.0 | 8.0 |

A = conventional accounting
B = conventional accounting plus HRA – cost method
C = conventional accounting plus HRA – replacement cost method
D = conventional accounting plus HRA – value method (discounted future earnings)

## SOCIAL REPORTS – THE PRESENT POSITION

The view of the UK government is that social reports should not be the subject of legislation. There should be a voluntary movement towards disclosure of information of a social nature. Given the widespread homage paid to the principle of wider disclosure, it is disappointing to note the almost universal disregard of that principle in the published reports of UK companies. The USA and some European countries are better served by their industrial undertakings. Indeed, nearly all the available examples of social accounting, in whatever form, come from US or German reports. Most of those examples have been reproduced in any number of papers and books on this topic so it is not thought necessary to duplicate those efforts here.

However, a number of UK companies have taken the plunge and produced statements detailing employee-related information and outlining corporate reaction to environmental and consumer pressure on topics such as pollution, minority employment, and so on. Additionally, UK companies have generally been conscientious in producing employee reports – albeit in differing degrees of quality and information content. For example, the employment report published by Crown House Limited with its accounts for 1978–79 is reproduced as Table 15.6. The report is a mixture of the quantitative and the monetary formats, and it represents perhaps the most advanced treatment of social information by UK companies to date. Many firms, of course, address themselves, usually in the chairman's statement, to problems of pollution or energy conservation, but such information is only rarely quantified and is, more often than not, accompanied by contentious political argument or special pleading. For many companies, the absence of legislation or regulation is equivalent to an instruction not to include social reports.[1]

There is an increasing tendency – for reasons not always altruistic – to reveal pension costs and to detail the specific provisions of individual pension plans. Even so, there is still a distinct paucity of employee-related or any other information in what might be seen as the social accounting catchment area. This is not to say that corporations are not socially responsible and, as has been said earlier, many

---

[1] For a discussion of the practice of British companies in providing employment reports and a proposed format for such reports, see Fanning, 1979.

companies have instituted social and accounting procedures for their own internal use. There are a number of inherent difficulties in designing and producing a social account, not least of which is the problem of identifying and quantifying social benefits and their associated costs. There is a growing disenchantment with the parameters and conventions of traditional financial accounting, and there is a growing call for more relevant information about a company's impact on its environment and its communities. A number of models have been proposed for social accounting, most of them advanced by US commentators but nonetheless worthy for that bias, and the literature abounds with peremptory guidelines and interpretative examples. The next section proposes a standard format for social reports.

**Table 15.6**
**Crown House Limited: employment report**

| | | 31 March 1979 | | 1 April 1978 | |
|---|---|---|---|---|---|
| | | Male | Female | Male | Female |
| 1 | Number employed | | | | |
| | (a) Total employees | | | | |
| | Full time | 5,205 | 896 | 4,969 | 935 |
| | Part time | 75 | 396 | 79 | 349 |
| | | 5,280 | 1,292 | 5,048 | 1,284 |
| | (b) Functions of employees | | | | |
| | Engineering and production | 4,697 | 616 | 4,457 | 568 |
| | Administration | 583 | 676 | 591 | 716 |
| | | 5,280 | 1,292 | 5,048 | 1,284 |

| | Engineering and production | Administration |
|---|---|---|
| 2 Location of employment at 31 March, 1979 | | |
| (a) UK | | |
| England | 3,511 | 1,045 |
| Scotland | 476 | 54 |
| Wales | 554 | 93 |
| Northern Ireland | 134 | 9 |
| (b) Overseas | 638 | 58 |
| | 5,313 | 1,259 |

| 3 Remuneration | UK | Overseas | Total |
|---|---|---|---|
| Gross pay | £24,582,312 | £2,167,916 | £26,750,228 |

| 4 Education and training | Hours |
|---|---|
| Total employee hours spent in training during the | |
| year within the company (excluding on-the-job training) | 328,026 |
| External training courses | 29,372 |
| | 357,398 |

| Cost of training | £000 |
|---|---|
| Training department | 54 |
| Wages paid during training | 322 |
| Training Board levy | 91 |
| External courses | 19 |
| | 486 |
| Less: Training Board grant | 144 |
| | 342 |

5 Trade Unions
As at 31 March 1979, the principal trade unions recognised by member companies of the group were:
Electrical and Engineering Staff Association; Electrical, Electronics, Telecommunications and Plumbing Trades Union; National Union of Sheet Metal Workers, Coppersmiths, Heating and Domestic Engineers; General and Municipal Workers Union; National Union of Flint Glassworkers.

6 Accidents
(a) Number of reportable accidents during the year 154
(b) Frequency of reportable industrial accidents
(accidents/1000 hours worked) 0.012

7 Disabled persons
At 31 March 1979, 66 disabled persons were employed by the group.

## A SOCIAL REPORTING MODEL

Table 15.7 shows the format and constituents of a proposed social accounting statement, based on the conventional profit and loss or income statement.

Taking the social benefits side of the equation first, the individual constituents can be defined and quantified as follows:

1 products and services provided (the present value of the entity's output, together with the value of facilities or services provided to other elements of society);

### Table 15.7
### Social reporting model

Responsible Undertaking Limited – social account

| | £ |
|---|---|
| **Social benefits** | |
| | |
| Products and services provided | XXX |
| Payments to other elements of society: | |
| Wages and salaries | XXX |
| Payments to suppliers | XXX |
| Taxes and rates, etc | XXX |
| Dividends and interest | XXX |
| | XXX |
| Additional employee benefits | XXX |
| Donations to the community | XXX |
| Environmental improvements | XXX |
| Ancillary benefits | XXX |
| | |
| Total social benefits | XXX |
| | |
| **Social costs** | |
| Goods and materials acquired | XXX |
| Fixed asset purchases | XXX |
| Labour and services used | XXX |
| Public services and facilities used | XXX |
| Payments from other elements of society: | |
| Customers | XXX |
| Investors | XXX |
| Lenders | XXX |
| | XXX |
| Work-related injuries or illnesses | XXX |
| Discrimination and disadvantage | XXX |
| Environmental damage | XXX |
| Other costs | XXX |
| | (XXX) |
| | |
| Social profit (or deficit) | XXX |

2 payments to other elements of society;
3 additional employee benefits (the value of fringe benefits, training programmes, recreational or social benefits – this should be the value to the employee, *not* the cost to the company, which is shown separately);

4    donations to the community (both money sums, whether by direct gift or sponsorship, and gifts in kind – the loan of an executive, for example, or the granting of time off for local council or voluntary duties);
5    environmental improvements (landscaping a gravel pit, for example, or providing a company bus service);
6    ancillary benefits (factory crèches or public education programmes, for instance).

Matching these benefits will be the categories of social cost, defined broadly as follows:

1    goods and materials acquired;
2    fixed asset purchases;
3    labour and services used;
4    public services and facilities used (the entity's share of the cost of the police and fire services, or the use of roads, parks, sewers and so on);
5    payments from other elements of society (customers, investors, lenders);
6    work-related injuries and illnesses (the present value of lost income);
7    discrimination and disadvantage (the present value of lost income, in cases of discrimination, and the extra cost caused by disadvantageous treatment);
8    environmental damage;
9    other costs (product shortcomings, for example, or undesirable attitude formation).

Much of the information needed for the compilation of a social account in this recommended format will already be available to management in conventional financial accounts. For the rest, most can be gathered with relatively little effort and minor modifications in the entity's information processing systems. Some of the information will be difficult to obtain and even harder to translate into monetary values. This may prove expensive for the organisation. However, the essence of this system is that the information network will only need to be established once. Replication of the process annually or regularly will reduce the unit costs considerably. The criteria to be adopted will vary according to the reporting firm's understanding of its social responsibility and its intentions: whether to report to the public its effect on society, or to produce an internal account of its overall effect on society.

In many cases, the value to be placed on a particular cost or benefit will be a subjective and sometimes haphazard figure. For example, in determining monetary values for social benefits or costs associated with the government sector, a company may take as a starting point the amount of taxes or rates it pays, and then adjust that figure by taking into account any additional demands it makes on public services or utilities – by having badly secured premises (inviting theft or trespass) or by transporting highly inflammable goods in unsafe containers. The reporting firm will also want to be aware of indirect benefits and costs, e.g. the air pollution caused by employees driving to work, or the noise pollution caused by customers playing the firm's stereo equipment – but this analysis must clearly not be taken to extremes. Standardised measurement techniques exist already or can easily be developed for many of the categories outlined, but a number will need to be of a specialised individual nature, even of a one-off kind. Where these are used, the social account will need to include some description of their nature so that users can judge their applicability and reliability.

Finally, with any social account there is obviously room for, and a need for, descriptive analysis of items which cannot be quantified or of items which reflect social concerns or changing public standards. For example, there was a decade or two ago a great concern with political donations by public companies and many a newspaper article was based on the practices of the larger companies. The emphasis of public interest has now moved on and, while all companies report their political donations or the lack of them, the matter is now somewhat demoded. It may well be that a number of the items presently fashionable in a societal view of the business enterprise will themselves be forced out of the limelight following the development of social disclosure.

## REFERENCES AND ADDITIONAL READING

Brummet, R. L., 'Human Resource Accounting' in Davidson, S. and Weil, R. L. (eds), *Handbook of Modern Accounting*, McGraw-Hill, 1977.

Dobbins, R. and Trussell, P., 'The Valuation of Human Resources', *Management Decision*, vol. 13, no. 3, 1975.

Fanning, D., 'Employment Reports – An Appraisal', *Employee Relations*, vol. 1, no. 4, 1979.

Flamholtz, E., *Human Resource Accounting,* Encino, Dickenson, 1974.

Likert, R., *The Human Organization,* McGraw-Hill, 1967.

McRae, T. W., 'Human Resource Accounting as a Management Tool', *Journal of Accountancy,* vol. 138, no. 2, 1974.

Seidler, L. J., 'Dollar Values in the Social Income Statement' in Seidler, L. J. and Seidler, L. (eds), *Social Accounting: Theory, Issues and Cases,* Melville, 1975.

Shanks, M., 'What is Social Accounting?' in *Social Accounting*, London, CIPFA, 1978.

# PART IV
# SPECIAL ASPECTS

## PART IV  SPECIAL ASPECTS

Many important aspects of business fit uneasily into the familiar classifications of planning and control. Thus tax management, which is the subject of the first chapter in this part, is at the same time an element of financial planning, a factor in the decision-making process and often a vital consideration in the management and organisation of a business venture. This is especially so where the operations are on an international scale and of which the implications for cash flow and profitability are often neglected. In Chapter 16 John Chown concisely explains how tax strategy is closely intermingled with decisions on such matters as: the sourcing of finance, exchange rates, variations in tax allowances from one country to another, differential interest rates, transfer pricing, and even evaluating the performance of overseas subsidiaries.

By way of contrast, Brian Murphy discusses the special management problems of the small business unit in Chapter 17. These problems are not always fully appreciated or acknowledged by financial executives in parent companies; nor by the managers in those concerns which, although they may not have an ostensible financial interest in a small business, may be relying on the services of small suppliers or the outlets provided by small retailers. Nevertheless the small business often contains the seeds of innovation in ideas and techniques which have great potential and are ripe for development.

There is no need to emphasise the growing importance of computerisation. In Chapter 18 Phil Jones not only foreshadows far-reaching developments still to come in this field but also argues that some existing systems of electronic data processing are misconceived and ill-planned.

Throughout this handbook the contributors refer to the effects of inflation on the aspects of planning, measurement, communication and control with which they are concerned. In Chapter 19 the diverse implications of inflation are brought together by Raymond Brockington in an appraisal of the different schools of thought on this vexed subject. The chapter includes an examination of the method of accounting laid down as a standard in SSAP 16 issued by the joint accountancy bodies in the UK.

# 16

# Tax Planning

**John Chown**

*This chapter is concerned with the effects of taxation on corporate financial decisions especially, but by no means exclusively, in relation to overseas trading operations. It deals not with the minutiae of tax calculations on a* post hoc *basis but with the factors which need to be considered* before *major decisions with a fiscal implication are made. As the author demonstrates, tax strategy can be a major element in financial planning. 'The tax planner has to look behind the conventions (of traditional accounting) to the real economic and cash flow effects of the decisions with which he is concerned'. We are thus reminded by yet another writer of the defects of historical cost accounting in the decision-making process.*

*Considerable attention is given in the chapter to the interaction of varying rates of interest, inflation and taxation rules in different countries. These factors are subject to rapid and often unsuspected change and thus need constant surveillance. The subject therefore becomes closely associated with problems of international financing and questions arising out of methods of transferring funds from one country to another.*

*The chapter contains much practical advice on, for example, such matters as the benefits and anomalies of UK stock relief, leasing transactions and capital investment decisions. Tax havens and transfer pricing are likewise given realistic treatment within the inevitable constraints of a single chapter on so wide-ranging a subject. The text is clarified by a number of practical examples which may cause the most experienced financial controller to think again about the tax consequences of many well established approaches to tax planning.*

In most countries, including the UK, companies have to pay over about half their profits as tax. Taxation therefore has an important effect on net profits, cash flow and the rate at which a company builds up its net worth. The difference between good and indifferent tax planning can make a lot of difference to the 'bottom line'. Reducing the total tax burden from 55 per cent to 45 per cent, would, for instance, increase the net earnings per share from 100 to 122.

This chapter deals only with taxes which fall on company profits. Readers will hardly need reminding of the substantial increase, in recent years, of the burden of National Insurance contributions, and local rates, nor of the problems of remunerating employees at all levels.

The central message of this chapter is that tax is too important to be left to the tax specialists. Taxation is an important component in cash flow and has to be treated as a major (but by no means the only) factor in general financial planning.

## INFLATION

This principle is particularly important today. The way in which tax interacts with inflation and with foreign exchange risk means that it cannot be considered in isolation. The old assumption that 'a pound is a pound is a pound' and the type of analysis based on historic cost accounts has to be thrown out of the window. The tax planner cannot afford to have his thinking restricted by the conventions of traditional accountancy. Accountants may, and for many purposes should, worry themselves about consistent methods of adjusting for inflation and if published accounts are to be comparable they must follow specific and stated rules.

Taxation is a real cash outlay, not merely a conventional accounting figure, and the tax planner has to look behind the conventions to the real economic and cash flow effects of the decisions with which he is concerned.

Another consequence of high rates of inflation (and therefore high interest rates) means the timing of tax payments is now much more important even than it has been in the past. Pushing a tax liability forward from one year to the next is today equivalent to a 4- or 5-point reduction in the tax rate. However, it is dangerous to become too preoccupied with the value of this type of tax saving as the 'leasing' example below shows.

In the UK 'rough justice' relief for the effects of inflation is given by stock relief. This concept is of central tax planning importance and should be considered by general management as well as by tax specialists. The UK is also the only country to grant 100 per cent first-year allowances on new plant and machinery. Capital investment decisions must, for this reason if no other, always be made in after-tax terms.

In an age of inflation, the real return through to the shareholder must be examined before that shareholder can be asked for new money. This may be very different from the apparent return at corporate level.

For example, a company has the choice between investing $1 million in Country A at a return before tax of 30 per cent or in Country B at a return before tax of 10 per cent. However, the higher return is because Country A is expected to suffer 20 per cent inflation. Assuming this expectation is in fact right *and* (which is by no means inevitable) the value of A's currency falls correspondingly; while B has no inflation and a stable exchange rate; the *pre-tax* returns to the parent should be about the same. If Country A has a 50 per cent tax rate and no relief for inflationary gains, the computation for the first year's trading might be as follows:

| | |
|---|---|
| Profits in local currency | 300,000 |
| Tax | 150,000 |
| | 150,000 |
| Net worth (local currency at year end) | 1,150,000 |
| Net worth at year end | $958,333 |

There is thus a *negative* return for the year of nearly 5 per cent compared with a *positive* 5 per cent return after tax in Country B, assuming a 50 per cent tax rate.

In the real world, the calculations will be much more complicated, but they should still be made. Country A *may* have measures for adjusting tax to inflation, and in any case, the tax liability is unlikely to be based on the increase in local-currency net worth. The position could be mitigated by ensuring that the subsidiary pays a dividend even out of its *nominal* profits (enabling double tax relief to be claimed) even though there is a loss in 'consolidated' terms. The investor's own country may be suffering from inflation. If local borrowing in Country B's currency is available, the use of this could dramatically improve performance. Conventional accounting (particularly under the notoriously unrealistic US FASB.8) seldom gives the right economic answer from a decision-making viewpoint. Differences between expected and outcome rates of inflation can dramatically offset the results: indeed, uncertainty about inflation rates is often a bigger deterrent to investment than inflation itself. Finally, foreign currency changes do not in practice follow inflation differentials at all closely: 'inflation risk' and 'foreign exchange risk' are imperfectly related and one cannot be used as a proxy for the other.

## STOCK RELIEF

Stock relief was originally introduced in 1975. It is a 'rough justice' method of giving relief from tax on the inflationary element in inventories.

In its original, and even in its amended form, it has several weaknesses. Relief is based on the total increase in the value of inventories at the year end without segregating the 'price level change' and 'volume change' element. Some companies get too much relief, while others, including banks, get too little to enable them to maintain their real net worth before tax.

Stock relief merely defers, when it should logically eliminate, tax. Whenever the trade ceases the whole amount of stock relief granted in respect of past years and not previously added back to income was brought into charge to tax in the year of cessation.

There was thus build-up of deferred tax liability which, if ever it came home to roost, could cause serious cash-flow problems and even bankruptcy. A lending banker will know that this contingent liability can rank ahead of his own claim and the 'balance sheet' effect may make it difficult for the company to borrow.

In 1979, the deferred tax liability problem was reduced a little (but by no means eliminated) by permitting any uncrystallised deferred tax liability arising out of stock relief granted six years or more before the beginning of a current tax year to be written off altogether.

The 1980 budget has introduced a second measure to mitigate the problem which was threatening to become acute as a result of declining output, especially in the case of steel-using industries which had been unproductive for an extended period due to the steel strike.

Because of declining stocks, many businesses faced the crystallisation of the whole or large portions of stock relief previously granted.

The budget therefore proposed that any liability to tax arising out of the drawback of stock relief due to a temporary fall in the value of stock at the end of a tax year should be deferred for one year and be brought into charge to tax in the following year or set against any increase in stock values (together with standard stock relief) at the end of that year, as the case may be.

This 'special deferral' will not be available on the cessation of the business or when there has been a transfer of the business or a change in the person carrying on the business. More important, perhaps, the special deferral will also not be granted where there has already been a fall in stock values in the preceding tax year. *This special provision is only intended to assist businesses whose fall in stock value is exceptional when set against a trend of general increases.*

There will only be a deferral of that portion of the decrease in value which exceeds 5 per cent of the value of the stock at the beginning of the tax year. Where stocks are financed by credit, the amount to be deferred will be restricted by the proportion which the value of net trade credit (i.e. trade creditors less trade debtors) at the beginning of the tax year ending in 1979/80 bears to the value of stock held on the same date. If, therefore, the value of net trade credit exceeds stocks on that date, no special deferral will be permitted. Conversely, if trade debtors exceed creditors at that date, this restriction on special deferral falls away.

The Chancellor has promised a Green Paper on the structure of corporation tax. This should appear towards the end of 1980 and will probably concentrate on 'inflation' aspects. It will doubtless take account of SSAP 16.


## INTERNATIONAL FINANCING

The international management of debt can be a powerful source of profit and, as many UK companies have found to their cost, a dangerous source of loss. A company needing to borrow to finance an overseas venture can arrange for the foreign subsidiary to borrow locally or can borrow at parent company level and transfer the funds to the subsidiary by interest-free loans, loans carrying interest, or equity shares. It can choose between short-, medium- and long-term debt and, significantly, between currencies to be borrowed. It used to be said that UK exchange control did not prevent UK companies investing abroad, but merely imposed restrictions on the ways in which the investments could be financed. With exchange control gone UK companies have a wider range of choices for financing and (significantly) refinancing which seem not yet to have been fully exploited. There are two tax factors: first, where is the best place to get a deduction for interest? Second, what is the tax treatment of profits or losses resulting from exchange rate adjustments? The first of these points is well understood; the second is not. Many UK companies entered into major borrowing commitments without being advised that any extra sterling cost of repaying an appreciated currency would not be deductible for tax purposes. This point is discussed at length in 'Corporate Finance under Floating Exchange Rates'.

Some years ago a US company took over a UK company. Instead of making the acquisition directly, they first set up a thinly capitalised company which borrowed $20 million from a group of banks in London with a parent company guarantee. The intermediate company then made the acquisition and the interest charged on the borrowing could be set off against UK profits. Good tax planning – at the time. Unfortunately, the venture was then caught in a squeeze. The falling value of sterling increased the sterling cost of servicing the dollar loan, while profits themselves did not come up to expectations and fell far below the level needed to service the interest. The only tax effect of the interest payment was to increase an already large carry-forward loss. Only when the company took strategic tax advice on a totally different matter, was it pointed out to them that in the changed circumstances, the loans should be renegotiated so that the parent company was the actual borrower and could claim the deduction in the USA. This change should have taken place two years earlier and every month's delay was costing them $60,000.

From a tax planning point of view, there are certain parallels between the management of debt and of licensing agreements. As with inter-company royalties, interest on inter-company debt can be a useful technique for the corporate tax strategist.

## TAX HAVENS AND TRANSFER PRICING

An obvious method of reducing the tax liability of an international group is for producing companies in the group to under-invoice exports to a tax haven affiliate, which then over-invoices to the sales subsidiaries in the country of destination. This is obvious – but dangerous. The Revenue authorities of the world are policing transfer pricing very carefully and invoking anti-avoidance measures to neutralise the advantage of tax haven subsidiaries.

There is no guarantee that attempting to apply strict arm's length rules to transfer pricing will keep a company out of trouble. Apart from the fact that the Revenue authorities at both sides of the transaction may take a different view of what is 'reasonable', transfer pricing affects tariffs, anti-dumping provisions, price control regulations and exchange controls. Transactions which shift profits from one jurisdiction to another may have consequences for internal management accounts and allocation to profit centres. What is reasonable in one context might be regarded as unreasonable in another.

In one case following a merger, it was decided to set up a group headquarters in a country where there was no material business interest. It happened to be a low-tax jurisdiction but tax avoidance was not the motive. Indeed, as a headquarters company had only expenses and no income of its own, there was a potential tax *disadvantage* in such a location. The only objective was a management one – to avoid any suggestion that any one of the national companies constituting the merger was in any way pre-eminent. The headquarters company, reasonably enough, sought to charge up the cost of its services to the various national companies and did so by allocating its total cost *pro rata* to turnover. Some Revenue authorities accepted this, but one in particular did not and insisted that the bill be itemised and that each individual item be justified as to its strict application to that national subsidiary. This was obviously impractical and any attempt to allocate the whole cost between the other operating companies would rightly have been attacked by their Revenue authorities. Either the company would finish up with having its head office expenses disallowed for tax purposes (and therefore twice as expensive) or it had to abandon the concept of managing from neutral ground. It chose the latter.

## CAPITAL INVESTMENT

Decisions to undertake new fixed capital investment are obviously affected by tax factors. In many countries, accelerated depreciation is available (indeed, in the UK the whole cost of equipment can be written off in the first year). In others, Australia and in the past in the Netherlands and the UK, the investor is allowed to write off more than 100 per cent of the cost of the equipment. The US 'investment tax credit' is arithmetically different: it is a reduction in the tax liability, as a result of the investment. The 'timing' effects of these factors should be, and generally are, built up into any capital investment decision model. This point is generally, but maybe not universally, well understood. An extreme example is the shipping industry where many of the traditional operators have seen their profits decline by failing to adapt to new opportunities while others have built major shipping fortunes on the basis of superb strategic tax and financial planning.

## LEASING

UK 100 per cent first-year allowances mean that fixed capital investment is a powerful method of postponing tax. In these circumstances a leasing transaction can benefit two parties. The *lessor* buys, and becomes the legal owner of capital assets which are then leased to a *lessee* for use in the normal course of business. The lessor gets the benefit of the capital allowances and postpones tax he would otherwise have to pay. The lessee typically has no otherwise taxable income (plenty of stock relief, or a new foreign-owned 'green field' venture) and gets the benefit of cheap finance.

The arithmetic is not always what is seems. It is worth taking a closer look. A recent leasing scheme offered to investors showed that the investor who invested £1,000 would receive 20 quarterly lease payments of £61.25. Each payment can be regarded as £11.25 'interest' on the average investment of £500 plus £50 return of capital. This is a 9 per cent return on investment ignoring tax and the tax advantages.

This return has to be compared with the return that could be obtained on bank deposits or gilts. At the time the example was quoted this was about 15 per cent.

Promoters of leasing schemes would say that the 'cost' of the investment (to a company paying tax at 52 per cent) was not £1,000 but £480 after tax relief. They would calculate the 'return on capital' on the figures and show that, allowing for tax, this was more attractive than gilts.

This is perfectly valid, but it is also interesting to treat the transaction as if the lessor is 'buying' a tax loss from the lessee. What does he pay?

The best way of calculating this is to discount the flow of returns. If there were no 'capital allowances' aspect and the transaction was a straight loan, each payment of £61.25 would represent £50 return of capital plus £11.25 interest, the latter being liable for tax at £5.85. The net of tax value of each payment is this £55.40. Discounting at 7.20 per cent per annum net (15 per cent gross) gives a present value of the net return from the lease at £940.22 compared with an investment of £1,000. The deficiency of £59.78 represents the net cost of leasing at 9 per cent as compared to an ordinary money market investment of 15 per cent.

The benefit comes from the tax postponement. The 'interest' element in the lease payments has already been analysed. Look now at the £50 representing capital.

As the first lease payment is made at the same time as the lease, the tax postponed is not £520 but £494 (52 per cent of £950). The schedule of tax payments is therefore:

|  |  | Discounted at 7.2 per cent |
|---|---|---|
| Year 1 | (494) |  |
| 2 | 104 | 97.01 |
| 3 | 104 | 90.50 |
| 4 | 104 | 84.42 |
| 5 | 104 | 78.75 |
| 6 | 78 | 55.10 |
|  |  | 405.78 |

The present value of the tax saving is therefore £88.22 (£494 saved in Year 1, less the present value of payments in years 2–6). This has to be compared with a cost of £59.78, leaving £28.44 net saving. The lessor has bought a tax loss of £1,000 on terms which show him a profit of this figure. It seems a little thin.

One way of making a comparison is to assume a 'one-off' operation in both cases and work out the effective discounted tax charge.

Assume £250,000 profit to 31 March, tax payable 31 December 1980, net rate of discount 7.2 per cent.

| 1 | No action | Present value |
|---|---|---|
| | Tax £130,000 due in 9 months | £123,395 (49.36 per cent) |

| 2 | Leasing | |
|---|---|---|
| | Present value of tax payable | £106,784 |
| | Present value of interest foregone | £ 15,732 |
| | | ———— |
| | | £122,516 (49.01 per cent) |
| | | ———— |

There seems little to choose. Leasing is attractive as a means of 'buying time' but of relatively little value as a long-term tax mitigation scheme. The lessee seems to get the best of the bargain!

## GROUP STRUCTURE

Should a company with a number of foreign subsidiaries group some or all of these subsidiaries under an intermediate holding company in a third country? There may be management advantages in doing this as it may be a good method of paving the way for the future flotation of parts of the business. There is seldom a dramatic tax saving and normally the decision stands or falls on commercial or management considerations. There are some tax traps, mostly minor, and these should be watched.

Sometimes, the traps can be serious. In two cases in the author's experience the companies may have been saved from expensive consequences by a matter of weeks. Each of the companies had trading activities in the UK, and also substantial overseas income which had been taxed in the country of source and on which full credit for overseas tax was available. This produced no problems so long as the UK company continued to be profitable. In one particular year the UK company had a trading loss of £1 million. In the normal way this would be available to be carried forward against future profits, and a return to profitability was confidently (and as it turned out, correctly) expected. Overseas income of £1 million gross, £500,000 after tax, was received in the same company. There would be little or no UK tax liability on this because of credit relief for the foreign tax. However, the rules require that the gross foreign income be first offset against the loss, eliminating the carry-forward. The credit relief would be wasted. When profits resumed the UK's company profits would be unnecessarily increased by £500,000! There was just time to save the situation and to arrange that the foreign income was received in a separate subsidiary. This subsidiary then itself paid no tax because of credit relief, but the parent UK company could then carry forward its own loss against future profits. Although a loss in one group company can be (and in normal circumstances is) offset against the profits of other group companies, this treatment is optional and requires a positive election by the companies. Simple – but it saved £500,000.

Another common type of case is where a company has two subsidiaries, A and B, in another country. Because there is no common parent in the country A and B are not a 'group' for tax purposes. This fact is only recognised, too late, when A makes a profit and B makes a loss and it is discovered that they cannot be offset. This has happened in the author's recent experience to large companies in the UK, the USA and Germany.

# 17

# Financial Control of the Smaller Business

**Brian Murphy**

*The following chapter, dealing with the financial management of the smaller business unit, may initially appear out of place in a handbook which is mainly concerned with the large or medium-sized business. But small businesses are in the nature of things the subject of a continuous process of acquisition by the larger undertaking, which is as a result bound to concern itself with the special problems of the former. The outcome of such an acquisition may indeed be that the small business disappears altogether as a separate unit, but in many cases it survives sustained by the parent company as ancillary to the main operations of the latter. The large company may be content with a substantial controlling interest in the small business which thereafter proceeds on much the same lines as before, except that it will enjoy greater stability and probably greater prosperity as a result of the financial support and access to specialised services from the parent.*

*For these reasons the purpose of this chapter is to inform – or perhaps merely to remind – financial managers of large companies of the particular attributes and problems of the smaller unit which comes within their responsibilities.*

*The long lists of subsidiaries associated with the great international groups may well include those which are little more than small workshops. The original motives for such acquisitions may have become purely a matter of history, and if this is the case the small subsidiary is unlikely to survive for long unless new and compelling reasons for its existence arise. In many cases there is a positive and enduring reason for maintaining the small subsidiary in a thriving condition. These reasons are diverse. One objective could be to protect the source of supply of what may be a comparatively minor but nonetheless vital material or component of a major assembly. Another reason could be to ensure the availability of a product which could be usefully included in the parent company's marketing package; or of a product, component or service which, if produced by the parent, would involve a costly diversion of managerial or technical skills. Acquisitions are made of small businesses to obtain control of a promising or competitive invention, process, method or operation; or with the ostensible or concealed purpose of securing managerial and innovatory talent of a unique nature. The acquisition may be defensive, expansionist or merely speculative.*

*Small businesses are of great importance to the economy in their own right, apart from their possible fate as subjects for take-over by large companies. As the author of this chapter points out, one-fifth of the UK gross national product emanates from the smaller business sector. This category of business has received intermittent attention from various governments in recent years, as indicated by the establishment of the small business centres, some alleviation of corporation tax, and the investigations of the Bolton Committee of 1972 and the Wilson Committee of 1978.*

*The author of this chapter, who works in an area where small businesses rub shoulders with great undertakings, makes the important point that sophisticated control techniques which may be in force in the parent company are quite inapplicable to the small subsidiary. He insists, nevertheless, that a financial control system of a simple and realistic nature must be applied in the small business if it is to be viable. At the end of the chapter he provides a factual case history which illustrates a simple but effective system of control.*

Political oratory in the late 1960s might easily have led one to believe that small business was on the decline and that this was not necessarily a bad thing. However, as a world recession began to develop and unemployment became more and more a problem needing urgent attention in a number of western countries, it became evident that small companies could probably provide as much new employment as larger enterprises. Increasingly, therefore, the slogan of the 1970s became 'small is beautiful' and positive steps were taken to encourage their development.

The private sector of most capitalist economies originated through the establishment and growth of small firms. Almost all the present large firms, with the possible exception of the great railway and some of the utility companies, started life as small firms and grew to their present size. The picture is, therefore, one of constantly changing patterns, some firms growing, some declining, but relatively few remaining static over long periods.

## WHAT IS SMALL?

In the UK the main investigation into the role of the small firm was undertaken by the Bolton Committee which reported in 1972. By 1980 small business in the UK probably employed in excess of 6 million people in nearly $1\frac{1}{2}$ million different enterprises. In every major industry there are successful small firms. Small business entrepreneurs operate manufacturing plants, retail stores, shops, construction firms and a host of other types of enterprises particularly in service industries. Although the fields of small business are similar to those of large business, in general smaller firms are relatively more important in some areas of the economy than others, for example, in manufacturing and retailing than in raw material extraction.

Approximately one-fifth of the gross national product is produced by the small-firm sector although the percentage of small firms in the UK is still significantly less than in France, Germany and the USA.

The Bolton Committee used a number of definitions of small firms relevant, as they saw it, to different industries. These were updated by the Wilson Committee in 1978 to accommodate changing money values, as shown in Table 17.1.

## EFFECTS OF SIZE AND OWNERSHIP ON FINANCIAL CONTROL PROCEDURES

The need for financial control procedures increases in direct ratio to the number of operating units and management personnel. A one-man business has little need for control data. The owner knows what he has done and has some idea of what he intends to do. His tendency is to rely on his business sense and hope that the majority of his decisions will pay off. However, it is often a mistake to distinguish sharply between size of enterprise in terms of one having different

**Table 17.1**
**Bolton Committee definitions of small firms**

| Industry | Statistical definition of small firms adopted by the Bolton Committee (turnover at 1963 prices) | Revised definition to allow for inflation (turnover at 1978 prices) |
|---|---|---|
| Manufacturing | 200 employees or less | – |
| Retailing | Turnover £50,000 p.a. or less | Turnover £185,000 p.a. or less |
| Wholesale trades | Turnover £200,000 p.a. or less | Turnover £730,000 p.a. or less |
| Construction | 25 employees or less | – |
| Mining/ quarrying | 25 employees or less | – |
| Motor trades | Turnover £100,000 p.a. or less | Turnover £365,000 p.a. or less |
| Miscellaneous | Turnover £50,000 p.a. or less | Turnover £185,000 p.a. or less |
| Road transport | 5 vehicles or less | – |
| Catering | All excluding multiples and brewery-managed public houses | – |

problems from the other.

One of the features of small businesses is that they are frequently family-owned. There may be one or more intermediate layers, e.g. supervisors or foremen, to interpret decisions, and in the larger firm certain specialised functions such as accounting or production may be devolved to senior employees, but it is the owners themselves who still take the principal decisions and exercise the principal management functions. In terms of using financial control techniques, research has shown that family-owned concerns are more reluctant to use them than non-family firms, and this may account for the relatively poor performance and success rate of the former. This is probably due, first, to the undue influence exercised by older members of the family who find it difficult to release executive power and, second, to the conflict of interests where decisions taken in the family interest are not necessarily in the interest of the business. Third, there are often a number of second- and third-generation managers who have little real interest in the family business but feel an obligation to continue in it. Small units may be subsidiaries of larger concerns and when joining the group they may have some difficulty in adapting to the parent control systems, particularly if administrative staff are limited or perhaps even non-existent.

## AWARENESS OF FINANCIAL CONTROL TECHNIQUES

It is, perhaps, particularly important in the small firm to understand the role which human relations plays in control systems. This may be illustrated by one of the most widely accepted financial controls, i.e. budgetary control. It is often found that many responsible managers dislike budgetary control because:

1  They object to their performance being measured against the goals set by this evaluation instrument.
2  By their nature, budgets tend to be formalised and are thought of as pressure devices. As such they produce the same kind of unfavourable reaction as do other kinds of pressure regardless of origin.
3  The subsidiary firm management may object to the parent setting targets, particularly if these targets have been set without prior consultation.

As the relationships between owners, managers and employees are likely to be much closer in the small business the 'negative' aspects of budgeting may be more noticeable.

One of the biggest problems facing small firms in relation to financial control is the lack of awareness of the techniques which are available. There is no doubt that there is an ever-increasing gap between theoretical knowledge and practical application of techniques by large firms and the use or awareness of techniques by the small firm. This gap is increased by the more sophisticated use of computing and micro-processing by the firms who can afford the initial outlay and the back-up services to run such systems.

Perhaps the seriousness of this point can be illustrated by Table 17.2 taken from a study concluded in 1973 by the author, involving a random sample of over 50 small companies, situated mainly in the Yorkshire and Humberside region.

From this study it might be concluded that a greater emphasis is placed on basic financial control techniques required for day-to-day control than on techniques concerned with the longer term. Although

## Table 17.2
## Summary of firms aware of and utilising
## techniques

| Technique | Awareness Size category Employees | | | | Utilisation Size category Employees | | | |
|---|---|---|---|---|---|---|---|---|
| | 11–50 | 51–100 | 101–200 | 201–500* | 11–50 | 51–100 | 101–200 | 201–500* |
| | % | % | % | % | % | % | % | % |
| Historical costing | 91 | 100 | 91 | 100 | 45 | 66 | 63 | 80 |
| Budgeting and budgetary control | 72 | 100 | 100 | 100 | 27 | 78 | 63 | 90 |
| Standard costing | 45 | 100 | 91 | 90 | 5 | 33 | 18 | 40 |
| Cash-flow forecasting | 59 | 89 | 91 | 90 | 32 | 67 | 27 | 70 |
| Credit control | 100 | 100 | 100 | 100 | 91 | 100 | 91 | 100 |
| Stock control | 100 | 100 | 100 | 100 | 14 | 67 | 54 | 90 |
| Capital investment appraisal | 32 | 67 | 67 | 80 | – | – | 9 | 30 |
| Internal check | 18 | 67 | 63 | 90 | 9 | 33 | 36 | 60 |
| Long-range planning | 32 | 44 | 45 | 60 | – | 22 | 9 | 30 |
| Marginal costing | 23 | 44 | 91 | 90 | 9 | – | – | 40 |
| Revaluation accounting | 5 | 33 | 27 | 60 | – | – | – | – |

* Not 'small firms' by Bolton Committee definition but included for purpose of comparison. Source: Murphy 1973.

the degree of both awareness and utilisation increases with the increase in firm size, there appears to be more reluctance on the part of smaller companies to utilise techniques of which they are aware. The utilisation of techniques such as standard costing, marginal costing and capital investment appraisal, which have received widespread publicity over the past two decades, is very low.

A further distinction between firms which are aware of and use financial control techniques and those which do not relates to whether the firm is a member of a group. There are obviously many variations in the relationships between group companies and their subsidiaries but because of necessity it is often the case that standard procedures will be laid down by the parent company for the control of group members. Weekly or monthly returns, stock control, cash management, debtor and creditor policies, are all areas where group control is likely to be evident. However, it is not unusual to find that although control techniques have been implemented by the parent company, the individual small business still has difficulty relating the techniques to its own operations and often regards the necessary form filling as an onerous chore.

## FINANCIAL MANAGEMENT

Some books and articles giving guidance on setting up small firms state that in the early stages the company's financial operations can be handled by a secretary or the owner's spouse, and only at a fairly developed stage is it suggested that an accountant should be employed. One must question whether this is good policy. It is a well established fact that one of the major causes of small business failure is the lack of financial control. It would, therefore, be a sound policy to obtain experienced professional advice from the outset and certainly from the point of take-over by a larger company, where such advice would be available.

The main complaint of small business is twofold: first, the difficulty in obtaining original capital to launch a new business; and second, the lack of support for business expansion. Various enquiries have tried to establish that there is really no lack of funds for both these purposes, but it remains the case that there is still a gap, perhaps a communications gap, between the sources of such funds and the firms who need them. In many cases the parent company will be the major supplier of finance but for this purpose it should require the same information as an external source. The parent may, as a matter of policy, insist that the subsidiary obtains its finance as an independent unit.

The specific nature of a business governs the nature of its capital needs. If the firm is a manufacturing plant, then financial planning must take account of the fixed capital needs, e.g. premises and machinery, working capital to cover purchases, wage payments and overheads prior to the receipt of funds. On the other hand if the business is in the service industry, say as a window-cleaning business, then the initial start-up capital is not normally large.

The initial capital base of the business is extremely important as it is that base which will determine the nature of all future financing. Too many small firms commence business undercapitalised. The only way in which a sound start can be made is to prepare a detailed cash plan for, say, the first two years of operation. This may be a daunting process if it is done correctly and includes assumptions which may not be accepted until experienced, e.g. that debtors do not pay on time, suppliers do not deliver on time, and the rate of interest paid on any overdraft is going to cost more than at first thought. If a company is taken over to operate within a group then the parent normally ensures that adequate funds are made available to continue and expand current operations.

As a company grows it will require additional funds. These will fall into two broad categories, long-term and short-term. The short-term funds will be needed mainly to iron out the fluctuations in working capital requirements frequently caused by the seasonal nature of many businesses. Such funds should be self-liquidating and if it is found that there is a constant need for short-term funds then this implies that the financial base requires expanding by the addition of longer-term capital.

The operation of the firm on a day-to-day basis will provide the short-term funds and to some extent the various components of the system can be manipulated to help smooth the peaks and troughs. Delay in payment of creditors, chasing collection of debtors, are two options, but it is vitally important that such actions do not damage the relationships between suppliers and customers which often take so long to establish.

The main source of short-term funds will be the firm's bank which will not necessarily be a branch of the parent company bankers. The firm should, therefore, build up a close relationship with the bank. The bank should have been involved from the outset of the business but it is important for the firm (and the parent company) to realise the limitations placed upon the local bank manager in terms of lending to unknown quantities. Documentation is particularly vital at this stage. The bank should be presented with details of the company structure, its objectives, its strategy on production and marketing, its staffing levels, details of capital to be provided by the owners, the two-year cash plan, and the security available to support any overdraft facilities sought, which may involve using a guarantee from the parent company if available.

When it comes to raising long-term capital the business should be aware of the sources of such funds. This information is now well publicised, but whichever type of organisation is going to be approached, the firm should ensure that once again its documentation is sound and demonstrates its awareness of the needs of such financing institutions. As a minimum the following information should be prepared:

1   Description of the company, its development so far, its present capital structure, its products, markets, competition, expansion plans, organisation chart.
2   Audited financial statements for the last three years.
3   Current unaudited financial position statement.
4   Profits and earnings forecasts for the next two years.
5   Cash flow forecast for the same period.
6   Amount of funds required and purpose for which they will be used.

One of the important considerations to establish before approaching a potential supplier of funds is to ascertain what are the likely requirements of the institution concerned. The management should draw up a shortlist of likely providers rather than shop around in a haphazard fashion hoping that someone will accept the proposals. It should also be remembered that the whole process of obtaining funds is a time-consuming business, not only from the firm's point of view in preparing the documentation and in the search process for a suitable recipient, but the lending institution is likely to take a considerable amount of time before committing its funds. This fact should be borne in mind if the small subsidiary has to seek long-term funds from external sources.

## ACCOUNTING AND CONTROL IN THE SMALL FIRM

Unfortunately most accounting systems set up in small firms have one objective only and that is to provide the necessary historical information to enable the financial statements to be prepared and, therefore, satisfy the legal requirements of, say, the Companies Acts if the firm is incorporated, and the Inland Revenue. Frequently the actual compilation of these statements is left to an external accountant and, therefore, the day-to-day control of operations through accounting procedures is minimal.

If it is possible from the start to encourage the small subsidiary's management to regard the production of accounting information as a basis for today's decisions which will be reflected in tomorrow's operations, then the control and forecasting aspect of accounting data is immediately recognised.

The accounting system should concentrate on the areas of operation which control the firm's profitability and growth. It should be recognised that different parts of the organisation require different types of information. Management, however defined, should have monthly operating statements which should be in sufficient detail to provide a good picture of performance during the month, together with an analysis of appropriate ratios such as profit/capital employed, gross and net profit percentages, operating costs as a percentage of sales, stock turnover, debtors' and creditors' ratios, current ratio showing the liquidity position. Relevant statements should be prepared for operating managers or supervisors to enable them to check on their progress and performance.

The recording of all financial transactions should be made in a systematic manner. To this end one of the most useful techniques is to operate a coding system. This may well be the system of the parent company if the firm is a member of a group. Specific types of income and expenditure will then be allocated to a specific code number allowing easy manipulation and analysis of the information. An appropriate coding system will facilitate mechanisation or computerisation of the financial records, particularly if the parent computer is to be used for data preparation and analysis. The number of digits in the code will depend on the type and variety of expenses, but a six-figure code would be a sound base for the system. A typical use of the six digits might be as follows: first digit for company number which would allow for company expansion and acquisition. The next two digits could be used for the cost centre allocations. A cost centre may be a physical location, a person, or an item of equipment to which costs can be allocated and used for control purposes. The last three digits would be used for categories of expense or income. Obviously the correct coding of income and expenditure is of extreme importance but it is usually surprisingly easy for personnel to familiarise themselves with coding systems.

A typical coding system might include the following:

| Cost centre | Code | Expense | Code |
|---|---|---|---|
| Press shop | 05 | Raw materials | 020 |
| Machine shop | 08 | Direct labour | 210 |
| Tooling | 10 | Gas | 620 |
| Repairs and maintenance | 12 | Rates | 680 |
| Marketing | 24 | Travelling expenses | 710 |
| Administration | 50 | Bank interest | 820 |

Individual expenses would now be represented by a code, e.g. 0105210 would be the cost of direct wages paid to employees in the press shop and 0108680 would represent the proportion of rates allocated to the machine shop.

The above shows only the way in which such a coding system would work and is not intended to be in any way comprehensive.

It will also be necessary to have suitable documentation to provide the control data, e.g. time sheets or piecework tickets, and stock recording and issuing information. Operating costs are frequently stated as falling into two main categories; 'variable costs' and 'fixed costs'. Unfortunately in the short term there is really no clear distinction between fixed and variable costs and perhaps the best approach is to have a system which provides management with a simple means of determining what changes will occur if certain decisions are made. The difficulty associated with cost determination may be illustrated by direct labour. Traditionally this has been regarded as a variable cost but because of a number of factors, not least of which is recent employment legislation, it is coming more and more to be regarded as a fixed expense. Few firms are now able to resort to a policy of 'hire and fire' as circumstances dictate, and such a policy has always been even more difficult to operate by the small company likely to be highly dependent on the skills of a workforce which would prove difficult to replace and train.

It is, however, a useful exercise for the management of a smaller company periodically to consider their cost analysis in terms of variable and non-variable headings in order to appreciate the effect which decisions in production and marketing will have on such costs.

## BUSINESS FORECASTING AND BUDGETING

Small firms have a tendency to be satisfied with the results produced by the installation of a historical cost analysis system as outlined above, and to neglect the need to forecast and budget for the future. Business forecasting attempts to ascertain the future course of business activity generally and also the likely trend of the firm's own activities. If such forecasts are not undertaken the preparation of the company budget becomes more difficult. It must be recognised that there are limitations on small firms in connection with forecasting. One of these is the inability of many small-firm managers to handle the inevitable quantitative analysis associated with the forecasting techniques used by large firms. A number of techniques require to be processed by computer and access to such facilities by small firms is likely to be limited. However, increasing use is being made by small businesses of systems packages available from computer bureaux and time can frequently be made available on the mainframe computer of the parent organisation. Moreover the rapid developments in mini and micro computers mean that small firms now have ready access to relatively sophisticated techniques (see Chapter 18).

It is in marshalling the actual data to be processed that the small firm has most difficulty, especially when considering possible movements within the economy overall. However, there are a number of information points available to the small firm either by way of trade associations or trade journals which can prove a valuable source of data. The business future of any firm is uncertain but it is up to the individual small-firm manager to make his forecasts from the latest data available and to use forecasting as a tool to aid his decision making. It may be valuable to second an accountant from head office to help with forecasting, if the business is part of a group.

A budget may be defined as a financial and/or quantitative statement prepared and approved before a defined period of time of the policy to be pursued during that period for the purpose of attaining a given objective. This definition is very much concerned with planning, and planning as such must form an important function of management, covering all aspects of business activity.

Despite the obvious advantages of budgeting, there are still many small firms which never use budgets. They claim that budgeting is not possible in their businesses because there are too many complications and uncertainties to make it worthwhile. Thus many businesses profess difficulty in estimating sales with any accuracy because of uncontrollable external influences, such as climatic changes. However, the preparation of a budget is itself extremely beneficial as it forces the person responsible for incurring expenditure or generating income to plan for the future, having regard to the uncertainty and complexity which this entails. Too frequently a small business is run on a day-to-day basis without any thought being given to the future. The firm is likely to finish up by fulfilling Mr Micawber's second prediction 'annual income twenty pounds, annual expenditure twenty pounds ought and six pence, result misery'. Even when a budgetary control system is in operation, it is essential that the budgets be revised at intervals to deal with unpredicted changes in circumstances or forecasting errors.

Control in a small business will be improved by flexible budgeting. A flexible budget may be prepared for varying levels of output 60 per cent, 70 per cent, etc. up to 100 per cent of capacity. It is desirable that expenses should be analysed into three distinct categories:

1   fixed expense, i.e. an expense which tends to be unaffected by variations in the volume of output;
2   semi-variable expense, i.e. an expense which is partly fixed and partly variable;
3   variable expense, i.e. an expense which tends to vary directly with variations in the volume of output.

Once this analysis is complete it is possible to prepare the different budgets for different levels of activity, thus allowing a greater degree of control to be exercised when the actual results are compared with the estimates.

An example of a flexed budget applied to a production department for control purposes is given in Table 17.3. It should be noted that budgeted fixed costs by definition remain unchanged irrespective of the level of production, whereas variable costs will tend to vary with the level of output. Since in our example the level of production attained was only 80 per cent of that budgeted it was necessary to adjust the budgeted variable costs in proportion to the level of actual activity attained in order to facilitate a fair comparison between actual costs incurred and budgeted costs.

Once the budget has been flexed in this way the analysis of variances is facilitated so that corrective action can be taken where variances are adverse. External factors may distort the budget and unless the system is flexible enough to take these into account it becomes an inaccurate yardstick against which to evaluate performance.

Another common weakness of small-firm budgets is a failure to include all the business activities within the budgetary system, i.e. failure to prepare a master budget. Budgets may be prepared for, say, cash, expenses and sales but if a capital budget is not included then the final budget is not a complete picture of all the interacting aspects of the firm which are relevant to its survival. Even in a small firm the preparation of the budget is not a one-man effort, nor can it be accomplished quickly.

It is important that management in a small firm should clearly distinguish between controllable and uncontrollable expenses. Stress should be laid on controllable expenses, e.g. once a lease is signed or a rental agreement made then there is little that management can do in controlling such costs, but the use of raw material, scrap rates and labour efficiency are items which should be within the control of management. Another important point is that with the limited amount of time available to management, attention should be focused on major items. It is useless for a manager to spend time on controlling minor items which results in savings less than the value of the time spent on achieving them. As an adjunct to budgetary control the small-firm manager should be involved in an expense reduction review to ensure that he is always achieving the best value for the resources being utilised by his firm.

## STANDARD COSTING

As was shown in Table 17.2, the actual operation of standard costing systems in small firms is not very high. Perhaps there is some justification for this as many small firms operate on a job order system, i.e. the make-up of materials, labour and overhead is different for each 'one-off' job and, therefore, difficult to control by use of predetermined standards, although it may be possible to have standard operations which can apply to a number of different jobs. Where standard costing is used the largest problem seems to be in keeping standards up to date or, perhaps of more importance, completely revising the standards at periodic intervals.

## CASE STUDY

The following is a case study involving the application of financial

## Table 17.3
## The Uno Brick Company production department X budget for the period ——

Budgeted level of activity: 100,000 bricks
Actual production achieved: 80,000 bricks
Actual activity percentage: 80 per cent

| Expense | Budgeted amount for 100,000 bricks | | Flexed budget for 80,000 bricks | | | Actual cost | Variances | |
|---|---|---|---|---|---|---|---|---|
| | Fixed | Variable | Fixed | Variable | Total | | Adverse | Favourable |
| | £ | £ | £ | £ | £ | £ | £ | £ |
| Direct labour | 1,000 | 7,000 | 1,000 | 5,600 | 6,600 | 7,000 | 400 | – |
| Direct materials | – | 4,000 | – | 3,200 | 3,200 | 3,600 | 400 | – |
| Production overheads: | | | | | | | | |
| Depreciation | 5,000 | – | 5,000 | – | 5,000 | 5,000 | – | – |
| Indirect materials | | | | | | | | |
| Supervision | 4,000 | – | 4,000 | – | 4,000 | 4,200 | 200 | – |
| Rates | 500 | – | 500 | – | 500 | 600 | 100 | – |
| Power | 400 | 1,600 | 400 | 1,280 | 1,680 | 1,250 | – | 430 |
| Heating and Lighting | 100 | 300 | 100 | 240 | 340 | 350 | 10 | – |
| Other expenses | 1,000 | 2,100 | 1,000 | 1,680 | 2,680 | 2,400 | – | 280 |
| | 12,000 | 15,000 | 12,000 | 12,000 | 24,000 | 24,400 | 1,110 | 710 |

control techniques to a small firm. The aim of the work was to introduce the necessary systems which would allow a reasonable degree of control to be exercised by management with the minimum of effort and expertise. By choosing a very small firm it was possible to show that the record system was a workable proposition and could form the base for a more sophisticated system in a larger company.

## History of the firm

The company was involved in making castings, both ferrous and non-ferrous on a job and batch basis. Its average labour force numbered twelve. The two directors were both involved in the day-to-day operation of the firm, one director acting as general manager responsible for the preparation of job estimates, cost records, pricing of sales invoices and payment of wages. In addition he frequently had to help out in the foundry as well as organise the work schedule. His wife was responsible for keeping the accounts of the firm, preparing the weekly payroll, paying creditors and banking receipts.

## Initial problems

From the original records it was possible to ascertain the cost of direct material but no records were kept of indirect material or labour costs, other than for jobs where a piecework system operated. Such rates were fixed for each job by the foreman on an arbitrary basis. The majority of the labour force were paid on a daywork basis. Estimates for job orders were calculated on a comparative basis of similar work and related to the weight of the finished casting. Management were interested in improving their costing system with a view to introducing a group bonus scheme for the employees in order to reduce employee turnover and absenteeism. However, the company was faced with a more immediate problem in the form of cash flow. The agreement with the bank was in two parts, a normal fluctuating overdraft with a limit laid down by the bank, and a loan arrangement which represented previous overdraft sums which had been taken out of the fluctuating arrangement to be paid off at a fixed quarterly rate. The company were under substantial pressure from the bank to reduce their overall liability to them. After discussions with the bank manager it was agreed that a new limit would be set on the fluctuating overdraft, the excess being transferred to the loan account which would be paid off by increased repayments made weekly. It was vital, therefore, to install a weekly system of forecasting cash flows and the bank supplied weekly statements to facilitate this task. A form (Form 1) was designed to enable the cash flows to be forecasted and a more formalised system of payment of creditors was introduced in order to aid forecasting.

## Form 1
## Weekly cash flow forecast

| Week | | | | Balance as per bank statement | | |

| Cheques issued but not yet presented | | Estimated expenses | | Estimated income | |
|---|---|---|---|---|---|
| Cheque no. | Amount | Item | Amount | Item | Amount |

Totals

Dr        Cr

Balance brought forward
Expenses for week
Income for week
Unpresented items

Estimated balance        Overdraft limit
at end of week.

Control accounts were established for both purchases and sales, and by the end of the three months of operating the system the manager's wife was able to reconcile the creditors, debtors, and wages control accounts and the cash book. The preparation of quarterly operating statements was now a simple task. From the creditors' and debtors' ledger two statements were prepared each month (Forms 2 and 3) and it became the practice to pay all creditors at the beginning of the third month after receipt of the invoice, thereby enabling cash flow to be more easily controlled.

## Form 2
## Monthly creditors' control

Month

| Folio | Name | Current month ( ) | Last month ( ) | 2 months' old ( ) | Over 2 months Month | Total £ p |
|-------|------|---------|---------|---------|---------|-------|
| | | £ p | £ p | £ p | £ p | |

## Form 3
## Monthly debtors' control

Month

| Folio | Name | Current month ( ) | Last month ( ) | 2 months old ( ) | Over 2 months Month |
|-------|------|---------|---------|---------|---------|
| | | £ p | £ p | £ p | £ p |

## Budgeting

As there was no formal costing system in operation it was necessary to devise a simple system which could be operated by the general manager in the limited time available to him for 'office work'. The purchases day book was redesigned to enable expenditure to be analysed at the time of entry under the main budget headings. From previous financial statements, an annual budget was compiled and then further sub-divided into quarterly budgets against which actual results would be compared.

## Costing system

In order to be able to establish the cost of each job on a prime cost and total cost basis, it was essential to have a record of the material and direct labour used. Castings are normally charged on the basis of weight, or per unit which in itself can easily be based on a weight measurement. Four new forms were, therefore, designed. Form 4 (job advice card) allowed each job to be recorded upon receipt of the order and was then used to enable the foreman to allocate work and to ensure that sufficient raw material was available. Form 5 (the daily time sheet) was used by the direct labour force and was completed in practice by the foreman. Because of the size of the concern, this produced no problems and piecework items were also entered on this sheet for convenience. Form 6 was used to indicate the weight of the finished castings. Any surplus metal which had been taken off a particular casting was normally re-usable and a loss in weight of raw material during processing had been calculated on a series of trials. The information from these tickets and the time sheets was then recorded on the job cost sheet (Form 7). Overhead percentages were calculated from the budgeted figures and in the initial preparation of

### Form 4
### Job advice card

Job no. ...............................................  O/N ......................................................

Customer  ...........................................  Date ...................................................

Description of work




Date required .........................

## Form 5
## Daily time sheet

Time sheet no. .........................................

Day ..................................................

Date ..................................................

Week no. ..............................................

| Name | Work done | Job no. | Time | | Hrs | Rate | Cost |
|------|-----------|---------|------|------|-----|------|------|
| | | | Start | Finish | | | |
| | | | | | | | |
| | | | | | | | |
| | | | | | | | |
| | | | | | | | |
| | | | | | | | |
| | | | | | | | |
| | | | | | | | |

Certified ............................................. ENTERED ON JOB CARDS

Foreman                           Date .............................................

these sheets, based on work currently being undertaken, wide discrepancies were revealed. It was then necessary to review the whole pricing structure and make adjustments where necessary. The contribution approach to pricing, particularly of gun metal castings, was used because of the strong competition in this particular type of work. As the budgets were revised on a quarterly basis, it was a simple task to ensure that the overhead percentages were also kept up to date and prices reviewed when necessary.

### Summary

It is appreciated that there is nothing new, sophisticated or novel about the systems introduced in this case study but it does show that

## Form 6
## Weight ticket

Job no. ............................ Ticket no. ........................ O/N ....................................

Customer .............................................. Date ......................................................

| Description of work | Type of material | Units | Weight |
|---|---|---|---|
| | | | |
| | | | |
| | | | |
| | | | |
| | | | |
| | | | |
| | | | |

Date ...................................................... Certified ..............................................

where the need for financial control is recognised, it can be operated with the minimum of time, cash outlay and expertise. It is admitted that the small firm manager must normally resort to a specialist to install the system, a task which it is felt should be undertaken by a firm's professional accountant in most cases or with the assistance of head office if it is a subsidiary. However, the operation of the system should be well within the competence of small firm managers. Perhaps the greatest benefit derived by the management in this case study was unquantifiable, namely peace of mind through being safe from the 'harassment' of the bank manager, and the knowledge that they were now aware of the current financial health of the business rather than having to wait at least six months after the financial year end before knowing whether a profit or loss had been achieved.

# Form 7
## Job cost sheet

Date _____ Order no. _____ Job no. _____

Customer _____

Job description _____

_____

_____

| Materials Type | Weight | | | Cost | | | Total cost £   p |
|---|---|---|---|---|---|---|---|
| | Ticket no. | Units | Weight | per 1 lb | per unit | | |

Labour
Detail                                        Time sheet no.

_____

_____

_____

_____

                                        Prime cost

Overheads

  Indirect material ............ % on direct material

  Works overhead ............ % on prime cost

                                        Factory cost

  Administration overhead ............ % on factory cost

                                        Total cost

                                        Profit

                                        Selling price

Estimate

# 18

# Computerisation of Financial Records

**P. V. Jones**

*The computerisation of a large variety of financial records is now commonplace for most substantial companies and even small organisations make considerable use of computers, usually but not exclusively through computer bureaux. Nevertheless, as the author of this contribution indicates, there is evidence for the belief that many of the modern developments in computer technology are by no means appreciated or utilised by many financial officers. The former constraint of expense on the wider use of computerisation has now been alleviated, particularly so far as hardware is concerned, and the advent of the mini and micro-computers, as well as developments in computer packages, have given a greatly enhanced availability to computer systems.*

*This chapter, which is firmly based on the realities of business financial operations, first discusses the potential uses of a computer in dealing with the simpler accounting routines. At the same time the dangers and illusions associated with such installations are clearly stated. The author emphasises the vital importance of user participation in the design stage of the installation and refers to 'unfulfilled expectations' arising from 'misconceptions as to the nature of the computer'. He acknowledges that 'often systems are developed for the wrong reasons' and that 'in the current state of the art a computer-based system is not always the best method'. He explains, on the other hand, how computerised systems may add immensely to the efficiency of financial data processing and reporting, not only for standardised clerical functions but also for the more sophisticated financial planning and control applications.*

*The chapter discusses the costs, both apparent and hidden, of instal-*

*ling a computerised system; the various schemes available for the purpose; training requirements; adaptation problems; and the essential prerequisite of management and staff acceptance. It concludes with some cautious forecasts with regard to data-based management information systems, networks of computerised systems; and the potential for the elimination of paperwork and routine manual operations.*

In the short time since the general-purpose computer came into being in the mid-1940s, it has found many applications in the field of accounting and finance. Ambitious claims have been made for the capabilities of computers and man's ability to use them, but with the passage of time some of these claims have been shown to be unreasonable or ill-considered. A realistic approach to current computer applications must begin by investigating the nature of this tool and its potential usefulness.

## WHAT CAN BE EXPECTED OF THE COMPUTER?

A computer may be considered as a device which can perform a great number of special functions beyond the scope of a simple calculator. These functions or instructions may be selected in a desired sequence to create a program. Here, the first benefit and the first constraint in the use of a computer are evident. The benefit is that once the sequence of instructions is defined, tried and verified, the computer can be relied upon to repeat the operation with unwavering accuracy. For many of the tasks of an accountant this is a major attribute. The constraint which is encountered lies in the difficulty of generating a precise definition and absolute verification of the instructions. The task to which the computer is applied must be definable as a series of discrete, detailed steps which will logically lead to the ultimate goals of the set of instructions. The computer, therefore, cannot be expected to do anything that has not been explicitly described as a set of detailed instructions.

While many activities in finance and accounting are apparently easy to define, the number of variations and exceptions that the accountant or clerk may be required to handle in a day's work, for even the simplest task, may be vast. The omission, or incorrect operation, of just one of these variations will render the computer system inadequate to meet the total demand made upon it.

The following are examples of simple but disruptive effects of system inadequacies.

*Example 1.* A gas consumer received a bill from the gas board produced by a computer demanding zero pounds for gas consumed. The bill was factually correct because in fact no gas was consumed in the period concerned. The bill was succeeded by reminders and other follow-up procedure apparently aimed at collecting zero pounds. As a result the customer was confused, the incident wasted time and paper, and tended to destroy the credibility of the computerised system. The fault should not, of course, have occurred in a well-designed computer program and is easily corrected.

*Example 2.* Ex-employees of an organisation continued to receive payslips for zero pounds after termination of their employment. The reason for this was that the computer record was not updated with the deletion of their records on termination of their employment. Each computer run still calculated the pay due for zero hours of work. The payslip was correct but should not have been a part of the computer run.

These examples are taken from actual system faults and exemplify just two of the vast number of conditions that a program must deal with. Many conditions are far more complicated.

The computer, therefore, must not be regarded as a 'magic black box' but as a piece of equipment needing great care in its use if it is to provide a useful service. The requirements which the computer program is expected to meet are known to the accountant but not to the systems analyst or programmer, therefore the system user, in this case the accountant, must be deeply involved with its design if the system is to be effective. A good computer application is normally achieved only after close cooperation between the accountant and the system designer to provide details of the procedures involved, the processes that the system will perform and the way in which the output from the computer will be used.

The precision with which the use of a computer must be planned and the way it must be operated may be seen as a constraint. It is also, however, a great benefit in that the necessary analysis of existing activity and the improvement of the method of work to suit a computer will themselves produce greater efficiency. In essence, the computer can only perform functions that are possible by manual processes but it can do those things faster, repeatedly and without complaint, if used as designed. Each accurate payslip, for example, may be calculated and printed in a small fraction of a second and therefore in great quantities in a short time. The payroll as an example illustrates the peripheral benefits of using a computer, such as those of typing the payslips within envelopes on special stationery, providing credit transfer and/or cash withdrawal information to the bank and all the analytical information required by the accountant. Obviously, these benefits may be even greater in more sophisticated accounting processes.

The major problems in such computer use lie in the possibility of equipment breakdown, of wrong information being used for input and of the computer meeting a condition which is not included in the program. These problems are becoming less acute with the advances in technology and improvements in the state of the art. The computer is becoming more reliable and, in the foreseeable future, breakdowns should become very rare. Also incorrect output is becoming less of a problem as direct entry of data from the point of its origin becomes more common. This is a matter of great importance to the accountant, especially in auditing, since direct data entry may replace production of auditable documents.

Direct data entry is an example of how the auditor may find that computerisation introduces considerable problems in the proper performance of the audit task, unless the computer system specifically allows for the audit function. The most obvious problem is created by the loss of audit trail which occurs when a number of processes take place within the computer. This removes the intermediate documentation which exists with manual processes. The auditor must be involved in the design of the programs to ensure that evidence of all processes and output is available for the purpose of the audit function.

In summary, the computer must be regarded as a tool with a number of very useful facilities but also with a number of possibilities for failure. An understanding of these factors has allowed many useful and profitable systems to be developed. However, unfulfilled expectations are often found to arise from misconceptions of the nature of the computer.

## BACKGROUND TO THE USE OF COMPUTERS IN ACCOUNTING AND FINANCE FUNCTIONS

Computers found their first major commercial uses in the field of accounting and finance. For this reason the computer systems department in many organisations is still part of the finance department. This has produced a bias in the use of the computer and attitudes to it within the organisation. It may be argued that a completely separate department for computer systems would be better for all concerned.

The first areas for application of computers logically comprised those tasks which were inherently repetitive and required large inputs of clerical labour, e.g. payroll, bought ledger, sold ledger and other easily definable routines. For reasons mentioned previously, even such standard procedures required considerable development to fit them to the computer. Companies employing computers for these operations began to experience real benefits in the cost and efficiency of the operations and began to look for other areas of work which the computer could accommodate. Up to this point, computer systems had been comparatively simple, in many cases being applied to running one program at a time. The desire to expand the use of computers coincided with a considerable reduction in their price due to the advent of the transistor. The state of the art of programming had also progressed and a technique called multi-programming made it possible to execute concurrently a number of different programs which made very much more effective use of the computer. For the accountant requiring large volumes of data to be processed, the concurrent execution of a number of programs brought about their timely completion with a minimum of computer usage. The remaining factor which increased computer use was the increased status achieved by a company using a computer. While these factors taken together contributed greatly to the development of computer systems, a large number of 'white elephants' were developed which considerably damaged the reputation of the computer. This situation is not entirely a thing of the past.

Often systems are developed for the wrong reasons. In the current state of the art, a computer-based system is not always the best method.

Apart from the simple systems mentioned, new techniques made possible a wide variety of applications that suited the finance function. One such technique is that in which the immediate updating of records is the predominant feature; 'a real-time system', as it is known, provides instant report facilities on various matters including financial reporting. Real-time systems represent a simple, but important, example of the potential that the computer offers the accountant.

It is, perhaps, of little value to discuss standard clerical functions except to say that these are ideal for execution by a computer. The major mistake that may be made here is to 'computerise' an existing procedure including all its inherent faults, redundancies and inefficiencies.

Potential offered by the computer is evident in such matters as costing, particularly material costing. In a manual system, the time delay in collecting and processing information about stocks received and stocks used for any given product, often makes costing a process which relates to long outdated information. A system which is based upon the computer may provide cost information which is in advance of the actual material usage. Such a report may be used for control purposes as manufacturing and sales activities proceed. Real cost control and accurate cost reporting become immensely more effective with instantaneous provision of data. For such a system, the major feature would be a stock-recording facility that identifies quantities and prices of stock, and books them against specific manufacturing tasks. This would take place not only as stock is issued from the stores but also when material requirements are being planned. Many other costing applications could be developed.

One of the most important functions of the accountant in industry is to appraise alternative proposals for investment and alternative courses of action. For this purpose he must construct budgets, models and projections to seek the optimum choice. The calculations may not be difficult but are often tedious. The computer is an ideal tool for the accountant in providing the answers quickly without tiresome clerical labour. In some cases, where a trial and error approach is appropriate, performance of a larger number of trials, which the speed of the computer permits without delay, means that the results produced are more soundly based than would normally be achieved manually. In this case, access to a simple computer input terminal could provide the service required. Alternatively, the request for the optimum or a range of variables to be used in calculation could be specified and the computer left to provide a printout as requested.

In both of these examples the computer acts as an assistant to the accountant, thus making him more effective. This is a more appropriate role for the computer than that of a direct replacement for people. The cost-effectiveness of the accountant using this powerful aid is of far greater significance than savings made by the 'number-crunching' activity of many machines. When considering the computer as an accountant's assistant, the possibility of the computer 'taking-over' can be ignored. The computer is not, at present, a 'thinking' machine and will not, in the foreseeable future, usurp the man for whom it works.

The examples above lead naturally to a discussion of some of the wide variety of possibilities offered to the accountant with regard to his main problem areas and control needs.

Representation in numerical form of the status of a company may be regarded as a model of its operation. The production of these data, in sets of accounts, is a major part of the accountant's role. From such a model, reports may be given upon status or, analytically, upon specified operating conditions. By forward projection an estimate of future status may be provided. Such a model can ideally be kept by a computer either in part, e.g. the payroll system, or more extensively, as a series of interrelated systems to make one integrated system. In this latter case, systems have been, and are being, developed to provide the output of all required accounts from input of the relevant raw data. These may also be linked with various other functions of the business.

The purchasing system, which often may be responsible for more than 50 per cent of the outgoing cash in an organisation, is a useful function to consider in this connection. Many of the decisions regarding replacement of consumables etc. are based solely on stock levels. The computer program can check goods issued and receipts, and compare with stock levels to initiate the issue of a purchase order. Other activities of purchase procedures can be handled by the computer, such as chasing receipt of goods and ensuring that payment is made at the correct time.

The spin-off from linkage into such a system is that all documents, such as purchase orders or payment cheques, may be printed by the computer from the data held. Such information, now held by the accountant's model, provides instant access to details of committed and available funds, either at the present time or at some given future time. While this is only one aspect of cash flow, it is evident that similar linkages with for example payroll and sales systems could provide a very accurate picture of cash flow from moment to moment. Within such a system, automatic checking could take place to perform tasks of maximising cost-effectiveness in such matters as ensuring payments where discounts are given or chasing selected debtors. A well-designed operation of this type may completely change the cash flow and profitability characteristic of a company.

Such a set of interrelated systems offers opportunities for accounting for inflation and for rapid update as circumstances change and the business of the company is transacted.

The reporting opportunities are such that either actual current status or future situations may be reported including possible changes in costs, inflation, etc. Variances may be calculated automatically, i.e. reporting against budget and progress against budget limits or usage rates.

It becomes increasingly evident that many aspects of the operation of a company could be related to the accounts model mentioned earlier. This would thus completely represent the activity of the organisation. It is observed that the computer would not perform manually impossible tasks but would make possible the speedy performance of tasks that would otherwise employ an army of manual operatives. The cost of these operatives may not be justified and their coordination would be very difficult.

This brief picture of the accountant's organisation model is not intended to be complete. However, it indicates the potential of the flexible model approach that may be taken to add a powerful and cost-effective tool to the finance operation. While the former high price of this tool has tended to make it the province of the larger organisation, the great reductions in price now occurring are changing this restriction. Further aspects of this change are discussed in the final section of this chapter.

## AVAILABILITY OF SYSTEMS

In addition to using computer systems, the accountant may well find himself appraising proposals for investment in computer systems in other parts of the organisation, e.g. in branches and subsidiaries. He will, therefore, need to be aware of two aspects of computer provision. One aspect is that, as a potential user of a computer system, he may be required to contribute to a committee made up of systems staff and user representatives who will work together on the design and development of procedural activities. The other aspect is that, for an effective appraisal of a project proposal, the general framework of computer system provision must be understood. The following briefly reviews the major aspects of computer systems.

## Hardware

At the centre of every system is the hardware, i.e. the physical parts of the computer. In most systems associated with pure information processing, four major types of equipment are encountered. The processor itself, which was at one time the major expense of the total system, has become a progressively smaller cost until it is now often the smallest part of the total cost. The high-volume storage devices, usually based upon magnetic tape and magnetic disc, are provided for systems which handle very large quantities of data. For entry of data, a very wide range of different mechanical, optical or tactile readers will be required. Finally, the hardware will need a device to output the reports and results of program runs. For high-speed printed output a line printer or fast character printer will be used and, for conversational input–output, a device rather similar to a typewriter using either paper or a 'TV-type' screen will be used. This latter device is usually called a terminal or teletype when used with a paper facility or 'hard copy'. When the 'TV-type' screen device is encountered, it is usually referred to as a visual display unit (VDU).

Other hardware items likely to appear in a project proposal would, normally, be electronics and equipment associated with the above. Two special associated items, which may often be significant costs in a proposal, are a maintenance contract and a computer room.

## Software

Another significant cost in most proposals is the software. The software consists of the programs which make the computer run. As development has taken place over the years, the cost of hardware has become much smaller with the advance in technology. The software, conversely, has become far more sophisticated and, while many useful developments have taken place, the advances in software have not made possible the same cost reductions as for hardware.

Before software can be discussed further, it is necessary to understand its purpose and nature. For the hardware to be used effectively, it is essential to produce a simple means of communicating with it. From the earlier description, it will be appreciated that the computer is a 'high-speed idiot', i.e. it can perform only simple tasks but at high speed. The easiest possible method is therefore required to create the many instructions to perform these simple tasks. The programs that are used to permit comparatively simple communication with the hardware are called systems software.

One of the most important aspects of computer software is the computer language. A selected set of instructions, which may be given to the computer, is specified and a program written. This will translate instructions in this 'language' into a code that the computer understands. Many such languages exist. Each has its own set of selected instructions suited to some given purpose. In reviewing a project proposal the accountant should expect the computer to have the appropriate language according to its proposed purpose or usage.

The correct software may be a major determinant in decisions regarding suitability of the computer for purchase. The software mentioned above is often a major selling feature and may be offered 'free' with the computer or charged per item purchased. It should be noted that different manufacturers will offer their own software or some internationally accepted standard type which has been applied to the given computer. All software so far mentioned is the system software required to make it possible to program the computer. The remaining software is that needed to enable the given user task to be carried out. Such software is called application programs. This may consist of a suite of many programs and files of data to cover all the functions of the given task. The design, development and maintenance of application programs is the major occupation of systems departments in companies.

## Design of a computer system

Before any activity can be computerised, the task and its peculiarities within a given organisation must be thoroughly investigated and a computer system designed. The designed system must be programmed and thoroughly tested with all expected conditions of operation and then implemented in the place of work. Some further aspects of this operation are included in a later section. For the moment, consideration is confined to the means of obtaining the services required to fulfil the above requirements.

The means used by larger companies is to employ a staff of systems analysts, designers, programmers and computer operators to provide and operate a computer owned by them. This needs substantial capital provision and a budget for staff and materials for which demand will vary considerably depending on the status of develop-

ment and the extent to which the system is used within the organisation. To support this level of staffing, an organisation must be continually developing and maintaining new and existing systems.
Otherwise, the staffing needs will be highly variable and the department subject to heavy cost penalties. The main benefits of operating
in such a way are that, for special tasks, it is cheaper to develop an
'in-house' system than to employ an outside agency to provide a
program 'package'; and the priorities of work to be carried out and
costs of system modification are more readily and cheaply controlled.

*How to economise on systems provision*

The purchase of a computer is often avoided to advantage by using a
leasing scheme which provides the 'in-house' availability of the
machine. In some cases where either an applicable cost-effective
service is availabe, or the full-time use of a computer is not required,
it is possible to purchase time on a commercially rented machine. To
obtain such a service, data may be sent periodically by some form of
messenger service to a computer bureau which will return the processed data. Alternatively, a terminal linked by GPO line to the bureau
of the user's choice may be owned or rented to provide direct data
transmission. This uses a small electronic communications device
known as a modem or acoustic coupler. This type of service is
particularly useful where an information service is to be accessed
which must be available remotely and even worldwide over the
international data networks.

Software to perform specific tasks is commercially available as
'packages'. Normally, a package will provide for a very wide range of
different options to allow the user to select those items suited to his
needs. In practice, such packages require the user either to tailor the
package to the needs of the company or to adapt the day-to-day
procedures of the company to suit the computer package. The package is very cost-effective in that it may be purchased at far less cost
than would be required for the user to develop it himself. This is
possible because the cost is spread over the many users that purchase
the same package.

In operation, the user will require some training in use of the
package but need have no knowledge of technical details. The disadvantages lie in the inefficiences that could exist in larger general-
purpose packages, the problems in package tailoring and difficulties
in obtaining suitable packages for all but the standard company
operations.

More recently, the sharp fall in hardware prices has made possible low-price 'turnkey' packages. The turnkey system provides all hardware, software and user procedures to perform a task. The user has no need to employ systems staff or to understand the technicalities of the system development. This does, of course, put the user in the hands of the package producer for the satisfaction of current and future requirements of this application. Turnkey systems have long been offered but are now more cheaply available.

The main impact of recent developments is that a cheaper more reliable computer can be used in more applications than was previously possible given the availability of suitable software.

## THE EFFECT OF SYSTEMS ON AN ORGANISATION

The description of computer systems has so far omitted one very important aspect of their operation – the effect of computer systems on the structure of the organisation and on the people who come into contact with them.

The basic premise must be that the computer provides for the needs of the organisation and its requirements. We must not, however, expect the computer to fulfil all the requirements of the organisation without some structural and procedural alterations to that organisation.

To achieve the balance between organisational change and tailoring the system to provide the ideal design to suit the application, attention must be given to the personnel in the system. In many cases, the ideal solution will require a number of changes in responsibilities and administrative groupings. This may mean that the structure upon which the accountant bases his activity will need modification. The computer system and organisation structure interact and must be carefully blended. This is particularly so when the computer is used to provide information intended to guide the processes of control both within and outside the organisation. The natural resistance to change which characterises most organisations can make such changes very difficult to perform 'at a stroke'. The preparation of personnel and phasing of system implementation is, therefore, as important as the systems design. In finance operations, which are often the longest established activities of an organisation, this is particularly relevant. Any approach to the personnel of an organisation, which in any way threatens their livelihood must, inevitably, produce resistance. It is often the cooperation of these members of the organisation which will ensure the effective design and use of the computer application. In the early stages of analysis of existing manual operations and design of computer systems, the current operator is a vital information resource. Reference was made above to the role of the computer as assistant and in most cases the individual will not become redundant as a result of the introduction of the computer system but the nature of the work may well be radically changed. Clerical functions may, perhaps, disappear and the computer take on mundane tasks.

A full appreciation of the role that the computer will play and the value and benefit that this will be to the individual and the organisation must be appreciated by the system user. This will mean that, from the earliest days of system design, the user should be consulted and involved. Alienation should be avoided by removal of threats to job security and by provision of full information to avoid unhelpful rumours. The earliest task of system analysis may be simply a feasibility study which could result in a decision not to use a computer. Rumours of an unhelpful nature will spread rapidly unless authoritative information and due consultation are provided.

A system imposed upon the members of an organisation may suffer from one or more of the dangers of the authoritarian approach. These dangers could be summarised as follows:

1   The system does not take into account the real needs of the user. The result of using such a system is often to generate more work for the user.
2   The output from a system does not present information in a way that may be either easy or possible to use. This will mean that the user may not use the reports at all, may have extra work to use the reports or may not receive full benefit from the reports.
3   The user does not understand the function of the system and is unable to use it effectively through failing to carry out the procedures required. Such a problem often renders the system practically useless.
4   The user will see the computer system as an alien force or a weapon to be used against him. The result of such an attitude is that the system and its equipment will be abused or not used at all.

To ensure that these problems are avoided a number of precautions must be taken in the development and implementation of a system. As previously mentioned, the user must be involved in the design of the system from the earliest possible time. This may be organisationally satisfied by forming a committee of a representative number of the users and of the computer system development team. Practically, user involvement will be satisfied when the user really contributes to the design. This may be in the form of providing local terminology, document layout, report style or procedure required.

These are simple examples of the type of involvement that will bring the user to see the system as his own and not as being imposed by some outside agency. A design developed in this way is more likely to be acceptable to the user. It is necessary to maintain this attitude throughout all stages of development of the design.

During the early days of investigation by the systems staff of current manual, semi-automated or computer-based systems, the majority of the work will be by interview of personnel and review of past documents. It is clear that co-operation of the user is of paramount importance if the correct perception of system needs is to be gathered by the systems designers. Such co-operation must extend throughout the next stages of verifying that design perception is correct, developing the programs and procedures and implementing the finished product.

Many attitudes must be accommodated and, so far, only the user attitudes have been considered. Those personnel indirectly associated with the system must also be considered, for example, the manager or supervisor of an accounting section.

The power and control which was once his will increasingly be handed over to the computer. The mystique which most people develop in performance of their daily work is often destroyed by the systems and procedures that accompany a computer system. For many people, a sense of personal achievement and job satisfaction are derived from their own job mystique. If they are deprived of this satisfaction then they must be given an alternative motivating force, e.g. the opportunity to work successfully with a large and powerful computer system.

It is very important that the system user is effectively included if a computer system is to be the exact tool required. Otherwise, the system will be the product of the computer department alone. With the best of intentions, such a system is unlikely to satisfy the needs of many of the likely users.

From this brief appraisal, it may be seen that the personnel element of a system could be the single most important feature dictating success or failure. There is certainly evidence of this in many installations where loss of user goodwill or staff and union resistance have destroyed all chance of efficient computer usage.

## FACTORS TO BE CONSIDERED BY THE USER BEFORE INSTALLATION OF A COMPUTER SYSTEM

The membership of the user steering committee is usually formed by a representative selection of both users and computer system designers. It is hoped that the accountant will find himself on such a committee, considering the factors that should be noted when installing and operating a computer system.

Many of these factors are a matter of making provision for necessary activities or expenditure. So often a computer system apparently costs more to install or to operate than originally anticipated. While cost inflation must take some of the blame, too often the major excess costs arise from a lack of understanding of the true costs to be incurred.

In addition to hardware and software requirements, many potentially expensive and sometimes long lead-time aspects of a system may be important. While many of these matters are the responsibility of the systems staff, in most cases the accountant or his departmental activity will be affected by them.

The location of the computer and the type of room to house it will, in practice, affect the ease with which the user may have access to it. A mini- or micro-computer may readily be used in an office environment with little or no special preparation of the area, but the larger mainframe device, which has some magnetic backing store apparatus, will require a large area which is dust-free and environmentally controlled.

A matter of importance is the time taken to transmit documents and data for processing and subsequently to receive results. Where a computer is sited at a distance, the availability of vehicles to transmit documents, as against preparation and transmission of data locally, are important determinants in the effective use of a system.

Every system user will need some training in providing data to the system and in making effective use of the results. Insufficient attention to training may render the user unable or even unwilling to use the system to its full potential. Training may take some time under the supervision of an adviser before all users are really competent.

The organisation of such training may be apparently costly and time-consuming but the high cost of operating a system badly is the result of inadequate training.

As a system is implemented, a number of processes must take place. The first is file conversion: converting all the data that a manual system user would require and transferring them to a form that the computer can read. The machine-readable form is usually based upon magnetic media. The process of extracting such data from records held, entering them on a form to be keyed in by a keypunch operator and carefully checking their accuracy, is a very lengthy operation. It can also be very expensive in systems where many thousands or millions of pieces of data are to be converted.

Another problem encountered by systems staff, and which may affect the accountant, is associated with the testing of programs during development. For a system of reasonable size, the time required for program testing will be very long. Unless this testing takes place outside normal working times or the computer has great spare capacity, any existing systems on the computer may be effectively slowed down. The task of testing programs is often seen only as the work of systems staff. This ignores the assistance that the user could give in defining test conditions.

The major problem in program testing is in ensuring that all likely activities and conditions are adequately treated. The precise nature of these test specifications can, therefore, be much more effectively defined if the accountant is involved in producing those specifications.

Finally, during the implementation stage, the computer system must where possible be run in parallel with a manual operation so that back-up services are available. It is reasonable to assume that some problems will arise to be dealt with. The parallel run will show that the system works and will effectively provide the final test of system capability. In many cases, the time for parallel run operations will be shortened by introducing the computer system in phases. The temptation to shorten the parallel run time to save costs must be weighed against the cost of launching a system before it is truly ready for use. This could mean the complete loss of a service if the computer system should stop without some back-up provision. The cost, in loss of user goodwill, difficulties during the period without the computer and problems in restarting, can be very high.

## THE FUTURE OF COMPUTERS IN FINANCIAL APPLICATIONS

One of the major factors affecting the future of computers in finance operations is the availability of cheap hardware. Until recently, a computer could not be considered for many tasks because the capital costs were too high. The equipment which can now be purchased for the price of several electric typewriters, offers great potential for many of the tasks encountered by the accountant.

A major stumbling block in the process of spreading the use of computers has always been the lack of suitable software. It can be seen that cheap hardware opens new markets providing higher sales potential and, therefore, greater motivation to develop software.

The future of computers could be radically altered by a new method of programming. While programming aids have developed over the years, the means by which a computer is made to respond to the user's needs requires a major change. Two developments in the state of the art contribute to these needs. One is the availability of database management systems which provide access to a vast data resource in any way specified by the user. The other development is in computer-based voice recognition. A development of these two concepts could allow the accountant to ask for a report of given information in a given format.

All the developments discussed in this chapter are likely to make considerable demands upon the accountant. The reaction to computers by the finance departments of organisations has been very variable and often, justifiably, very suspicious. To realise some of the potential that has been mentioned in this chapter, the accountant will be faced with difficult decisions of acceptance of wide-ranging computer-based systems. Some will undoubtedly be 'gadgets and toys', others will be potential contributors of great effectiveness in the tasks of accountancy, but the profession will require positive evidence of the usefulness of these tools. The best results will be achieved with a sound balance between caution and willingness to take a limited risk where a need is obviously going to be satisfied by the use of a computer.

The closer relationship that the accountant is likely to have with the computer due to its falling cost and ready availability will improve his knowledge of systems. In setting out tasks for programming and for developing procedures the attitudes which were previously the domain of the systems man must play a considerable part in all aspects of accountancy. The future for the accountant will be in dealing with more locally available computers to provide local services. These computers will be linked to a central computer to deal with centralised issues and to other computers to transfer information. Such networks are already in the early stages of development. The term 'distributed processing' is used to describe the large number of computer systems based on a central computer with a number of remote local stations. The transfer of money between computers in banks and associated systems has been happening for some years.

The logical conclusion of this trend is to remove the paperwork from within and between organisations. This will have a profound effect on the work in finance departments. Major problems are to be overcome in the areas of social acceptability and in the adequate development of computers and systems to deal with such demands. The ultimate result of such developments will be to remove all routine labours and leave the accountant as the intelligent decision-making component of a system. The nature of his work will continue to make him a pioneer in the use of computers.

## REFERENCES AND ADDITIONAL READING

Anderson, R. G., *Data Processing and Management Information Systems*, Macdonald and Evans, 1979.

Clifton, H. D., *Business Data Systems*, Prentice-Hall, 1978.

Higgins, J. C., *Information Systems for Planning and Control: Concepts and Cases*, Edward Arnold, 1976.

Lambourn, S., *Computer Applications in Business*, Longman, 1974.

# 19

# Inflation Accounting

**Raymond Brockington**

*The author underlines the importance of inflation accounting in rela-
tion to financial planning and control by his statement that its introduction is 'one of the biggest responsibilities which the accounting profession has ever undertaken'. This chapter carefully examines the nature
of inflation and critically reviews the long discussion on the subject and
the numerous reports, exposure drafts and statements of standard
accounting practice issued by accountancy bodies.*

*Inflation is an effect of relative values which are changing even in a
barter economy. In a money economy they are changing 'in a fashion
to which a particular perception is imparted by our insistence on the
adoption of a specific unit of account'. Inflation, maintains the author,
is essentially an accounting problem and in the absence of explicit
accounting adjustments an individual's assessment of the effect of
inflation can be incomplete and highly subjective. The chapter cites the
illusory pictures of growth and prosperity presented by accounts based
on the historical cost convention and acclaimed with pride by company
chairmen. It indicates how the holding of current assets causes loss but
credit creates gain.*

*The doctrines of the two schools of thought, current purchasing
power and current cost accounting, are examined and contrasted, and
particular attention is given to the principles outlined in the Sandilands
Report. The author finds much to approve in both these schools and
concludes that 'the profession is right to move with all the caution and
conservatism which its friends and critics alike are prone to impute to it.'*

The reader will not have come this far without encountering, in many forms, manifestations of the problems in accounting caused by inflation. Although business management is concerned with the organisation and optimum use of real scarce resources it can plan, control and report on these things only after translating them into financial terms. This chapter is largely concerned with the reporting problems caused by inflation and hence with a consideration of relevant accounting standards and proposed standards. These are applied to the published accounts and are therefore a primary responsibility of the financial accountant and of the auditor. No financial manager dare, however, regard this as being outside his field. For one thing, any variation in the method of accounting used in external reporting is bound to spread backwards into the records on which it is based and hence to those on which also is based planning and control information. For another, the financial manager's ability to raise external finance, his planning of financial structure and his determination of his cost of capital, amongst many other things, are closely bound up with the information provided to external decision makers.

The chapter is organised as follows. First a general outline establishes what inflation is and puts the view that it is much more of an accounting problem than an economic problem. If the former could be resolved so that the reality of the underlying situation could be precisely conveyed then, it is argued, the economic consequences of inflation would largely cease to exist. Then some of the more important distortions in reporting which arise when the conventional historic cost (henceforth HC) method of accounting is used against an inflationary background are examined. This is to establish that the problem has quite profound consequences and that its solution is not merely a matter of pedantic nicety. Third, the two main schools of thought concerning inflation accounting, those of current purchasing power (CPP) and current cost accounting (CCA) will be considered in theoretical terms. Finally there is a review of practical developments to date from early Recommendations on Accounting Principles to the Accounting Standards Committee's S.S.A.P. 16.

## INFLATION – AN ACCOUNTING OR ECONOMIC PROBLEM?

An elementary text on economics will say that money has several important functions. It acts as a medium of exchange, as a store of value and as a unit of account. In such an elementary treatment there is unlikely to be discussed the very important issue of how *good* money is at performing these functions. It is in its deficiencies that the problems which inflation accounting seeks to resolve are created and, before consideration of that resolution, there should be careful attention to the precise nature of the problem.

It may charitably be assumed that if modern man wished for the first time to create money he would be able to design something which fulfilled its purposes wholly perfectly. This, however, is not the case. Money was born into the world for the same reasons and in the same way as any other commodity and, as such, it carried with it the congenital condition common to them all but which in money becomes a disease. Value in economic terms is determined by an interplay of a commodity's scarcity and of its desirability. Even in a barter economy relative values are constantly changing. A cow may cost three sheep one day but may exchange for only two on the following day. Where all commodities are of equal standing this relative change will be seen for what it is. It will be no more meaningful to say that cows have fallen in value than to say that sheep have risen in price.

A change in the analogy may make the point plainer. If one car travelling at 40 m.p.h. is overtaken by another travelling at 45 m.p.h. both drivers will recognise that each continues to make progress but at different speeds. The first driver will fall neither into the error of believing that the other is travelling at only 5 m.p.h. nor, still less, that of believing that he himself is moving backwards at that speed. If one or other car were arbitrarily designated and accepted as a new standard of rest, however, the perception would be quite changed.

In economic terms, once more, if sheep be designated as the commodity which henceforth is to act as money, the standard of value, it will then be declared unequivocally that the price of cows has fallen. The problem all starts, then, when one point in a turmoil of confused motion is arbitrarily selected as the datum from which all other movements are to be measured. The possibility that the datum itself moves is thereafter precluded from consideration. The creation of money in the way described did not, of course, occur in an instant but there was a gradual development over a very long period. During this time certain commodities, usually the uncommon, durable and attractive metals, came to be desired for their usefulness as money above their usefulness in the direct satisfaction of human wants.

With one or two relatively shortlived reversals of the secular trend, inflation, the constant relative decline in the value of money or, as it is observed, the constant upwards movement of all prices, has persisted ever since. Why the movement is generally in one direction is a question beyond the present scope. It might be fair to suggest, however, that an impetus to this is that money (whether it be gold or banknotes) is a durable commodity of which, therefore, the available supply gradually increases over time as more is created than is consumed. Moreover, once such a trend has been established, expectations that it will continue must be a very powerful influence towards ensuring that in fact it does so.

The bearing of all this on the work of the accountant is that it will lead to a definition of inflation which is crucial to the formulation and understanding of processes designed to account for its effects. Inflation is not merely that 'prices are rising' or that 'the purchasing power of money is falling'. It is that relative values are changing in a fashion to which a particular perception is imparted by our insistence on the adoption of a specific universal unit of account. This gives rise to what is often termed the 'money illusion'.

Inflation is thus quite uniquely an accounting problem. It is because of the discrepancy it creates between perception and reality that it has such undesirable effects and for no other reason. If it were possible to account for inflation adequately, there would be no need to cure it although, as will be seen, the former is not necessarily the easier of the two to achieve.

The stock argument used in the past against making adjustment for inflation has been that it is unnecessary because inflation is so well understood a phenomenon that people automatically make their own mental adjustment for it and read figures in that light. To some extent this is demonstrably true. If a man goes into a shop to buy a pair of shoes and he is quoted a price which is double what he paid for similar shoes five years previously, he does not immediately assume that he is being overcharged. He looks at prices around him and makes appropriate allowance for the inflation of the five years. Again, a housewife does not refuse to buy food because she now spends in a day what her mother used to spend in a week. Some adjustments, thus, clearly are routinely made. On the other hand a unit trust management company is able proudly to advertise that the value of its units has doubled in the last ten years without at the same time pointing out that this actually represents a loss to the investor in real terms. Again, the houseowner is able to continue to complain about the struggle to meet his mortgage repayments even though inflation is rapidly lifting the real burden of the charge from his shoulders. The problem is that, in the absence of carefully designed explicit accounting adjustments, those adjustments which are made are incomplete, highly subjective and selective.

Consider how people might cope if there were inflation in the units of length rather than those of currency. A glazier measuring up a window frame for a pane of glass would find that the glass supplied in the centimetres of today would not fit the frame measured in the centimetres of yesterday. In this situation no vague understanding that inflation was taking place followed by a rough and ready mental adjustment to allow for it would serve. Nothing less than a very precise knowledge of the extent of the change and a careful evaluation of its full effect would do. Clearly, then, there is a *prima facie* case which says that inflation will cause accounting statements to distort our understanding of the real situation.

## DISTORTIONS IN REPORTING

It will be helpful now to present a rather fuller case by giving some important specific examples of distortions caused in HC accounts where no subjective judgement can be expected to give any adequate adjustment. The importance of these examples is that they arise in a situation which is commonly met and which commonly leads to errors of interpretation of accounting statements. Company chairmen are very fond of calling the attention of shareholders to an impressive growth record which they will frequently exemplify by reference to figures drawn from successive accounts over a period of time.

The following table and chairman's statement relates to the imaginary company, Avocado Ltd.

'In the last decade we have seen a most encouraging growth in our business. In that time our capital employed, a measure of the total

| Year | 1969 | 1970 | 1971 | 1972 | 1973 | 1974 | 1975 | 1976 | 1977 | 1978 |
|------|------|------|------|------|------|------|------|------|------|------|
| Capital employed (£ million) | 20.0 | 20.6 | 21.6 | 22.3 | 23.3 | 25.2 | 28.2 | 30.5 | 32.9 | 34.2 |
| Profit (£ million) | 2.2 | 2.3 | 2.6 | 2.7 | 3.0 | 3.5 | 4.3 | 5.0 | 5.8 | 6.3 |
| Dividend per share | 5p | 5p | 6p | 6p | 8p | 8p | 8p | 10p | 10p | 10p |

resources over which we have control, has increased steadily until it now stands at 1.7 times what it did in 1969. As might be expected this has brought a steady increase in our total profit. What is particularly gratifying, however, is that this has grown faster than capital, implying a substantially improving profitability as we have grown in size. Our profit represented a return on capital of 11 per cent in 1969 but by the year just past it had risen to 18 per cent. Whilst making appropriate retentions out of profit to finance our growth we have passed on a substantial part of the benefit to our members who now, after three increases in their dividend over the decade, enjoy an income which has doubled.'

Such figures supporting such statements are a commonplace in the financial world and yet, where the figures have been prepared by conventional accounting methods, every one of the chairman's statements is completely invalid as will now be shown.

The official Index of Retail Prices, used here as a convenient measure of inflation, averaged 68.7 in 1969 (January 1974 = 100) and it rose every year subsequently to a level of 197.1 in 1978. In order to retain its purchasing power of 1969, therefore, the company's profit would need to increase to £2.2 × $\frac{197.1}{68.7}$ million by 1978. This gives a figure of £6.3 million which was, in fact, just achieved. Thus, we would argue, the chairman should have said 'Profit has remained stationary through the past ten years.'

Applying the same calculation to the dividend, this, in order to maintain its purchasing power, should have risen to 5 × $\frac{197.1}{68.7}$ p by 1978, i.e. a level of 14.34p. The actual dividend is just under 70 per cent of this and the chairman might have said 'Because inflation has placed a considerable strain on our cash resources we have found it necessary to curtail dividends by a little over 30 per cent during this difficult decade'.

The imaginary chairman made an approving comment on the company's return on capital and here the position is even more confused. The discrepancies caused within a conventional accounting system by inflation arise fundamentally because the unit of currency has a value here and now determined by its current market rating but accounts are dominated by a principle in which money is deemed to retain a value determined by some past market rating. This is the more complicated in that, although there is only one present moment, there is an infinity of past moments and different ones of these condition different parts of the accounts.

It may be supposed that the amount of the inflationary effect is related to the time elapsed since the historical moment when the recorded value was determined. Because fixed assets are relatively long lived the average time elapsed since the values in that account were determined will be relatively long. The profit and loss account contains one item, depreciation, which is as old as fixed assets but other figures are much newer. For this reason, in an inflationary period, reported profits might be expected to respond more quickly to the upward pressure of prices than do most of the assets. The lag of asset valuations behind profit and loss valuations will lead to an observed increase in the rate of return on capital – precisely the effect commented on by the chairman. The distortion cannot be quantified by a simple transformation of the figures given. It can, however, be said that the chairman has certainly overstated the position. Nor, it should be noted, is doubt being thrown merely on the trend which he has observed. The absolute level of the rate of return which may be used in, for example, evaluating alternative forms of investment, is also subject to distortion.

There is an equally important phenomenon where the facts themselves are influenced by inflation. Because some money values are free to float in a market and others are fixed by contract or by law, inflation will lead to arbitrary redistributions of wealth. The market value of a company's stock or of its fixed assets are free to rise in money value so that, other things being equal, there are no inflationary consequences of such investment in real terms. The value of debtors, bank balances and cash, however, are fixed in money terms and will, therefore, decline in real value causing the company an actual loss. By a similar argument a company under inflation will gain in real terms at the expense of its creditors and its suppliers of loan capital both of which will again have fixed money values.

Consider the following simple balance sheet for Mango Ltd at 1 January 1974.

| Share capital | £1,000,000 | Physical assets | £1,500,000 |
| Loan capital | 1,000,000 | Cash at bank | 500,000 |
| | £2,000,000 | | £2,000,000 |

Suppose that, for the sake of simplicity, the physical assets are non-depreciating, that all loan interest is promptly paid, that all profits are distributed as earned and that there are no debtors nor creditors. The balance sheet, on conventional HC principles, will remain unchanged over time. We will look at the position at the end of September 1978, by which time the general level of retail prices had doubled. A balance sheet based on a fresh valuation of Mango's position at that time would appear as follows:

| | | | |
|---|---|---|---|
| Share capital and reserves* | £2,500,000 | Physical assets† | £3,000,000 |
| Loan capital | 1,000,000 | Cash and bank | 500,000 |
| | £3,500,000 | | £3,500,000 |

\* including revaluation reserve  † estimated current value

Note that the inflation-adjusted balance sheet shows a dramatically different picture from the HC balance sheet. The equity share in the business is up from 50 per cent to over 70 per cent. Overall solvency is greatly improved but liquidity is down. These improvements in the position have been *concealed* by a failure to account for inflation in the balance sheet and *caused* by a failure to account for inflation in dealings with the outside world.

Thus the existence of inflation where a conventional HC-based system of accounting is in use will have two effects. It will cause redistributions of interests between equity holders and debt holders and between goods owners and cash owners and it will distort the perception of reality so as to invalidate almost any observation which might be made in the interpretation of accounts. This is why the point was made earlier that inflation is wholly an accounting problem. If it were resolved then the distortions in the interpretation of data would be avoided. It is also impossible to believe that the massive capricious redistributions of income and wealth which occur now would be tolerated once they were revealed clearly for what they were. A satisfactory solution to the problem is not, however, easy to find, as the story of practical attempts to do so, to be told later, confirms.

## TWO SCHOOLS OF THOUGHT

At a theoretical level, however, the argument can conveniently be divided between two main schools of thought illustrating the main consequences of the use of each.

## Current purchasing power

The first, that associated with the current purchasing power (CPP) concept, argues that the relationship between a 1978 pound (say) and a 1969 pound (say) is not unlike the relationship between a pound and a dollar. They differ, that is, in terms of their purchasing power and can be converted one into another by means of an appropriate factor. Just as, on a particular day, we can accurately say that £1 = $2 so, it is argued, we can equally accurately say that

$$(\text{since } \tfrac{68.7}{197.1} = 0.35) \; £_{1978}1 = £_{1969}0.35$$

There is, however, one important reservation to make. Whereas there is a market which says that £1 = $2, there is no market as between $£_{1978}$ and $£_{1969}$. The rate of exchange is imputed from a consideration of index numbers as a measure of purchasing power. The selection of some specific index for this purpose carries an unavoidable implication as to how the uses to which the money will be put are seen. Use of a retail price index, as here, for example, implies an interest in purchasing power as applied to the range of goods and services offered in the retail market. Had the interest been in money as used for stock market investment (arguably more appropriate in the context of company finance) share price index (of which there are several – not all in agreement) might have been used. Had the concern been with the use of money to purchase business fixed assets an index of freehold buildings or of plant and machinery prices might have been selected. Had the focus been on ability to finance stock an index based on raw material prices might have been used. It is thus a practical flaw in the CPP concept, though not necessarily a destructive one, that there is no universal measure of purchasing power which is free of all implication about the specific use to which money might be put.

Look again at Mango's balance sheet as it would appear in September 1978 if prepared on CPP principles, e.g. see overleaf.

Some important points should be noted. All amounts not fixed by contract or by law, i.e. all non-monetary amounts, are indexed according to the selected measure of general inflation. The fact that 'Physical assets' now stands at £3 million, therefore, does not mean that these are deemed to have a market value of that figure. It means that at some historic time the acquisition of these assets absorbed a quantity of purchasing power assessed in terms of alternative goods

| Share capital | £2,000,000 | Physical assets | £3,000,000 |
|---|---|---|---|
| Profit due to inflation* | 500,000 | Cash and bank | 500,000 |
| Loan capital | 1,000,000 | | |
| | £3,500,000 | | £3,500,000 |

| * Profit from loan capital finance | £1,000,000 |
|---|---|
| *Less* loss from holding cash | 500,000 |
| Profit due to inflation | £500,000 |

and services which assessed now in terms of those same alternative goods and services would have a money valuation of £3 million. The physical assets *may* have a market value of this figure, as indeed was supposed in the earlier reference to the company, but this will be merely fortuitous and not a universal experience with CPP.

Monetary items, e.g. loan capital, creditors, debtors and cash, are not indexed and this leads to a 'difference' in the balance sheet identifiable as net profit or loss due to inflationary movements. This is shown on the balance sheet and an analysis of it follows. It is useful in emphasising the consequences during a period of inflation of holding idle cash balances, which lose value, and of debt financing, which gives rise to inflationary gains.

CPP accounting is in many ways an attractive and logical extension of HC accounting. The so-called capital maintenance concept has always been at the heart of the latter in that profits are so computed that, after all have been distributed, including any on realisation, liquidation would enable the repayment to the investor of his original cash subscribed. Obviously when inflation has taken place this repayment will be less valuable in terms of other goods and services which it will command than was the original amount invested. Under CPP when all reported profits have been distributed, including inflationary gains and, again, those on realisation, liquidation would enable a repayment to the investor of the same amount of purchasing power, though more money, as he forwent when making his original subscription. It should be emphasised that the investor is not better off in aggregate by these manipulations. Under CPP lower profits would be reported and this retention would be the source of the higher money payout on liquidation. The concern here, however, is with accurate reporting and the contention is that historic cost, by ignoring inflation, has overstated profits.

Here is an example which contrasts HC and CPP. Satsuma Ltd. started in business on 1 January with a share capital, fully subscribed, of £500,000 and loan capital of £200,000. It immediately purchased stock for £600,000. On 31 December the stock was sold for £1,000,000, interest at the rate of 25 per cent for the year was paid on loan capital and the whole of the net profit was distributed as a dividend. The company was then liquidated. Prices, as measured by a general index, had risen by 20 per cent during the year.

Satsuma Ltd – Profit and loss account for the year ended 31 December

|  | HC | CPP |
|---|---|---|
| Sales | £1,000,000 | £1,000,000 |
| *Less* cost of sales | 600,000 | 720,000 |
| Gross profit | 400,000 | 280,000 |
| *Less* interest on loan capital | 50,000 | 50,000 |
| Net profit on trading | £350,000 | £230,000 |
| Inflationary gain on loan capital |  | £40,000 |
| *Less* inflationary loss on cash |  | 20,000 |
|  |  | £20,000 |
| Total profit distributed as dividend | £350,000 | £250,000 |
| Realisation at 31 December Cash available after payment of dividend and interest | £700,000 | £800,000 |
| Paid to holders of loan capital | £200,000 | £200,000 |
| Paid to shareholders | 500,000 | 600,000 |
|  | £700,000 | £800,000 |

## Current cost accounting

CPP's main rival is current cost accounting, CCA. The basic argument underlying this is that inflation causes reporting problems because of the multitude of valuation occasions used under HC. The way to deal with this is to maintain all accounting values at up-to-date figures. For historic cost, the amount that was paid for resources, is substituted current cost, the money amount which would now have to be paid for the resources. An advantage which is claimed for this method is that the balance sheet becomes a statement of true values rather than a mere list of unexpired balances and that this makes it of real use in determining the relative merits of alternative uses of funds. One point should be made quite clear, however. CCA is more than a means of accounting for inflation. It is a different system of accounting based on a quite different principle from HC. It deals with inflation almost incidentally and cannot distinguish between general inflation and market price fluctuations.

Suppose there is a period of price stability and that a business is operating at a constant level of activity. HC, CPP and CCA will all report similar profits and will show constant financing. Then comes a period of general inflation. Under HC enhanced profits will be reported (because selling prices will rise in advance of historically based costs) but increased finance will be seen to be required (whether this be acquired by new issues of capital or by voluntary retention of profit). Under CPP and CCA lower profits will be reported and, given the constant level of activity, no extra finance will be shown to be required. CPP and CCA thus (broadly) agree with one another and disagree with HC. Suppose now that, instead of general inflation, there are specific price rises due to relative scarcity in the assets in which the company deals. Now HC and CPP will agree with one another that additional finance is required, although they may not agree on the precise extent of it. CCA will, however, show constant financing but lower profits. It is a matter of argument as to which is right but there is some intuitive appeal to an argument which says that a pocket of scarcity in an otherwise inflation-free economy would require extra finance in its exploitation. If this is correct then CCA is wrong in denying it.

Now look at Satsuma Ltd again to see what its accounts would look like under CCA. For this is needed one new piece of information. The replacement cost of the stock had risen to £690,000 by 31 December. The HC figures are repeated for purposes of comparison.

## Satsuma Ltd – Profit and loss account for the year ended 31 December

|  | HC | CCA |
|---|---|---|
| Sales | £1,000,000 | £1,000,000 |
| *Less* cost of sales | 600,000 | 690,000 |
| Gross profit | 400,000 | 310,000 |
| *Less* interest on loan capital | 50,000 | 50,000 |
| Net profit distributed as dividend | £350,000 | £260,000 |
| Realisation at 31 December |  |  |
| Cash available after payment of dividend and interest | £700,000 | £790,000 |
| Paid to holders of loan capital | £200,000 | £200,000 |
| Paid to shareholders | 500,000 | 590,000 |
|  | £700,000 | £790,000 |

The two ideas explored can fairly be characterised as follows. CPP is investor-centred and seeks to preserve the investor's capital in all its alternative uses. It seems ultimately, therefore, to envisage the liquidation of the company, the antithesis, that is, of the going concern concept. CCA, on the other hand, is company-centred. It values resources in their existing uses and capital is maintained in the sense of being able to support the current level of real resources actually employed.

CCA, in the pure form illustrated here, has an important weakness where general inflation exists. Although it recognises that the increased prices of non-monetary assets require an increased money capital, it does not recognise that this is also true of monetary assets. If prices have doubled so that physical assets have doubled in money value, the company will certainly also need to maintain a doubled cash balance and allow its debtors to double as well. CPP allows for this by computing the loss due to holding cash and debtor balances but CCA, in its basic form, does not.

## ACCOUNTING FOR INFLATION IN THE REAL WORLD

It has already been said that the solution is not a simple one and the story of attempts to formulate it reflects this. It is a story which is not yet ended and which is likely to continue for some time.

The problem found quite early recognition in recommendations issued by the Institute of Chartered Accountants in England and Wales. Recommendation 12 (1949) and Recommendation 15 (1952) referred to the problem but ended by endorsing the HC method. Not until January 1973 were any forceful proposals for action placed before the accountancy profession. Then the Accounting Standards Committee issued Exposure Draft (ED) 8, 'Accounting for changes in the purchasing power of money'. Before ED 8 could crystallise into a standard the government had announced the establishment of its own committee to look into inflation accounting under the chairmanship of Sir Francis Sandilands. The standard based on ED 8 was, therefore, pending the report of that committee, issued as a provisional standard only. Provisional Statement of Standard Accounting Practice 7, as it was numbered, was issued in May 1974.

The important provisions of this standard can be summarised quite shortly. Historic cost accounts were to continue to be prepared as heretofore and inflation-adjusted statements were to be produced as supplementary statements to those accounts. The method of adjustment was to be CPP using the general index of retail prices. All non-monetary assets and the share capital and reserves were to be revalued by reference to changes in the index since acquisition or issue and the difference was to be interpreted as the gain or loss due to inflation. The virtues of (P)SSAP 7 would appear to be that it offered a very rapid and easily calculated adjustment for inflation and that it retained the well-understood system of HC at its base. A weakness seemed to be that by producing in effect two sets of accounts each purporting to present a true and fair view it seemed likely that confusion would be caused.

In the event (P)SSAP 7 became a back number before it had been implemented by more than a handful of companies. The Sandilands Committee reported in September 1975 and with recommendations quite contrary to the proposals of the Accounting Standards Committee. The report envisaged the replacement of the HC method of accounting entirely by a CCA method. The concept of current cost which it proposed was that of value to the business or deprival value. This is a somewhat difficult concept to put into practice involving, as it does, the selection of the appropriate measure of value for each asset from a choice of economic value, realisable value and replacement cost.

An example will make this principle clear or, at least, highlight the complexity of it. Value to the business can usefully be thought of as the amount which would be needed exactly to compensate for the loss of the asset. If an item had a replacement cost of £4,000, an economic value (discounted expected cash flow) of £2,000 and a realisable value of £3,000 then the value to the business would be £3,000. The argument is that a rational company would be seeking to sell rather than use such an asset and would certainly not replace it. Therefore the proceeds of realisation is the relevant measure of value. If the figures had been replacement cost £1,000, economic value £2,000 and realisable value £3,000, value to the business is only £1,000 since replacement can be effected at that figure and would be worthwhile. Generally value to the business is the *lower* of two values. One of these values is replacement cost and the other is the *higher* of economic value and realisable value. The report, it should be added, after establishing the principle of value to the business, accepts that in a very large proportion of cases replacement cost will be the only figure which can feasibly be determined and that this would generally be used.

The Sandilands report proposals began to take practical shape when the Accounting Standards Committee issued ED 18 in November 1976. Its main feature was the adoption of value to the business as a basis of valuation in accounts to replace historic cost completely. Revaluation was to take place annually on the date of the balance sheet and the surplus thereby created was to be taken to a revaluation account. The depreciation and cost of sales figures used in the profit and loss account were to be the value to the business of the resources used at the time they were used. The revaluation account would notionally represent the necessary augmentation of money capital to enable the current level of investment in physical resources to be maintained. The surplus was then to be taken to an appropriation account where a transfer to permanent reserve would be made of an amount determined at the discretion of the directors. Under ED 18 no provision was made for increased requirements of net monetary resources.

In the calm words of the Accounting Standards Committee (ED 24, paragraph 6), 'It became clear that the Sandilands recommendations, and ED 18 which stemmed from them, were not acceptable.' It is perhaps inappropriate that more than this should be said about the events which led to a vote by the members of the Institute of Chartered Accountants in England and Wales massively rejecting, against strong advice to the contrary from the Council, the abandonment of HC. There were several important objections to ED 18. One was that it was dangerous to replace HC with the untried CCA without some experimentation and research to test its utility. Another was that the ED 18 proposals were very complicated and thus difficult and expensive to put into operation (ED 18 ran to 332 paragraphs as against PSSAP 7's 44 paragraphs). Yet again the omission of any adjustment in respect of net monetary items was seen by many as a basic weakness.

The collapse of ED 18 was followed by the introduction of the stopgap 'Hyde' proposals which were then themselves displaced by ED 24. This exposure draft experienced a relatively easy transition into a definitive standard, SSAP 16. SSAP 16 tries to avoid the faults of ED 18. First of all it does not propose the replacement of HC accounts by CCA. The CCA accounts are to be supplementary statements. Second, it allows for the effects of inflation on net monetary assets.

The steps in implementation are as follows. There is first calculated by conventional means a profit, the historical cost trading profit. Three adjustments are then made to this: a charge to allow for the greater current cost of sales over historic cost of sales; a charge to allow for the excess of current cost depreciation over historic cost depreciation; and an adjustment in respect of monetary working capital. Monetary working capital is defined in the Standard as trade debtors less trade creditors but may also include cash and bank balances where their exclusion is likely to be misleading. These adjustments lead to what is termed the current cost operating profit.

It is then further recognised that to the extent that finance is by means of loans fixed in money terms there is an additional benefit to equity holders. This is represented by a gearing adjustment which, in effect, writes back that proportion of the previous adjustments which would have been attributable to debt holders had their investment been index-linked. All surpluses relating to these adjustments are credited to a capital maintenance reserve.

What ultimately emerges as the definitive way of dealing with, or of avoiding, the problem of inflation in accounts will be a consequence of historical processes which can now probably not be greatly influenced by any single individual. Perhaps the ideal method could be approached more nearly by an amalgam of the CCA and CPP principles which might exhibit the hybrid vigour which is the characteristic of a successful union. The suggestion is of a system of CCA with the incorporation of a careful segregation of gains and losses attributable to a background of general inflation. The figures for Satsuma Ltd will once again serve for illustration.

It is contended that this company engaged in a number of activities each with its own separate outcome. It carried on a trading activity. This led to a profit which can be appropriately evaluated in CCA terms. It held cash. Inflation meant that a loss was caused by this activity and CPP provides a convenient way of evaluating this. The company owed money. Inflation makes this a profit-making activity. Finally it held stock. This is a neutral activity where stock price rises are exactly in line with general inflation but either a profit- or loss-causing activity where this is not the case. The profit or loss can be determined by comparing CCA and CPP figures.

On these principles Satsuma's accounts look as follows:

Satsuma Ltd – Profit and loss account for the year ended 31 December

| | | | |
|---|---|---|---|
| Sales | | £1,000,000 | |
| Less current cost of sales | | 690,000 | |
| | | 310,000 | |
| Less interest on loan | | 50,000 | |
| Trading profit | | 260,000 | (as per CCA) |
| Gain on borrowing | | 40,000 | |
| Less loss on holding cash | £20,000 | | |
| Loss on holding stock* | 30,000 | 50,000 | |
| Net loss due to inflation | | (10,000) | (as per CPP) |
| Available for distribution | | £250,000 | |

* £720,000 (CPP valuation) — £690,000 (CCA valuation)

The realisation at 31 December is as for CPP.

The essence of the method can be seen by looking at a comparison of the treatment of stock by four methods. This was bought on 1 January for £600,000 and had a replacement cost on 31 December of

£690,000 by which time the general price level had increased by 20 per cent. There is a money gain of £90,000 on the stock holding which may be treated as follows:

|                                                                        | HC      | CCA     | CPP       | Hybrid    |
|------------------------------------------------------------------------|---------|---------|-----------|-----------|
| Not segregated, appears as increase (decrease) in trading profit       | £90,000 | –       | (£30,000) |           |
| Augmentation of money capital to preserve purchasing power             |         | £90,000 | 120,000   | £120,000  |
| Segregated as specific inflationary profit (loss)                      |         |         |           | (30,000)  |
|                                                                        | £90,000 | £90,000 | £90,000   | £90,000   |

The introduction of inflation accounting is one of the biggest responsibilities which the accountancy profession has ever undertaken. Historical cost accounts were in origin statements of stewardship, that is they were a straightforward account of how entrusted funds had been deployed. If the world chose to use them for other purposes, including valuations and assessments of economic performance, then it did so at its peril and it was a fair defence for any shortcomings that the accounts had never claimed to have been designed to bear that load. Inflation accounting is to be introduced, however, specifically to remedy the defects of HC in satisfying users' current needs for information. It has to be accepted that any new system carries an implicit warranty of fitness for this purpose. The accountant cannot thereafter shelter behind the principle of *caveat emptor*. In these circumstances the profession is right to move with all the caution and conservatism which its friends and critics alike are prone to impute to it.

# Index

# Index